A READER IN LATINA FEMINIST THEOLOGY

A READER IN LATINA
FEMINIST THEOLOGY

RELIGION AND JUSTICE

MARÍA PILAR AQUINO,
DAISY L. MACHADO,
JEANETTE RODRÍGUEZ
Editors

UNIVERSITY OF TEXAS PRESS
AUSTIN

LIBRARY OF CONGRESS CATALOGING-IN-PUBLICATION DATA

A reader in Latina feminist theology : religion and
justice / María Pilar Aquino, Daisy L. Machado,
Jeanette Rodríguez, editors.—1st ed.
    p.   cm
  Includes bibliographical references and index.
  ISBN 978-0-292-70512-8

  1. Feminist theology   2. Mujerista theology.
3. Hispanic American women—Religious life.
I. Aquino, María Pilar.   II. Machado, Daisy L.
III. Rodríguez, Jeanette, 1954–

BT83.55—R39   2002
230′.082—dc21   2001041439

We dedicate this book to all women and men who struggle everywhere to overcome all forms of kyriarchal domination and violence.

To all Latina women who have preceded us in the struggles for *un mundo nuevo*, a new creation. *Ustedes nos han heredado visiones de justicia y liberaci n.*

To all Latina feminists, *campesinas y escritoras, afanadoras y poetas, cocineras y maestras, estudiantes y activistas, secretarias y analistas, catequistas y sanadoras, amantes y pensadoras, madres y comadres, y muchas m s* who inspire and encourage our theological commitments.

A nuestras compa eras latinoamericanas que luchan a diario contra la pobreza y la exclusi n. Con ustedes, nuestro empe o no conoce fronteras.

CONTENTS

FOREWORD

OLGA
VILLA PARRA

It is indeed an honor for me to write this foreword. About thirty-five years ago, when I gave one of my first Latina feminist talks at a small college in Iowa, I declared, "We are going to look into the future of Latinas and imagine many voices contributing to our understanding of God, justice, and feminism. We Latinas cannot be divided and scattered into many pieces and still be Latinas, Christian, and committed to justice." Little did I understand that one day I was going to be asked to write a foreword for what will become a powerful set of conversations in the theological world, particularly for Latinas.

Latinas in the United States performing ministry carry out their baptismal call with profound, quiet spirituality and endurance in environments often plagued with challenges, obstacles, and contradictions. Today, fresh new voices of Latinas doing critical analysis and scholarship in theological and intellectual arenas are emerging. These Latina scholars bring to the table of scholarship an understanding of liberation that is integral and holistic. To some it may appear as a sense of *bendito coraje*, or "blessed anger." At the same time there is a sense of deep, reflective feminist spirituality which is a mixture of new and old perspectives. This includes a fresh and vibrant analysis which both challenges and inspires us to see things in new ways. This reader gives us a foundational affirmation of and deep affinity to these fresh voices.

This collection of essays combines the voices of established and emerging Latina scholars. It is worth noting that this is the first collaborative work focusing on the feminist theological exploration of the lived experience of Latinas and using it as the starting point and key source for theological insight. As a whole, this volume continues the tradition of bringing together our resources, strengths, and visions, as they are culturally mediated, and which characterize Latina scholarship in general and Latino/a theology in particular as joint theories and theologies, *teorías y teologías de conjunto*. As a shared effort, this volume enriches, deepens, and develops further the *teología de conjunto* tradition by framing it within distinct feminist struggle and thought. This manner of scholarship highlights not only the connection of our common endeavors to the reality of our communities, but also our shared commitment to the goals of human dignity for all and greater justice for women. As such, our endeavors demonstrate a relational character and a communitarian orientation.

As the subtitle reads, the significance of this book is the systematic approach that the various contributors take to examine the relationship between religion and justice from the social and cultural context of Latino/a life. More significantly, this reader makes the point that religion and theology can and must be related to the history of struggle and hope, of suffering and survival, of poverty and social change, of injustice and liberation in our plural communities. A theology that refuses to be touched by these past and present histories becomes an empty and alienating religious ideology. Certainly, from the point of view of liberating Christianity, religion and the struggle for justice cannot be separated. The various essays included in this book adopt multiple feminist methods and address a diversity of topics. However, in my opinion, what provides unity to the book is the coherent way in which the contributors approach the relationship of religion and justice from a feminist perspective. The plurality of methods and topics does not hinder but rather enriches the ecumenical conversation about intercultural and interdisciplinary theologies.

The theological world has been waiting for this conversation. Crucial to this dialogue is the intersection of traditions, values, theology, and social justice. Oftentimes, we Latinas who have walked with the poor have lacked confidence in our ability to articulate our vision of humanity, or our theological method and our claim to justice both at the national and international levels. This reader moves beyond these fears and initiates a diverse and ecumenical conversation with a wider community. It will give scholars, especially feminist scholars of religion, as well as theology and ministry students, church congregations, pastors and priests, students in various related fields, and, most importantly, the international community, an opportunity to read and understand Latinas in the United States.

INTRODUCTION

MARÍA PILAR
AQUINO,

DAISY L.
MACHADO,

AND JEANETTE
RODRÍGUEZ

This collection of original articles represents the critical reflections and voices of Latinas engaged in theology in the United States of America. Other well-known feminist anthologies have brought together and identified the "experiences of women." However, the experiences presented in those anthologies continue to be dominated almost exclusively by Euro-American or Afro-American women. This collection is an attempt to add the perspectives of U.S. Latinas to that feminist religious intellectual construction. This reader includes contributions from Latinas who live all around the United States of America, who are not only ethnically diverse but ecclesiologically diverse as well, and as such they are representative of the Latina mosaic that is a reality in our communities. We lift our voices to share the variety of issues that interest us, trouble us, challenge us, and motivate us. We are aware of how important it is for women to hear one another's voices to enhance the work that needs to be done. The addition of our Latina voices, as expressed in our diverse methodologies and approaches, provides to the national tapestry of "women's experiences" the missing textures, colors, shapes, and shades that are created by our Latina context. By adding the experiences of Latinas we seek to transform and enlarge that tapestry and create a bridge that connects to the work of our feminist and womanist sisters. In this anthology we not only acknowledge the great diversity of approaches to the feminist religious language but also the unity of themes found among U.S. Latina feminists.

This is a feminist Latina reader. This collection articulates the theological reflection of Latinas in the United States of America on the realities, struggles, and spirituality of women. We understand theology as a dynamic and critical language with which we express our religious vision of a new paradigm of civilization that is free of systemic injustice and violence due to kyriarchal domination.[1] Empowered by this language, we seek to affirm new models of social relationships that are capable of fully sustaining human dignity and the integrity of creation. Beginning with the religious practices and imagination of our Latina communities, the feminist religious language allows us to say who we are and how we seek to affect the present and future direction of society, culture, churches, and the academy. As women engaged in theology, whether in the church or in the academy, we acknowledge the importance of claiming a space for our voices to be heard and for collaboration among women to be achieved. With the emergence and growth of the feminist theologies of liberation, we no longer wait for others to define or validate our experience of life and faith. Women, and in fact all who are in a constant struggle against oppression, have decided to interpret and to name themselves. We want to express in our own words our plural ways of experiencing God and our plural ways of living our faith. And these ways have a liberative tone. In the midst of a reality in which "women of color" continue to be excluded, as noted by M. P. Aquino, doing theology "is not a luxury, but a necessity and a right to be claimed."[2]

The task of theological reflection is never done in a vacuum, and it builds on the reflections and learnings of other women who journey with us. That is why we acknowledge the important work and contributions of Ada María Isasi-Díaz in developing what she has defined as *mujerista* theology.[3] However, we have opted to name ourselves Latina feminists. Since the power of self-naming is so crucial to the experience of women, particularly non-white women of grassroots provenance, this decision represents our effort at self-identity in the public sphere.[4] It also represents our effort at establishing conversation with the rich tradition of Latina/Chicana feminism in the United States of America. As Latina feminists, what we offer in this reader is what Cherríe Moraga has called "a theory in the flesh," which because of the "physical realities of our lives—our skin color, the land or concrete we grew up on, our sexual longings—all fuse to create a politic born out of necessity."[5] This theory in the flesh is also plural and multivocal. Because the Latina community in the United States of America is a *culturally plural* and a *mestizo/a* community present in all colors of the human rainbow,[6] the articles in this reader also represent the variety of voices and realities of *Chicanas (or Xicanismas), Puertorriqueñas, Cubanas, Mexicanas,* and *Sur Americanas.* Our common bond is that we live in the United States of America (our physical reality), where we have all experienced racism, sexism, devaluation, and exclusion by a culture and a society that cannot seem to move beyond the white/black focus of its national discourse on race and national identity.

As Latina feminists, we are presenting a critical framework from which we analyze the realities of Latinas in the United States of America. In doing this, we examine inequalities along lines of race, class, poverty, citizenship, gender, and religion as they affect us and our communities. With these articles we hope to challenge Euro-American feminists and womanists to rethink the issues that directly relate to the ongoing and developing discourse of women in both the secular world and the theological academy. We understand that the dominant feminism, Euro-American and womanist, in the United States of America represents only one type of what Chéla Sandoval calls "oppositional consciousness,"[7] also found in other liberation movements and ideologies. Therefore what we bring to the feminist and womanist discourse is a pluralism that goes beyond the white/black agenda. The articles in this reader focus on issues that are relevant and pertinent to Latinas yet are also of concern to our national agenda. The articles in this collection reflect on the themes of the Latina reality, whether it be the issue of identity or the importance of popular religion in Latina communities or the situation of undocumented women who live within U.S. borders. We find in this collection of writings evidence that what Ivone Gebara has said is true for Latinas in the United States of America: "Feminist theological expression always starts from what has been lived, from what is experienced in the present."[8]

The theology in this reader is one that takes seriously the relative autonomy as well as the integration of theory and practice while reflecting on life. As a result, it is a theology that is in the process of

xvi   A READER IN LATINA FEMINIST THEOLOGY

redefining reason itself. Our task as Latina scholars is not to give up reason or neglect skill development in favor of social justice, but to demonstrate that *how* we think counts as reason. How we think arises from our plural practices and lived experiences. We want to be able to tell our own history and speak about our condition and our expectations. That is why the Latina feminist language we are presenting cannot overlook or dismiss the issues of nationalism and the geopolitical configurations of the nation-state as analytical categories. The history of Latinas is interconnected with the history of conquest and domination of the southwestern reaches of this country, as well as of the Spanish-speaking Caribbean, by an ever-evolving United States of America. This is a national story as well as an international one in which the United States of America would seek to dominate an entire hemisphere—militarily, economically, and racially.

Latinas share a common history of *conquista* and *reconquista*, of colonization and domination. We know what it means to be seen as intruder and alien on our own land; we know what life is like as a daily cultural, social, and racial "border crosser." It is this national/international reality that is unique and important to the Latina feminist, while it also serves to focus our writings on relations of power. In these relations of power the Latina uses her social position as well as her gender and cultural location (language and skin color) as the place to begin her analysis. The result is a process that empowers and decolonizes. That is why the issue of justice remains central to our analysis. As a result of our shared history of conquest and colonization, Latina feminists use their theological reflection to move in new and liberating directions in which justice is also interpreted as a Christian vision of a new humanity in a new social order. The quest for justice, for social transformation, gives Latinas the power to challenge the dominant culture's devaluation of our own culture, language, and indigenous intellectual legacy while affirming our self-worth.

As Latina feminists we are also trying to formulate what can be called "marginal" theories because they are partially outside and partially inside the Western frame of reference. We are articulating new positions that examine the "in-betweenness" of Latinas who live in this country. As Gloria Anzaldúa says, the Latina lives in a "borderland world of ethnic communities and academies, feminist and job worlds."[9] In this in-between existence we move across racial, cultural, economic, and idiomatic boundaries. We may be citizens, but we continue to have outsider status. We may be a part of the academy, but our research interests continue to be labeled "special topics." We may be members of a parish, but our styles of worship continue to be considered nontraditional and ethnic. The ministries to our communities continue to be underfunded and overlooked in denominational planning. We are daily border-crossers who must learn early on to interpret life on both sides—life in the dominant culture and life in the Latina community—in order to survive. The pages of this book give the reader a glimpse into the experiences and patterns of life we have uncovered, and we offer our own theories to help understand and interpret a reality that touches the lives of the more than thirty-five million Latina/os living in this country. In our reflection/writing there is also an obligation and a sense that our primary responsibility, accountability, is to our people, our communities, our children. Therefore, we challenge the prevailing view of scholarship as a fundamentally individual activity undertaken in isolation from community. We further question the mind-set that too readily pits the individual against society, affect against intellect, subjectivity against objectivity, science against theology, and faith against religion. Our faith is at the root of our struggle *and* our reflection.

This collection is divided into two sections. The first contains six articles that focus on the source or locus of Latina thought and insight: religious practice. Beginning with historical contextualization, Michelle González writes about Sor Juana Inés de la Cruz and her legacy of writings, which provide a clear example of how the religious practice of Latinas does have a feminist intellectual history. The article by Teresa Delgado examines the writings of Puerto Rican women as they struggle with their national reality as *colonia* and how those writers offer a new source for feminist liberation theology. Gail Pérez examines the *cuentos* of Chicana writer Ana Castillo, arguing that she uses the popular religion/folklore of Chicanas as a tool to interpret the reality of class, race, and oppression. Leticia Guardiola-Sáenz explores the concept of identity and the ways it is used as a hermeneutical lens for a liberating reading strategy. Anna Adams focuses on Latina Pentecostals, a rapidly growing group, by examining the context of one geographic setting, Allentown, Pennsylvania. In the final article of this section, Jeanette Rodríguez looks at the context in which Latinas live out their faith and how that faith fuels their commitment to justice.

The second section has as its focus the methods and insights of

Latina feminists on two levels. The six articles in this section not only establish a deliberate yet critical conversation with the existent U.S. Latina feminism, but they also examine the reality of Latina life. María Pilar Aquino's article explores the central features of our theological activity, including its understandings and orientations, context of reality, preconditions and characteristics, key principles, and its major tasks. Daisy L. Machado writes about the undocumented women who live in this country, using the biblical image of the Levite's concubine to examine relations of power and nationhood. Carmen Nanko examines how the Latina/o theologian must rethink the concept of a "preferential option for the poor" that is central to Latin American liberation theology, so that such an option can give voice to the reality of the U.S. Latina community. Nora Lozano-Díaz writes about the Virgin of Guadalupe from a Protestant perspective; she examines whether *la virgencita* has been ignored by Protestant Latinas. Gloria Loya explores the many contributions of Latinas to what she calls "an ever-evolving *mestiza* feminist theology." And finally, Nancy Pineda-Madrid develops a "ChicanaFeminist epistemology," describing the major themes of this epistemology and their importance for the intellectual work being produced by Latina theologians.

Before closing this introduction, we would like to say a little about the journey of Latinas in theology. The reality is that Latina/o theology is just beginning to take hold within the academy and the Church as a result of the books and articles that the Latina/os in the theological community have produced in the past decade. We are an emerging community that has only recently begun to give voice to our theological reflection and experience. This anthology has Roman Catholic and Protestant contributors, and while we may struggle together, each denominational community also has had its own particular journey and realities. The Roman Catholic U.S. Latinas trace their first steps as a group to the creation of ACHTUS (Academy of Catholic Hispanics in the United States), which officially began in 1988. Five years later, María Pilar Aquino became the first female president of ACHTUS, giving evidence that Latinas have been integral to the burgeoning Roman Catholic Latino/a theology right from the beginning. Protestant Latinas, while still fewer in number than their Catholic sisters, are also making great strides and creating a much-needed space for their theological voices. As a minority within a minority, Protestant Latinas have forged friendships and crossed boundaries with their Roman Catholic Latina sisters, which has created an awareness of the value of both perspectives as well as the importance of all our contributions to theological activity.

And now some words of gratitude. The editors want to say a heartfelt "thank you" to our colleagues who also contributed to the realization of this project. They offered their work with a sense of selfless giving, knowing that we did not have any kind of funding to compensate them for their work. Their goal was to make their voices heard by a larger and more diverse audience. These writers also represent a newly emerging community of younger Latina scholars, many of whom have only recently entered the academy. *A cada una de ustedes, ¡Muchas gracias, hermanas!* This book is the realization of a dream, of OUR dream. María Pilar Aquino's work in the editorial process and her chapter in this book were possible thanks to the Louisville Institute, which, through its Christian Faith and Life Sabbatical Grants Program, allowed her the time to participate in this project. We thank the Louisville Institute for its support. We are especially grateful to Theresa J. May, assistant director and editor-in-chief of the University of Texas Press, for making the publication of this book possible, and to the readers involved in this project for their helpful suggestions. We are also grateful to our colleagues at the University of San Diego, Brite Divinity School, and Seattle University for their support.

Our hope with this anthology is to offer a collection of articles written by Latinas in our search for innovative intercultural explorations for feminist theological methods. We came together driven by our desire to actualize our "anthological imagination." It has taken more than three years for this project to come to fruition, but we celebrate the journey, and we hope that this book will be a bridge to a more open and diverse feminist/womanist dialogue. As Cherríe Moraga has said, "We do this bridging by naming our selves and by telling our stories in our own words."[10]

NOTES

1. On the meaning of *kyriarchy* as analytical category, see Elisabeth Schüssler Fiorenza, *Rhetoric and Ethic. The Politics of Biblical Studies*, 5–6, and *Jesus Miriam's Child, Sophia's Prophet. Critical Issues in Feminist Christology*, 14.

2. María Pilar Aquino, *Our Cry for Life: Feminist Theology from Latin America*, 68.

3. Ada María Isasi-Díaz, *En la Lucha. In the Struggle: Elaborating a*

Mujerista Theology and *Mujerista Theology: A Theology for the Twenty-First Century.*

4. As editors of this book we acknowledge that the term *mujerista* was coined in Peru as the name for a sectarian gynocentric group that, inspired by an essentialist ideology about women, turned away from the powerful Peruvian feminist movement in the late 1970s and gradually disappeared in the late 1980s. See Documento Final, "Del amor a la necesidad. A Julieta Kirkwood. IV Encuentro Feminista Latinoamericano y del Caribe. Taller: La política feminista en América Latina hoy," in *Caminando: Luchas y Estrategias de las Mujeres. Tercer Mundo,* María Antonieta Saa, Isis Internacional, Ediciones de las Mujeres, vol. 11 (1989): 9–13.

5. Cherríe Moraga, "Entering the Lives of Others. Theory in the Flesh," in *This Bridge Called My Back: Writings by Radical Women of Color,* ed. Cherríe Moraga and Gloria Anzaldúa, 23.

6. See Gloria Anzaldúa, *Borderlands/La Frontera: The New Mestiza;* Daisy L. Machado, "Latino Church History: A Haunting Memory," *Perspectivas,* Hispanic Theological Initiative, no. 1 (fall 1998): 22–34; Jeanette Rodríguez, "U.S. Hispanic/Latino Theology: Context and Challenge," *Journal of Hispanic/Latino Theology* 5:3 (1998): 6–15; María Pilar Aquino, "Directions and Foundations of Hispanic/Latino Theology: Toward a Mestiza Theology of Liberation," *Journal of Hispanic/Latino Theology* 1:1 (1993): 5–21.

7. Chéla Sandoval, "Mestizaje as Method: Feminists-of-Color Challenge the Canon," in *Living Chicana Theory,* ed. Carla Trujillo, 355, 359; and "U.S. Third World Feminism: The Theory and Method of Oppositional Consciousness in the Postmodern World," *Genders,* no. 10 (spring 1991): 1–36.

8. See Ivone Gebara, "Women Doing Theology in Latin America," in *Feminist Theology from the Third World: A Reader,* ed. Ursula King, 55.

9. Gloria Anzaldúa's introduction ("Haciendo caras, una entrada") in *Making Face, Making Soul. Haciendo Caras. Creative and Critical Perspectives by Feminists of Color,* ed. Gloria Anzaldúa, xxvi.

10. Moraga, "Entering the Lives of Others," 23.

PART I

SOURCES, THOUGHT, AND PRAXIS OF LATINA FEMINIST INSIGHT

CHAPTER 1

SEEING BEAUTY WITHIN TORMENT

SOR JUANA INÉS DE LA CRUZ AND THE BAROQUE IN NEW SPAIN

MICHELLE A.
GONZÁLEZ

Very few women's voices emerge in the history books and theological texts of colonial Latin America. Many, in fact, would argue that there are few substantial figures in this region whose impact is significant beyond their local context. Latin America has historically been set apart from the remainder of the New World and, as a consequence, all of Europe. As Octavio Paz writes in his monumental work on the life, work, and culture of Sor Juana Inés de la Cruz, "Our history, from the perspective of modern Western history, has been ex-centric. We have no age of critical philosophy, no bourgeois revolution, no political democracy: no Kant, no Robespierre, no Hume, no Jefferson."[1] The difference of Latin America's history has been historically judged as lower or less than the Anglo-European dominant group. Since we *seemingly* have no Kant or Jefferson, we are seen as having nothing to contribute to other cultures and nations intellectually. Paz does not find the equivalent of the traditional philosophical greats in the Spanish New World. I disagree.

I maintain that we can find in Latin America our Kants and Jeffersons. Due to the marginalization of Latin American culture, history, and scholarship, these voices have been ignored and invalidated. As George Tavard notes in his work *Juana Inés de la Cruz and the Theology of Beauty: The First Mexican Theology:*

Well known in her native Mexico and in the generality of the Spanish-speaking world, Juana Inés de la Cruz has remained largely unknown to the educated public of English-speaking North America, in spite of the fact that good scholarly investigations of her life and works have been done in the United States . . . Undoubtedly, the disregard of a major literary figure from South of the Rio Grande proceeds in part from the traditional indifference of the English-speaking populations of North America to speakers of the Spanish language.[2]

Granted, these intellectuals and scholars appear in different guises than their European and North American counterparts. Since they do not carry the prestige and weight of European history behind them, and they are seemingly insignificant, or solely significant on a highly contextualized level. Their impact resonates in less obvious ways.

It is my contention that Sor Juana Inés de la Cruz, a seventeenth-century nun from New Spain,[3] is such a figure. Her writings may not have aided in the founding of a nation, but her voice speaks of the birth of a people. A study of her writings reveals not only a substantial source of creative philosophical and theological thought but also a vital historical resource for feminist scholarship.[4] The very act of "un-covering"[5] this resource is an empowering act for Latina Americans, whose contributions are often overlooked in the pages of mainstream history. Therefore, to retrieve Sor Juana's voice is to recognize the omission of Latinas as an androcentric and ethnocentric oversight.

The primary purpose of this study is the introduction of Sor Juana's writings as a vital resource to U.S. Latina/o theology, feminist theology (both Latino/a and non-Latino/a), and the larger theological community. Through her life and work Sor Juana confronts assumptions that Latina Americans do not have an intellectual history, specifically in the fields of theology and philosophy. This study will be threefold, beginning with a brief examination of the Baroque in New Spain. Second, I will provide a biographical sketch of Sor Juana's life, followed, third, by some initial explorations into the theology of Sor Juana. I will conclude with a preliminary examination of Sor Juana's work in dialogue with contemporary Latina/o theology, offering some horizons for future study.

Building on the methodological insights of Latina theology, theological scholarship on Sor Juana exhibits a subversive hermeneutic that challenges the androcentric Western philosophical and theological tradition through the very form and content of her work. In a similar vein, Sor Juana offers us a window through which to explore a colonial feminist in the Americas.[6] Without imposing contemporary categories upon a seventeenth-century figure, we shall see that many of the concerns and themes developed in Sor Juana's work mirror her contemporary Latina American counterparts.

THE BAROQUE IN NEW SPAIN

In comparing the histories of Latin America and the United States, one finds the shared influence of religion behind the colonization of the "New World." Yet while the English fled in search of religious freedom, the Spanish *conquista* was rooted, in part, in a commitment to spread and maintain orthodox Roman Catholic faith. This distinction, coupled with the distinctively Spanish Counterreformation, produced what we today call the Baroque in New Spain. Historian Irving Leonard sets the Baroque's parameters: "The chronological limits of the Baroque are roughly set from the mid-sixteenth to the mid-eighteenth centuries, reaching a peak around the middle of the seventeenth."[7] Leonard best expresses the spirit of the Baroque when he writes:

In contrast to the more northerly parts of Europe the Hispanic people reacted to humanism by trying to reintegrate a medieval religiosity with science, but the end result was largely a blend of the two intellectual movements. A neoscholasticism became the methodology of a neo-orthodoxy without diminishing the dilemma of Christendom . . . The effect was a tendency to shift from content to form, from ideas to details, to give new sanctions to dogmas, to avoid issues, and to substitute subtlety of language for subtlety of thought; it served to repress rather than liberate the human spirit, and to divert by spectacles, by overstatement, and by excessive ornamentation. Such, in essence, was the spirit of the so-called "Baroque-Age" as manifested in the Hispanic world.[8]

In his discussion of the longevity and intensity of the Baroque's impact on Latin American cultures, Leonard provides various factors that must be considered. They are as follows: Spain's isolation of the New World from other European influences during its formative years; the Church's massive influence and control in the New World, even in "secular" society; and the Church as the patron of the arts. The repressive Baroque spirit that Leonard highlights has a concrete effect on the life and work of Sor Juana.

The Baroque was a time of paradox. This is due in part to the attempt in Baroque times to resolve and maintain the medieval worldview that was slowly deteriorating in the wake of scientific, political, and economic revolutions throughout Europe and the Americas. It is interesting that within this chaos Louis Dupré, in his work *Passage to Modernity: An Essay in the Hermeneutics of Nature and Culture,* finds "a comprehensive spiritual vision" uniting Baroque times. This vision, as highlighted by Dupré, is the attempt to maintain the unified Medieval worldview of the secular and sacred. "In its successful achievements, the horizons of immanence and transcendence become totally fused."[9]

The society of New Spain was constructed in such a way as to mirror Spain. In this era, Spain saw itself as the Kingdom of God that was up against the Kingdom of Man, the rest of Europe. It therefore attempted to shut out any Enlightenment ideas, which were seen as tinged with Reformation ideologies. While this proved an extremely complex task within Europe, the isolation of New Spain made it easier to contain the cultural and political influences on its intellectual life. It is perhaps for this reason that Paz does not see an age of critical philosophy in Latin America. However, to judge the development of Latin American philosophy based solely on androcentric European philosophy is to claim such thought as universally normative.

In her work *Razón y Pasión de Sor Juana,* Anita Arroyo describes the Baroque as an era in which:

The most contrary political, economic, religious, and social interests clash. The great values of the spirit are in crisis. Faith erodes, the ancient philosophical edifice collapses. The consequence of this total change of the historical conditions is the transformation of the spiritual attitude of the human, and as it has been well said, the style is a result of all these complex cultural factors, and this change produces the baroque style.[10]

The Baroque was a new way of dealing with the sharp contrasts and contradictions of life: the rich and the poor, morality and barbarism, idealism and realism. The comprehensive manner in which this occurred, touching practically every aspect of culture, caused an utter transformation of society.

The social hierarchy of New Spain was extremely immobile. The structure remained firmly in place based on birthplace and skin color. These two factors are difficult to hide. I would also add the factor of biological sex to this formula. This was truly a world where most women had minimal influence and autonomy. Some women, however, were able to flourish intellectually and impact significantly the world and culture around them. One such woman was Sor Juana Inés de la Cruz.

A VOICE FROM NEPANTLA, A VOICE IN NEPANTLA[11]

Sor Juana was born sometime between 1648 and 1651 in Nepantla, Mexico.[12] The daughter of unwed parents, her mother was a *criolla*,[13] and her father a Spanish military officer. Around the age of thirteen Sor Juana went to live in the court of the viceroy of Mexico, as the lady-in-waiting of Marchioness of Mancera. She stayed there for three years. Her relationship with the viceregal court, which next to the Catholic Church was the most powerful force in New Spain, would prove a vital association throughout her life. In 1666, she entered into the very ascetic, cloistered Order of the Carmelites. Unable to withstand the rigors of Carmelite rule, however, she became ill and returned to the court. In 1669, she entered the convent of Saint Paula of the Order of San Jerónimo in Mexico City, where she would remain for the rest of her life.

It is always difficult, when examining a historical figure, to resist the impulse to place her in our contemporary categories. One must also avoid excessive psychological analysis and caricature. Sor Juana scholarship is saturated with attempts to understand the internal drives and desires that motivated her. This desire to insert Sor Juana's writings into contemporary models is best exemplified in the title bestowed on her as "First Feminist of the New World."[14] In a recent article, Alicia Gaspar de Alba reconfigures Sor Juana as a "Chicana lesbian feminist."[15] While it is inevitable that we examine Sor Juana through our eyes, we must not, however, imply that her life and her work neatly fit into our modern/postmodern theoretical constructs. Retrieving her as a theologian, a foundational impulse in this essay, is in fact for me a subversive principle. As I will demonstrate in my concluding comments, Sor Juana as a theologian challenges our twenty-first-century constructs of what is defined as theology.

At a young age Sor Juana was extremely interested in intellectual pursuits. As Leonard notes, "She had devoured any and every book that came within her reach. At the age of fifteen she had already established a reputation as the most learned woman in Mexico . . . It was because of her learning that she gained a position at the vicere-gal court."[16] Learning was her first love. In her most explicitly auto-biographical piece, *The Answer to Sor Filotea*, she tells of begging her mother to allow her to dress as a boy in order to enter the university (her mother refused), spending her youth studying in her grandfather's library, and learning Latin at an early age.

Attending a university was not an option for women in seven-teenth-century New Spain, even for a woman renowned for her ge-nius. Sor Juana's decision to enter the convent is a point of heated de-bate for *sorjuanistas*.[17] Some, such as Dorothy Schons, frame Sor Juana's decision in the context of the limited options for a woman in seventeenth-century Mexico. Short of marriage, as a *criolla* she had little other option. "She was, therefore, practically forced to choose convent life, or be at the mercy of the world . . . We may safely con-clude that the deep, underlying reason for Juana's retirement from the world is to be found in the social conditions of her time."[18] Implicit in this analysis is trivialization of Sor Juana's sense of vocation.

More recently, Patricia A. Peters disputes this claim as reduction-ism, offering what I see as a more comprehensive look at Sor Juana's entry into convent life. Peters highlights the historical caricature of Sor Juana as an unsuitable woman religious.

Sor Juana has been found wanting as a nun by many of her male critics such as Ermilio Abreu Gómez, editor of the first critical editions of her work, who wrote in 1934 in a long prologue that hers was a fake vocation by which she deceived others to satisfy her own intellectual needs. Thirty years later, she was posthumously analyzed by Ludwig Pfandl, who saw her devotion to books as a sexual aberration and accused her of penis envy and menopausal neurosis . . . More recently, her biographer Octavio Paz, after claiming her as one of Mex-ico's greatest poets, found her guilty of narcissism, devoid of religious calling, and in the habit of unhealthy sexual sublimation.[19]

In such assessments and Schons's comments, Peters sees an overall superficial analysis of Sor Juana's vocation and devotion.

According to the biography of her confessor, Sor Juana hesitated to enter the convent, fearing that life there would impede her studies.[20] This documented fear could lead one to suspect that for Sor Juana, re-ligious life was a mere façade to allow her to pursue her studies. Per-haps it is best to turn to Sor Juana's thoughts on this matter. She writes that she entered the convent because "it would, given my ab-solute unwillingness to enter into marriage, be the least unfitting and the most decent state I could choose."[21] She hesitated at first, for she feared that the obligations of convent life and the noise of her community would distract her from her studies.

A cursory glance at her words could lead one to believe that Sor Juana in fact had very self-gratifying reasons for taking the veil. This reading, however, fails to take into account how Sor Juana herself viewed her intellect. For her it is a gift from God:

For ever since the light of reason first dawned on me, my inclination to letters was marked by such passion and vehemence that neither the reprimand of others (for I have received many) nor reflections of my own (there have been more than a few) have sufficed to make me abandon my pursuit of this native impulse that God Himself bestowed on me.[22]

One must also consider Sor Juana's Thomistic understanding of the hierarchy of knowledge. After being publicly reprimanded by her bishop for her "secular" plays and poetry (ironically this occurs as a result of Sor Juana's first and only explicitly theological essay), Sor Juana defends her actions, for they were rooted in her desire to eventually write theology.

I went on in this way, always directing each step of my studies, as I have said, towards the summit of Holy Theology; but it seemed to me necessary to ascend by the ladder of the humane arts and sciences in order to reach it; for who could fathom the style of the Queen of Sciences without knowing that of her handmaidens?[23]

For her, theology, as the "Queen of Sciences," is, in a Thomistic fashion, the perfection of secular knowledge. As a nuanced interpretation of her entry into the convent, I offer Sor Juana's inclination to follow what she held as God's vocation for her in the pursuit of her studies.

For the most part, Sor Juana's poetry and plays were commissioned. Her services as a poet were very much in demand. She composed poetry for both church festivities and court occasions. She states that she never wrote for herself and felt extremely inadequate in her work. "I have never written a single thing of my own volition, but rather in response to the pleadings and command of others."[24] Because her work was commissioned, we find in it the excessive ornamentations and praises to God, Jesus, the saints, the Church, and members of the court. The very nature of her work required the excesses of the Baroque. In Sor Juana's dramas, for example, the lives of the saints are illustrated in a lively fashion to make it interesting for the viewers. Much like the architecture of the Baroque era, Sor Juana's writings are lavish and ornamented. As George Tavard writes, "She literally decorates the spiritual edifice that is the Church in Mexico, and, more generally, the Church in all Hispanic lands."[25]

The first volume of her works was published in 1689 in Madrid, sponsored by the wife of the viceroy. In 1692, a second volume of her work was published, again with the vicerine's aid. The third volume of her work was published posthumously in 1700. Included in the second volume is Sor Juana's theological critique of a forty-year-old sermon written by the Jesuit Antonio Vieira that emerged in Mexico in 1690. The critique had been distributed without her authorization and given the title *Carta Atenagórica* (Letter worthy of Athena). This essay, in which Sor Juana criticizes Vieira's opposition to Augustine, Aquinas, and John of Chrysostom's interpretations of the finesses of Christ's favor and love, would prove to be detrimental to her situation with ecclesial authorities in Mexico.[26] Her response to the letter's unauthorized publication, *La respuesta a Sor Filotea de la Cruz* (The answer), was published the following year. Within four years of the publication of her answer, Sor Juana completely renounced her public life. "She also had all her books and instruments sold, and the money was given to the poor. She never wrote another line for the public."[27]

An account of her renunciation cannot be fully explored without momentarily backtracking to the ecclesial environment under which Sor Juana lived and wrote. One must remember that as a former employee of the viceroy's court, Sor Juana had connections and relationships with many people in power, especially her close relationship to the viceroy's wife, the Condesa de Paredes (María Luisa Manrique de Lara y Gonzaga, Marquesa de Laguna). Her friendship with this woman often protected Sor Juana from Church reprimands and warnings.

Though Sor Juana belonged to a cloistered order, her friendships and the popularity of her works enabled her to live a very public life, with a flow of daily visitors at her convent. To ecclesial authorities, Sor Juana's life was too public. As Schons notes, "Her worldly life brought down upon her the criticism of the more sinister, more fanatical element in the church."[28] The controversy surrounding her theological critique emerged after the departure to Spain of her most loyal and powerful friends (including the *condesa*). Her relationship with her confessor, Father Nuñez, deteriorated—a significant and perilous occasion in her life. He was extremely powerful in the Mexican Church, and his disapproval of her resulted in disastrous effects.[29]

It is apparent that prior to this renunciation she was under extreme pressure from ecclesial authorities to curtail her public life and scholarship. During that time she wrote: "But all this has merely led me closer to the flames of persecution, the crucible of affliction, and to such extremes that some have even sought to prohibit me from study."[30] She grew to believe that the gift of her intellect was alienating her from her duty to God. In the end, Sor Juana was never formally told to cease her studies. Her bishop, however, recommended that she refocus her life primarily on religious works, not intellectual pursuits. In 1694, she signed a statement of self-condemnation, devoting the rest of her life to self-sacrifice. The next year, 1695, Sor Juana died in the convent from an affliction.

Sor Juana suffered from an internal conflict that mirrored the struggles of colonial Spain: the desire to gain knowledge and the constraints of the means to do so. Octavio Paz rightfully notes, "Sor Juana affirmed her times, and her times affirmed themselves in her."[31] We see in her the struggle between the secular and the sacred, the Church and the State. We also find in her their tumultuous unity, the fragile unity of the Baroque. Mariano Picón-Salas praises this attribute:

Sister Juana Inés de la Cruz's work, more than any other, seems to bring into peculiar focus the values and enigmas of the Baroque century . . . Scholastic philosophy, music, mathematics, and the subtle psychological analysis of current Jesuit theology, all found a place in the Baroque content of her verse.[32]

THE BEAUTY OF GOD, THE BEAUTY OF CREATION

Sor Juana's extensive literary, philosophical, and theological background is revealed in the various forms of her writings: her poetry, plays, and essays. Pamela Kirk, in her recent monograph, *Sor Juana Inés de la Cruz: Religion, Art and Feminism*,[33] notes that two-thirds of Sor Juana's work is religious and that those writings "occupy a middle place between literature and theology."[34] In a particularly helpful passage Kirk also highlights the pluralistic forms of Sor Juana's writings as representative of the theology of her era:

This remarkable variety of literary expressions offers a challenge to the theologian because of contemporary expectations of the genre of theological discourse as prose reflection and critical argumentation. Sor Juana's age was accustomed to receiving religious content not only through sermons, works of theology, and books of devotion, but also through sacramental dramas . . . Because she was adept at using these popular forms, consideration of her theology from this angle can also be instructive for the theology of our time in its search for alternative expressions of theological content.[35]

As Kirk suggests, a study of Sor Juana's theological writings is a useful means of pursuing constructive, alternative theological forms, both as we study the past and as we turn toward the future. Of special note is Sor Juana's *auto-sacramental El Divino Narciso* (The divine Narcissus). This play is the most theological of Sor Juana's writings.[36] Therefore, as a preliminary investigation into Sor Juana's theology, to this text we turn.

An *auto-sacramental* is a play performed during the feast of Corpus Christi. "The *autos* derived from medieval religious theater, which was still pervaded with ancient ceremonies and pagan festivals. These sacred mysteries, accompanied by games and pantomimes, were performed in the atriums of churches."[37] Often, Greek mythology was used in Spanish dramas in the seventeenth century. The plays were used as catechisms, to educate Catholics and fortify their beliefs. The *auto-sacramental* always ended with the triumph of the Eucharist over the misery of life. *The Divine Narcissus* was written around 1688. It appears in a volume of Sor Juana's works published in 1692.

All of Sor Juana's *autos-sacramentales* are preceded by *loas*. As defined by Paz, a *loa* is "a brief theatrical piece played as prologue to a principal play, often in praise of visiting or newly arrived dignitaries or for royal anniversaries."[38] The four main characters of the *loa* for *The Divine Narcissus* are Occident, America, Zeal, and Religion. Occident and America are *indios* (natives). Zeal represents the Spanish military force. Religion is Roman Catholicism as represented by a Spanish lady.

America and Occident are celebrating the feast of the *dios de la semillas* (god of the harvest), one of their pagan gods. Zeal and Religion arrive on the scene, each with a very different agenda. Zeal wants to attack and kill the two *indios*, while Religion wants to convert them to Christianity. After some debate, Religion convinces the two *indios* that their god is but an anticipation of the Christian God, who is the great God of all gods. In order to better explain the beauty and glory of the Christian God, Religion decides to teach them about Christianity through the play *The Divine Narcissus.*

In Octavio Paz's analysis of this *loa,* he notes that one of its major themes is that "early pagan rites contained signs that, although encoded and allegorical, foreshadowed the Gospel."[39] This is clearly seen in Religion's affirmation to Occident and America that their god of the seeds is contained within the Christian God. Sor Juana, knowing of an Aztec ritual characterized by creating and eating a figure of the god Huitzilopochtli, links this as a precursor to the Eucharist. We see this in the *auto* itself, which ends with praise of the Eucharist. Also contained in the *loa* is a subtle argument for the use of drama as a theological resource. As Pamela Kirk writes, "All three of the one-act plays with which Sor Juana prefaces her sacramental dramas are designed to point up the limits of the 'discussion of the schools' in theological debate and to plead gracefully for drama as a more appropriate form for the communication of theological truths than rational discourse because of the very nature of 'divine things.'"[40] I will return to this point in my concluding comments.

Was Sor Juana perhaps in some way trying to validate the indigenous people's religious practices? Based on these preliminary findings, I believe so. This was a dangerous endeavor, for Aztec rituals were greatly feared and condemned by the Church. Sor Juana engages this directly. As Alejandro López López highlights, "The Tenth Muse, courageous and audacious, doubtlessly elaborates the beliefs of the indigenous and confronts them with the ideology of Catholicism."[41] Zeal, for Sor Juana, represents the irrational, militaristic arm of the conquest. Religion, on the other hand, represents the compassionate, loving side.

The Divine Narcissus is inspired by the tale of Echo and Narcissus, as written by Ovid in *Metamorphoses.*[42] Sor Juana transforms Ovid's myth into an allegory of Christ's passion, death, and resurrection. In the context of the *loa,* the *auto-sacramental* is used for catechetical purposes. The use of a pagan myth to tell the story of Christ reaffirms Sor Juana's belief that there is something redeemable, pre-Christian within pagan religions.

The main characters of the *auto-sacramental* are: Gentile (Gentilidad), who represents the ancient pagan world; Synagogue (Sinagoga), representative of the ancient Hebrew world; the celestial Narcissus, who is Christ; Human Nature (Naturaleza Humana); Echo (Eco); and Pride (La Soberbia) and Self-Love (Amor Propio), who accompany

Echo. Lastly, there is God's Grace (Gracia), who helps Human Nature find Narcissus. The play opens with Gentile praising humanity and her sister, Synagogue, praising divinity. Human Nature, their mother, overhears them and offers the story of Narcissus to explain to them what she intends to demonstrate, the reconciliation of both her daughters' love and adoration, the praise of divinity and humanity. In other words, Sor Juana does not hold an explicit and radical separation between the human and the divine, based on the incarnation and on humanity's creation in the image of God. Also of note is Sor Juana's reaffirmation of the dramatic as a theological vehicle in her introductory comments by Human Nature.

The story proper of Narcissus begins with Echo in love with Narcissus and following him around the forest. Yet hers is an impure love, full of self-gratification and selfishness. Echo, Pride, and Self-Love form an "unholy" trinity motivated by egoism and self-gratification. Jealous of any other potential lovers for Narcissus, Echo's goal is to prevent an encounter of Narcissus and Human Nature. Echo is convinced that if Narcissus sees an unsullied image of Human Nature, he will recognize himself in her and fall in love. This would lead him to redeem humanity. In the play, salvation is defined as Narcissus seeing his beauty reflected in Human Nature and becoming incarnate in her. This in turn would lead to his passion, death, and resurrection.

Echo's intention is to soil all the waters where Narcissus seeks his image to prevent him from seeing Human Nature in his reflection. The particular character of Human Nature, in Sor Juana's play, is representative of all of humanity. Human nature is in its fallen state yet retains its resemblance to the divine. The *imago dei* continues to exist within us, though it is sullied by our self-love and arrogance. Echo, as a character operating with these motivations, can be seen as representative of those impulses within humanity that cloud our *imago dei*.

There are two operative theological themes that are significant to raise at this juncture, for they underlie the entirety of the play. Mauricio Beuchot, in his theological analysis of Sor Juana's three *autos-sacramentales*, highlights one of these themes, Sor Juana's engagement in the perennial debate surrounding the one and the many.[43] Beuchot notes that in transforming the myth of Narcissus into an account of the incarnation and the Eucharist, Sor Juana enters into this recurring theme in classical and medieval philosophy.[44] The Narcissus of mythology falls in love with himself as an individual. The new

Narcissus, as the Son of God, falls in love with himself as a member of the human race and, consequently, falls in love with humanity. It is through the encounter with the individual character of Human Nature that Narcissus falls in love with humanity in its entirety.

The second theme significant to highlight is the role of theological aesthetics in Sor Juana's play. As the embodiment of divine beauty, Narcissus is Beauty, not a mere reflection of beauty.[45] Likewise created in the image of God, Human Nature also embodies this beauty. Echo's fear that Narcissus will see beauty in the face of an unsullied Human Nature, a fear that is realized in the play, is based on the beauty of humanity. Humanity's beauty, however, is only complete with God's Grace. As we shall see, it is only with the gift of God's Grace that humanity's beauty fully comes forth.

Narcissus is found sitting in the forest, which George Tavard proposes as symbolic of Jesus's temptation in the desert. Echo torments and tempts him. Human Nature, also in love with and in search of Narcissus, wanders the forest. Much of Human Nature's speech, as Tavard notes, is lifted from the Song of Songs.[46] She exalts his beauty and proclaims her similarity to him. "Oh, with what reason all adore you! But that the sun's intensity has marked me need not dismay you; Behold, though soiled, I am beautiful, because your countenance I bear."[47] Human Nature, in other words, is on a quest for divine beauty, yet she is frustrated that she cannot find it. At this point God's Grace arrives on the scene to help Human Nature directly. God's Grace shows Human Nature a spring unsullied by Echo, a fountain that is unblemished. Tavard interprets the fountain as representative of the Virgin Mary. "It is one of the more notable features of *Divine Narcissus* that although the Virgin Mary is not represented by an actress she is nonetheless present at the climax of the play: she is the well with clear water. Bent over it, looking into it, Narcissus will see his perfect image."[48]

Human Nature and God's Grace hide and await Narcissus. God's Grace tells Human Nature to make sure her face is seen in the water so that Narcissus will see himself in her and fall in love. He approaches the fountain and within it sees his reflection in the water. "Narcissus sees Nature and Grace together, or, better, he sees Nature through Grace, as their reflected images now form only one beauty in the Virgin Mary."[49] Narcissus falls in love with his image, Human Nature purified in the divine spring with the help of God's Grace. In other words, it is in recognizing that his Beauty is shared with humanity that the incarnation occurs. Sor Juana's Christology and consequently anthropology are based on this theme. Our *imago dei* is Beauty. We share in divine *hermosura*.

The result of this love is a transformation of Narcissus. However, the joy surrounding his love is shortlived. It soon turns to sorrow, for he realizes that he must die for his love. At the end of this scene he passes away. After his death, an earthquake is heard. Listening to the turmoil of nature, Echo proclaims Narcissus as the Son of God. Human Nature is extremely upset and mourning the death of Narcissus when God's Grace appears and tells all to stop mourning, for Narcissus is alive. Narcissus then appears and asks Human Nature why she is sorrowful. She explains her sorrow surrounding Narcissus's death. Like Mary Magdalene in the Gospels, at first Human Nature does not recognize the risen Savior.

When she does identify him, she wants to embrace him, but he refuses because he is on his way to his Father's heavenly throne. Human Nature begs him not to leave her, for she is worried Echo will try to tempt Human Nature away from Narcissus. God's Grace consoles her, promising to remain by her side. Narcissus assures Human Nature that he is leaving something to help her when her faith is faltering, the establishment of the Church and the sacraments. The play ends, in the true form of an *auto-sacramental*, with the Eucharist. The introduction of the Eucharist, along with the affirmation through the Church and other sacraments, demonstrates that Human Nature has a participatory role in salvation history. The image of the divine Narcissus is not merely imprinted in Human Nature unconditionally, nor is it a fleeting moment. Instead, Human Nature is an active expression of God's glory. Human Nature remains human at the end of the play, yet it is a humanity that has been revealed as the gift of God's Grace and Beauty. Echo's pride and egoism can no longer conquer the human spirit. Our "image" can no longer be "distorted" by the egocentricity that Echo represents.

The Divine Narcissus offers us a complex theological vision containing christological and anthropological themes. The genius lies in its transmittal both through a pagan myth and within the context of a dramatic work. As Octavio Paz notes, "Sor Juana's originality lies in her transformation of the pagan myth: Christ does not, like Narcissus, fall in love with his own image, but with Human Nature, who is and is not himself."[50] The use of a Greek myth, while characteristic of the literature of her time, is a significant methodological gesture, especially for Latina/o theology. Various scholars, including Margo Glantz and Marie Bénassy Berling, have documented Sor

Juana's sympathy toward the indigenous populations of New Spain. Sor Juana directly addresses, explicitly in the *loa* and implicitly in the *auto-sacramental*, indigenous religious practices and interprets them as prefiguring Christianity. Perhaps in our day this view of non-Christian religions seems imperialistic. However, in Sor Juana's time this view was quite progressive and dangerous when one considers her position as a woman. As a theology that privileges *mestizaje/mulatez* as a theological locus, Latina/o theology should find in Sor Juana's writings on these themes an interesting theological resource.

Also prominent in this work is Sor Juana's understanding of the incarnation, as Tavard historically situates it:

Juana does not side exactly with either of the two medieval answers to the purpose of the incarnation. She does not, with Anselm, Bonaventure, and Thomas Aquinas, understand the incarnation as primarily remedial, chosen by God to undo the effects of sin by way of redemption. Juana comes closer to John Duns Scotus' idea: the purpose of the incarnation is that humankind should give God the highest possible glory. Yet her view cannot be identified simply with this. Rather, the purpose of the incarnation—identical to that of creation—is the ultimate union of two kinds of divine beauty: the beauty of the eternal Word and the beauty that has been given to creatures.[51]

Key to this theme is the understanding of the incarnation as an event of universal redemption. Sor Juana's Christ/Narcissus is an event for all of humanity, not solely Christians. It is therefore an event for humans in their plurality and difference, as a community of God's creatures. In seeing the beauty that is God, and in seeing the beauty of creation, Sor Juana places herself in a centuries-old tradition of theological aesthetics which culminated in the twentieth century in the work of Hans Urs von Balthasar. Tavard notes, "As has been shown by Hans Urs von Balthasar, the perception of the glory of God has inspired the Christian search for beauty. The history of Christian theology can be seen as a history of attempts to express the glory of God in successive styles and theories of beauty. Although Juana Inés is not mentioned by Urs von Balthasar, she deserves a prominent place among those who have seen the divine beauty in creation."[52]

CONCLUDING COMMENTS

The glory of Sor Juana's works, the passion of her writings, and the pain and struggles of her life demonstrate both her genius and her identity as a Baroque figure. As Picón-Salas writes, "No other artist suffered nor better expressed the tragic drama of the artificiality and repression of our Spanish American baroque than did this extraordinary Mexican nun."[53] The life of Sor Juana is representative of the life of a culture, a people. Through her, Latinos/as find a part of ourselves and the complex labyrinth of our history.

In a brief article on the theological contribution of Sor Juana, Beatríz Melano Couch writes, "Scholars who have studied Sor Juana speak of her greatness as a literary figure, philosopher, and woman of science. My study of her works has brought me to the conclusion that she was also a theologian: indeed, the first woman theologian in all the Americas."[54] Couch's claim is reaffirmed in the above-cited monographs of Kirk and Tavard. As a Latina American,[55] Sor Juana's contributions must be engaged in conversation with Latina/o theology. As a way of offering some concluding comments, I offer two areas in which I find Sor Juana's work to be of particular use: theological method and theological anthropology.

In its response to the demands of the scientific and rationalist worldview produced by the Enlightenment, theology has suffered a great loss. It has, to resonate the thought of von Balthasar, lost its "form." As Latino theologian Roberto S. Goizueta writes,[56]

One of the most devastating consequences of Western rationalism has been the divorce between theological form and content . . . In turn, the traditional forms for communicating such knowledge—symbol, ritual, narrative, metaphor, poetry, music, the arts—are necessarily marginalized as unacademic and unscholarly, that is, as pure (aesthetic) form without (conceptual) content.[57]

Goizueta describes a profound loss in modern-day theology. In its struggle to become an "academic" discipline, theology has lost its form, its beauty, and consequently its ability to reflect the glory of the God whom it claims as its focus. As a result, Goizueta continues, theology has lost the ability to speak with a significant voice. "[W]e have become irrelevant to the faith communities that we claim to represent, and, therefore, increasingly desperate in our attempts to say *something* that actually *matters* to people—not least of all to ourselves. Theology has indeed become academic."[58]

Goizueta's recent work in theopoetics, along with the scholarship of Alejandro García-Rivera and of Peter Casarella, is representative of a turn toward theological aesthetics in Latino theology.[59] In this field, a Latina voice is lacking. Sor Juana's writings, and my intended scholarship surrounding her work,[60] offer a Latina theological aesthetic. Sor Juana scholarship, in addition to contributing to the aesthetic emphasis of some recent Latino theology, also resonates with the hermeneutics of Latina feminist theology. This is most sharply revealed in the work of María Pilar Aquino.

Aquino's theological method is governed by a hermeneutics of suspicion and retrieval that is characteristic of feminist theologies. Applying her method to the Eurocentric mythology surrounding the conquest in the Americas, she notes,

The great European invasions did not *discover* but rather *covered* whole peoples, religions, and cultures and explicitly tried to take away from the natives the sources of their own historical memory and their own power . . . [W]e seek to *un-cover* the truth and bring to light our collective will to choose a different path.[61]

This insight demonstrates the subversive hermeneutics operating in Aquino's work. A similar insight arises when Aquino turns to the colonial period in Mexico. Noting that for many women in the colonial era the patriarchal religious and political structures isolated women to the private sphere, Aquino emphasizes that this was not the case for all women. Citing Sor Juana Inés de la Cruz's writings, Aquino uncovers the agency maintained by women, for example, in convent life.[62]

In addition to these methodological insights, the content of Sor Juana's theology reveals a theological anthropology compatible with themes developed by various Latino/a theologians. Sor Juana's vision of humanity as created in the image of God is posed in contrast to an egocentric understanding of the self (Echo—Pride—Self-Love). Though Sor Juana does not explicitly state this, for she examines the human in light of the gift of God's grace, an intersubjective and relational human is the modern-day opposite of the clouded image of humanity personified in Echo. This image of humanity is seen in the egalitarian anthropology of María Pilar Aquino,[63] the intrinsic role of community in the anthropology of Roberto Goizueta,[64] and the relational anthropology of Ada María Isasi-Díaz.[65]

With these remarks in mind, it is my hope to pursue more extensively the contributory impact of Sor Juana's theological aesthetics on contemporary Latino/a theology and beyond. Much deeper analysis of the complexity of both Sor Juana's writings and Latina/o theology is needed.[66] The present work is intended to begin this much-needed conversation. The "un-covery" of Sor Juana offers the promise of a critical engagement between historical and contemporary Latina/o theological resources and the recovery of a lost theological form.

NOTES

1. Octavio Paz, *Sor Juana: Or, the Traps of Faith*, 16.

2. George Tavard, *Juana Inés de la Cruz and the Theology of Beauty: The First Mexican Theology*, 1. Stephanie Merrim, in her recent study of Sor Juana, notes that this bias pervades women's studies, which has yet to seriously engage the Hispanic context. Stephanie Merrim, *Early Modern Women's Writing and Sor Juana Inés de la Cruz*, xiv.

3. New Spain is a designation for colonial Mexico.

4. With regard to specifically Chicana thought see Alicia Gaspar de Alba, "The Politics of Location of the Tenth Muse in America: An Interview with Sor Juana Inés de la Cruz," in *Living Chicana Theory*, ed. Carla Trujillo, 136–165. Gaspar de Alba explores the complexity of Sor Juana's life and work, with special emphasis on the heterosexism that has plagued modern Sor Juana scholarship, and the classism, racism, and dichotomous gender constructs that shaped Sor Juana's life.

5. The technical use of this term will be examined in the conclusion.

6. See Ana NietoGomez, "Chicana Feminism," in *Chicana Feminist Thought: The Basic Historical Writings*, ed. Alma M. García, 52–57.

7. Irving Leonard, *Baroque Times in Old Mexico: Seventeenth Century Persons, Places, and Practices*, 29.

8. Leonard, *Baroque Times*, 27–28.

9. Louis Dupré, *Passage to Modernity: An Essay in the Hermeneutics of Nature and Culture*, 240.

10. Anita Arroyo, *Razón y pasión de Sor Juana*, 131. Unless otherwise indicated, translations are my own.

11. Nepantla is the Nahuatl word for "land in the middle."

12. The date of Sor Juana's birth is disputed. Her biographer, Father Diego Calleja, gives the date of 1651. A baptismal certificate that is most likely Sor Juana's, however, dates her birth in 1648. See Alfonso Méndez Plancarte's introduction to *Obras Completas de Sor Juana Inés de la Cruz*, vol. 1, LII–LIII, note 1.

13. A *criollo/a* is a person born in the Americas of Spanish/European parents.

14. Stephanie Merrim, preface to *Feminist Perspectives on Sor Juana Inés de la Cruz*, 7.

15. Gaspar de Alba, *Sor Juana's Second Dream*.

16. Leonard, *Baroque Times*, 39.

17. *Sorjuanista* is the term for Sor Juana scholars.

18. Dorothy Schons, "Some Obscure Points in the Life of Sor Juana Inés de la Cruz," in *Feminist Perspectives on Sor Juana Inés de la Cruz*, ed. Stephanie Merrim, 46–47.

19. Patricia A. Peters, introduction to *The Divine Narcissus/El Divino Narciso*, xv. In this introduction Peters cites Ermilio Abreu Gómez, *Sor Juana Inés de la Cruz, Biografía y Biblioteca* (Mexico City: Secretaría de Relaciones Exteriores, 1934); Octavio Paz, *Sor Juana Inés de la Cruz o las Trampas de la Fe* (Mexico City: Fondo de Cultura Económica, 1982); Ludwig Pfandl, *Sor*

Juana Inés de la Cruz, la décima musa de México: su vida, su poesía, su psique (Mexico City: Universidad Nacional Autónoma de México, 1963).

20. Leonard, *Baroque Times*, 40.

21. Sor Juana Inés de la Cruz, *The Answer/La Respuesta*, 51. The original Spanish text can be found in Juana Inés de la Cruz, *Obras Completas*, vol. 4, pages 440–475.

22. Sor Juana, *Answer*, 47; original Spanish in *Obras Completas*, lines 188–193.

23. Sor Juana, *Answer*, 53; original Spanish in *Obras Completas*, lines 312–317.

24. Sor Juana, *Answer*, 97; original Spanish in *Obras Completas*, lines 1263–1265.

25. Tavard, *Juana Inés*, 53.

26. Ironically, when this critique was distributed in Spain, many rose to Sor Juana's defense. Its publication in 1692 was authorized by Spanish ecclesial authorities.

27. Tavard, *Juana Inés*, 7.

28. Schons, "Some Obscure Points," 47.

29. In "Some Obscure Points," Schons writes, "Father Nunez was one of the most powerful ecclesiastic in New Spain . . . There is plenty of evidence to show that all important cases of the Inquisition passed through his hands. The break, therefore, between him and Sor Juana was a most serious matter" (47).

30. Sor Juana, *Answer*, 73; original Spanish in *Obras Completas*, lines 732–735.

31. Paz, *Sor Juana*, 110.

32. Mariano Picón-Salas, *A Cultural History of Spanish America: From Conquest to Independence*, 102–103.

33. Pamela Kirk, *Sor Juana Inés de la Cruz: Religion, Art, and Feminism*.

34. Ibid., 10.

35. Ibid., 12–13.

36. This is affirmed by Tavard, *Juana Inés*, 104.

37. Paz, *Sor Juana*, 338.

38. Ibid., 513.

39. Ibid., 346.

40. Kirk, *Sor Juana Inés*, 38.

41. Alejandro López López, "Sor Juana Inés de la Cruz y la loa al *Divino Narciso* (Raíces autóctonas en los escritos de Sor Juana)," in *Memoria del Coloquio Internacional Sor Juana Inés e la Cruz y el Pensamiento Novohispano*, Biblioteca Sor Juana Inés de la Cruz (Toluca, Mexico: Instituto Mexiquense de Cultura, 1995), 225.

42. Due to space constraints and familiarity, I felt it was unnecessary to include the story of Echo and Narcissus as told by Ovid. For a complete account of the myth see Ovid, *Metamorphoses*.

43. Mauricio Beuchot, "Los Autos de Sor Juana: Tres Lugares Teológicos," 353–392.

44. Ibid., 362.

45. I would like to thank my advisor, Dr. Alejandro García-Rivera, for this insight.

46. Tavard, *Juana Inés*, 119–120.

47. Sor Juana Inés de la Cruz, *El Divino Narciso*, in *Obras Completas de Sor Juana Inés de la Cruz*, vol. 3, pages 3–97. See original Spanish in *Obras Completas*, lines 1036–1040.

48. Tavard, *Juana Inés*, 121.

49. Ibid., 125.

50. Paz, *Sor Juana*, 352.

51. Tavard, *Juana Inés*, 118.

52. Ibid., 186–187.

53. Picón-Salas, *Cultural History*, 105.

54. Beatríz Melano Couch, "Sor Juana Inés de la Cruz: The First Woman Theologian in the Americas," in *The Church and Women in the Third World*, ed. John C. B. Webster and Ellen Low Webster, 54.

55. "Latina American" is a term coined by María Pilar Aquino in her essay "The Collective 'Dis-covery' of Our Own Power: Latina American Feminist Theology," in *Hispanic/Latino Theology: Challenge and Promise*, ed. Ada María Isasi-Díaz and Fernando Segovia, 240–258.

56. Roberto S. Goizueta, "U.S. Hispanic Catholicism as Theopoetics," in *Hispanic/Latino Theology: Challenge and Promise*, ed. Isasi-Díaz and Segovia, 261–288.

57. Ibid., 261.

58. Ibid., 262.

59. Peter Casarella, "The Painted Word," *Journal of Hispanic/Latino Theology* 6, no. 2 (November 1998): 18–41.

60. The theological aesthetics of Sor Juana Inés de la Cruz, in conversation with the work of Hans Urs von Balthasar, is the intended focus of my dissertation.

61. Aquino, "Collective 'Dis-Covery,'" 241–242.

62. Ibid., 247.

63. María Pilar Aquino, *Our Cry for Life: Feminist Theology from Latin America*.

64. Roberto S. Goizueta, "*Nosotros:* Toward a U.S. Hispanic Theological Anthropology," *Listening* 27, no. 1 (winter 1992): 55–69.

65. Ada María Isasi-Díaz, "Elements of a *Mujerista* Anthropology," in her *Mujerista Theology: A Theology for the Twenty-First Century*, 128–147.

66. Sor Juana's contribution, however, is not solely in Latino/a theology, but also in a larger theological arena. In the spirit of the twentieth-century *ressourcement* movement in Roman Catholic theology, which calls us to return to original sources to inform our contemporary understandings, Sor Juana scholarship offers a vital resource for historical theology. In addition, the very form of her writing, as literature, forces us to broaden our understandings of what constitutes the discourse of systematic theology. Sor Juana's dramatic and poetic theology is an inroad for a Latin American *ressourcement*.

CHAPTER 2

PROPHESY FREEDOM

PUERTO RICAN WOMEN'S
LITERATURE AS A SOURCE FOR
LATINA FEMINIST THEOLOGY

TERESA
DELGADO

The prophet lives in the future. She sees the semblance
of life which shines on the surface of the graveyard: too
much talking, too much doing, eating and drinking
before the flood, towers which are built to reach
heavens. But she is an exile, she lives in a different
time, her nest is built in the future . . . The poet plays
her song to the living ones.

But when she sings her song to the dead, she
becomes a prophet . . .

The prophet invokes the Wind. She calls the untam-
able. There are no birds in her cages, no swords in her
hands, no wisdom in her mouth. She is empty, like the
dead. She speaks and hopes that the Wind will come, to
resurrect the Dead.[1]

RUBEM A. ALVES, *The Poet, The Warrior, The Prophet*

In his controversial and still relevant book of
essays titled *The Docile Puerto Rican*, author,
playwright, and literary/cultural critic René
Marqués identifies the mission of the writer as
one who aspires "to defend humanistic values,
to search for the truth, the truth of his own circumstances, to be a rebel, to be free and therefore never to abandon the cause of freedom.[2] It is
in this search for the truth, always elusive and
never fully grasped, that the mission of the creative writer and that of the theologian intersect.
Although the devices and methodologies may
differ, the purpose is the same. Good writing and

good theology, inclusive of the discourse between them,[3] do not claim to be the final word; rather they open our souls to the possibilities, to the questions of ultimacy that our human existence and experiences reflect. David Jasper, in his concluding remarks to his edited volume *The Study of Literature and Religion,* makes this point:

In literature we glimpse, at times, the fulfillment of our nature, cast in the imaginative genius of great art, and continuing to persuade us of the value and ultimate truth of the theological enterprise as a seeking for utterance of the divine mystery as it is known and felt in our experience.[4]

What can these stories by Puerto Rican women writers—Nicholasa Mohr, Judith Ortiz Cofer, Esmeralda Santiago, and Rosario Ferré—emergent from our experience as Puerto Rican people and rich in theological possibility, tell us, as Latinas, about our relationship with God? How can we know the divine in our midst, even through our history, in a way that is unique and which reflects the uniqueness of our experience? Once understood in relation to our God, in whom many of us as Latinas so strongly believe, can these theological themes reflect a more universal story of the God-human relationship? And finally, will such reflection shed light on our own identity as human beings, as Latinos/as, as Puerto Ricans in the United States? I would not be engaged in this enterprise if I were not confident that these questions can be answered in terms of our experience as Puerto Rican people, and specifically as Puerto Rican women.

With creativity and vision, as Alves and Marqués describe, these contemporary Puerto Rican women writers are engaging in a process of "prophetic imagination" through their literary production.[5] It is prophetic because their *cuentos* (short stories and novels) proclaim the coming of a new era for Puerto Rican people and reveal messages that are both disturbing and necessary for Puerto Ricans to hear. It is imaginative because these same *cuentos,* while emerging from the lived experience of Puerto Rican people, create a vision of what does not exist in the lives of Puerto Rican people as a collective: the possibility of freedom, dignity, and justice.

I believe these Puerto Rican women writers are prophets for the Puerto Rican people, specifically, and for Latinos/as in general. As such, their stories provide us with a *critical source* for the development of Latina feminist theology, in particular, and for U.S. Latino/a theology in general. They are presenting a vision of what has been made of us and what we have made of ourselves; they are allowing us to glimpse what will become of us if we continue on the same course. They are not prescribing solutions, nor are they giving us an ethical mandate. They are using the form of the narrative, the story, which has been so central to maintaining our tradition and our culture, to undercut the complacency that has become a part of that tradition and culture. They are pushing us toward the edge of a cliff, a cliff which we are already approaching with certainty. But through the storytelling process, these women are presenting Puerto Ricans with two options: reality/status quo, from which we can only fall, in despair, to a certain death; or imagination/risk, from which we can soar on wings we fashion for ourselves, with faith that God will breathe the wind, to resurrect the dead.

SPEAKING TRUTH TO POWER: PUERTO RICAN LITERARY LEGACY

It is no mere coincidence that the relationship between creative literary production and freedom is such a close one; in fact, one seems to necessitate the very existence of the other. The literature of Puerto Rico and, more recently, of Puerto Ricans on the U.S. mainland has been one of the very few areas in which freedom of content and form has continued to be exercised within Puerto Rican scholarship. This connection between the creative act of writing and independence of thought without fear of reprisal (although reprisal has come to many of our writers) is a constitutive element for the Puerto Rican writer. Again René Marqués, in his essay "The Function of the Puerto Rican Writer Today," makes this point clearly:

The writer has to be free to be able to struggle against that web which others fashion to impede [her] search for the truth. And, in effect, [she] feels free, [she] knows [her]self to be free. This is a natural feeling, since [she] has the experience of creation; [she] knows, because [she] has experienced it in [her] own flesh and spirit, that the act of artistic creation is an act of supreme liberty . . . The writer, who knows freedom not as a political concept or as a philosophical abstraction, but as a vital experience, will love liberty for [her]self and, by extension, for others.[6]

Thus the very act of writing is an act of rebellion, evidence of a revolutionary spirit and impulse in a repressive environment where the silence of those numbed by the weight of colonialism is preferred. Puerto Rican journalist Roberto Santiago said of the works he compiled in the anthology *Boricuas*, ". . . [I]t isn't possible to separate Puerto Rican art from its politics. Strip one aspect away and you're left with an incomplete portrait."[7] Rosario Ferré, in her essay "The Writer's Kitchen," states similarly, "[I]magination is irreverence to the establishment . . . [it is] always subversive."[8]

The creative writer, or any writer who understands her creation in this way, does not attempt to reach the absolute truth or solutions to the contradictions she witnesses and experiences in her community and her life. From the Puerto Rican context, these creative writers have positioned themselves outside of the realm of solutions and finality. For them, good writing is not prescriptive, but it is more than descriptive as well. The Puerto Rican women writers, through the process and content of description and storytelling, speak a prophetic word to the reader with the hope, I believe, that the reader will spread and act upon that prophetic word. "Take heed," they seem to tell us, "we are living in a time of crisis and some action is required if we are to be faithful to ourselves, to our children, and to our God." Through their gifts of imagination, they are calling us into action by their critique. They are speaking truth to power: the abusive power of those who oppress; the transformative power of those who hope.[9]

Before explicating the direct relationship between the four Puerto Rican women writers I have chosen for this essay and the spirituality reflected in their work, I must first make clear five critical presuppositions I hold regarding literature, spirituality, and theology and how these are held in tension in my own work. First, as I have illustrated above, particularly through the influence of René Marqués's critical writings, literature by Puerto Ricans has continued a tradition of subversive rebellion, critique, and freedom; it has served the purpose of waking the sleeping conscience of Puerto Rican people. Thus understood, the tradition of Puerto Rican literature has maintained a tradition of Puerto Rican anticolonialism, sovereignty, and self-determination. This is not to say that all Puerto Rican authors, or even the ones I will focus on here, are *independentistas*. Regardless of whether she openly expresses her political beliefs, each of these writers shows a preoccupation with the issue of freedom and, in particular, what that means for Puerto Rican women.

Second, creative writing, inclusive of prose, poetry, *cuento*, and novel, shows us the contradictions evident in the context of the writer specifically and of the human community in general. The most memorable literary creations are the ones which are parabolic, as John D. Crossan describes in *The Dark Interval*—they push us to the edge of our reality and leave us there with the responsibility of a conclusion.[10] They expose these contradictions at work in the lives of the characters we read about and quite possibly in our own lives in ways that may have gone unrecognized before. Contemporary Puerto Rican writers, as they lift up these contradictions and expose them in full color, raise existential questions about our human condition in a Camusian sense: Is hope possible in the midst of utter despair?

Third, I believe that our response to those contradictions, to the disjuncture between our reality and our conviction of how things "ought to be," forms a foundation for our theology as Puerto Rican women in particular and Latinas/os in general. The way in which we live out a hope/doubt/search-filled faith in the midst of those contradictions is a fundamental aspect of a theology that is active as well as reflective, that responds to as well as perceives our earthly condition. Jon Sobrino, Salvadoran Jesuit priest, activist, and theologian, affirms three prerequisites for a genuine and concrete spirituality; I believe these are applicable to a genuine and concrete theology as well: (1) honesty about the real—a willingness to look the contradictions squarely in the eye, to confront the ugliness of our situation, with hope; (2) fidelity to the real—a recognition that faithfulness to eradicating the contradictions will likely lead to carrying burdens that those who choose to "escape" from reality do not, a burden of love; and (3) participation in the "more" of reality—a willingness to be an active player in building a more just society, our ethical mandate to strive toward the "ought."[11] For Sobrino, a more just society is one which understands and tries to live out a profound notion of freedom. I believe this hermeneutic is useful for the development of a Latina feminist theology emergent from our experience and thus reflected in the literature.

Fourth, a theology emergent from a Puerto Rican context that maintains the prerequisites Sobrino describes must also embody liberative action, a theology that is made flesh. In this sense, our Puerto Rican literature is testimony of our passion for justice and freedom; to write, as Marqués claims, is to choose to see oneself as a free being, free to create and to determine one's creative destiny. Our creative writers have not, in general, separated the spirituality of the people from their political expressions or desires as have the institutional churches.[12] They have maintained that to be faithful to our interconnected Christian and cultural roots,[13] we cannot ignore the political/economic "king-dom" which has served to numb our senses, crush our spirit, dull our vision, and separate us from ourselves and threatened our cultural identity as a Puerto Rican people with freedom of will and a will for freedom.

Finally, a theology emergent from a Puerto Rican context will be experienced through the connection of cultural identity and ritual (religious and "secular"), both of which can only be fully encountered within community/relationship. For example, the ritual of a shared meal on Sunday in many Puerto Rican communities is one imbued with cultural and religious significance such that, as with art and politics, one aspect cannot be separated from the other without distorting the meaning of the whole. But the ritual has changed, from within and without: the barrio apartment may not accommodate as many people as did the house in the hills of Puerto Rico; the men may be cooking alongside the women (perhaps this is just my prophetic hope); the *platanitos* may now be baked, not fried. Issues of poverty, sexism, and health emerge from this example and serve to illustrate the changing response of our community. This changing response is reflected in the storytelling process as a way to maintain viable cultural norms by passing them on as well as to communicate changes that benefit that culture for our community. The stories allow us to look at ourselves in a new way because a fundamental presupposition of the creative freedom in literature allows the writer to self-critique as well. In fact, the complex and ambiguous sociopolitical and socioreligious reality of Puerto Rican people, marked by marginality and reflected poignantly in our literature, lends itself well to self-scrutiny and critique.[14] Our theology, emerging in part as a response to the ethical, moral, and spiritual contradictions and ambiguity we face, also changes. The literature, as a written stream of Puerto Rican consciousness and consciousness-raising, *is central* to our spirituality as a people as well as a source for our theology in that it (1) reflects our will to be free and our free will, (2) helps us maintain a hermeneutics of suspicion[15]—a grounding element of our living faith—toward all that may diminish our spirit, (3) passes on our cultural tradition, with change and dynamism, despite attempts to exterminate, domesticate, or prostitute that tradition, and (4) acts as a form of resistance that, as our history has borne out, cannot be defeated.

THE PROPHETIC IMAGINATION OF MOHR, ORTIZ COFER, SANTIAGO, AND FERRÉ

I have chosen to examine the works of four Puerto Rican women writers because of my own feminist conviction to lift up the voices from the margins of the margin, those who are doubly silenced, whose spirits are relegated to the shadows of our invisible history. But I look to the stories told by women for another reason: it has been the women of the Puerto Rican communities in Puerto Rico and on the mainland United States who have passed on the spiritual traditions and rituals, often not associated with the institutional churches, that reflect our communal spirituality. The literature of Puerto Rican women writers, then, serves a dual function of describing and challenging the reality in which we live as well as the spirituality that forms a response to that reality. These writers are no exception in the ways they describe and challenge:

1. cultural norms/traditions, including but not exclusive to the *machismo/marianismo* dynamic, that oppress women's fullness of being;
2. elements of our religiosity/spirituality, whether from indigenous or institutional church sources, that are not faithful to our freedom;
3. external forces that inhibit free expression of a self-determined cultural identity and spirituality.

For these reasons, these writers truly stand on the margins of the margins, but they continue to give voice to what would otherwise remain unspoken.

I have stated that the Puerto Rican women writers to be examined here are engaging in a process of prophetic imagination through their literary production, understanding the prophet as one who "reveal[s] the will or message of God."[16] My interpretation of God's will, based on Roman Catholic tradition and the Puerto Rican embodiment of that tradition, as well as from the influence of theologies of liberation from various cultures and denominations, centers on two focal elements: love and justice. I believe the scriptural tradition bears witness to the tension and interplay of God's love and justice and that each is dependent on the other for us to live out God's will in fullness. While the limitations of this essay do not allow me to delve into the historical or scriptural tradition that informs such an understanding, I use this to undergird my belief that the prophetic imagination of Mohr, Ortiz Cofer, Santiago, and Ferré communicates God's will to love and do justice for and with the Puerto Rican community and thus cannot be ignored as a critical source for Latina feminist theology in particular and U.S. Latino/a theology in general.

THE WILL TO LOVE: NICHOLASA MOHR AND JUDITH ORTIZ COFER

Nicholasa Mohr speaks of a profound will to love, and a desire to be loved, through her short stories, particularly *In Nueva York* (1993) and *Rituals of Survival: A Woman's Portfolio* (1985).[17] In each of her stories, Mohr captures the humanity and "ordinariness" of Puerto

Ricans living in the United States (mostly in New York), trying to survive with dignity and grace. Like the old cat that appears in every story of *In Nueva York*, Puerto Ricans have at least nine lives, Mohr seems to suggest, in all that they endure; despite the taunts, harassment, banishment, poverty, like the cat they search for a place to live in peace. In the story of "Old Mary," the title character likens herself to the cat in the ways they have both been tenacious survivors:

Go on! I ain't gonna do nothing to you. Besides, look at you. No use even bothering about you. You're a mess, filthy and you're half bald. Your ears are chewed off! Your eyes are running with some sort of disease; you're practically blind. Bah! What a sight you are. Look, you got half a tail left and your belly droops! . . . You're still lusting around and fighting. You know what you are? A survivor, that's what you are—like me.[18]

Old Mary endures with hope as she awaits the change of luck for which she has been praying: the arrival of her son from Puerto Rico, the child she bore as a result of rape at age thirteen and left with relatives to care for with money she earned as a domestic. With hopes of saving enough money to send for her son and raise him with opportunities, she came to New York. But her story is that of so many Puerto Rican women who came to the big city during the Great Migration[19] and live to tell only of their struggles—economic, spiritual, political—to survive. The thought of her son was the only hope she was left to hold on to, a life fulfilled not in herself but through a child.

It is Old Mary's son, William—nicknamed Chiquitín because of his dwarflike appearance—who, throughout all the stories in *In Nueva York*, shows the most compassion and understanding, particularly for the women who must endure oppressive situations. Chiquitín, as a literary character for Mohr, illustrates how the perception of our people even among ourselves has been so negative, as if we are less than human. Chiquitín may be perceived to have a physical "deformity," and yet he is the most human as intended by God: with the will/willingness to love. By showing our humanity, even to ourselves, the stories can serve to combat both our internalized self-hate and the hatred others direct at us.

Mohr's stories are full of examples of Puerto Rican people who choose to love themselves and others with the fullness of their being. They are stories that, for the most part, don't make it onto the evening news because they reflect our goodness as a people; as such, they remain invisible to the wider community. Particularly poignant are the stories of those who show deep compassion for gay and lesbian Puerto Ricans, whose lives are even more invisible and silenced within our community. Mohr is one of the very few Puerto Rican authors who deal with heterosexism, homophobia, and homosexuality in the context of their writings.[20]

Yet, Mohr's stories also illustrate the difficulty that comes with choosing whose rules best serve the interests of the community at a given time and who defines those interests. Rudi, the owner of the luncheonette that provides a common backdrop to all of the stories in *In Nueva York*, characterizes the clash of cultures that so permeates the Puerto Rican reality on both the island and mainland: the American culture that places priority on economic advancement and the rule of law, and the Puerto Rican culture that places priority on communal responsibility and the will of God. Rudi's luncheonette is robbed by two Puerto Rican youths; he pursues the thieves and shoots one of them, who subsequently dies from the gunshot wound. Rudi is cleared of manslaughter (his gun had a legal permit), but the young man's mother is not satisfied with the ruling of the court. She believes Rudi holds some responsibility for the death of her son, even while she admits the boy's wrongdoing:

Listen! Listen to me! Tomás Ivan Rodriguez was fifteen. Fifteen years was all that he was allowed to live in this world before he was shot down like a dog and buried without a marker! I am all alone. I cannot have his father make things right . . . He must have a headstone to show that he was part of this world. Dios mío . . . God in Heaven has to help me reach that man who shot my boy!

After a confrontation with Rudi, who makes it known that he was cleared of all charges by the court, Mrs. Rodríguez continues:

You shot my boy . . . He's not coming back to harm you no more. I don't care who cleared you. You have an obligation to my son! You shot a boy, not an animal! You say the courts cleared you, eh? But . . . What about God? Are you cleared with Him? Listen to this hardhearted man who won't listen to a mother's lament for her dead son!

. . . "All right . . . What do you want? For God sakes, why are you here after three months? What do you want from me?" Rudi shouted. "What does this woman want from my life?" A headstone! Roberta Rodriguez's shrill voice sounded . . . A headstone, Mr. Padillo, so that everyone will know that my son Tommy once lived, and so I will have a place to go and mourn him, a place with his name.[21]

This scenario illustrates the difficulty of maintaining competing allegiances, of individual versus communal rights, of economic advancement/prosperity versus familial responsibility. To do both—carve a space in a new culture and maintain the spiritual foundation of the old—is no simple task, as these stories reflect.

Mohr shows us what happens when we, like Rudi, forget the will to love within our own culture; that is, even without the cultural clash of American and Puerto Rican values, there are ways in which the culture prohibits a large majority of its people to express the fullness of their being, namely women. Mohr's collection of *cuentos, Rituals of Survival: A Woman's Portfolio,* is a testament of the Puerto Rican woman's struggle to survive both the sexism that permeates the community and the oppression involved with managing new expectations and pressures in an unfamiliar and often hostile environment without the communal support network of previous generations. The portfolio motif of the title suggests the various aspects of an artist's work, the many faces that express the soul of the creator. In this sense, every story has a name of its own (Zoraida, Carmela, Virginia, etc.), but each story can be every woman's story when understood as their attempt to express themselves freely, to be free to love and be themselves fully.

We see, through each story, that when women are not permitted to shape their own destinies, to be autonomous moral agents in their lives, they must find avenues of escape in order to survive. Without these rituals, their spirits are dulled numb beyond recognition; for their own sake and, in some cases, for the sake of their children, they maintain a "spirituality" of survival, a way of life in the shadow of death.

Each story reflects the particular struggle for Puerto Rican women living in the United States to keep their spirit alive; and, in many ways, it is the story of every woman's struggle for self-determination and personal freedom against patriarchal dominance. It is a struggle that parallels that of the Puerto Rican community for self-determination and freedom from colonial dominance. The spirituality of survival reflected in Mohr's writing is not an individual struggle; it is one that strives to maintain genuine and mutual communal relationships based on love and respect rather than on fear and power. The stories show our capability for such relationships and evidence of their existence; the stories also give voice to the experiences of those who are victimized by the absence of such relationships.

Similarly, Judith Ortiz Cofer deals with the tension of culture and tradition in the expression of personal identity. Ortiz Cofer's short stories and novel reflect the reality of the migration experience so prominent in her own life. Born in Puerto Rico in 1952, Ortiz Cofer traveled back and forth as a child from Puerto Rico to Paterson, New Jersey (her family's home base), while her father was stationed overseas in the U.S. Navy. Ortiz Cofer examines themes of cultural and geographical flux through her novel, *The Line of the Sun*, and her prose/poetry collection *The Latin Deli*. In both works, it is the process—of storytelling, of migration, of movement[22]—that proves to be the moment of greatest freedom: "the instability itself becoming the source of creativity."[23]

Perhaps the greatest movement in Ortiz Cofer's literary production is the movement toward freedom, a freedom that comes from reconciliation and love of oneself, of living in the flux amidst the ambiguity and confusion and somehow emerging to tell about it. As a storyteller, she often takes on the persona of one-in-relation; that is, her characters are often those of child in relation to parent, mother in relation to child (daughter in her case), wife in relation to husband, grandchild in relation to grandmother, and so forth. In the context of these relationships, we see a woman struggling to come to terms, in resistance and acceptance, with the ways the other impacts upon *her* life. Through the eyes of the narrator, we can see her attempt to redefine and reinvent herself by reflecting upon the relationships which have shaped her and by constructing something that honors the authenticity of their influence without restricting the new creation: herself. That is, through her writing, Ortiz Cofer brings the reader into her own struggle for self-definition while illustrating that one can still love with depth and profundity in the midst of that struggle and ambiguity. She seems to suggest that we are most destructive to ourselves and others when we refuse to acknowledge the contradictions we live and embody and when we equate reconciliation with negation and denial.

As a child of a diaspora, the author reflects the anguish caused by migration on those who had no choice in the matter, the children. Throughout her stories and novel, she seems to confront those in positions of authority for not taking the responsibility and care to prepare the next generation for the difficulties they were bound to face in a new environment. The author is left only with the construction of story because she has been given no other resources from which to build a positive identity. As such, she raises the issue of betrayal—parental as well as national—as a means of asking the question, "How can we now use the past to heal in the meantime?"[24] For the children, the parental dream of returning to Puerto Rico is meaningless; their lives have been shaped by a new reality, and they will be as much in exile there as here.

In her only novel to date, *The Line of the Sun*, Ortiz Cofer introduces the narrator, Marisol, the daughter of Ramona, around whose family the story revolves. Although born in the house of her grandmother, Mama Cielo (Mother Heaven/Sky), Marisol moved with her mother to meet her father stationed at the Brooklyn Navy Yard when she was only two years old. For her, the necessity of capturing the life stories of her parents, her uncle Gúzman, and her grandparents emerges from a desire to understand herself and grow roots into unsteady ground:

Gúzman's story took a long time to tell; in fact, it is not, nor will it ever be, finished. My mother told me her story throughout the long, lonely first season of our newest exile . . . In the years that followed I concluded that the only way to understand a life is to write it as a story, to fill in the blanks left by circumstance, lapses of memory, and failed communication. Gúzman's story did not end happily at the altar as all good fairy tales and love stories should. It continued through my mother's letters and in my imagination until one day I started writing it for him.[25]

The reconciliation of the old and new customs, of *el campo* and *el building*, is the task of all Puerto Ricans who wish to do more than simply survive; it is a prerequisite for carrying out our understanding of God's will to love ourselves and others. The process of reconciliation is just that, a process, without finality or absolution. It is ongoing, just as the story will never be finished. When we try to take a way of life and transplant it in a new environment without reflecting upon its necessity for change in light of that new reality, without attempting to reconcile the contradictions we embody, Ortiz Cofer suggests we will end up in disaster.

An example of such a disaster occurs in *The Line of the Sun*: the apartment building where Marisol lives is set ablaze when a spiritist meeting turns chaotic. On the eve of an impending strike organized by many of the poorly paid Puerto Rican laborers who live in the building, the women hold a spiritual gathering to invoke blessings on all those involved and to try to gain some control, via the spirits, over their own destinies. Elba, the *santera*/priest who presides over the ceremony, dies as the blaze, inadvertently ignited by lighter fluid and throngs of candles, envelopes the apartment.

This incident illustrates the author's prophetic call for reconciliation in a number of ways. The spiritist meeting itself occurred without any consideration of the new environment. Whereas one can light a bonfire to invoke the spirit of Chango in the countryside of Puerto Rico, one must consider the hazards of doing the same in a crowded apartment in New Jersey. The medium, Elba, who bestowed her benediction on the people "like a big-breasted pope dispensing her blessings, hugging and kissing her flock while they wept away a week's misery,"[26] failed to reflect upon whether the situation could be made right by simply enacting the age-old rituals without being faithful to the "real," as Sobrino suggests. This is not to pass judgement on the medium, in this case Elba, who had no choice but to hold the ritual in her apartment. Yet the importance of the inferno points beyond the spatial limitations: it suggests the need to reconfigure the means/methods of healing that are relevant to a new reality without losing the authenticity of the process itself, so that true healing can take place.

The burden of the medium, as the title and content of Ortiz Cofer's last poem in *The Latin Deli* suggests, is to give voice to the anguish, to be "tormented by the knowledge" of another's pain and live to tell about it so that others may continue to live in hope. The burden is to tell the story in such a way as to provoke some response, a healing response that must change given the change of circumstances and forces against us. In turn, the one who invokes the response, the medium, must also invoke a changing spirituality as a "way of life," a responsibility to the ongoing process of reconciliation. As such, Marisol, not Elba, is the true medium of healing and hope because she tries through her narration to reconcile her own spirit with the traditions of her family. In order to survive in new circumstances and to be truly free to love and create, we, like Marisol, must confront the contradictions and live through them; this is of particular importance for women whose silence and invisibility are usually deadly.[27]

Thus the author, through the character of Marisol, embodies prophetic hope in the midst of exilic despair. The name Marisol merges two prominent images/symbols: Maria/Mary the mother of Jesus, the passive vessel in traditional Catholic doctrine; and the sun, the aggressive fire deity Chango of African traditional religion. When her palm is read by Elba, Marisol learns that she bears a strong "line of the sun," an indication of natural gifts. Yet, the line of the sun is also the borderline between old and new, south and north, Puerto Rico and the United States, that come together in her very being. She must carry the burden of contradiction as well as the hope of living freely amidst the uncertainty and continuous redefinition that such embodiment entails. And so from her attic bedroom looking out onto an old oak tree in the silence of suburbia, Marisol writes the stories to reconstruct herself for herself and her children:

In a trunk I kept at the foot of my bed I stored Gúzman's life—all the letters, the childish journals I had kept in the years after the fire at El Building; the pages written under the gaze of the witch at my bedroom window in our house in the suburbs. One day I would have the courage to put it all together, I thought: a puzzle that would reveal many things about my own life. Perhaps I would start the story in the present and go back, giving myself more and more freedom to invent ways of telling it.[28]

THE WILL TO DO JUSTICE:
ESMERALDA SANTIAGO AND ROSARIO FERRÉ

The writing of Esmeralda Santiago, particularly her novel *América's Dream*, communicates a prophetic call to do justice on many levels, including the personal, relational, and national. Her first publication, an autobiographical account titled *When I Was Puerto Rican*, details Santiago's youth in rural Puerto Rico, the culture shock of moving to New York, and her coming of age amidst the adversity of straddling two cultures, to find herself graduating from Harvard University with highest honors. Her autobiography props up the myth of the American dream: poor immigrant country girl overcomes all the odds and climbs the ladder of societal success to the highest rung. Her story sets itself up in support of the myth of meritocracy: if you work hard and sacrifice enough in American society, you will certainly succeed. Myth, according to John Dominic Crossan, leaves us feeling at ease, our conscience assuaged, because "what myth does is not just to attempt the mediation in story of what is sensed as irreconcilable, but in, by, and through this attempt it establishes the possibility of reconciliation."[29] For Santiago, the myth of the American dream is made reality for her through the telling of her life story, or so it seems.

The title of her second publication, *América's Dream*, plays into this American mythology; but now the dream is pursued by America with a Spanish accent. The protagonist is América González, a single mother working as a maid at the only hotel on Vieques, an island which is part of Puerto Rico but off the coast. Santiago opens the novel with the words "It's her life, and she's in the middle of it." The story begins with América's fourteen-year-old daughter, Rosalinda (Beautiful Rose), running away with a young man. The daughter's impulsive action stands in the tradition of similar conduct taken by América and América's mother, Ester (Star); Rosalinda is but the latest in a long line of fatherless daughters of cleaning women.

América is abused, physically and otherwise, by Rosalinda's father Correa (Belt/Strap). Ten years her senior, he impregnated but refused to marry her when she was fourteen. While married to another woman, with whom he had three children, Correa continues to possess/oppress América. Even the slightest provocation, interpreted as such through his *machista* paranoia, could lead Correa to beat América. But he always does his penance; Ester's house (where América and Rosalinda live) is full of his penitential offerings: "Electronics typically mean he knows he's really hurt her, but chocolates always mean she deserved it . . . A coffee brewer for a split lip. A toaster oven for a black eye. A rocking chair for a broken rib that kept her out of work for a week."[30] Correa, with all his charm and good looks, is the quintessential abuser; América is the archetype of the battered woman.

Without giving away the entire story, its ending appears all too familiar. Now in New York with Rosalinda and working as a maid in an exclusive midtown hotel, América looks at her mirror reflection; noting the changes on her face after her many dances with death, the narrator has this to say:

It's a reminder of who she is now, and who she was then. Correa's woman was unscarred, but América González wears the scars he left behind the way a navy lieutenant wears his stripes. They're there to remind her that she fought for her life, and that, no matter how others may interpret it, she has the right to live that life as she chooses. It is, after all, her life, and she's the one in the middle of it.[31]

The story seems to end as it begins; despite all that she has done—escaping (albeit tentatively) from Correa, relocating to New York City, reclaiming her daughter—América remains in the same psychological state as before. There is no transformation or reconciliation in the story itself. *América's Dream* is no myth; rather, it is a parable.

"Parable is always a somewhat unnerving experience," Crossan says. "You can usually recognize a parable because your immediate reaction will be self-contradictory: 'I don't know what you mean by that story but I'm certain I don't like it.'"[32] While myth mediates reconciliation, or at least its possibility, parable undercuts reconciliation, showing that it too is a myth of our own making. Again, Crossan's definition is useful for a deeper understanding of this Puerto Rican novel: "The surface function of parable is to create contradiction within a given situation of complacent security but, even more unnervingly, to challenge the fundamental principle of reconciliation by making us aware of the fact that we made up the reconciliation."[33]

Considering the earlier claim that Puerto Rican art cannot be separated from its politics or, I would add, politics from theology, I believe this story is a parable about and for the Puerto Rican people; to state it in the form most readily recognizable, "Puerto Rico is like a battered woman." We are, the story suggests, victims, survivors, and accomplices of our current conditions. From the names alone, we can understand the parallel Santiago makes with the history of Puerto Rico—the "shining star of the Caribbean" (Ester), the island paradise in full bloom (Rosalinda), America with a Spanish accent—and América's story, shared with her mother (past) and daughter (future). Correa is the (Operation Boot) strap that binds, cutting off circulation, squeezing out the breath of life; when pulled up by the bootstrap, so to speak, one finds oneself in target range of being struck down again.

How América and Puerto Rico/Puerto Ricans have been victimized is obvious through the story and history; how she, and we, continue to survive is evidenced by our living to tell the story, a formidable task in itself. But can we say América and Puerto Ricans act as accomplices to our own victimization and struggle to survive? This is not what we are prepared, nor wish, to hear. But this is the message we must hear if we are to have an authentic response to the prophetic imagination of the author. It is precisely this prophetic message that jolts our complacent consciousness, that makes us think about our condition in a new way but that refuses to prescribe an easy solution. To say we are accomplices in our continued captivity is, at the very least, to acknowledge the theft of our spirit, and, more importantly, to recognize our inner, collective power, our moral agency, to get it back.[34]

In a 1993 essay titled "Island of Lost Causes," published in the

New York Times opinions section the day of the plebiscite that would recommend independence, statehood, or commonwealth status for Puerto Rico, Santiago wrote:

We are taken for granted by the U.S., and that sharpens in us a stubborn nationalist streak—yet we don't demonstrate it at the ballot box. In our hearts, we want to believe independence is the right choice, but our history forces us to see it as a lost cause. Still, we are not willing to give up so completely as to vote for statehood. It would be the ultimate statement of our surrender.

This is why so many Puerto Ricans will vote for the status quo. It fosters the illusion of choosing a destiny, neither capitulating nor fighting. But it continues to evade the question of who we are as a people.

An elusive cultural identity lies at the heart of our unwillingness to declare ourselves either a nation or a state. A vote for the commonwealth insures that we don't have to commit one way or the other.

Ironically, neither violent insurrection nor the democratic process seem able to solve that question . . . We need to look at ourselves hard and stop hiding behind the status quo. It is not a choice. It is a refusal to choose.[35]

The refusal to make a choice is, as América's story reveals, as deadly as choosing the path of life and freedom could be. Her story illustrates how the silence that envelopes such a refusal slowly but certainly leads to greater isolation and alienation. América hardly communicates her inner thoughts and feelings to her mother or her daughter; she is resentful and suspicious even of them, thus severing all possibility of mutual wisdom gained from relationship. Her involvement in any meaningful community is nonexistent; she listens to the sermons of the Pentecostal preacher from her porch as they are broadcast to the neighborhood on a Saturday night. When América comes to New York to work as an au pair for a wealthy white family in Bedford, she is cautious of the other *empleadas* she meets at the playground. While they share the same child care and housekeeping tasks, they are different, she reasons, since they are Latin American and she is American. Like Puerto Rico in relation to Latin America, América González fears relationship because it will somehow break the silence of her true condition of oppression and domination, a condition that she has escaped temporarily and superficially.

América's silence and self-perpetuated isolation, fueled by justifiable fear, put not only herself at risk but those for whom she is responsible: the children she cares for and her own daughter. Without a support system, a community of solidarity, she becomes an island unto herself ("It's my life and I'm in the middle of it") without recognizing that her life is also those who will come after and that she is still responsible for their well-being. While it is true that "it is all up-hill from *Esperanza* (Hope) to *Destino* (Destiny),"[36] each need not be exclusive of the other when the path is paved with the wisdom of community. By viewing her own life as a cycle of dependency devoid of the hope for freedom, América places her daughter into a situation that will make it difficult for the girl to break a cycle of destiny without hope.

Santiago conveys the incredible hardship of breaking such a cycle, given our history of oppression. Can we expect anything more from América, or Puerto Rico, considering the circumstances? Can we call her an accomplice after acknowledging her victimization and survival? Her story is truly a tragedy.[37] Yet the author allows us to catch glimpses of revelatory moments in América's life: for five days a month, when she takes her blue placebo birth control pills, she is in tune with her natural hormonal cycle and true emotions. She is reflective of her situation; she cries tears of "hurt and anger, fear and frustration."[38] But on the sixth day, she goes back to her usual self: humming and singing, sedated from her reality, numbed. In these bursts of revelation, América talks to herself more and seems sure to make some change; she even fights for her daughter to stay when Correa has made plans to take her away. These moments, however short-lived, carry the seed of transformation; they are nonetheless ineffective because they are not witnessed or testified for others to hear and participate with her in the transformative process.

This novel is acutely prophetic of God's will for humanity to do justice for a number of reasons. First, through the form of the parable, it allows us to see the condition of Puerto Rican women in particular and Puerto Rico in general as unjust to the core. There are no illusions to suggest otherwise. While we have been treated unjustly, we have also participated in the unjust treatment of ourselves by failing to recognize the grace-filled moments of revelation that startle our consciousness out of stupor.

Second, the author leaves us and the story unreconciled. Reality has been presented, imaginatively and in sharp relief, with no conclusion nor the possibility of conclusion in ways which will ease our conscience. We are forced to make a choice, to confess our complicity on many levels and either to live like América, allowing circumstances to govern her destiny, or to understand our destiny in relation to God's will for justice.

Third, when we choose to do God's will for justice, we are forced into action. Santiago has given us the big picture, the panorama of our existence; she is asking us the question, "Given what we now know of ourselves, do we have the will from within to do justice?" We are poised to respond. Through her prophetic imagination of authorship, she has broken América's silence; she has testified and we are her witnesses, a new community. Now in communion with the prophet's message, our response constitutes our spirituality, our fidelity to the real and our will/willingness to participate in the "more" of reality: the building of a more just society. To refuse a response is to turn our backs on our very spirit, to negate the tradition of freedom of our people, and to sacrifice ourselves to the status quo. América's world is devoid of spirit because she cannot/will not respond. The abuser winds up for the ultimate blow.

Finally, Santiago shows us our future, as women and as a community, if we refuse to choose the path of freedom which is God's will for justice: our children will suffer an even worse fate because they will know our betrayal of them and their destinies. But if we share our struggles with them, allow them to see the contradictions we embody in ourselves as América and Correa concurrently, and communicate our most profound visions and deepest fears, we will have given them tools to break the cycles of despair and confusion; they will struggle valiantly for their right to create themselves because they will have seen the destructive elements of themselves. Only when confronting and then overcoming fear and death, our theological/spiritual tradition attests, can life be made new.

Myth vindicates the world we know; parable subverts that world.[39] Taken together, Santiago's literary works act in tension with one another; as an author, she justifies herself while undermining herself. This is the very contradiction faced and embodied in all Puerto Ricans and in Puerto Rican women in particular. The story/history may be one of despair, a lost cause, but our response to it need not be. And it is our response—a lifelong task—to that contradiction which will bear the fruit of justice, of living out the will of God.

In many ways similar to those of Santiago, Rosario Ferré's ever-growing literary contributions are a commitment to living out the will of God to do justice. Her life and work are parabolic in the sense Crossan describes, as she and her literary creation embody contradiction; push us to the limits of language/comprehension; make us uncomfortable in the face of reality seen with new eyes; and make no apology for paradox. Born into the bourgeois elite of Puerto Rican society in 1938, Ferré witnessed and lived the contradictions resultant from the merging of two societies, two languages, two cultures, and a multitude of colors and influences, all within her own home in Ponce. As is evidenced in her literary production for children and adults, Ferré was greatly influenced by Puerto Rican folkloric tradition—as passed on by her financier father[40] and her black nanny—as well as by the fairy tales of American/European culture (Grimm, Anderson, Carroll, etc.). Through these, and an apprenticeship with Latin American literary notables such as Mario Vargas Llosa and Margot Arce de Vásquez and her exposure to the independence of thought in Puerto Rican literature, Ferré developed a sophisticated literary style which challenges and critiques all levels of social injustice.[41]

Like Santiago, Ferré's art cannot be separated from her politics of personal, relational, and national freedom. While for the purpose of this essay I have chosen to examine only one novel, *The House on the Lagoon*, all of Ferré's stories convey a desire for freedom and independence, for the assertion of self and group identity, and for self-determination. As a Puerto Rican woman, Ferré attempts to illustrate the nihilistic quest for self-preservation that leaves women empty of true selfhood. Her work is consistent with the postmodern dilemma of acute literary self-consciousness as described by Robert Detweiler:

Novelists are writing stories about novelists writing stories; characters watch themselves intently; images of mirrors, reflections, echoes, doubles abound. But they do so precisely because the concept of the self is fading. The eagerness to portray the self indicates a sense and fear of its imminent loss. This compulsive and anxious self-consciousness expresses itself in a vigorous "historicizing" effort, because if the self can identify itself historically, in factual time and space, it can reinforce its reality. At the same time, this . . . effort also encourages the self toward group-hood, for in locating oneself historically one also places oneself in the context of others.[42]

Ferré, now living in both Puerto Rico and Washington, D.C., is acutely aware of this sense of loss in relation to a particular Puerto Rican identity.[43] Her novel *The House on the Lagoon* follows Detweiler's description accurately. It is set in Puerto Rico, is animated with history and folklore, and tells the story of a woman, Isabel Monfort Antonsanti, writing the recollected stories of her family and the family of her husband, Quintín Mendizabal, that they shared with each other before their marriage. Ferré presents to us the finished product of Isabel's creation: an interweaving of her storytelling, her first-person voice as commentary, and Quintín's third-person commentary as notes in the margin. We are thrown on waves which vacillate between fact (Quintín is an historian) and fiction (Isabel is a novelist), and we are left to wonder whether either distinction makes any difference to the true purpose of the story: the emancipation of the self, as individual and in relation. For Ferré, the assertion of the self is a life-or-death mandate for women; through the story of a woman, she, like Santiago, makes that claim for Puerto Rico as well. The issue of the Puerto Rican woman's identity does not arise in opposition to that of national/cultural identity; rather, Ferré's novel illustrates that both must be integrated to do justice for and with Puerto Rican people.[44]

All of Ferré's stories, without exception, illustrate the need for our lives to be in balance; that is, we cannot live fully if we are cut off from our own spirit. This is particularly deadly, and more commonplace, for women. In an oppressive environment which tries to maintain itself through the bifurcation of life and spirit, women who assert a balance between the life they lead on the surface and the journey of their inner spirit are usually severed, maimed, or tricked—physically and otherwise—into perpetuating the status quo of alienation. The same can be said for Puerto Rico: that is, when Puerto Rico has allowed its inner spirit of emancipation to emerge, it has been repeatedly squelched and repressed.

The House on the Lagoon is replete with cases of severance, repression, and alienation. Early in the story, and told within the context of Puerto Rican slave history, we meet Barnabé, whose name means "son of prophecy"; he had been a chieftain of his tribe when stolen from Angola, "a spiritual leader whose duty was to look out for [his] people."[45] He maintained his native language and by virtue of it was able to organize a rebellion with other slaves without "dutiful and docile" *criollo* (mixed) slaves discovering their plans. After the insurrection was aborted, Barnabé was sentenced to a special punishment: his tongue was cut off. "One's tongue," Isabel tells us when speaking of Barnabé's language, Bantu, was so deeply ingrained, more so even than one's religion or tribal pride; it was like a root that went deep into one's body and no one knew exactly where it ended. It was attached to one's throat, to one's neck, to one's stomach, even to one's heart.[46]

As Jean Franco observes, "The repressed in Ferré's stories always returns with violence."[47] The physical and psychological severance, maiming, and trickery against the spirit that chooses to live out in the open is thus forced into a subterraneous and subversive life; it too can re-emerge violently in an attempt to do justice (or seek revenge) for itself, as the stories reflect. But justice encompasses a meaning other than "equity" or "balance"; Ferré insinuates through her work that to do justice is also "to approach with proper appreciation; [to] enjoy fully."[48] She wages a fierce critique at the upper classes of Puerto Rican society who, in the unfair privilege of class usually reserved for the lightest-skinned and "purest bred" Puerto Ricans,[49] fail to do justice for/with the working-class and poor Puerto Ricans of more obvious African descent.[50] Her stories and their attention to the history and current reality of black/mulatto Puerto Ricans break the silence and invisibility that has characterized the official history of the island. Ferré suggests it is those on the margins of society, in this case blacks, who understand deeply the question, "Does the outward living of your life do justice to your spirit?" This is not to say that those of darker skin automatically live out the balance that Ferré seems to advocate. Rather, societal racism—in its overt and covert expressions—has not afforded darker-skinned Puerto Ricans the same "opportunities" to be lured into the seduction of an alienated life in a sociopolitical or economic sense. The alienation has come via other means—substance abuse, gang violence, disease—which plague the poorest communities on the island and mainland. Las Minas, the slums on the other side of the lagoon, are built on a foundation of polluted water whose stench can be detected from a distance; alienation from the life-giving aspects of the water mirrors the spiritual pollution of people's self-consciousness with despair and desperation seeping from the conditions around them.

Still, Ferré's work continues to hold those of African descent in high esteem; they constitute the spiritual foundation throughout her stories. This is nowhere more obvious than in *The House on the Lagoon*, where Petra Avilés, the *santera/curandera* is truly the rock upon which the story is built. She lives in the dirt-floor cellar with the other domestic laborers who access the lower level of the house from the lagoon. Ferré's attention to the character of Petra, her function in the family, and her spirituality constitute one way in which Ferré's authorship is prophetic: she is questioning and challenging the validity, the assumed security, upon which the house (as the archetype of the condition of one's psyche, one's relationships, one's nation) has been built. This formidable piece of architectural mastery that is the Mendizabal home is built on a swamp; but only those who enter by way of the swamp (the servants) are fully aware of its impermanence. The water is the true foundation; long after the house is gone, water remains. It is no mere description that the house was built originally over an underground spring; this fact is central to understanding that what is on the surface is illusory and that which is closer to the water is more authentic to our intended humanity. Petra lives on the level of the spring; her subterranean existence is closer to our spiritual origins. Those who avail themselves of her wisdom, who enter the underground cell that shelters the spring, come closer to mending the wounds of lifelong maiming and scarring. Those who pay attention to their healing processes can then bring that wisdom to the surface; the wisdom cannot remain underground if it is to change the world order.

Understood allegorically, Ferré's story challenges the foundations of our national identity as Puerto Ricans; in a sense, she is questioning the political and economic foundations of our colonial relationship to the United States as if to say, "What is really at the core of who we are as a people, and how do we restore that?" Her prophetic call forces us to determine whether we have the will to do justice to that core identity, even if it means destroying the false construction that has been a theft, a plagiarism from the start.[51] The storyteller within the story, Isabel, comes closer to restoring her own identity and voice as her relationship with Petra blossoms. As the migrant, a vehicle and translator between their worlds, Isabel tries to integrate the two by giving voice to their tension, interplay, and interdependence. Only then can the story be told.

Ferré's work is also prophetic in its challenge of the "set in stone" ideologies which have bolstered the construction of a false identity, including nationalism, capitalism, racism, and even feminism: ideologies which, if unaccepting of the flux of history and the changing needs of people, become destructive of the very spirit they intend to reflect.

What I believe is most visionary, most prophetic in Ferré's work is her challenge to the Christian understanding of creation, of human origins, and thus of the foundational architecture of our spirit. On Ash Wednesday, Christians are reminded that we are created of dust and to dust we shall return. Ferré's illustration of dust shows it to be anything but fecund; it has no creative potential devoid of spirit, which is water. Infused with water (and perhaps some manure), dust can become fertile soil in which new life can be planted and grown. Dust alone, as demonstrated in her tales "The Dust Garden" and "Marina and the Lion,"[52] makes it difficult to breathe; it chokes us and blinds our vision. It is associated not with creation but with the forces of industrialization that have stripped the island of *its* healing potential; we are left with a wasteland. With regard to women's condition, dust—that is, the removal of it—is our perennial domestic chore; it binds us to continuous and repetitive action without the space for creativity or reflection. Dust is the cloud that eclipses our self-consciousness and prohibits our self-determined creation, our identity, from living or thriving.

It is Willie Mendizabal, the epileptic son of Quentín and Petra's granddaughter (by rape) with the use of only one eye, who truly understands Petra's assertion that everything begins and ends in water. In a conversation with Isabel after Petra's death, Willie says:

Maybe I had to become partially blind to understand what she meant. When I realized I might never be able to paint again, I cried so much I couldn't believe the body could hold so much water. Tears, saliva, semen, blood—our bodies are mostly water.

Petra knew that water is love . . . Every time we wet our feet or wade into the sea, we touch other people, we share in their sadness and their joys. Because we live on an island there is no mass of mountains, no solid dyke of matter to keep us from flowing out to others. Through water, we can reach out and love our neighbors, try to understand them . . .

Water permitted the Avilés family to travel from Morass to Alamares Lagoon in the first place . . . After all, I was conceived in the swamp, isn't that right, Mother? And it was in the mangroves that Carmelina Avilés fell into Father's arms.[53]

The image of water as the medium of creation (beginnings/birth) is also the medium of destruction (endings/death). The water is always changing that which comes into contact with it. The house on the lagoon did not require a final inferno to ensure its demise; the water would have eroded it over time. Likewise, our personal and cultural identities as Puerto Rican women and Puerto Rican people in general have been changed by water: Spanish and American ships which have sustained 500 years of colonialism were brought to us by water, over which our newest migrations have also traversed. The water that has now divided Puerto Ricans on the island and the mainland will help us forge a new identity, even with the knowledge that this definition will always be elusive. The water is both boundary and access.

In Santiago's novel, water is feared by América as a destructive force that washes away everything in its path; tears blind rather than enhance spiritual vision. Water is seen through the lens of death without the balance of life. Ferré's novel does not negate death but illustrates the tension of love and justice that we are required to embody if we are to remain whole and in balance with our spirit. Forgiveness and reconciliation hold love and justice in proper balance: a love devoid of justice becomes anemic, and justice devoid of love runs the risk of vengeance. Ferré's stories, as archetypal visions of who we have become, also present us with the possibility of the new identity we are empowered to re-create fully.

Ferré seems to suggest that the question of Puerto Rican identity is not primarily a political one—that is, statehood, independence, or commonwealth—although we must face this issue directly as well. But if we are a faithful people who treasure those things that have not been defeated through our history—the gifts of life and love, our freedom of will, our voice, our ability to face death and survive—then we will live in dignity in whatever political structure we determine is best for us to maintain those aspects of our identity. The political decision will not lead to harmony in itself; the balance, and our will to do justice to it, must first be sought within. And this balance is based on love and justice, reflected in our ability to embrace the contradictions and paradoxes we embody. The water instructs us to wash away those aspects of ourselves which no longer do us justice, that no longer afford us, as women, as Puerto Ricans, as Latinos/as, as humans, a proper appreciation of what God has created and to enjoy that creation fully. This understanding echoes the image of water in Christian scriptural tradition: the water of the flood and the water of baptism are both evidence of God's justice and righteousness.

CONCLUSION: CIEN AÑOS DE SOLEDAD

The Puerto Rican women writers I have examined in this essay, in all their variety, simplicity, and profundity, come to me as voices crying out in the wilderness proclaiming to and with Puerto Rican people, women and men, that we must see ourselves with new eyes, we must create a new vision for our future in feminist terms. If not, we will fade into oblivion, sink back into the ocean, as the song goes in "West Side Story." The impact of U.S. colonialism, including the migration experience, will have been, at the dawn of a new millennium, more than "one hundred years of solitude" imposed upon our psyches, our culture, our language, our nation; the entirety of our humanity is, as reflected in Ferré's novel, compressed in that warp of time. Will we be given a second opportunity on earth, a better fortune *(buenaventura)* than the Buendías of García Márquez's classic tale? The stories beg yet another question: Who are we as Puerto Ricans, and how will that identity inform the way we do God's will in the world to ensure a future? I do not claim that this essay has approached an answer to those questions, but I am sure that a critical feminist examination of our stories, our experiences, our lives—especially as interpreted and voiced by those historically silenced—allows us to glimpse the prophet's vision of self-determination and freedom: a freedom *from* that which severs us from our spirit; a freedom *to* love and do justice as our God has willed us to do. If we respond to the vision—the prophetic imagination—I believe the theology that emerges will compel us to tell a different story in yet one hundred years' time.

NOTES

1. I have changed the gender pronouns in this quote to make the more obvious connection to the Puerto Rican women writers I will discuss in this essay. Rubem A. Alves, *The Poet, The Warrior, The Prophet,* 137.

2. René Marqués, *The Docile Puerto Rican,* xvi.

3. Gregory Salyer, in his introduction to *Literature and Theology at Century's End,* co-edited with Robert Detweiler, speaks of the literature and theology dialogue/enterprise as "a viable hermeneutical avenue because it values the inherently self critical dimensions of life on the borders" which will continue into the coming century because of "its refusal to proclaim itself in its various incarnations as the final word" (3–4).

4. David Jasper, ed., *The Study of Literature and Religion,* 138.

5. A volume by Walter Brueggemann, *The Prophetic Imagination,* shares this phrase but focuses primarily on the ministry of the Church, which must

respond with justice and compassion in order to remain faithful to the Mosaic/prophetic covenant with God. While this theme resonates with my work in this essay, I have not depended on Brueggemann's analysis for my own.

6. René Marqués, "The Function of the Puerto Rican Writer Today," in his *Docile Puerto Rican*, 115. Again, I have changed the quote to the feminine pronoun to make a more obvious connection to the writers examined in this essay.

7. Roberto Santiago, introduction to *Boricuas: Influential Puerto Rican Writings—An Anthology*, ed. Roberto Santiago, xxi.

8. Rosario Ferré, "The Writing Kitchen," *Feminist Studies* 2 (summer 1986): 243–249.

9. See Robert MacAfee Brown, *Persuade Us to Rejoice: The Liberating Power of Fiction*, 20–29.

10. John D. Crossan, *The Dark Interval: Towards a Theology of Story*, 1–30. Related to the effectiveness of "story limit," René Marqués in his essay "Literary Pessimism and Political Optimism" describes a study in which an educational pamphlet geared toward country-dwellers in Puerto Rico presented two stories, one ending in reconciliation and the other in open-ended tragedy. The people were more affected and responded more acutely to the latter, in which no solution/conclusion was provided. In Marqués, *Docile Puerto Rican*, 22–23.

11. Jon Sobrino, *Spirituality of Liberation*, 14–20.

12. See Samuel Silva-Gotay, "The Ideological Dimensions of Popular Religiosity and Cultural Identity in Puerto Rico," in *An Enduring Flame: Studies on Latino Popular Religiosity*, ed. Anthony M. Stevens-Arroyo and Ana María Díaz-Stevens, 133–170.

13. These interconnected Christian and cultural roots are grounded in our understanding of Jesus as brother whose life, death, and resurrection reflect God's commitment to restoring love and justice within God's "kin-dom."

14. Salyer's introduction to *Literature and Theology* is informative, as he highlights the task of theology and literature as a discipline. I believe Puerto Rican literature, particularly those examples I have chosen for this essay, works well into the literature/theology enterprise because of the "borderland" existence of Puerto Rican people, from a sociopolitical perspective, and Puerto Rican literature, which remains on the fringes of American literature.

15. The philosophy of Paul Ricoeur has been fundamental for the discipline of literature and theology, particularly his theory of interpretation, in which he identifies distinct hermeneutic styles such as the hermeneutics of suspicion and the hermeneutics of restoration. See Charles E. Reagan and David Stewart, eds., *The Philosophy of Paul Ricoeur*. While I have yet to delve fully into his volumes of postmodernist philosophy, my initial and cursory investigation of Ricoeur's *The Symbolism of Evil* identified many useful tools for future theological analysis of Puerto Rican women's literature and Hispanic women's literature in general.

16. *American Heritage Dictionary of the English Language*, 1998, s.v. "prophet."

17. I have analyzed two other literary pieces by Mohr—*Nilda* (1973) and

El Bronx Remembered (1975)—in "A Latina Theology of Story as Reflected in the Works of Julia Alvarez, Sandra Cisneros and Nicholasa Mohr" (master's thesis, Union Theological Seminary, 1993).

18. Nicholasa Mohr, "Old Mary," *In Nueva York*, 6.

19. "More than a half-million Puerto Ricans left their tiny Caribbean island to come to New York City from 1946 until 1964 . . . [This] eighteen-year period . . . represents the Great Puerto Rican Migration, which has for-ever transformed the life of Puerto Rico's people." Ana María Díaz-Stevens, *Oxcart Catholicism on Fifth Avenue: The Impact of the Puerto Rican Migra-tion upon the Archdiocese of New York*, 12–24.

20. Yet dealing with such issues is common among the Puerto Rican women writers; three of the four authors examined in this essay deal specifically with gay/lesbian themes in their work. See Rosario Ferré, "The Other Side of Paradise" and "The Fox Fur Coat" in *The Youngest Doll*, and "Pico Rico Mandorico" in *Reclaiming Medusa*, ed. Diana Vélez; Nicholasa Mohr, "A Brief Miracle (Virginia)" in *Rituals of Survival*; and Judith Ortiz Cofer, *The Line of the Sun*.

21. Mohr, *In Nueva York*, 175–177.

22. "The Habit of Movement" is both a poem and a section title of Ortiz Cofer's *Reaching for the Mainland and Selected New Poems*.

23. Nicolás Kanellos, "Judith Ortiz Cofer," in *Bibliographical Diction-ary of Hispanic Literature in the United States*, 62. "In the novel [*Line of the Sun*] . . ., she delves into the theme of the individual set adrift between two cultures and two languages, attempting to find, if not acceptance or answers, at least a means to express herself in art. The novel begins with the two words, They Say, which emphasize the storytelling tradition to the author" (63).

24. Two pieces in *The Latin Deli* reflect this sense of parental betrayal poignantly. The short story "By Love Betrayed" tells of a young girl's love for her father even as she discovers his infidelity and must cope with the mixed emotions which ensue. The poem "Guard Duty" describes the nighttime fear of a young child placed under the watchful eye of a print hanging over her bed titled *"El Angel de la Guardia"* (The guardian angel). The military refer-ences and repressive tone allude to the "cruel indifference" not only of the parent/child relationship but also of the U.S.-Puerto Rican relationship.

25. Ortiz Cofer, *Line of the Sun*, 286, 290.

26. Ibid., 241.

27. For examples of what happens to women when we are silenced with-out an identity of our own making, see Ortiz Cofer's poem "The Lesson of the Sugar Cane" and short story "Nada," both in *Latin Deli*, 36 and 50–60, respectively.

28. Ortiz Cofer, *Line of the Sun*, 287.

29. Crossan, *Dark Interval*, 32–37.

30. Esmeralda Santiago, *América's Dream*, 91.

31. Ibid., 325.

32. Crossan, *Dark Interval*, 39.

33. Ibid., 40.

34. Throughout the writing of this essay, I have been nurtured, sustained, and brought back by Clarissa Pinkola Estés's work *Women Who Run With the Wolves*. The notions of capture, theft, and returning to the self resonate throughout her work but are brought into sharper focus in her chapter "Homing: Returning to Oneself," 255–296.

35. E. Santiago, "Island of Lost Causes," reprinted in *Boricuas*, ed. Roberto Santiago, 24.

36. E. Santiago, *América's Dream*, 19. Esperanza and Destino are two towns on Vieques and highlighted in the novel; América physically walks away from the former to the latter.

37. Nathan Scott says of tragedy, "In the tragic universe, life is experienced as having broken down: that the congruence between the highest aspirations of the human spirit and its world environment, apart from which existence seems utterly futile, is no longer discernable." In *The Broken Center* (New Haven: Yale University, 1966), 122. He claims it is the communion of the Eucharist, the celebration of tragedy's defeat, that mediates/reconciles the tragic vision. In this sense, the community of those who maintain the memory, like those who read/know América's story, can respond in spite of tragedy.

38. E. Santiago, *América's Dream*, 78–79. The motif of the birth control pill is significant for the Puerto Rican woman, since reproductive rights have been exploited through forced sterilization and unethical "experiments" with birth control pills on Puerto Rican women by U.S. pharmaceutical companies. See Edna Acosta-Belen, ed., *The Puerto Rican Woman: Perspectives on Culture, History and Society*; and Cynthia T. García Coll and María de Lourdes Mattei, eds., *The Psychosocial Development of Puerto Rican Women*, 147–148, 217.

39. Crossan, *Dark Interval*, 40–45.

40. Her father, Luis A. Ferré, was an industrialist who, after building his wealth financing construction projects (primarily roads and bridges), held the highest political/social position in Puerto Rico as its governor from 1968 to 1972, advocating statehood through the New Progressive Party.

41. Julia M. Gallardo Colón, "Rosario Ferré," in *Biographical Dictionary of Hispanic Literature in the United States*, ed. Nicolás Kanellos, 99–105.

42. Robert Detweiler, "Theological Trends of Postmodern Fiction," *Journal of the American Academy of Religion* 44, no. 2 (1976): 225–237.

43. In an essay discussing her translation of her own work from Spanish to English, "On Destiny, Language, and Translation; or, Ophelia Adrift in the C. & O. Canal," Ferré states: "Coming and going from south to north, from Spanish to English, without losing a sense of self can constitute an anguishing experience . . . Those who come [to the United States] fleeing from poverty and hunger . . . are often forced to be merciless with memory, as they struggle to integrate with and become indistinguishable from the mainstream. It is for these people that translation becomes of fundamental importance . . . Obliged to adapt in order to survive, the children of these Puerto Rican parents often refuse to learn to speak Spanish, and they grow up having lost the ability to read the literature and the history of their island. This

cultural suicide constitutes an immense loss, as they become unable to learn about their roots, having lost the language which is the main road to their culture." In Ferré, *Youngest Doll*, 163.

44. René Marqués, in *The Docile Puerto Rican*, claims that *machismo* was the last, and a necessary, cultural bulwark to resist U.S. imperialism and Puerto Rican docility. These women authors challenge assumptions that the self-determination of women and Puerto Rico are mutually exclusive and that to critique Puerto Rican sexism is to negate Puerto Rican culture. See Diana L. Vélez, "Cultural Constructions of Women by Contemporary Puerto Rican Women Authors," in *The Psychosocial Development of Puerto Rican Women*, ed. Cynthia T. García Coll and Maria de Lourdes Mattei, 31–59.

45. Ferré, *House on the Lagoon*, 59.

46. Ibid., 60.

47. Jean Franco, foreword to Ferré, *Youngest Doll*, xiii.

48. *American Heritage Dictionary of the English Language*, 1993, s.v. "(to do) justice."

49. "Purest bred" Puerto Ricans are those who can trace their ancestry back to Spain with little or no intermingling with African or Taíno blood— or so they believe.

50. I say "more obvious" here because I believe that all Puerto Ricans have African blood running through our veins, regardless of whether our physical features reflect this fact in lesser degrees. Puerto Rico's slave history, as well as the forced and consensual interrelationships which have marked our history since, bear witness to this reality.

51. In the novel, the house was designed by an architect apprentice of Frank Lloyd Wright, who stole some of his designs and recreated them in Puerto Rico where the people were not "sophisticated" enough to recognize his theft.

52. Both stories in Ferré, *Youngest Doll*.

53. Ferré, *House on the Lagoon*, 389.

CHAPTER 3

ANA CASTILLO AS *SANTERA*

RECONSTRUCTING POPULAR

RELIGIOUS PRAXIS

GAIL PÉREZ

**Storytelling: her words set into motion the forces that
lie dormant in things and beings.** TRINH MINH-HA

In June 1997, an item appeared in the *San Diego
Union Tribune* that recounted the miraculous
appearance of the Virgin of Guadalupe in Mexico City's Hidalgo Subway. Spotted by a fifteen-
year-old girl who was mopping the floor, the Virgin has attracted hundreds to the site, who
come bearing candles and flowers to Our Lady.
Their responses to this people's miracle replay
the contestation of meanings, both hegemonic
and counterhegemonic, generated not only in
Mexico since the original apparition in 1531
but in subsequent apparitions throughout the
American Southwest. Of the "Metro Miracle,"
working women said, "This is telling us that
there is divine light, that we are not alone," and
"She is here . . . You can see her if you have
faith." A student was more skeptical: "Let's see
what the government has invented for us now."
Rather predictably, the archbishop gave the
final word: "It is not a miracle." The history of
Our Lady of Guadalupe demonstrates that her
cult was initially opposed by the Franciscans as
obvious indigenous atavism until her image
was later recognized by the hierarchy as a useful instrument of conversion. However, her apparition continued to grace indigenous revolts

throughout eighteenth-century Chiapas, the Yucatán, and Morelos, often in highly syncretic forms. It was on the foothills of the volcano Popocatépetl that Antonio Pérez in the 1760s found an image of the Virgin that inspired a millennial movement to rid local peoples of a corrupt clergy and Spanish *hacendados,* all in the name of the Christian Virgin. "God," Antonio announced, "is the ear of corn, and the three ears of corn, the Holy Trinity."[1] Indigenous revival movements were motivated by the deep sense that both Christians and their own gods had abandoned them. So profound is this legacy of both political and ironic hermeneutics that locals in Mexico City interpreted the eruption of "El Popo" on the eve of the 1997 elections as a sign that the god/mountain was angry with the PRI, the ruling party.

I am indulging in precisely the amused, faithful, political interpretive practices of popular religion/folklore that is the subject of Ana Castillo's *cuento* (or better, *metacuento*), So Far from God. Published at about the same time as her book of prose, *Massacre of the Dreamers,* the novel recounts the miraculous doings of a poor, female-headed household in the old Penitente town of Tomé, New Mexico. Four hundred years ago, Juan de Oñate made his *entrada* into New Mexico, then a distant outpost of New Spain and later of Mexico. The legacy of Franciscan missions, Indian enslavement, and cultural syncretism provides an ideal site for the re-imagining of Chicano/a culture from a feminist (or Xicana) perspective.[2] (Of course, isolation and the neglect of church and state have played and still do play a role in Chicano/Hispano cultural production. Thus, Chicanas/os are so far from God.) As Castillo relates in *Massacre of the Dreamers,* miracles still have their place within our five hundred years of struggle; in 1992, the Virgin appeared on an oak tree during the mostly female-led cannery strike in Watsonville, California:

The response of the Mexicanas to the apparition of the Virgin's image on the oak tree is, to my mind, an indication of a need for spiritual consolation and material relief. Again, it is not so much a manifestation of the Church but of the women's culture and ethnic identity. Above all, I see the Guadalupan Cult as an unspoken, if not unconscious, devotion to their own version of the Goddess.(48)[3]

The novel, then, is embedded in a long tradition of voicing struggle and oppositional consciousness in the language of miracle and popular religion. Whatever the "real" status of the Metro or oak tree miracles, Castillo's concern (and ours) should be the social and political struggles motivating each community of interpreters—in this case, the plight of contemporary Chicanas. The women in Mexico City interpret the sign as showing they are "not alone," not abandoned; just as indigenous leaders felt their apparitions testified to their suffering under the ontological abandonment of the conquest; just as the cannery workers struggled, often abandoned by the men who should have supported them. While *Massacre of the Dreamers* proposes a serious Xicana spirituality, in the vein of Luisah Teish's *Jambalaya* or Gloria Anzaldúa's *Borderlands/La Frontera*, the novel is about the process of interpretation and the invention of culture and ethnicity within the praxis of the everyday lives of working-class Xicanas. Because Castillo has done such a meticulous job of research, each allusion in the allegorical narrative tends to endlessly reverberate with historical/mythical meanings. The text forces us to enact its theme— recovery through *re*-covery and *re*-memory of the past. Reconstituting female power relies on an act of cultural memory that excavates the untold story of female agency, indigenist revolt, and woman-centered spirituality.

Given Castillo's subject matter—the possibility of Chicana resistance to the interlocking systems of late capitalism, religion, and family—I hope that it is clear why this discussion must be wide-ranging. One system of oppression inevitably leads us to another. Concerning family, Cherríe Moraga complains in her comments on the 1990 Chicano Art: Resistance and Affirmation (CARA) exhibit that Chicano art has not really engaged in the "breakdown and shake-up of La Familia y La Iglesia."[4] Castillo bravely takes this on in light of the current debate about the "Latino" family as the new "model minority" with strong family values. This discourse erases the reality of the exploitation of Third World women in a restructured economy and feeds the cultural defensiveness of Chicanas/os who seek to counter racist discourse with our traditions of family and spirituality, but who also are thereby reluctant to spill the beans about sexism and abuse within the family. Carlos Vélez-Ibáñez's commentary on Hispano/Mexicano households in the Southwest outlines the crucial role of family and kin networks in economic and psychic survival: "At the household level, the main struggle of the members is to defend themselves against repeated attempts by the state and/or market to exert complete control over their labor and productive capacities."[5] "Thick" or multiple-kin relationships, clustered households, especially around the grandparents, and ritual cycles of exchange help families share knowledge, resources, family history, and cultural practices. Baptisms, *quinceañeras*, Tupperware parties, and holidays ritualize relationships and keep alive cultural practices. Most crucially, within the households occur cultural conflicts; children are being socialized in the values of mainstream individualism and consumerism while being asked to participate in cooperation and sharing at home. These positive values may not be viewed as such by children indoctrinated into Anglo values of "self-serving vertical mobility": "These deny the cultural efficacy of the population by framing them within derogatory stereotypes."[6] Children exist in a world which they simultaneously deny, and this alienation from one's own sources of power is one of Castillo's important themes. Obviously, as Vélez-Ibañez points out, "Mexicanas are the primary agents of change and stability," although he leaves it at that. Even more surprising, he finds that after an initial period of individualistic social mobility, the young tend to return to the family and maintain the religious and cultural rituals even into the second and third generations. Given this absolutely critical role of social relations, Vélez-Ibañez asks that we not deny patriarchy, but that we view it within the broader context of survival.

It is precisely this role of "survival," however, that really prevents the question of gender from ever arising. Castillo foregrounds the role of women as cultural producers, demanding that we interrogate the religion and the definition of motherhood that is being "transmitted." By not unmasking gender inequality as we unmask the racial/cultural stereotyping Vélez-Ibañez refers to, we are maintaining the family as the refuge in a heartless world instead of transforming the world. This, I'm afraid, is what he refers to as "gender posturing" in "academic hallways." Castillo makes the point in *Massacre of the Dreamers* that women create children, but they do not create the world the children come into: "If we believe in a value system that seeks the common good of all members of society, by applying the very qualities and expectations we have placed on Motherhood to our legislature and our social system—to care selflessly for her young, to be responsible for her children's material, spiritual, and emotional needs—we are providing for the future" (187). If we focus on survival, we never need ask what creates the evil we survive, in this case the global capitalism and competitive individualism that are bolstered by traditional gender roles. Vélez-Ibañez's sample also ignores the fact that overall, the number of female-headed households went up during the 1980s, and he cannot account for the social forces behind this.

Patricia Zavella[7] has studied the electronics and garment industries in the Rio Grande Valley (the site of Castillo's *So Far from God*)
and argues that the employment boom there for Chicanas came at
some cost. Relying on gender divisions of labor already in place
throughout these industries worldwide, Chicanas were the preferred
labor force. As traditional male-dominated industrial jobs declined,
women did move up as some men moved down. Gender analysis here
is not "posturing" but absolutely central to understanding why
women are the preferred labor force in non-union, often paternalistic
and exploitative assembly plants worldwide. The Albuquerque Mexi-
cana whom Zavella profiles briefly participated in the "boom," but
her "traditional values" (the very ones Vélez-Ibañez celebrates) include "deference to her wealthy Anglo benefactors, repression of her
anger toward her ex-spouse, and reliance on self and kin rather than
on institutional support."[8] In other words, she has no public power
to demand that institutions meet her needs, in spite of the help that
her kin offered.

As for "Iglesia," the Church, Chicano culture and Catholicism—
so intimately intertwined—are situated within the household space
where these social/economic transformations occur. Social mobility
for Chicanas, of which Castillo is herself an example, must reveal the
contradictions within the "ritual cycles of exchange" as their experiences in the workforce and in higher education "conscienticize"
them.[9] Furthermore, I think that Castillo's artistic representation
concerns a certain group of Chicanas; *Massacre of the Dreamers* focuses on working-class women and the canneries, factories, and fields
that are the sites of their struggle. It is within the context of their
praxis that cultural reinvention and interpretation occurs. In *Sunbelt
Working Mothers*,[10] the authors emphasize the new anthropological
view of culture as not simply static, but a site of improvisation and
agency within existing norms. These improvisations are driven by
survival: "We see women as active agents who develop strategies for
managing their everyday lives."[11] The problem I have noted in terms
of positive cultural norms (Vélez-Ibañez) and female agency (Zavella)
is that these behaviors, because of sexism and racism, are not always
viewed as positive, as oppositional, as empowering.

Castillo's revisionist Catholicism, as interpreted within the praxis
of working-class Chicanas, initially seems to fix her thought within
the emerging body of work by Latina theologians. Ada María Isasi-
Díaz radically reinterprets Catholic tradition in light of the survival
practices of Latinas, including their naming of their own reality and

their understanding of God, of the saints, of liberation. Like Castillo, she insists on solidarity with working-class women. Only by creating a society that gives them actualized being and not simply existence will true social transformation occur: "This option (for the poor) is grounded in the belief that from their marginality, the poor and oppressed can see a different future, a better future for themselves, and, in the long run . . . a better future for all."[12] Noting the extreme marginality of Latinas, both within the Church hierarchy and socially, Isasi-Díaz acknowledges the power of popular religion to contribute to theology and the liberation of Latinas. Their insights are to be judged not according to doctrinal scrutiny, but according to the broader Gospel message of "Justice and Love."[13] The importance of this movement is that it gives (or purports to give) the woman in the Mexico City subway the authority to reinterpret the sacred, according to her needs and in the woman's voice that the Church labors to exclude.

All of this introductory discussion speaks to the special significance of the home and of women as cultural agents. Rowe and Schelling's *Memory and Modernity: Popular Culture in Latin America* provides an analysis particularly relevant to Castillo's project.[14] In the ongoing conquest of the Americas, the clash between indigenous and European worldviews continues, just as it does in contemporary New Mexico.[15] While church and state promulgate official history and memory, there remain sites of alternative cultural memory. Cultural memory is a practice that occurs within social spaces; eliminating such spaces creates a kind of public amnesia, eradicating other political and cultural alternatives. In colonial Mexico, the space that best eluded the destruction of native practices was the home, especially concerning matters of healing, love problems, birth, and the general amelioration of misfortune. While the total Amerindian worldview behind such magical practices tended to disappear, it was women who passed on this "counteracculturation." In the home altars of women, the Church's monopolization of the sacred (we recall the archbishop's pronouncements in Mexico City) was broken. This cultural transmission, Rowe and Schelling argue, occurred "between tactical obedience and pragmatic evasion: *'obedezco pero no cumplo.'*"[16] Latina theologians such as Isasi-Díaz embrace the Indian and African strands of popular religion as long as it is "good and life giving," but they cannot do what I believe to be the project of writers like Castillo, Cherríe Moraga, and Gloria Anzaldúa. And that is to pull out the subversive "forgotten" memories of another worldview, the suppressed countervalues of women and Native peoples. A final function of the home, then, is to provide the social space that articulates indigenous values, chiefly in the healing practices of *curanderismo*.

Castillo's tale of a multigenerational family of women is also a way of confronting her own Catholic mother and all the attendant anxiety about gender, culture, and identity. In an interview with Marta Navarro,[17] Castillo expresses her deep ambivalence, on the one hand admiring her mother's labor and suffering (survival), and on the other realizing that her mother's religion and investment in traditional roles would condemn her own quest for wholeness. In the essay "La Macha: Toward a Beautiful Whole Self," she castigates the misogyny and antisexuality of the Church and prefigures the theme of *So Far from God*; practices such as the cult of the saints send repressive messages: "What kind of convoluted message do we give young Catholic women when we teach them to be obedient and submissive and yet to protect their virtue even on the pain of death?"[18] Castillo's literary/cultural project, I argue, is not that of the new Latino/a theologians. With great respect, she will reject the Catholicism of the mothers for the *curanderismo* of the grandmothers: "Although the Catholic Church as an institution cannot for a number of reasons guide us as Mexican/Amerindian women into the 21st century, we cannot make a blanket dismissal of Catholicism either. Rejecting the intolerant structure of the church does not automatically obliterate its entrenchment in our culture."[19] One could argue, as I think Castillo's art exemplifies, that Mexican Catholicism is also the cultural space (especially in the figure of Our Lady of Guadalupe) in which the indigenous world view survives.[20] The spirituality of the *abuelas*, then, is potent for its indigenous strand of curing and unconditional love: "So certain feminists of that form of activism, are recalling the folkways of their grandmothers while altering the Catholic Faith of their devout mothers."[21] This revisionism is very movingly stated in a recent essay in the anthology *Goddess of the Americas*.[22]

As I have noted, the home is also the site of indigenous practices that can be recuperated into an alternative spirituality. This is very much in line with the earliest Chicano/a cultural projects, such as Luis Valdez's Teatro Campesino. In her brilliant book on the *teatro*, Yolanda Broyles-González quotes Valdez on the "brown face beneath the white mask": "Frijoles and tortillas remain, but the totality of the Indio's vision is gone. Curanderas make use of plants and herbs as popular cures, without knowing that their knowledge is what remains of a great medical science."[23] Castillo's allegory, I argue, uncovers alternative worldviews—precisely non-Christian—to serve as utopian, oppositional standpoints. As a work like the Mexican anthropologist Guillermo Bonfil Batalla's *Mexico Profundo* makes clear, our *mestiza* grandmothers might not fully understand their own practices, but they are part of a different worldview which is everywhere alive in Mexico, if we have eyes to see it (especially in collective community practices). This alternative vision defines our relationship with nature in a very different way: "In this civilization, unlike that of the West, the natural world is not seen as an enemy. Neither is it assumed that greater human self-realization is achieved through separation from nature."[24] The other deeply non-Christian element of popular religion is the notion of immanence, the effective presence of the divine in the image of the saints (or gods!)—in other words, magic. As Rowe and Schelling point out, popular religion rejects Christian notions of "moral perfection" for the more important everyday "livelihood of self and family for whose benefit the assistance of the saints is sought."[25]

Castillo's time in New Mexico has allowed her to locate her "vision in which brown women refuse to work for a system that renders us ineffective and invisible except to serve it" in a site that recapitulates the conquest of indigenous peoples by the Spanish, the Mexicans, and the Anglo-Americans. The contemporary unholy mix of New Mexican culture—from La Conquistadora, the Virgin who presided over the reconquest of New Mexico's Indians in 1692, to New Age vision quests—provides a final theoretical challenge for Chicana/o artists. The historian Ramón Gutiérrez refers to the conscious use of pageantry in the conquest of New Mexico in 1598 by Juan de Oñate, who went so far as to restage the conquest of Tenochtitlán for the benefit of the Pueblo Indians.[26] The question has always been how women and other subaltern peoples have staged their own resistance within the imposition of Christian forms. Yolanda Broyles-González demonstrates how the Christian shepherds play, the *Pastorela*, was staged by indigenous performers to parody Christian theology. "Traditional" Southwestern cultural forms—*dichos* (proverbs), dramas, *cuentos*—are all too often taught in a way that erases their subversion. Why not view the appearance of the Virgin of Guadalupe as the Indians' first countermiracle? Instead of viewing the miraculous as a sign of mystification, one could view it in the way the critic Michel de Certeau does: "He conceptualized miracles as an affirmation of a utopian space full of possibilities, as a counterdiscourse and countermemory in the life of the oppressed."[27] Castillo's artistic problem is to deploy the fantastically overmediated and commercialized remnants of contemporary Indo/Hispano culture in the name of her Xicana agenda. Will her novel take its place next to the turquoise coyotes of Santa Fe boutiques, or will it illustrate a process of cultural reappropriation, giving Chicanas the last laugh?

THE MIRACLES IN TOMÉ

So Far from God opens with the death and resurrection of Loca, the fourth daughter of Sofi, a single mother who runs a *carnicería* (butcher shop) with her three other daughters—Fe, Esperanza, and Caridad. Tomé, a former stronghold of the Penitente Brotherhood whose history permeates the novel, has run on hard times, being a little too far from the tourist industry and too close to the high-tech boom of the Rio Grande Valley. Much of New Mexico has been poor, and as the land grant revolt of Reies Tijerina in the 1960s reminds us, the memory of losing the land is an enduring one. For Sofi, the loss of her child is just one more "punishment" in the martyrdom of her life—martyrdom being especially enforced by the notorious Penitente flagellations on Good Friday. To everyone's surprise, the baby rises from her coffin, floats to the church roof and gives, in a bilingual rendition, the story of her Christlike journey to hell and back. When Father Jerome suggests there might be something devilish in all this, Sofi stands by her interpretation of the miracle. Somehow the words of the eighteenth-century Mexican nun, Sor Juana Inés de la Cruz, come to her: "And this is a miracle, an answer to the prayers of a broken-hearted mother, 'hombre necio, pendejo . . .'" (23). Sor Juana's poem—"*Hombres necios que acusáis/a la mujer sin razón/sin ver que sois la occasión/de lo mismo que culpáis*"[28]—points out that the frightful image of woman that men fear is itself a male construction. So the church's devils, as we shall see, are patriarchal reinscriptions of female and indigenous wisdom. If popular religion has always been a site of resistance, with this first domestic miracle, female spirituality has begun to evangelize the church. As the resurrected little Loca says to the priest: "Remember, I am here to pray for you." And we do remember. We remember that in 1531, the Virgin of Guadalupe appeared to an Indian, whose task it was to evangelize the church, turning it, according to Virgilio Elizondo, away from the urban center to the impoverished barrio of Tepeyac.[29] This hermeneutic struggle always resonates with the ongoing historical conquest of America.

Early reviews of the novel, like Ray González's in *The Nation*,[30] demonstrate a lack of understanding of Castillo's project. He charges her with "reckless fantasies" in a novel full of "stories told by too many characters who fade in and out of the vague plot." "Predictable figures like mother Sofia and her daughters . . . are too 'ethnic' for their lives to be believable, even in the supernatural world Castillo sets in New Mexico" (772). González is free to dislike the novel, but it is deeply ironic that he accuses Castillo of "reckless fantasies" in just the way that Father Jerome accuses Sofi. Sometimes I think that people haven't any sense of humor. Castillo is not writing a realistic novel; her literary sources are the lives of the saints, the New Mexican *cuento*, and the discourses of contemporary Chicanas, whether as *chisme* or tales from the Oprah Winfrey Show. In a press release for the novel, Castillo describes her inspiration: "I read the *Dictionary of the Saints* as research for the novel . . . when I finished reading it, I wrote the first chapter of the novel in one day." This generated the character La Loca Santa. "With great care I attempted to bring together and *re*tell in my own way many of the stories I learned concerning New Mexico, historical, legendary, mythological and contemporary, a collapsing of realities that exploded in my imagination like fireworks at the fiesta. I do believe that while we are laughing and crying when hearing stories we are being given lessons which we may choose to heed or not." Américo Paredes has written an ethnographic essay about all-male joking sessions concerned with the magic/trickery of *curanderos*.[31] The humor reflects both skepticism and cultural pride in the wit of *curanderos*, even if it omits the fact that most of the jesters were probably cured at home by women. He notes that the joking both mocks and continues the tradition of *curanderismo*. The jesters cling to Mexican-American culture "in great part because Anglo-American culture rejects part of themselves" (62). Similarly, Castillo creates a community of female storytellers who revise patriarchal attitudes in the saints' lives and in traditional figures such as La Malinche, La Llorona, and other figurations of motherhood and martyrdom. Their telling is admittedly ironic, but it also performs a kind of resistance to cultural assimilation.

We should view the novel as invoking oral traditions in the spirit

of *relajo*, defined by Broyles-González as "disruptive group cheeki-
ness," as parody and joking that can "magically subvert the existing
order, that could open up new vistas of freedom for the Chicano(a)
collective" (29). As she points out, the use of an occasional miracle in
such burlesques, say the appearance of an indigenous deity, could
"question and challenge the established order" (30). Laughter has a
utopian function because it is based on seeing the familiar in a new
way and is thus a "rehearsal of freedom." This is precisely the quality of the novel and it in no way obscures the serious analysis. Perhaps the most important quality of storytelling is the emotional effect, the attitude toward life it creates in the listener/reader. As was
said of the sacro-profane spectacles of Amerindians: "With the sol-
emn the Indian always unites the frivolous, in loving harmony, as in
life itself."[32]

The plot of the novel, then, is extremely allegorical, a quality evident in both the traditional *cuento* and the saint's life. Besides Loca,
there are Fe, Esperanza, Caridad, and various men who wander through
their lives trailing fragments of Chicano history. Fe, like someone
who walked out of *Latina Magazine,* is the believer in the American
Dream and her own "Spanish" heritage. She dies a cruel death in one
of the new military-industrial plants and "stays dead." Caridad, a
nurse's aide and *puta,* is miraculously healed by Loca after an attack
by the mysterious *malogra.* Drawing on elements from St. Clare's life,
Castillo reconfigures Caridad as a *curandera* (traditional healer) who
finally undergoes not a Christian but a Native American assumption
back into Mother Earth. She is loved by Francisco Penitente, and their
story symbolically comments on the interactions of Christianity and
indigenous religion. Esperanza is a survivor of the Chicano Movement, politicized but wounded by the ongoing sexism not only of the
movement (through her boyfriend, Ruben, aka Cuauhtémoc), but also
in her journalistic profession; she is martyred as a correspondent in
the Gulf War. Tomé itself is losing its children to "better lives" and
is slowly giving in to poverty and gossip. The core story, however, is
Sofi's, the wisdom of the mother that must discover its own wisdom.
Invoking important groups such as the Mothers of the Plaza de Mayo,
the Mothers of East L.A., and women within such organizations as
the Southwest Organizing Committee in Albuquerque, Castillo lo-
cates the salvation of the community in Sofi's ability to reconfigure
the martyrdom of her children. Sofi's central act is to *re*-remember
her own history; she is not *La Abandonada,* as the neighbors and her

own indoctrination would have it. Long ago, it was she who got rid of her husband, Domingo (a compulsive gambler), and by recalling her own agency she is able to renew her community. Obviously, it is patriarchal history and Christian myth that revise our female creativity. Castillo quite explicitly intends to revise yet again this initial Christian revisionism. She describes her project in *Massacre of the Dreamers:* "We must take heed that not all symbols that we have inherited are truly symbolic of the life-sustaining energy we carry within ourselves as women; so even when selectively incorporating what seems indispensable to our religiosity, we must analyze its historical meaning" (145).

The quality of compassionate laughter in the novel is very close to the spirit of the New Mexican *cuento.* Collections of these stories emphasize the wit, common sense, and magic that made survival possible in lonely Hispano villages.[33] *Dichos* and *cuentos* bind communities together to this day and keep alive the spirituality of communities that have been notoriously neglected by the clergy (hence the rise of the Penitente Brotherhood). All such stories are didactic, but most of all they embody the life-affirming values of the community.[34] Castillo updates this tradition in her tale of contemporary small-town Chicanas. If she misses anything here, I think it is what Vélez-Ibañez points to in his discussion of family as a defense against oppression. Some of the Penitente stories such as "Doña Sebastiana" are deeply subversive. Like all systems of popular religion, the *cuentos* insist on a personal and reciprocal relationship with the saints. A *cuento* like "Parading a Santo" shows a happy mixture of indigenous magic with the Christian procession, as the local Indians use an image of the Baby Jesus to bring rain and then send out the Virgin Mary to dry things up.[35] In "Doña Sebastiana," a poor farmer refuses to share his meal (which he has stolen!) with both Christ and Mary because, he tells them, "You have created an unjust and unfair world . . . On the one side are those who are wealthy and beyond all worth and justice, and on the other are the poor and miserable beyond all compassion and understanding."[36] But when Death (Doña Sebastiana) asks for a share, he complies because death treats all equally. For this sensible response, the farmer is made a healer, a *curandero.* While there are no direct analogues to this tale in the novel, the symbolism of its plot is everywhere. Those who stand up to the Church, call the priest a *pendejo,* and voice injustice are given the gift of healing (on the condition that they do not use it for selfish ends). Castillo casti-

gates the logic of martyrdom of the Penitentes, but her characteriza-
tions of men don't seem to acknowledge that women's traditions are
embedded in broader communal traditions of resistance. The Penitentes, in fact, cooperated with groups like *Las Gorras Blancas* in resisting Anglo encroachment on communal grazing lands in the 1880s
and enforced an ethic of cooperation and respect vital to the survival
of local communities.[37] While the Penitentes are noted for dragging
Doña Sebastiana's death cart in their Good Friday processions, their
subversive tale is not so well-known.

The brilliance of Castillo's family allegory has a more localized focus. In the opening of the novel, the women exist within the ideology
of the church and traditional roles. Within this interpretive frame,
Sofi (wisdom) is not wise, but simply a sad case. Doña Felicia's healing powers are confined within the acceptable role of *curandera*, and
she herself has long since stopped challenging the church. Her hard
life is not, of course, *felíz*. Loca is simply crazy and not holy. Fe and
Esperanza live out the narrative of the American Dream, surpassing
their mother professionally and economically, and yet are devastated
by its destructive logic. This martyrdom will inspire the reevaluation
of the "backward culture" of Tomé. After all, if the American Dream
can't save us, what can? Sofi runs a *carnicería* but under the social
rules of patriarchy has been "abandoned" by her husband. In "La
Macha," Castillo argues that it is just those women who are single,
lesbian, or female heads of families who point the way to "transformation of *our* culture" (45). First, stereotypes about traditional roles
within Chicano families belie our own history; historian Richard
Griswold del Castillo has found that 31 percent of households in Los
Angeles in 1880 were headed by females.[38] This was largely due to the
migratory labor possibilities open to men. In spite of traditional roles
and family values, Isasi-Díaz finds, "the figures are equally dismal today: in 1991, 28 percent of all Hispanics were poor and 23 percent of
Hispanic families were headed by women."[39] Second, constructions
of motherhood in Mexican/Chicano culture define the role as asex-
ual, as essentially that of nurturer and mediator for males. It is no coincidence that the "bad" mothers of Chicano culture—La Llorona, La
Malinche—were women who acted on their own behalf. To transform culture, the *mujeres solas*, including nuns and virgins, must be
given power and voice to articulate an existence outside of the male
gaze, but first they must be conscienticized to understand that their
power is always already there.

Without foregrounding gender and what Castillo defines as the Amerindian worldview that "all things created in the universe are sacred and equal," patriarchy and capitalism cannot be changed. Chicano families will continue to produce exploited workers. Thus, her novel is a profound antimobility myth. The "Decade of the Hispanic," Raul Izaguirre's misnomer for the 1980s, actually produced very uneven development; marginal labor participation increased for Chicano workers in spite of gains in the professions.[40] What especially concerns Castillo is that the hypocritical rhetoric of family values is accompanied by the massive exploitation of Third World women in the new global factory. Fe's martyrdom to toxic poisoning in a Sunbelt munitions factory recalls Annette Fuentes's and Barbara Ehrenreich's exposé, *Women in the Global Factory*. In the early 1980s, 40 percent of electronics workers in the United States were immigrant women, and the multinationals demonstrated a preference for a workforce that was "docile, easily manipulated and willing to do boring, repetitive assembly work."[41] Fuentes and Ehrenreich also noted the continuity between the patriarchal family and the preference of factory management for young women willing to take orders from men. Here "private" and "public" oppression coincide in a way that refutes the corporate myth that work will liberate women. One corporate executive enthused, "The benefits and freedom to be gained by these women from their employment in these new industries are almost always to be preferred to the near slavery associated with the production of classical goods such as batik."[42] Economic power has clearly benefited some women and has clearly challenged gender roles at home,[43] but corporate logic still prefers female workers precisely because of their historically subordinate status. We must get over the notions that insistence on gender is "posturing" and that the Holy Family is somehow innocent of the workings of capitalism and the state. As Patricia Zavella makes clear,[44] "Latino family values" are used as an alibi by policymakers to ignore the needs of poor families and to mask the economic restructuring that underemploys men and sends women into the service economy. Third World women are now the surplus army of labor.

Contrary to the assimilationist mythology of capitalism, capitalism itself creates the very marginality that makes mobility a joke; it also keeps alive notions of gender and ethnicity for its own purposes. Castillo insists on gender and ethnicity as sites of oppositional consciousness precisely because (and in spite of the postmodern insistence on the instability of identity) "the ethnicization of capitalism on a global scale," in Appelbaum's words,[45] continues to maintain a racial and gendered hierarchy of labor. Since global capitalism continues to "reinvent ethnicity," it is vital that women of color create an oppositional culture. As Norma Alarcón puts it, we must "work with literary, testimonial, and pertinent ethnographic materials to enable Chicanas to grasp their 'I' and 'We' in order to make effective political interventions."[46] The new interest in popular religiosity[47] teaches us to view popular miracles as interventions and not merely as the opium of the people;[48] such a so-called enlightened view itself continues the "imperial gaze." Fuentes and Ehrenreich explain how eruptions of the magical among workers can be resistance: "In Malaysia, a woman may suddenly see a hantu or jin, a hideous mythological spirit, while peering through a microscope . . . Within minutes the hysteria spreads up and down the assembly line. Sometimes factories must be closed for a week or more while the evil spirits are exorcised" (28–30).

For Castillo the process for Chicanas of grasping the "we" must begin with a reformulation of family (the novel only implies reformulation of society in general). How can the family move from being "mother-centered" to the very different notion of "woman-centered"? How can *comadres* cease commiserating, especially over men (a real miracle), and begin empowering each other? How can children dying to leave home not return as the dead, martyred to a larger world the parents do not understand? Only a reformulation of mothering can accomplish these ends by (1) making nurturing reciprocal so that women, too, are nurtured; and (2) by establishing a new relationship between the woman-centered home and society at large. Like a loving *santera*, Castillo resemanticizes the existing logic of martyrs and saints, not as ways to dignify female powerlessness through Christian suffering, but to reveal the goddesses beneath such images who are capable of exerting agency. Ultimately, we need activists and not martyrs, but hopefully one can lead to the other in the conscientization of our Catholic mothers. For these reasons, the novel must ultimately be about mother Sofi (wisdom) and Loca (principle of female creativity).

A brief explanation of the martyred sisters reveals the logic of this social reformulation. Fe (faith in the American Dream) and Esperanza (hope for political change) illustrate the lingering post–Chicano Movement structures of exploitation. Esperanza has been silenced not only by the sexism/racism of the "system" but also in Tomé, where the *comadres* consider her a *mitotera* (gossip) who probably got what she deserved for making trouble. Significantly, Esperanza sends La Llorona to tell Loca of her fate in the Gulf War, and the allegorical resonance is dazzling. Esperanza's political message simply cannot be heard by the community; a sighting of La Llorona is more believable than the logic of the Pentagon(!). But as Chicanas come to understand systems of exploitation in the dominant culture, they will not simply abandon "quaint" figures like La Llorona: they will also rehabilitate them as they come to see that the merely "mythic" is also the language of suppressed history. Llorona is both Malintzin (Cortez's Amerindian translator/lover) and the archetypical lower-caste *mestiza* of the folktale whose act of infanticide was more than simple revenge against her upper-class betrayer. Llorona dared to appropriate male property—her children.

The question of betrayal must be at the center of Chicana cultural revisionism. The reconstruction of Malintzin/Malinche has been so extensive that it need not be gone into detail here.[49] As Adelaida del Castillo argued so long ago, Malintzin was certainly the mother of La Raza and possibly prophetic of a new world order under the more peaceful aegis of Quetzalcóatl. All women who speak their resistance are potential *Malinchistas* (traitors); of course, it is Ana Castillo's thesis that it has been female wisdom that was betrayed. Even the "Spanish" Fe believes that by following the standards of Anglo culture, rejecting her "Indian flat butt" and her "dysfunctional family," she can make it. Jilted by the convenience store manager, Tom, Fe finds happiness with Casimiro ("I almost see"), who is perfect except for the congenital bleating he shares with his sheep-herding ancestors,[50] and in her new job in a very toxic military parts plant. Castillo uses Fe's horrible death by cancer and her shift from *gritona* (victim of love betrayed) to *macha* (resister) to express the plight of all women in the global factory. In 1984, in fact, a cancer suit was brought against Southwest Electronic, where women like Fe were poisoned by a gluing operation.[51] Fe's voice, damaged by the great *grito* (scream) over lost romance, still has the strength in the end to express her outrage. In the allegory of the plot, Fe's faith in work, consumerism, and the "Dream" is utterly betrayed because of the contradictions in the Dream itself.

Unless we are in solidarity with working-class women of color, what Isasi-Díaz calls the *proyecto histórico,*[52] a plan to transform op-

pressive situations for all, will not occur. The ideology of the Dream—
that any hard-working individual can succeed *within the present
order*—obscures structural practices of exclusion. The destruction of
the *agringada* Fe in the new Sunbelt industries factory demonstrates
how the equation of race, gender, and exploited labor simply moves
around, rather than being confronted, in this postindustrial and post-
movement era. Fe's quest for material success and romance are clev-
erly linked to the folktale of Juan Soldado's mine. To the degree that
she partakes of the conquistador's love of gold and loves men "also
lost in the mine," she will lose her soul in materialism and "stay
dead." If her family is *loca*, it is less so that the "incomprehensible
world that Fe encountered that last year of her pathetic life" (172).

Fe's fate is in marked contrast to Caridad, who lives through her
heart (Corazón is her horse) and whose martyrdom comes through
abortion, betrayal by men, and, finally, assault by the *malogra*, a creature straight out of Hispano lore: "an evil spirit which wanders about
in the darkness of the night at the crossroads. It terrorizes the unfor-
tunate ones who wander alone at night, and has usually the form of a
large lock of wool."[53] Castillo rewrites the creature to represent the
conquest, placing Caridad in the place of the raped earth and indigenous woman: the monster is "made of sharp metal and splintered
wood, of limestone, gold, and brittle parchment. It held the weight of
a continent and was as indelible as ink . . . It was pure force" (77). The
gold and parchment suggest the bitter struggle over land grants in
New Mexico, heavy as history itself, a struggle that oppresses Caridad but is only available to her as myth.

Caridad has another aspect that is also deeply rooted in New Mexican history and myth: she is the counterpart, the St. Clare, of Francisco Penitente's St. Francis. Her role, as the feminine has always
been throughout history, is to be the whore of his sexual fantasies
and the virgin guiding his own personal salvation. Francisco practices
the artistic traditions of the "Brotherhood of Light," including the
making of wooden *santos* and the singing of *alabadas* (hymns).
Castillo explicitly rejects the *morada* (meeting house) and its female
auxiliaries' sites of cultural renewal. By the time Francisco begins his
pursuit of her, Caridad has been healed from the *malogra* by the prayers of Loca and is deep into her vocation of *curandera* under the guidance of Doña Felicia. In the relationship between Caridad and Francisco, the battle of the saints really takes place. As Barbara G. Walker
points out,[54] early Christian saints were themselves transformations

of pagan deities. Santa Barbara, "the Divine Barbarian," was originally a goddess in her sacred mountain before she became yet another martyred virgin murdered for refusing to renounce Christianity. Santa Barbara was invoked to provide protection from lightning, and perhaps this led to her association with Shango, the West African *orisha*. Amusingly enough, Caridad's own "conversion" experience at the sacred site of Chimayó has to do with falling in love with a woman from Acoma Pueblo. Redemption, we are to understand, involves loving her indigenous self in the person of Esmeralda. Caridad retreats to a cave for a year, like a divine mountain goddess, to think things over. There, she performs her first local miracle and indeed comes closest to sanctification, even if as a distinctly Indian goddess.

The Penitentes who stumble upon Caridad in the mountains literally cannot budge her, a miraculous act that places her in the weighty company of saints such as Lucy and Clare. An explosion of local theologizing ensues. Although our narrator/*comadre* won't say it, the Penitentes are in the mountains during this Holy Week to perform their forbidden acts of flagellation. Catholics and Indians alike refuse to go to Easter Mass; they make a pilgrimage to La Armitaña, Caridad, interpreting her in light of their needs and cultures. The Indians believe she is Lozen, Spirit Woman of the Apache, who "vowed to make war against the white man forever"; and one Hispano claims she was the Virgin of Guadalupe who "relieved him of his drinking problem" (90). Our coy narrator ventures an opinion: "Yes, perhaps this mountain woman was not the one the Penitente brothers thought her to be, but a spirit memory, and that was why she was not overcome by them" (88). Like the European goddesses, perhaps Caridad is *prior* to Christianity. Every saint embodies layers of meaning and history that do not speak until we remember; and in Caridad, Castillo asks us to recall our indigenous selves.

Francisco tracks down Caridad and her beloved Esmeralda to Acoma Pueblo. Francisco hides in a crowd of tourists, resembling a "coyote" and "vulture." What drives the two women over the edge (literally, and like Thelma and Louise) is also a conversation Esmeralda has with her grandmother and a secret she knows about Francisco. We are never told what this is, so I am going to make something up, because the whole point of the novel is to force us to be creative interpreters of the miracle of existence, just as women have always been. Perhaps Francisco told Esmeralda of his time in Vietnam and of his feeling for Caridad, whom he loves like a virgin—in other words, his own sad, sad story. On her way to sanctification, this is Caridad's "Last Temptation": to pity this man and fulfill her role. Perhaps the Keres grandmother told Esmeralda what happened to Acoma in 1599 under the Spanish and Franciscans, when a Spanish force murdered eight hundred, enslaved the survivors, and cut off one foot of every man over twenty-five.[55] Perhaps she remembered that the Franciscans used flagellation as part of the spectacle of superior "magic" that kept them in power and that one memorable medicine man jeered, "You Christians are crazy,"[56] just as the Indian Sullivan jeered at Francisco for not fulfilling his all-too-evident sexual desires. Perhaps the cross on Francisco's back at Easter represents the weight of historical contradictions of the Church in the Americas, at once the voice of social justice and the institution that refused to create a female or native clergy and, indeed, wrote women and Indians out of theology and history.

At any rate, the women take one look and jump over the side of the mesa, not to death but back to earth where they "would be safe and live forever" (211). Tsichtinako, the Keres creatrix, has called them, and they have resisted the virgin/whore dichotomy that disallows Chicanas from reclaiming their sexual and intellectual power. The Virgin of Guadalupe, of course, best illustrates the initial reinscription of the Aztec goddess Coatlicue as Our Lady, a mediator and not a creator. As the critic Tey Diana Rebolledo explains, Coatlicue was "independent, wrathful, competent; her power to create and destroy was autonomous, as was that of most of the Nahuatl deities; it was a power not emanating solely from a central male figure."[57] The Keres people are remarkable for their all-female trinity, which represents a recognition of the female principle that embraces the earth and woman as both intellectual and biological creatrix.[58] Caridad and Esmeralda remember, as we are supposed to, female wholeness in a world where capitalism and patriarchal religion dismember the feminine (and actual women). This world cannot be fixed by being good workers and good girls. Because the indigenous world lacks a notion of sin or evil, even Francisco could assume a place in it, as coyote/trickster, the haphazard but necessary agent of creation. Unmasking the indigenous identities of Caridad and Francisco might also reveal them to be sacred twins (both were "raised" by Doña Felicia). Their conflict could be reinterpreted as the more indigenous notion of continual transformation through opposing forces, and not as a dualistic clash of good and evil.

In Sofi's conscientization, however, and in the creative wisdom of La Loca lies the unexpected answer to social transformation, right in the domestic space where the children left it. Sofi's liberation is an act of memory; she is not "abandoned" but kicked Domingo the Gambler out. This awakening, however, must be preceded by her activism in Tomé; she has "forgotten" because the culture has no name for her agency, her empowered role, just as it has no name for her outspoken daughter, Esperanza, but *mitotera*. One must literally create a new language for the female repressed, and certainly all the new *santas* of the novel are doing precisely that.

Capitalism, as noted, depends on the underdevelopment of some social sector, especially female labor; therefore, radical change can only come from empowering those left at the bottom of the socioeconomic ladder. Tomé represents the homes and communities of those "left behind" but also the very real attempt of small New Mexican towns to revitalize their economies and culture, especially through the manufacture of folk art. These are just those "classical goods" our corporate executive related to systems of slave labor. By fixing the screen door that Domingo never does get around to fixing, Sofi is inspired to become "mayor" of Tomé and creates a weaving cooperative that educates and socializes the community in ways from which they can actually benefit. The mothers of Tomé replicate all the revolutionary mothers of the past decade from Argentina to Chile to East Los Angeles. In all these cases, the educated, visionary, and acculturated children were martyred (though not to the same degree), and their very sacrifice radicalizes the mothers. As the Mothers of the Plaza de Mayo (Argentina) put it: "Our children begot us. You stop being a conventional mother when you give birth to children who think and work for something beyond their narrow personal goals."[59] Like Sofi, these women were forced into seeking to transform social institutions as their children were "disappeared" during the Dirty War in Argentina between 1976 and 1983. This violation of the "public" and "private" spheres reveals the reality that the home is not private and is in fact deeply embedded in broader social structures. Marguerite Guzmán Bouvard explains: "The Mothers have transformed themselves from women seeking to protect the sanctity of the mother-child bond within the existing political system to women wishing to transform the state so that it reflects maternal values."[60]

Similarly, Castillo argues in *Massacre of the Dreamers* that the home culture and not assimilation into dominant culture provides the source of "an alternative social system" (220). Only when Sofi extends her housekeeping into the community—creating a new weaving cooperative, revising the Penitente Easter procession into something a little closer to an eco-Xicana protest march, and instituting MOMAS (Mothers of Martyrs and Saints)—does she begin to create a world where her children might be safe. Under the spiritual guidance of her dead or *loca* children, she does these feats in culturally specific ways. Through death, the daughters fulfill their names of Faith, Hope, and Charity by incarnating Xicana power (not Christianity): popular culture, indigenous spirituality, and activism. Of course, the martyrdom, sanctification, and general destruction of the children could have been avoided if the generations had communicated in the first place. The first cultural/political intervention must take place within the Chicano family. And as Norma Alarcón insists, women must be foregrounded: "The lure of an ideal humanism is seductive; but without female consciousness and envisioning how as women we would like to exist in the material world, to leap into humanism without repossessing ourselves may be exchanging one male ideology for another."[61]

The Holy Friday procession that closes the novel demonstrates the complex cultural reinscription that is, I argue, the real subject of the novel. The very use of the fantastic, the comic, and the magically real calls all beliefs into question. It is not simply what we believe that is relevant, but how beliefs are deployed, how they are constructed around the liberatory praxis of women. Dean MacCannell, whose work addresses the challenges of Native American artists working within the intense co-optation of the Santa Fe art scene, defines tradition in a way that might suggest how agency and culture among Chicanas/os might be maintained: "Tradition is the challenge to the living by the dead to keep on living."[62] Processions in New Mexico (and the entire Southwest) are enduring sites of cultural contestations, from the highly problematic annual fiesta and procession of La Conquistadora in Santa Fe, to the yearly Easter pilgrimage in Chimayó, traditionally hosted by the Penitentes. Marta Weigle describes how the handsome young man bearing the cross at Chimayó has been fully reconstituted in the media's gaze: "At that moment, amid much dust and noise, the Sky 7 helicopter arrived, and the reporters . . . asked him to pick up the cross and step across the entrance once more."[63] For this moment, however, the people of Tomé capture public space to stage their own understanding of oppression. The fourteen stations of the cross reinscribe the body of Christ as the people and as the earth: "Nuclear power plants sat like gargantuan landmines among the people, near their ranchos and ancestral homes. Jesus was nailed to the cross."[64] This demonstration is less for the benefit of the outsider than it is for the community itself. As a prelude to political action, the contradictions and fears within the community must first be resolved. Loca, not a handsome man carrying a cross, leads the way in her jeans with the patch pulled off (probably referring to the protests in San Antonio against Levis for shutting down a plant that employed fifteen hundred women). Political transformation here occurs within the existing religious vocabulary; interpretive communities abound, both in terms of the commodification of popular religion (i.e., in products like "La Loca Santa and Her Sisters' Tarot Deck") and in terms of the conscientization of Tomé itself. All products and artifacts are haunted by history and by lost social relations that it is our job to restore. Commodification of radical spirituality is simply inevitable.

Loca is the key here. In the novel's allegory, her life most clearly parallels Christ's, and in the procession she will be crucified by AIDS (which she has mysteriously contracted). But she is not Christ, and throughout her short life the community has sought to interpret her. Is she a devil as the church insinuates, or is she a *loca* in the sense that the Mothers of the Plaza de Mayo were called *Las Locas?* Without any "education," Loca excels in all aspects of female culture, and "for a person who had lived her whole life within a mile radius of her home . . . she certainly knew quite a bit about this world" (245). She has no fixed signification for two reasons: first, there is no social inscription for a working-class Chicana intellectual; and second, she is the spirit of Xicana creativity itself. Thus, after her second and final death, she is commemorated as the Fool, the 0, of the "Loca Santa Tarot Deck." As Castillo defines La Xicanisma in *Massacre of the Dreamers*, it creates "a synthesis of inherited beliefs with her [La Xicana's] own distinctive motivations" (13). If she is a reinscription of the Holy Spirit, she embodies the principle of survival within the historical unmaking of women by the erasure of their labor, subjectivity, and sexuality. I am reminded of Paula Gunn Allen's words: "We know this: in the void reside the keepers of wisdom. It is we, perhaps because we are nothing ourselves, who stalk the void and dance the dervish of significance that is born through our parted lips and legs."[65]

Our survival depends on our ability to reinvent ourselves, a process impossible without the recovery of all aspects of the *santas* and the history encapsulated in the myths we seem to prefer. Loca is La Vida Loca itself—improvisation and intuition. Beautifully stated in the novel, the Fool walks "without fear, aware of the choices she made in the journey of life, life itself being defined as a state of courage and wisdom and not an uncontrollable participation in society" (250). It is not a coincidence that as Loca dies of AIDS, she is visited by the Lady in Blue, a Franciscan nun from New Mexican lore who is said to have catechized the Indians *before* the arrival of the official clergy.[66] Allegorically, this makes the point of the novel, which is that the marginalized—women and indigenous peoples—have their own *sheroes*, saints, agency, and especially dispensation of grace outside of patriarchal institutions. Most beautifully, Loca parades through Tomé wrapped in Esperanza's blue bathrobe, the color of the mantle of Our Lady of Guadalupe, but also of the Aztec creator Ometéotl, "mother-father of the Gods and the origin of all the natural forces and of everything that was."[67] The image conflates the hope for justice in ordinary life with the principle of the divinity of life itself.

Any good saint's life must end with canonization, and the MOMAS convention is the final spoof. Historically, groups like the Mothers of East L.A. have challenged local government. In this case, a parish in Los Angeles was the base for a coalition of activists and women who protested the construction of a prison in their neighborhood. Father Moretta's naming of the group was directly inspired by the Mothers of the Plaza de Mayo.[68] Why Castillo focuses on the religious society of the women of Tomé and not on social renewal is hard to say. Perhaps she is showing how the mechanism of institutionalizing religion inevitably perverts its message, thus pointing to the limits of our mothers' Catholicism. Or she might be asking whether female-dominated institutions would be an improvement and is taking her final shot at the supportive (and subordinate) role of women in the Church. First, only a group of empowered working-class Chicanas, with the support of a female clergy and corporate sponsors, could institutionalize the suffering of Latinos through new saints and martyrs (thus creating the MOMAS convention). Given the fact that Latinos are 30 percent of the Catholic Church and only 3 percent of the clergy, this isn't likely. Then there is the question of whether the Mothers would run things any differently; the closing joke about the legendary Pope Joan (AD 854), whose existence prompted a test to show that all papal candidates had testicles,[69] suggests that women would not perpetuate such dualisms and simpleminded inversions. The marketing of candles and T-shirts at the convention indicates that we have come full circle: the voices of the *santas* have fallen silent again in the reified object. Next, the women begin to fight over whose child is the real saint. Perhaps Castillo is making a final dig at Catholicism. The whole need to prove anything—that one is a saint, Chicana, woman—is ridiculed, essentially undermining the whole logic of martyrdom. The martyrdom of children can cut two ways: we can give meaning to their sacrifice and act, or we can confirm our masochistic role as suffering mothers. Again, what will determine if women's spiritual practices are hegemonic or liberatory will be praxis; and given that "local or federal government" greet the advice of the martyred children with "skepticism," their political efficacy is open to doubt.

When we reflect on Castillo's experiment with the novel, we understand how she is attempting to use the form as a way to access oral traditions, collapsing the oral and written in a way that also replicates the generational and educational differences among Chicanas. She is *santera*/novelist, obliged to tell healing truths, just as she herself was healed by her *abuela*. The meanings of *santera* are multiple—priestess of the *orishas* in Santería and maker of sacred images in New Mexico. Castillo is thinking of both as she excavates the feminine repressed in popular religion and in the domestic sphere. Like our own female power, the goddess Tonantzin/Coatlicue, *curanderismo*, and the general invention of domestic arts are latent in our lives and sacred images.[70] Unfortunately, women's culture has been created within the vicious circle of domination: (1) traditional healing and spirituality enabled those abandoned by social institutions to survive, yet (2) the same creativity is stigmatized as superstitious or inferior by dominant cultural institutions, thus justifying further domination. Castillo's novel represents what is happening to the popular expressions of subordinate ethnic groups: "mixing" with elements of dominant culture does not necessarily defeat them. As San Diego activist Mary Lou Valencia says, tradition is whatever contributes to survival, and thus survival will continually redefine value. *Santera* also implies that a woman now controls the creation of sacred images (and perhaps has some clout with New York publishers), and these counterinterpretations of tradition are bound to offend. Women who reinterpret the spiritual and who call the priest a *pendejo* now have the social power to begin to make their interpretations heard. The point is that the essence of the popular is its effective deployment by subordinate groups. Clearly, Castillo is saying that Xicana art implies more than "making it." Viable art will depend on more than scholarly reclamation of culture; it will depend on the survival of self-identified communities.

Finally, the most recent news on the Virgin of the Mexico City Metro is that the city has agreed to construct a *nicho* (chapel) around her astonishing image.

Note from the editors. This article was previously published in a longer version by the Chicana/Latina Research Center in *VOCES: A Journal of Chicana/Latina Studies* 2, no. 1 (1998): 64–101. Reprinted with permission.

NOTES

1. Enrique Florescano, *Memory, Myth and Time in Mexico*, 161–165.
2. I use the term Chicana to refer to women of Mexican descent who reside in the United States. *Xicana* is Castillo's term for a new feminist consciousness. She explains it best: "The search for a term which would appeal to the majority of women of Mexican descent who are also concerned with the social and political ramifications of living in a hierarchical society has been frustrating. In this text I have chosen the ethnic and racial definition of Mexic Amerindian to assert both our indigenous blood and the source, at least in part, of our spirituality . . . I introduce here the word, *Xicanisma*, a term that I will use to refer to the concept of Chicana feminism," 10. (My italics).
3. Throughout this chapter, numbers in parentheses indicate the page number of the book under consideration.
4. Cherríe Moraga, *The Last Generation*, 72.
5. Carlos Vélez-Ibañez, *Border Visions*, 137.
6. Ibid., 180.
7. Patricia Zavella, "Living on the Edge: Everyday Lives of Poor Chicano/Mexicano Families," in *Mapping Multiculturalism*, ed. Avery Gordon and Christopher Newfield, 362–389.
8. Ibid., 380.
9. "Conscienticized" refers to Paulo Freire's notion of *conscientazaçao*: "The term refers to learning to perceive social, political, and economic contradictions, and to take action against the oppressive elements of reality." *Pedagogy of the Oppressed*, 19.

10. Louise Lamphere, Patricia Zavella et al., eds., *Sunbelt Working Mothers.*

11. Ibid., 17.

12. Ada María Isasi-Díaz, *En la Lucha. In the Struggle: Elaborating a Mujerista Theology*, 179.

13. Ada María Isasi-Díaz and Yolanda Tarango, *Hispanic Women: Prophetic Voice in the Church*, 70.

14. William Rowe and Vivian Schelling, *Memory and Modernity: Popular Culture in Latin America.*

15. Ramón A. Gutiérrez, *When Jesus Came the Corn Mothers Went Away.*

16. Rowe and Schelling, *Memory and Modernity*, 23.

17. Marta Navarro, "Interview with Ana Castillo," in Carla Trujillo, ed., *Chicana Lesbians: The Girls Our Mothers Warned Us About.*

18. Ana Castillo, "La Macha: Toward a Beautiful Whole Self," in Trujillo, ed., *Chicana Lesbians*, 33.

19. Ana Castillo, *Massacre of the Dreamers: Essays on Xicanisma*, 95–96.

20. The anthology edited by Tey Diana Rebolledo and Eliana S. Rivero, *Infinite Divisions: An Anthology of Chicana Literature*, gives endless examples of excavating the indigenous "goddess" as "a site of a female power."

21. Castillo, *Massacre of the Dreamers*, 153.

22. Ana Castillo, ed., *Goddess of the Americas: Writings on the Virgin of Guadalupe.*

23. Yolanda Broyles-González, *El Teatro Campesino*, 87.

24. Guillermo Bonfil Batalla, *Mexico Profundo*, 27.

25. Rowe and Schelling, *Memory and Modernity*, 70.

26. Ramón A. Gutiérrez, *When Jesus Came.*

27. Broyles-González, *Teatro Campesino*, 65.

28. Sor Juana Inés de la Cruz, *The Answer/La Respuesta*, 156.

29. Virgilio Elizondo, *La Morenita: Evangelizer of the Americas*, 117.

30. Ray González, "A Chicano Verano," *The Nation* 7 (1993): 772–774.

31. Américo Paredes, "Folk Medicine and the Intercultural Jest," in *Folklore and Culture on the Texas-Mexican Border*, ed. Richard Bauman.

32. Garibay quoted in Broyles-González, *Teatro Campesino*, 68.

33. Nasario García, *Recuerdos de los Viejitos*; Angel Vigil, *The Corn Woman.*

34. Vigil, *Corn Woman*, xx.

35. Nasario García, *Recuerdos.*

36. Vigil, *Corn Woman*, 27.

37. Marta Weigle, *Brothers of Light, Brothers of Blood.*

38. Richard Griswold del Castillo, *La Familia.*

39. Isasi-Díaz, *En la Lucha*, 22.

40. Rodolfo Acuña, *Occupied America*, 413.

41. Annette Fuentes and Barbara Ehrenreich, *Women in the Global Factory*, 12.

42. Ibid., 15.

43. See Lamphere and Zavella, *Sunbelt Working Mothers.*

44. Patricia Zavella, "Living on the Edge."

45. Richard Appelbaum, "Multiculturalism and Flexibility: Some New

Directions in Global Capitalism," in Gordon and Newfield, eds., *Mapping Multiculturalism*, 308.

46. Norma Alarcón, "Chicana Feminism: In the Tracks of the Native Woman," 254.

47. Popular religion (and Catholicism) do not refer to the production of mass culture. Among Latino/a theologians such as Jeanette Rodríguez, it has the following meaning: "When I speak of Catholicism in relationship to the Mexican-American culture, I am not referring to the institutionalized version of Catholicism, but to popular Catholicism, handed down through generations by the laity more than by the recognized and/or ordained clergy." Jeanette Rodríguez, *Our Lady of Guadalupe: Faith and Empowerment among Mexican-American Women*, 144. Such a tradition emphasizes the spontaneous expressions of faith by a particular ethnic group.

48. Orlando O. Espín, *The Faith of the People: Theological Reflections on Popular Catholicism*; Rodríguez, *Our Lady of Guadalupe*; Isasi-Díaz, *En la Lucha*.

49. Adelaida del Castillo, "Malintzin Tenepal: A Preliminary Look into a New Perspective," *Essays on La Mujer*, ed. Rosaura Sánchez and Rosa Martínez Cruz; Norma Alarcón, "Chicanas' Feminist Literature: A Re-Vision through Malintzin, OR Malintzin: Putting Flesh Back on the Object"; Rebolledo and Rivero, *Infinite Divisions*.

50. For the bleating shepherd, the *jornada del muerto*, and other references to New Mexican folk culture, see Marta Weigle, *The Lore of New Mexico*.

51. Lamphere and Zavella, *Sunbelt Working Mothers*.

52. Isasi-Díaz, *En la Lucha*.

53. Ruben Cobos, *A Dictionary of New Mexican and Southern Colorado Spanish*, 104.

54. Barbara G. Walker, *The Woman's Encyclopedia of Myths and Secrets*.

55. Gutiérrez, *When Jesus Came*.

56. Ibid., 89.

57. Rebolledo and Rivero, *Infinite Divisions*, 190.

58. Paula Gunn Allen, *The Sacred Hoop*.

59. Marguerite Guzmán Bouvard, *Revolutionizing Motherhood*, 179.

60. Ibid., 187.

61. Alarcón, "Chicanas' Feminist Literature," 188.

62. Dean MacCannell, "Tradition's Next Step," in *Discovered Country: Tourism and Survival in the American West*, ed. Scott Norris, 176.

63. Marta Weigle, "Selling the Southwest," in *Discovered Country: Tourism and Survival in the American West*, ed. Scott Norris, 219.

64. Ibid., 243.

65. Paula Gunn Allen, "Border Studies: The Intersection of Gender and Color," in *The Ethnic Canon*, ed. David Palumbo-Liu, 35.

66. Weigle, *Lore of New Mexico*.

67. Elizondo, *La Morenita*, 83.

68. Rodolfo Acuña, *Anything but Mexican*, 66.

69. Walker, *Woman's Encyclopedia*.

70. Monica Sjoo and Barbara Mor, *The Great Cosmic Mother*.

CHAPTER 4 **READING FROM OURSELVES**

IDENTITY AND HERMENEUTICS
AMONG MEXICAN-AMERICAN
FEMINISTS

LETICIA A.
GUARDIOLA-
SÁENZ

As one of the few feminist voices from the racial and ethnic minorities doing biblical studies
in the United States, often I have felt alienated
from the Western academic dialogue. When it
comes to reading and interpreting the Bible
from my own perspective, I find that there are
not enough critical approaches that respect the
validity and relevance of minority and non-
Western perspectives.

However, this scenario of a monolithic Western perspective has been changing over the past
thirty years. The irruption of non-Western voices
into the academic arena has made evident the
multiplicity of readings and interpretations of
the biblical text that expresses the diversity
and difference of readers. One of the elements
acknowledged as a catalyst in this variety of
readings is the identity of the readers. In this
postmodern era, freed from the ghost of univer-
salism and objectivism, the subjective identity
of the reader plays a major role in the process of
reading and interpreting a text.[1]

Therefore, in an effort to develop my own
alter/native hermeneutical model, one that is
cognizant of the sociocultural context of the
Mexican-American community in the United
States, I explore in this article the concept of
identity in the writings of some Mexican-
American and Latina feminists and the ways in

which this concept can be used as a hermeneutical lens. Ultimately, my aim is to establish the grounds for a liberating reading strategy, used as a "transformative practice" to empower minority populations in their task of being agents of historical change.

I use cultural studies as my methodological approach to read the selected feminist writings and to read myself. The flexibility and openness of this paradigm allows me to integrate my cultural context and my experiences as a real flesh-and-blood reader, the very elements that constitute the lens of my hermeneutical model. As a flesh-and-blood reader, I define and explore the scope and influence of my identity, in order to take responsibility for the ways in which I read, the lenses that I use, and the interests that I pursue in my readings. Consequently, when I read the selected feminist writings and myself, I focus on issues of social location, identity, subjectivity, and hybridity.

This article is organized into five sections. First, I introduce a brief historical account of the Mexican-American community in the United States. The story of its ambiguous existence can be helpful in understanding the complex identities that can be found in this hybrid community. Second, I present an overview of cultural studies as the mode of inquiry under which I explore the concept of identity and emphasize some of its critical aspects in the construction of the subject. Third, I classify and appraise the writings of some Mexican-American and Latina feminists according to the ways in which their dialogue contributes to the formation of a Mexican-American feminist identity. To do so I use the concepts of cultural identity defined in the second section. In this third section I also present some of the conflicting issues between Mexican-American feminists' discourse and Anglo-American feminists' discourse regarding the ways in which they perceive and construct their subjectivities. The main purpose of doing so is to find clues, signs, and models of how some Mexican-American feminists construct their identity; how they use it to read their texts; what similarities or dissimilarities appear between my identity and theirs; how agency can be found in the community's identity; and how this can be used as a "transformative practice" for social change and historical revolution. In the fourth section I describe the autobiographical conditions of my own struggle in defining my identity as Mexican-American and its implications for my reading strategy. Finally, by way of re-reading a biblical story, I evaluate identity as a hermeneutical lens, exploring its role in the process of liberation, and acknowledging the agency it confers to the subject to produce historical change.

LAND, HISTORY, AND IDENTITY

The face of the world has changed dramatically during the past two centuries. Nations have emerged and have fought to defend and define their boundaries and their power to control them. No territorial encroachment has gone unnoticed. In a way, the power of a nation to defend and retain its boundaries—and expand them when possible—gives pride and dignity to its people as a nation. Every border, frontier, or limit moved either way, to gain or to lose territory, becomes an indelible scar or a glorious memory in the identity of a nation.

The identity of the Mexican-American community in the United States, as is almost universally true, has been shaped by the history of its land. In 1848, with the Treaty of Guadalupe-Hidalgo, the life of the inhabitants of the old northern states of Mexico changed drastically. The unjust appropriation of half of the Mexican territory gave birth not just to a new population with an ambiguous identity, but to a new reality: the unique world of the northern Mexican borderlands, a place where the dreams of many poor Mexican people come true, or become their worst nightmares.

Ever since Mexico lost this enormous territory, the feeling of displacement and dispossession has been present, and it materializes into the continuous border-crossing of thousands of Mexicans who come to this land every year to claim a better life in restitution for the seized territory. The influx of the boundary-crossers never stops; no law or border patrol can repress the dreams and hopes of those who, poor as they are, have nothing to lose. Their stubbornness in crossing the border in spite of all the failed attempts has become part of the identity of this community that feels somehow at home in its ambiguous and divided life.

It is difficult to define the characteristics of the Mexican-American community; so many different realities, motives, and agendas make any definition fragmentary and fluid. Culturally rooted in Mexico, the community has formed in stages over time. It is a community of multiple faces converging from all the different stages.

Although the history of the Mexican/Hispanic presence in what is now U.S. territory could be traced back to the sixteenth century, I will start my story at a critical point that defined the geographical identity of both countries and therefore the identity of their people.

The first critical stage of the process of formation of the Mexican-American community was the territorial annexation of 1848 in which Mexico lost to the United States half of its territory, along with the inhabitants of those lands. The second stage of formation was the recruitment of workers to labor in railroad construction at the beginning of the twentieth century. The third main stage was during the time of the Mexican Revolution, from 1910 to 1920, when thousands came looking for a safer place to live, looking for a new beginning after losing everything, or hiding from the violence of the revolution.

Beginning in World War II, the United States needed laborers, and through the Bracero Program (1942–1964), the U.S. and Mexican governments established some visiting worker agreements through which a large number of Mexicans were recruited for seasonal agricultural work at low wages. But just in the same way they were brought, they were discarded. As soon as they were not necessary and useful to the United States, or when they became a burden during economic downturns, they were deported. At some point, even those Mexican-Americans who were legal citizens, those who lived on the land before it was taken, were deported just like the rest, with no respect or recognition of the legal status granted to them.[2]

By and large, the relationship of the Mexican-American people with the United States from the mid-nineteenth century to the mid-twentieth century has corresponded to utilitarian demands of the United States.[3] After a long history of labor activism, fighting for their rights at their workplaces in mines, meat-packing houses, pecan-shelling and garment industries, among others, Mexican-American workers finally achieved a milestone. In 1965, thanks to the leadership of César Chávez, Dolores Huerta, and others, the United Farm Workers Union was created. The Mexican-American/Latino workers began to have a face and an identity. It was a paradoxical juncture: the very land that was stolen became fertile ground for recovering the lost identity of the hard-working people who labored on it and who thus began to assume a new face in the twentieth century. Thanks in great part to these farmworkers, the Mexican-American community began gaining public identity and a face of its own. The community is getting stronger and, through education and political participation, some battles have been won.

Gloria Anzaldúa writes of the awakening of the community, "Chicanos did not know we were a people until 1965 when César Chávez and the farm-workers united and *I Am Joaquín* was published and *La Raza Unida* party was formed in Texas."[4] From that moment in history, the Mexican-American population started raising its voice through the creation of organizations that the Chicano movement has promoted. This movement has been committed to obtaining civil rights and respect for Mexican-Americans and their culture.

The Mexican-American population is large and diverse. We have come to the United States for different reasons and with different agendas, but because of our closeness with Mexico, there is always a certain ambiguity about our identity, a bicultural life always present. For many poor people in Mexico, coming to the United States represents the hope of claiming a better life and the sense of getting even for the past loss. This situation has promoted a part-time lifestyle for many Mexican-Americans who live some of the year in the United States and the rest in Mexico. Those who live this bicultural/binational life learn to be alert to their surroundings and—like a chameleon—trick the system by making quick changes. Life in the borderlands is a constant metamorphosis and a game of masks. Smuggling has become the ethos of survival. What is at stake is not just the material smuggling of goods but the lives of those who are at risk every time they cross the borderlands. As Gloria Anzaldúa writes, "To survive the Borderlands you must live *sin fronteras,* be a crossroads."[5]

A glimpse of the many reasons and agendas underlying the Mexican-American presence in this country can be seen in Anzaldúa's self-definition:

We do not identify with the Anglo-American cultural values and we don't totally identify with the Mexican cultural values. We are a synergy of two cultures with various degrees of Mexicanness or Angloness . . . sometimes I feel like one cancels out the other and we are zero, nothing, no one. When not copping out, when we know we are more than nothing, we call ourselves Mexican, referring to race and ancestry; mestizo when affirming both our Indian and Spanish (but we hardly ever own our Black) ancestry; Chicano when referring to a politically aware people born and/or raised in the United States; Raza when referring to Chicanos; tejanos when we are Chicanos from Texas.[6]

The complexity could be increased if we considered that she is just talking about that part of the population that was born in the United States. If we also consider those of us who came to the United States as adults, or even younger, who might want to stay or leave or be commuting between worlds, the identity of the community gains complexity.

Diverse political, economical, historical, and cultural situations have brought us to be part of this ambiguous Mexican-American population. As such we have suffered discrimination, segregation, and many other problems, like the rest of the Latino/a minorities, but somehow, through the organized movements that fight for civil rights and through the education of our people, the Mexican-American community is getting stronger. As long as we insist on affirming our identity and our roots, there is hope for the entire Hispanic community of becoming agents of historical change.

CULTURAL STUDIES AND IDENTITY: A FRAMEWORK

Cultural studies could be defined as a vast interdisciplinary field of study that encompasses various theoretical approaches and addresses diverse questions, all of which is done within a political context. Thus, cultural studies is not a discipline per se, but rather a mode of inquiry that challenges institutionalized disciplines. It has no particular theories or methods, but it appropriates and works with the theories and methods from social science disciplines, the arts, and the humanities, using them for its own purposes.

The fact that cultural studies does not have a specific subject area or a particular object of study makes it difficult to establish a comprehensive definition. However, there is a point of departure that is crucial to doing cultural studies: the concept of culture. Culture in cultural studies is not defined aesthetically, but politically, as the texts and practices of everyday life. And since different meanings can be ascribed to the same texts or practices, there would always be resistance from minority groups against dominant groups and their imposition of meanings. Therefore, culture as the terrain where meaning is incorporated or resisted becomes the battlefield where hegemony is won or lost. From this point of view, culture becomes highly political.

Cultural studies is not a value-free scholarship; it is a practice committed to social reconstruction by critical political involvement, exposing power relationships and the ways they influence and shape cultural practices. In that sense, culture is analyzed within its social and political context in order to understand and change the structures of dominance. Some of the central elements in cultural studies used to contest the dominant structures are the notions of race, identity, and difference.

Identity is constituted by power relations, usually defined in relation to the outsiders, the others. In cultural studies, identity is described as a process, ever changing, not unified. The subject is in constant flux.

I want to highlight three main ideas from this theoretical background which I find important for reading and constructing identities. First, identities are constituted by power relations: they are created in relation to outsiders, the "other" (Western representations of the non-Western, in terms of ethnic identities, seen often as subordinated to the West).[7] Second, identities are not unified: they are fragmented, ruptured, discontinued, and contradictory. We are split among political allegiances, and we have multiple identities that struggle within us. Third, identities are constantly in flux: they are not final productions but productions in process.

In what follows, I use this postmodern view of identity and culture to examine the ways in which identity is used as a primary hermeneutical key in the feminist selected writings. In so doing, I seek a common bond among Mexican-American feminists which will help me to construct my own reading and hermeneutical strategy.

IDENTITY AMONG MEXICAN-AMERICAN FEMINISTS

The feminist dialogue in the United States has been mostly dominated by Anglo, academic, middle-class women. However, in the past two decades, thanks to the challenges and criticism that women of color have presented to the Anglo feminists' discourses, the panorama of dialogue is changing. These changes are not surprising, nor can they be taken as a given but as the result of long battles that most minorities in this country have fought, every step of the way, to gain basic human rights.

The Chicana feminist movement was strengthened by the struggles for life that the Chicano workers' community engaged in during the 1960s.[8] The consciousness of being a people with a long history in this country, but still experiencing discrimination, segregation, and no recognition in its efforts to build up and contribute to this nation's economic life, awoke the community. Progressively, the Chicano identity has become visible, recognized, and respected in forums such as academic departments at universities; business, societal, and economic life; governmental positions; the arts; and the religious arena.

Chicana feminist activists, empowered by this consciousness, continued to struggle to have a voice of their own and to transform the patriarchal history and structures of the Latino/a community and of society and the Church at large. These feminists created organizations such as Las Hermanas (founded in 1970) and Mujeres Activas en Letras y Cambio Social (founded in 1983 at the University of California, Berkeley) to continue "our mothers' struggle for social and economic justice."[9]

As a Mexican, born and raised in Mexico, technically I am not considered Chicana. However, as a border-crosser living now in the United States, I discovered myself as being part of the community—by race and cultural and ethnic origin—and therefore in need of a better understanding of the Chicana/o community. Somehow, my subjectivity, identity, and agency, whether I accept it or not, are linked to the struggles of this community. Therefore, by analyzing the concept of identity in the writings of some Mexican-American and Latina feminists, I attempt to affirm my hybrid identity, define my hermeneutical lens, and understand the agency with which my socially constructed site provides me to intervene in the production of our reality as Latino/a community.

The background readings that inform this section are a small sample of the work done by some of the Mexican-American and Latina feminists in the United States: Gloria Anzaldúa,[10] Norma Alarcón,[11] María Pilar Aquino,[12] Ada María Isasi-Díaz,[13] Beatríz M. Pesquera and Denise M. Segura,[14] Jeanette Rodríguez,[15] and Chela Sandoval.[16]

In my search for common traits of identity within the selected readings, I identify at least three phases in the formation of the complex concept of identity among Chicana feminists. I divide the material according to what I see as three types of dialogue which I perceive to be at work in these readings. The first type comprises what I call the *inner dialogue,* and it is illustrated in the writings by Gloria Anzaldúa on *mestizas* and borderlands and by Norma Alarcón on Malintzin. The second type of dialogue that I observe at work is the *community dialogue,* which I identify in the writings of Jeanette Rodríguez and Ada María Isasi-Díaz. The third type of dialogue, which I call the *outward dialogue,* is expressed in the articles by Chela Sandoval, in Norma Alarcón's second article, and in articles by María Pilar Aquino and by Beatríz M. Pesquera and Denise M. Segura. Focusing on identity, its construction and representation by Chicana feminist writers, I understand these three types of dialogue as part of the formation of a Mexican-American feminist identity.

The first type, the *inner dialogue,* represents a more cultural and personal formation of identity. Anzaldúa and Alarcón both dig deep into our cultural heritage, going back to the history of the indigenous people and their mythology, to trace their identities as Chicanas and *mestizas.*[17] They reclaim the empowering visions and traditions of the times previous to the Western European conquest, previous to any encounter of our people with invaders or intruders. They also acknowledge the mixture that has become part of who we are in order to accept that as people, we belong to a special race named *raza cósmica* because it is "una raza hecha con el tesoro de todas las anteriores, la raza final, la raza cósmica" (a race made from the treasures of all those who went before it, the final race, the cosmic race).[18]

Anzaldúa and Alarcón describe their identity, our identity, as a heritage of integration and of fusion[19] that existed long before our identities were defined by the present invasions of Anglo-American feminists and their discourses of "difference" regarding the identity of "minority" women.

This inner identity that comes not just from the past but from a previous spatial existence gives to the Chicana's identity the power to exist as other and to define herself in her own terms and space. By going to the mythical place of Aztlán, or to the spatial dimension of our ancestors, Chicanas can claim an identity that existed before the invasions by conquerors who wanted to label our identity through their eyes.[20] This self-definition from a past and a space unknown to the oppressor breaks with the negative identity mediated through categories of difference. Through this heritage of a *spatial face,* we can produce an identity from our own originality; we can gain agency by affirming our own place in culture and society now, supported by a different way of being. An identity that we have forged on our own can give us the agency to transform our history in a way that an identity that has been imposed on us cannot.

The second type of dialogue that I see in these readings is the *community dialogue.* Exploring the religious dimensions of the community, its spaces of worship, its spaces as family, Isasi-Díaz, Tarango, and Rodríguez present a face of our identity as Mexican-American women that is also outside the categories of difference in relation to other communities. The voice of women from the community, the one that emerges as a communitarian voice, is the one that finds identity in their common struggles, their common experiences. Our identity is not unified. It is complex. We are also collective voices that strengthen our individual voices.

I should mention that the scope of the women presented by these three feminists has a common religious background: a Catholic background. By using the spiritual dimension of the community, the identity of Chicanas acquires a *communitarian face* that breaks with the logic of individuality from the modern concept of identity and enables the community to have agency as a community and to struggle together for historical change.

The third type of dialogue that I find in the readings is the *outward dialogue,* which can be recognized in the articles by Alarcón, Aquino, Sandoval, Pesquera, and Segura. What I call the outward dialogue is the dialogue that Mexican-American and Latina feminists have with Anglo-American feminists, or the dialogue that is mainly open to engage the academy. The language and terms these Mexican-American and Latina feminists use are evidently standardized to the common jargon in order to avoid excuses, such as lack of understanding of our discourses or lack of communication due to the usage of terms and language not common to the English-speakers.

In this third type of dialogue, the writers compare and contrast the ways in which Chicana identity has been presented, and they expose how most scholars, whether Anglo-American women or men, have not engaged them in dialogue or responded to their calls and voices. This lack of response is often because such scholars have excluded from their terms of conversation the realities entailed in the categories of race, ethnicity, and class by centering their terms of dialogue on gender. By engaging scholarly dialogue through the category of gender only—thus ignoring race, ethnicity, and class—those scholars limit their understanding of the other and change dialogue into monologue. This monologue uses identity in a binary oppositional way as it centers in defining women as different than men due to gender, and it denies possibilities of dialogue among women through the categories of race, class, and sexual orientation.

The outward dialogue challenges the logic of difference and invites a logic of otherness. It presents the *face of otherness.* In this third type of dialogue, the identity of Chicanas is opening the door for historical change in which one accepts the other on her own terms, resisting and countering the negative identity imposed by those who would dominate the dialogue.

By analyzing and constructing identity from the postmodern perspective of cultural studies, being aware of power relationships, the fragmented view of identity, and the constant process involved in the production of the self, this reading of some feminist writers offers a new hermeneutical lens to the Mexican-American and Latino/a community. It is a hermeneutical lens that offers the possibility of reading from ourselves as a valid and respected perspective, grounded in the experience and heritage of a community with self-identity.

Although what I present in this paper is my overall evaluation of the feminist writings through these three types of dialogues, it is important to read each of these authors to better grasp the core of the Mexican-American/Chicana movement. I do not believe that I have exhausted such a core but merely grasped it. The way I divided the readings into a three-level dialogue is my personal preference, but I do believe that many more ways of reading them can be found. In fact, they are not mutually exclusive, but inclusive and interchangeable.

THE BRIDGE: STRUGGLE, RUPTURE, AND HYBRIDITY

As a Mexican woman, born and reared in the bicultural neo-colonialist context of the Rio Grande Valley borderlands and now living as a resident alien in the United States, I am aware of my particular situation and of the fact that I represent just another segment of the present postmodern plurality. I am also aware that both the space I inhabit and my hybrid identity help me to read and interpret reality in a particular way. This way needs to be acknowledged as valid and legitimate just as any other perspective and hermeneutics are. I celebrate my biculturalism as a vantage point that allows me to evaluate and respect the presence of the multiple realities that coexist in this country.

By acknowledging the complexity of my context and by listening to other Mexican-American feminists' voices, I can understand better the perspectives and the sources of my identity and the ways in which I can use them as hermeneutical lenses.

I grew up in Reynosa—a Mexican town on the border with Texas—in a bicultural context, well informed of my Mexican roots and at the same time acquainted with the history of the United States of

America. I recall being aware, even as a child, of the historical struggle hidden (historically and symbolically) behind that International Bridge just ten blocks from my home. In a way, that bridge represented the negative result of the rupture Mexico suffered as a nation at the hands of its imperialist neighbor. Paradoxically, the bridge also represented the source of a new connection—a hybrid culture coming out of the encounter of two worlds, one struggling for survival under economic oppression, the other seeking to invade.

In my childhood I did not know the complexity involved in a label such as Hispanic or Latina. At that time, the only "Hispanics" I knew were Chicanos/as and Puerto Ricans, and I associated the United States with good things only, such as candies, toys, vacations, and having a good time with my family. For various reasons, back then I never thought of living in the United States myself. First, I was aware of the negative historical background of the U.S.-Mexican relations. Second, I experienced racism firsthand during the years that I lived in the borderlands. Third, I knew personally of the oppression and cruelty inflicted upon grassroots Mexican people as they were searching for jobs on the U.S. side of the bridge to better their families' quality of life.

These experiences, however, were one-sided, and I had to adjust them when I moved to the United States in 1988. Only on the north side of the Rio Grande was I able to understand what being a U.S. Latina woman meant. My decision to move to the United States was difficult indeed. I temporarily lost the freedom, mobility, and agency that I felt I had within the familiar space. However, I must also say that I have acquired a better perspective and a greater awareness of my *mestiza* identity as a Mexican and now as a U.S. Latina living in this alien context. While I was living in Mexico, I took such identity for granted.

My condition as an alien in the United States has helped me to go back to my history and become more aware of the political location in which I stand now within my hybrid identity. The roots of our identity as Mexican-Americans and as Latina women, as I see it, have their origin in the imperialistic move by the United States to incorporate not only the northern region of Mexico but also the population living there at the time. José David Saldívar writes, "In 1848 U.S. imperialism created a group of second-class citizens within the belly of the beast."[21] In a first instance, our presence within "the beast" is due to its imperialistic desire to control and absorb as much territory as possible. But it is also important to acknowledge that our presence in the United States is a response to various other forces. Among these, the economic factor certainly plays a central role, given the present process of impoverishment experienced by the majority in Latin America due to the imposition of neoliberal global capitalism. Fernando Segovia has defined well this segment of the Hispanic/Latina/o population that has immigrated to the United States as "the diaspora (which) represents the sum total of all those who presently live, for whatever reason, on a permanent basis in a country other than that of their birth."[22]

The experience of imperialism lived by the Mexican-American population has been complex both historically and religiously. First, Spain came with its evangelization project that demolished the religious systems of our indigenous ancestors. The Spaniards utterly ignored and disregarded native cultural and religious beliefs, resulting in an ontological oppression that threatened indigenous identity.

Then Protestant missionary groups came from the United States with their evangelizing projects, which had a destructive effect similar to that of the first evangelization of Mexico conducted by the Roman Catholic Church under Spain. These evangelists espoused a supposedly universal way of reading and interpreting the Bible. Such a "universal way," however, only encouraged an Anglo-European experience of Christianity that brought to those being evangelized a second alienation from their cultural identity.

In spite of the inculturation brought through these waves of Eurocentric evangelization, in many ways the Mexican-American community has persistently returned to its indigenous heritage, recovering pieces from that cultural identity and integrating them into its present reality. In some cities where the concentration of Mexican-Americans has a strong presence, the identity of the community is constantly reinforced by means of the special celebrations that bring memories of Mexico; by stores and restaurants that sell Mexican products, by churches and museums that celebrate the rituals and symbols of the ancestors; and by creating and participating in coalitions that give voice to the community. All these means reenact, in a way, the life that the community or their forebears once lived in Mexico.

The bridge, as a site of struggle, rupture, and hybridity, represents for me not just the broader picture of the oppression of the Mexican-American population, but also a place of dialogue and construction from which Mexican-American women can construct our identity, denounce oppression, and call for liberation.

CROSSING BORDERS WITH THE CANAANITE:
A READING FROM MYSELF

Being able to evaluate some key elements that form the identity of Mexican-American women through their written experiences has helped me to recognize the power for change behind the construction of my own identity. I believe that it is precisely the ambiguous identity of the community, the history of displacement that our people have suffered, and the shifting of places between here and there (United States and Mexico) that help us to use our hybrid identity as a strategy for reading and interpreting. Such strategy is demonstrating its ability and potential to open dialogue with other readings, likewise influenced by their own contexts and histories. Defining myself as other, with an ancestral lineage that can be traced long before the arrival of the oppressor, helps me to break the binary oppositions and read those who surround me also as others, under their own terms.

I believe that another key element in using identity as hermeneutical lens is that identity is understood in terms of community, not just in terms of individuality. It is the singularity of being part of a community that enables us to work for historical change. By acknowledging our complexity and fluidity we can be open to change and reconstruction.

Both Anzaldúa and Isasi-Díaz present a project as part of their invitation to work as community as a way of gaining a new consciousness as *mestizas* and as a way of building a better future; this is undertaken as a *proyecto histórico* by the community. Through my analysis of the articles by Latina feminists, I understand my need to continue to develop my own definition of identity in the various types of dialogue in which I participate. By using identity as a hermeneutical lens to approach and understand my reality, I aim at the construction of reading strategies that will support a practice for historical change and social transformation.

The following notes from a reading of the story of the Canaanite using my border-crossing perspective might help to illustrate how my hermeneutical lens and reading strategy could work.

Read through my experience, the story of the Canaanite woman is the encounter of two peoples, two cultures in contest. It is a story of borderland conflicts between the original inhabitants and those who have dispossessed them, with a long history of struggle, rupture, and hybridity. But it is also a romantic view of "the other"—the submissive image depicted by those in power—which needs to be unmasked and retold from the grounds of a postcolonial world. A text that conceals the ideology of manifest destiny and chosenness of people, which allows the displacement of *others* from their own land and does not condemn such ideology as oppressive, cannot be a liberating text when it is interpreted by those who want to keep the power for themselves.

It is only by listening to the voice of the other in the text, the one who has suffered the unjust invasion and oppression, that one can construct a liberating story, by reading between the lines and listening to her own construction of identity.

When I read Matthew's story, I do it with a spirit of dispossession, the one I *assume* the Canaanite woman had when she approached Jesus, a spirit of protest and reclamation. She was determined to take the bread from the table of those who had displaced her, knowing that in a household where even the *dogs* get to eat what the masters waste, there must be some extra bread for the neighbors, precisely those neighbors whom the masters have dispossessed.

In my socio-historical condition of dispossessed neighbor from the borderlands of the U.S. empire, I am certainly determined to take the bread from the table and not wait until the crumbs fall from it. It is only at the level of the table "as equals" and not under the table "as inferiors" that a constructive dialogue and a fair reconstitution of the world can be achieved.

A cultural text—Matthew's story in this case—should be read not just for the history that it reflects but for the history that it makes: the political, moral, economic, and social consequences that the text has brought about in the culture. As such, the text is borderless and can speak to all who read it and transform it into a "text."

I believe that if the ideology of chosenness has proven to be exploitative to two-thirds of the world's people, then it is an ideology that needs to be challenged by all those who read for liberation. Even if this ideology belongs to the very sacred text that has been used by Western Christianity to supposedly save the Two-Thirds World, it needs to be contested as any other cultural concept or ideology that has been constructed to exploit and subjugate people.

Thus, in my reading of the Canaanite woman's story, I argue that the Matthean ideology of chosenness is dismantled by the story's plot itself. The very presence of the Canaanite woman, who is used by the author to affirm the chosenness of his people, makes the ideology collapse when she comes precisely to confront the one who has advised his disciples to "go nowhere among the Gentiles."

As such my reading is an act of self-affirmation and solidarity with the Canaanite woman as other. It is an effort to construct not just my own otherness through the reinterpretation of the story but also to construct the otherness of the Canaanite woman by defying the harmful borders of the biblical text. This will be part of my liberating reading strategy against imperialistic practices. It is a step forward in the process of decolonization and liberation, a process that cultural studies has brought into biblical criticism by means of the contextualized flesh-and-blood reader. As a real reader, my reading of the Canaanite woman's story is an act of re-appropriation of the text, a move to rewrite the story from the reverse of history. My reading is a story retold by the defeated, rewritten from the perspective of the postcolonial reader. This recasting of the story is also a way of speaking from the borderless biblical text that has been inscribed in cultures for centuries. From this angle I am now able to raise questions: What if . . . the Canaanite woman was aware of her dispossession? What if . . . she was not begging Jesus for a favor but demanding restitution? What if . . . she was not worshiping Jesus but defying him? What if I recast the story? Would that attempt change the history of exploitation and destruction that the ideology of chosenness has endorsed?

As a Mexican-American I read the Canaanite woman's story as the rhetoric of the other against the rhetoric of Matthew and its readers. I hold that the Canaanite woman is not a humble dog begging for crumbs. She is a dispossessed woman who has awakened from her position as oppressed and now is coming to confront the empire and demand her right to be treated as human. By asking Jesus to heal her daughter, the Canaanite woman is asking for a replevin which will not just vindicate her as other but also will vindicate her oppressor as her equal, as other. The presence of the woman as the resistant oppressed who has gained consciousness of her oppression is breaking the dominant system. She is confronting the oppressor. He in turn realizes on account of her presence as other that he has overridden her rights and ignored her existence, but now he has been humanized by her presence. The other whom he treated as a dog is now giving him a lesson of human courage and love for life. The Canaanite woman comes to break the bread together with him as an act of restitution and humanization.[23]

Reading from ourselves, with a clear awareness of the power relations that we need to defy in order to define our own identity, with the awareness of our fragmented identity that can be strengthened by acknowledging both its multiplicity and its incompleteness, and with the understanding that we are in process, that we are constantly hybridizing in our interactions with others, will empower us to cross the borders that we need to challenge in order to bring about transformation through the agency of our self-defined identity.

NOTES

1. On the emergence of the real reader within the critical paradigms used in biblical criticism see Fernando F. Segovia, "And They Began to Speak in Other Tongues," in *Reading from This Place: Social Location and Biblical Interpretation in the United States,* ed. Segovia and Mary Ann Tolbert, 1–32.

2. See Denis Lynn Daly Heyck, *Barrios and Borderlands: Cultures of Latinos and Latinas in the United States,* 6. Also in Heyck's book see "My Roots Are Not Mine Alone: La Identidad Cultural," 370–449.

3. Heyck, *Barrios and Borderlands,* 5–8.

4. See Gloria Anzaldúa, *Borderlands/La Frontera: The New Mestiza,* 63.

5. Ibid., 195.

6. Ibid., 63.

7. In this article I use the concept of "the other" following Fernando Segovia's nomenclature. The use of "other" in quotation marks implies a pejorative meaning, the definition of the other that is imposed from outside. The use of other without quotation marks has a positive meaning, the self-definition of the other. See Segovia, "Toward a Hermeneutics of the Diaspora: A Hermeneutics of Otherness and Engagement," in *Reading from This Place,* 58, note 2.

8. See the impressive anthology edited by Alma M. García, *Chicana Feminist Thought: The Basic Historical Writings.*

9. Rafaela Castro, "MALCS Declaration," in *Chicana Critical Issues. Mujeres Activas en Letras y Cambio Social,* ed. Norma Alarcón, Rafaela Castro et al., vii.

10. Anzaldúa, *Borderlands,* and "La conciencia de la Mestiza: Towards a New Consciousness," in *The Woman That I Am: The Literature and Culture of Contemporary Women of Color,* ed. D. Soyini Madison, 540–572.

11. Norma Alarcón, "Chicana's Feminist Literature: A Re-Vision through Malintzin/or Malintzin: Putting Flesh Back on the Object," in *This Bridge Called My Back: Writings by Radical Women of Color,* ed. Cherríe Moraga and Gloria Anzaldúa, 182–190; and "The Theoretical Subject(s) of *This Bridge*

Called My Back and Anglo-American Feminism," in *The Postmodern Turn: New Perspectives on Social Theory*, ed. Steven Seidman, 140–152.

12. María Pilar Aquino, "The Collective 'Dis-covery' of Our Own Power: Latina American Feminist Theology," in *Hispanic/Latino Theology: Challenge and Promise*, ed. Ada María Isasi-Díaz and Fernando F. Segovia, 240–258; and "Perspectives on a Latina's Feminist Liberation Theology," in *Frontiers of Hispanic Theology in the United States*, ed. Allan Figueroa Deck, 23–40.

13. Ada María Isasi-Díaz, *En la Lucha. In the Struggle: Elaborating a Mujerista Theology*. Although Isasi-Díaz is Cuban, the results of her book give a glimpse into the Mexican-American identity, as she interviewed Mexican-American women for her research.

14. Beatríz M. Pesquera and Denise M. Segura, "There is No Going Back: Chicanas and Feminism," in *Chicana Critical Issues*, ed. Alarcón, Castro et al., 95–115; and "With Quill and Torch: A Chicana Perspective on the American Women's Movement and Feminist Theories," in *Chicanas/Chicanos at the Crossroads: Social, Economic, and Political Change*, ed. David R. Maciel and Isidro D. Ortiz, 231–247.

15. Jeanette Rodríguez, *Our Lady of Guadalupe: Faith and Empowerment among Mexican-American Women*. Rodríguez, an Ecuadorian writer, speaks of the experience of Mexican-American women in chapter 4 of her book and in "Sangre llama a sangre: Cultural Memory as a Source of Theological Insight," in *Hispanic/Latino Theology*, ed. Isasi-Díaz and Segovia, 117–133.

16. Chela Sandoval, "U.S. Third World Feminism: The Theory and Method of Oppositional Consciousness in the Postmodern World," *Genders* 10 (1991): 1–24.

17. Alarcón, "Chicanas' Feminist Literature," 187.

18. José Vasconcelos, *La Raza Cósmica: Misión de la Raza Iberoamericana*, 50.

19. Anzaldúa, *Borderlands*, 47.

20. Ibid., 3–5.

21. José David Saldívar, "Américo Paredes and Decolonization," in *Cultures of United States Imperialism*, ed. Ami Kaplan and Donald E. Pease, 299.

22. Segovia, "Toward a Hermeneutics of the Diaspora," 60.

23. For an extended exegesis of the Caananite woman's story see Leticia Guardiola-Sáenz, "Borderless Women and Borderless Text: A Cultural Reading of Matthew 15:21–28," *Semeia* 78 (1997): 69–81.

CHAPTER 5

PERCEPTION MATTERS

PENTECOSTAL LATINAS IN

ALLENTOWN, PENNSYLVANIA

ANNA
ADAMS

The phenomenal growth of Pentecostalism in Latin America has had a significant effect on Latin American societies in recent decades. Edward Cleary notes in his introduction to *Power, Politics, and Pentecostals in Latin America:* "Without this understanding [of Pentecostalism] one has an incomplete view of Latin American culture and will enter ill-prepared upon any analysis of contemporary Latin American politics."[1] Recent scholarship on Pentecostals reexamines two areas of conventional wisdom regarding them: their political involvement and the status of Pentecostal women. The traditional view on Pentecostals' political involvement held that they did not participate in so-called worldly matters and that this nonparticipation gave tacit conservative support to the political status quo. For example, in 1980, Anthony La Ruffa observed that Pentecostals in Puerto Rico upheld the commonwealth status or saw statehood as the only alternative. Independence, they believed, would inevitably lead to another communist Cuba.[2] Pentecostalism's continued growth, however, has led to newer scholarship that challenges this assumption. John Burdick, Rowan Ireland, Kathleen Harder, and Paul Freston have shown that to varying degrees Pentecostals have indeed become involved in some sort of political activity. Pentecostals in

Brazil, according to Freston, changed a slogan in 1986 from "Believers don't mess with politics" to "Brother votes for brother." In 1993, seventeen Brazilian Pentecostals were federal deputies and senators.[3]

The growth of Pentecostalism has also prompted scholarly examination of women and the status and influence they hold in this very patriarchal church whose doctrine holds that women are naturally inferior to men. In Pentecostalism's divinely conceived hierarchy, power and authority rest with men and God, and church doctrine imposes strictures on the behavior and appearance of women. And yet, studies have shown that Pentecostal women find liberation in their religion. They claim to be better off than non-Pentecostal women or than they were before their conversion. As early as 1975, Cornelia Butler Flora's study of women Pentecostals in Colombia concluded that a gain in the individual status for women can be seen as a result of the Pentecostal movement.[4] More recently, the works of Elizabeth Brusco, Cecilia Mariz, and Carol Ann Drogas on Pentecostal women in Latin America also point to an increased status for women, at least within the context of family and church.[5]

Elizabeth Brusco's study of male/female relationships in Colombian Pentecostal families indicates that women enjoy more equality and higher status in Pentecostal families. She has found that the aspirations of men and women seem to coincide more when life centers on church and family. Pentecostal men spend their free time at home instead of in bars. For many women, their husband's conversion can mean literally the difference between life and death: the men stop drinking, stop beating them, and bring home a paycheck that puts food on the table. These changes improve women's status within the family and also the entire family's economic status.

Carol Ann Drogas likewise attributes improved status for women in Latin American Pentecostal families to men's participation in the private sphere of the home and their forsaking of the public sphere of potential vices and temptations. She has found that improved status comes not from women sharing equally in the public world of men, but from men sharing in the private world of women.

As Pentecostalism becomes more mainstream and as a second generation of Pentecostals comes of age, the churches have become less removed from society, more active in the civic and political lives of their communities. Pentecostalism is no longer exclusively a religion of the poor and marginalized. In 1980, Anthony LaRuffa wrote of Pentecostals in Puerto Rico:

One of the most striking aspects of Pentecostalism is its accommodating propensity-adaptability to changing socio-cultural conditions. Although beginning as a religion of the poor and oppressed, it can readily adjust itself to more affluent conditions. Some Pentecostal churches in Puerto Rico, for example, have a constituency which is part professional and fits into the middle and upper middle class." [6]

ALLENTOWN, PENNSYLVANIA

This work grows out of earlier research (1994–1995) in which I used Allentown, Pennsylvania, as a case study to compare Pentecostalism in a U.S. Latino/a context with Latin American Pentecostalism.[7] Allentown is one of the "gritty cities" of the northeastern United States. It is the fourth largest city in Pennsylvania. Allentown's Latino community has grown from approximately 100 people in the early 1950s to more than 12,000, or approximately 15 percent of the city's population. (At this writing, incomplete 2000 Census data indicate significant growth in Allentown's Latino population. It is possible that some of this increase is a result of earlier undercounting.) The majority are Puerto Ricans who came originally as migrant workers after World War II and stayed to work in the growing textile industry. Allentown's Latinos have not been warmly welcomed. After almost fifty years in the city, they remain on the margins of society, resented by many of the older Pennsylvania Dutch inhabitants who blame them for the increase in crime and the deterioration of the city. As the number of Latinos increases, so does the number of their Pentecostal churches. The first Spanish-speaking Pentecostal church was founded in 1967. Today there are more than twenty.

Approximately 16 percent of Allentown's 12,000 Latinos attend one of the twenty or so Spanish-speaking Pentecostal churches, which provide a sense of community for people who have been assigned outsider status in a city whose tradition is unwelcoming to foreigners. At their exuberant services, Latinos feel at home in a church where the prayer is spontaneous and intense, the music is loud and rhythmical, the other worshipers are warm and loving brothers and sisters, and the pastor is a caring father. My surveys show that 83 percent of churchgoers attend regularly at least three times each week. Clearly, religion plays an important role in their lives. For many, social life also revolves around the church and church activities such as evangelizing crusades, Sunday school teaching, retreats, and the planning of worship services. Although the majority of Allentown's Latino Pentecostals are poor, living on welfare or disability insurance, there

are also solidly middle-class longtime churchgoers whose involvement is steady and fervent. Most of the churches are located in small
storefronts furnished with folding chairs and make-do furniture, but
there are several in former Anglo church buildings purchased by
middle-class Pentecostal congregations.

In my 1996 study, I found that the character of Latino Pentecostalism in Allentown, with regard to political participation and the status of women, generally follows the patterns established thus far in
the literature of Latin American Pentecostalism. However, there are
two very important, related differences: Allentown's Pentecostal
churches appear to have almost as many men as women. Perhaps this
is because there are few comfortable places for Latino men in a hostile city like Allentown, where most Latinos have experienced both
blatant and subtle discrimination. Samuel Soliván has noted that
Latinos in the United States see the roots of their oppression in
racism, whereas Latin Americans see them in poverty. He points to a
Latino theology that "emerges *from* the margins and speaks on behalf
of those on the periphery."[8] In the cities of the Northeast, this periphery is not necessarily inhabited only by the economically disad-
vantaged. It is not surprising, then, that Latinos in Allentown find
community in Pentecostal churches. They know that they suffer discrimination not necessarily because they are poor but because they
look different, speak Spanish, and hold different cultural values.
Some have lived for generations in Allentown and, though they are no
longer poor or uprooted, they are still marginalized. Pastor Edwin
Colón of the First Corinthians church describes the effect on the men
in his congregation: "El hombre hispano va a la iglesia con todo el
bagaje de sus problemas con la lengua, con el trabajo. La misión aquí
es mucho más difícil que en Puerto Rico"(The Hispanic man comes
to church with all the baggage of his problems with the language,
with the job. The mission here is much more difficult than in Puerto
Rico).[9] This fundamental difference in the location of their oppression may mean that Pentecostalism will be longer-lived among Latinos in places like Allentown than among upwardly mobile Latin
Americans.

This paper is based on my observations of church services and on
oral history interviews with five pastors and nine Pentecostal
women. Some of the women were raised as Pentecostals, while others had converted as adults from Catholicism to Pentecostalism.
When queried, the women said that as Pentecostals they shared a
more equal relationship with men and that Pentecostalism was liber-

ating to them *as women*. Others, through their words and/or actions, demonstrated a departure from traditional women's roles. The structure of the church, the strictures it imposes, and even the words that the women used to describe their experiences might seem to contradict this belief, yet I believe it is significant that these women *perceive* that their religion can be liberating and can provide a more egalitarian relationship between men and women. It seems to me that women's perceptions of their reality must be taken into account in any analysis of their spiritual life, even if we grant that those perceptions are culturally bound. It is important to listen to their voices, to go beyond considering only empirical evidence that points to Pentecostalism as a patriarchal system. These women's words tell how women adapt to, challenge, or even resist that patriarchy as feminists define it.

The lives of the four women presented here illustrate how ideology and structure of the churches both support and contradict their perceptions of equality. I believe that the perception can be an important vehicle for change, and I will attempt to draw some tentative conclusions about the potential for Pentecostal women in the context of their perceptions. Furthermore, I believe that LaRuffa's observations about the adaptability of Pentecostalism are germane.

Several aspects of the Pentecostal churches' structure support the women's notions of their equality in the church. Although generally there are no women pastors in Allentown's Pentecostal churches, women play an active role in church governance and leadership. Some of them have attended Bible institutes to prepare for a role in church leadership. Women are active participants in missionary work and in evangelizing campaigns. In the churches I attended, women serve in elected positions and as deacons. In some, women are responsible for planning and leading the services. At all the services I attended, women either led the group in prayer or song, preached, gave testimony, or led Bible study. Many spouses attend church together, sit together, and share the care of the children. Family life is a common theme in the testimonies of men in church. Often they describe the importance of the church and the family in their fight against Satan's temptations. The strong family orientation of the churches, the many hours that families spend together in church, and the public sharing of child care support the perception of the women that they share a more equal relationship with men.

Several factors in church ideology also contribute to notions of equality between men and women: because of the very personal nature of the relationship with the Lord, Pentecostalism empowers believers equally. The belief in a priesthood of all believers and the absence of a male priestly interpreter gives men and women equal access to the Lord. This direct access is an important part of daily Pentecostal life. As Nora told me, "I'm not a fanatic, but I love God and I need to talk to him every day. Just like I love my husband and I want to talk to him."[10] María, who converted from Catholicism when she was fifteen, told me: "I don't go to a statue like before. They used to tell me, 'vaya a la estatua y la estatua habla con Dios,' pero ahora hablo con Dios directamente" ('go to the statue and the statue talks with God,' but now I talk with God directly). María's concept of the role of saints and images may differ from the religious beliefs of popular Catholicism, yet it is her perception, however ill-informed, that is important here. Furthermore, even though most Pentecostal Latinas were brought up in a culturally Catholic society where the ideal woman is defined by the patient, suffering, morally superior Virgin Mary, the de-emphasis of the Virgin in Pentecostalism, as Flora wrote in 1975,[11] gives men and women equal moral potential. There are two more important differences between Pentecostalism and Catholicism vis à vis women: because Pentecostalism has no prohibitions against birth control, women have at least the possibility to control their own fertility; and Pentecostalism allows for divorce if a husband (or wife) has been unfaithful or abusive.

In many churches the pastor's wife is as important as the pastor. In fact, she is generally known as *la pastora,* and if women in the congregation feel the need to talk about very personal issues (marital problems, for example,) they go to *la pastora.* One woman explained, "We don't have confession, so the man pastor is not as important." While it may be true that women and men have equal access to the Lord and share more in family and household matters as well as church governance, it is also true that Pentecostalism is a patriarchal religion with a male-centered image of God. It presupposes the superiority of men and the belief that women should obey men.

Although the behavior of men and women is strictly defined by Pentecostalism, which prohibits drinking, smoking, dancing, and infidelity to both sexes, the churches dictate to varying degrees even more structures that apply only to women. Doctrinal differences between churches are described solely in terms of how liberal or conservative a congregation is with regard to women's dress codes. In the most conservative churches, women are not permitted to cut their hair or wear pants, makeup, or jewelry. When I asked about this apparent contradiction between church doctrine and the belief that women and men are treated equally, several women insisted that the restrictions on women's dress are not so much a question of church doctrine as of what women feel. One woman told me that one time when she wore a short skirt, she was so uncomfortable that she had to get rid of the skirt. As for haircuts and makeup, she said women shouldn't change the appearance that God gave them. These rules, another woman told me, "come from the Bible, not from men, and I comport myself according to the Bible because men change and the Bible never does."

I will turn now to four oral histories to illustrate how the women's words and experiences both support and contradict their perceptions of equality and liberation. As you will see, their stories also show how within their religion some have indeed reconceptualized church doctrine and women's traditional roles. Some have begun to move away from literal, fundamentalist interpretations of the Bible, particularly with regard to their physical appearance. I chose these four stories not necessarily because they were typical, but because they illustrate different possibilities for Pentecostal women. I will call the women Marta, Dorotea, Elsa, and Maribel.

MARTA: FORMER DRUG ADDICT

Marta is the volunteer supervisor of a church-sponsored shelter and rehabilitation center for drug-addicted women. She is a very intelligent, well-spoken, and street-wise woman of about forty who, until three years ago, was a drug addict herself and had spent more than twenty years on the streets, buying, selling, and stealing drugs. During those years, she managed to hold down various jobs in social services for brief periods—she even worked as a drug and alcohol counselor while she was addicted to heroin. "I was taking more drugs than my clients. I was guiding them right to hell."

Born and raised in New York, Marta married at age sixteen, dropped out of high school, and had three children. Her drug-addicted husband got her started on heroin and then left her. In 1980, believing she had to go somewhere where nobody knew her, so she could "go right and find God," she came to Allentown, Pennsylvania. She did well for a while, until she began meeting the "wrong people." She started taking drugs again and became involved with a drug addict who beat her and stole her money. "I believe now that all these men were put there by Satan to destroy me. The primary reason for my destruction was always a man. It seemed like whenever I was on my own, I was doing better than when I had a man." For the next ten years, Marta lived between Allentown, Puerto Rico, New Jersey, and Florida, following some men, running from others, trying unsuccessfully to break her heroin addiction, and "looking for something spiritual within me so I could feel God." For a while she practiced Islam. "In all this time I kept asking God to send me a man to take care of me, not knowing that God would take care of me."

Marta's dramatic conversion occurred in Allentown when she met her former babysitter, an old friend of her mother. The woman invited her to accompany her to church. "I used to wear a lot of jewelry—thick chains and a ring on every finger. This woman said to me 'Jesus has been calling you for a long time—you have a special calling, and today is your day. All those rings on your fingers will be taken off.' I laughed—nobody's going to take my jewelry. I went to church and kept hearing her words. Listening to the preacher's testimony, I began to cry because it was like my own. Every time I tried to change, I couldn't. He said, 'If anyone here is feeling like this and you want to stop . . .' Yes, I wanted that, and my hands got all swollen. One of my rings broke, and I remembered my words that nobody would take my rings. I opened my heart to the Lord, and I felt so warm and peaceful."

The center that Marta runs now is one that she says she envisioned before her conversion. She believes that the Lord was speaking to her by sending her visions and that her various jobs in the social work field were the Lord's way of preparing her for this mission. She prepared herself to teach Bible studies by attending a biblical institute. She is a deacon of the church. The women who come to the shelter must adhere to its strict rules and tight schedule. They may communicate only with their legal husbands. They may not wear skimpy clothes, only long dresses. They may not leave the shelter except to go to church. Their days consist of prayer, Bible study, chores, and church. Marta explains the dress code: "It gets ladies back into being ladies." Her new husband, a former gang leader who met the Lord while in jail in Puerto Rico, helps her with the center and holds down two other jobs. Having tried many other methods, they both believe that Jesus is the only way to kick the heroin habit.

Marta's life has drastically changed since her conversion. She has found personal and economic stability and love with a man who shares her past trials and her present success. Together in an equal partnership they have dedicated their lives to helping other addicts to cure themselves through the Lord, a task they now believe the Lord was preparing them for during their addicted years. As the head of the center and a deacon in the church, Marta enjoys high status in her community. She feels liberated from a past of dependency on drugs and on the men who introduced her to drugs, men whom she now views as Satan's tools. Through the prism of her new life, she understands that she did not need men to protect her, that in fact she had always been better off alone.

DEDICATED DOROTEA: SERVANT OF THE LORD

Dorotea was born in Puerto Rico sixty-five years ago to poor parents. Her mother practiced *santería*. In retrospect, Dorotea says that as a child, she always felt an inexplicable emptiness until, when she was thirteen, friends took her to church. There she accepted the Lord as her savior. Her mother was furious, but Dorotea chose the Lord anyway. She may have lost her mother, she now says, but she got the Father, the Son, and the Holy Ghost in return. When she was twenty-two, Dorotea moved to New York, where she worked as a domestic under slave conditions. She knew that her prayers for escape had been answered when she met and married a man from her church. Unfortunately, within seven years, he contracted multiple sclerosis and was confined to a wheelchair for the next twenty-eight years. When the Lord called Dorotea to do missionary work in Honduras, she left her invalid husband for three months to save souls.

In 1980, Dorotea and her husband moved to Allentown, where her husband died two years later. Now she lives with her son's family in a comfortable house in a nice neighborhood. While they are all devoted Pentecostals attending church several times each week, Dorotea does not attend the same church as the rest of her family. The van from her church calls for her daily, permitting her to live a fairly independent, church-centered life filled with daily prayer, door-to-door missionary work, visiting the sick, and teaching Bible classes. In fact, the week after our interview, the rest of the family was going on vacation to Disney World, but Dorotea chose to stay home. "I can't be away from the church for two weeks. The church is my life."

ELSA: PENTECOSTAL REBEL

Elsa is a twenty-three-year-old college graduate who works as the director of educational services at a Latino social services agency. She is a devout Pentecostal who converted from Catholicism at age twelve. She and her husband attend church together Tuesdays, Thursdays, and twice on Sundays. Like many young, professional couples, they share household chores and are putting off a family until they are more financially stable. In fact, she is not even sure that she wants children: "I never envisioned myself as a mother." She thinks that if they decided to have children, they will adopt.

Elsa thinks of herself as an independent woman, and that makes her a rebel in her church. She believes that the direct access to the Lord that her religion gives her empowers her to be independent. Elsa goes to one of the more conservative of the Pentecostal churches, but she wears modest makeup and loose-fitting trousers (never to church), and her long hair is slightly layered. These transgressions mean that she is not allowed to stand in front of her church to sing, preach, or give testimony. However, she believes that if God had a problem with her appearance, he would tell her directly. "I pray every night and every morning, and I tell God to let me know if he doesn't appreciate my wearing pants." Even though the Bible says that "el pelo es el velo de la mujer" (her hair is a woman's veil), Elsa thinks that slight modifications will not offend God. And even though she is not permitted to stand in front of the congregation, she has been asked to represent the church to the outside world. Her fluent English, education, and job-related connections in city hall helped her church to purchase its new building. Does this seeming hypocrisy bother her? "It's fine. God uses me for my talents. As in the larger community, we all have our roles and all are necessary." The church has denied her a leadership role within the institution because of choices she has felt free to make, yet she has not been shunned or excommunicated. On the contrary, her expertise and abilities are utilized and respected by the church.

Elsa's professional involvement with the poor Latino community of Allentown has led her to question other church teachings. She points out that it can be dangerous nowadays to live by the Bible. The Bible says that married women may not refuse their bodies to their husbands, yet with the prevalence of AIDS, Elsa believes that women should have the right to refuse sex with unfaithful husbands. She has suggested to her pastor that he give a sermon on the subject of AIDS and safe sex within marriage.

Pentecostalism appears not to have limited Elsa's development as a professional woman. As the only woman in her congregation with a college degree, she has taken it upon herself to encourage and help other young women (including the pastor's daughter) to go to college. She does not see her religion as an obstacle to success, but rather believes that it gives her the strength of character to do her job well and that in her work and in her life she is serving God.

MARIBEL: PENTECOSTAL REVOLUTIONARY

Maribel heads Lehigh County's Human Services Information and Referral Unit. She has a degree in psychology and has worked as a caseworker and casework supervisor for various governmental agencies. Although she describes herself as a devout Pentecostal, she has short hair, pierced ears, and wears pants.

Maribel was born and raised in the 1950s in New York in a Puerto Rican family. Her mother taught her three daughters to be independent. "Getting an education is more important than getting married," she told them. Maribel's parents were not Pentecostal but sent their girls to the very conservative neighborhood Pentecostal church four times a week because it had the restrictions they wanted for their daughters—"it made us good girls." Her mother's insistence that her girls have an education conflicted with the traditions of their church that discouraged education for women. A good Christian woman's work was to care for her family. Maribel's two older sisters studied nursing, an acceptable career for women if they insisted on having one, but Maribel was drawn to psychology. Her mother was opposed to her working with "crazy people," and her culture generally had difficulty acknowledging psychological problems, but, though it took her eight years, Maribel completed her degree.

After twenty-five years in the same church in New York, where Maribel met her husband, Juan, the family moved to Allentown and joined another conservative Pentecostal church. But she did not have the longtime personal ties to the new church. The strictures began to seem senseless to her. "My relationship with God was being stifled with ritual and ceremony." Transgressions such as trimming her hair or shaving her legs led on several occasions to "disciplinary processes." During those times, which lasted up to a year, she was "inactivated." While she had to go to church, she had to sit in the back without participating. "You were there, but not there" is how she describes it. She thought back to her days of teaching Sunday school in New York, and she began to think about church doctrine. When she asked her pupils what the doctrine was, the children responded, "You can't do this and you can't do that." She realized that everything was negative. Maribel wanted to raise her three children differently, to show them the positive side of their religion.

Maribel and Juan joined a liberal Pentecostal movement in Colum-

bus, Ohio, studied through correspondence courses, and were ordained. Three years ago, they opened their own church with thirteen
members. In their new church, now with close to one hundred members, doctrine is not important. Men and women are treated equally.
Maribel and Juan both preach what they see as the positive aspects of
their religion, the tenets of faith, loving God, serving God. Their
main message is tolerance. She quotes Paul: "In Christ Jesus we are
all the same, rich and poor, gentile and Jew, men and women."

Maribel agrees that Pentecostal wives are better off because their
husbands haven't spent half their salaries on the way home from
work, but she says, "Women are still thinking *family*. They are not
thinking 'what about *you*, who are *you?*' Personal fulfillment is as important to women as it is to men." In Maribel's church, young girls
are encouraged to go to college and to be independent, productive
members of society.

Maribel's beliefs go beyond her church. At home, her sons and
daughter cook and do laundry. She and her husband contribute to the
family income and share the household tasks. There is no sexual division of labor in their home. It is their belief that true religion must
also serve the greater community. "Most of the churches are isolated,
segregated, and only meet the needs of their own membership. We envision a church that has a food bank, a clothing bank, that meets the
social needs of the community. How can I speak to you about spiritual needs when your material needs are not being met?" Besides her
demanding job and the time she spends in church, Maribel has played
an active leadership role in Allentown's Latino community as a member of the mayor's advisory council on Latino affairs and as a member
of the board of directors of a social services agency.

Do you think of yourself as a feminist? I asked. "No, although
some people might call me that." Why not? "A lot of what I have accomplished is because my husband has stood by me. He is the priest
in our house." Is your church the future of Pentecostalism? "Women
have a very strong presence in our church. They have no authority,
even though they are the majority. I think that as women start to
grow and see different possibilities of relating to God, they will have
no choice but to change."

CONCLUSIONS

Because Pentecostal church doctrine provides not only a religious
framework, but strict paradigms for life, it has brought a dramatic improvement in the material as well as spiritual lives of thousands of

men, women, and families. In the material realm, the strict doctrine that prohibits drinking and infidelity often enhances the socio-economic status of the family. In fact, although Pentecostalism is often associated with the poorer sectors of society, many Latin Americans see it as a route toward upward mobility, a way of distancing themselves from the poverty they associate with Catholicism. Pentecostalism's ability to adapt to changing sociocultural conditions has helped to ensure the survival and growth of the church. Maribel's church, in fact, is bilingual to accommodate second- and third-generation Latinos who do not speak Spanish.

Pentecostal churches in Allentown are becoming involved in their communities at the informal level by providing various social services and publicly protesting what they see as injustices to their churches. Several pastors are active in community affairs. At least one has invited political candidates to speak in his church and urged the congregation to vote. Some individuals are involved in the formal political structures, such as Maribel's participation on the mayor's council. The continued growth of Pentecostalism in Allentown, even among the youth, indicates the vitality of the church.

The churches are somewhat less flexible with regard to women. While they may have changed vis à vis their attitudes toward involvement in the greater society, most seem less willing to relinquish the doctrine which controls women's appearance. Nevertheless, the religion seems to hold enough attraction to keep women faithful in their way. Maribel and Elsa, because they felt free to interpret church doctrine for themselves, have been censored. Elsa chooses to layer her hair, knowing that she will be denied participation in services. Maribel's rejection of doctrine finally led her to establish her own church. Neither woman left Pentecostalism, and both believe that their religion is what liberates them to change. Church ideology that stresses personal relationships with the Lord appears to have given these women the freedom to interpret doctrine for themselves. This theology of equality, as they perceive it, undermines the overtly androcentric doctrine of the church.

In their article on Pentecostal women in Brazil titled "God Is More Important than the Family," Cecilia Loreto Mariz and Maria das Dores Campos Machado wrote that it is the process of individuation, coupled with the assertion of a primary responsibility to God, rather than to spouse and family, that transforms women into active, responsible agents.[12] Dorotea's narrative is illustrative of this process.

Elsa believes that if God had a problem with her hair, he would let her know. Maribel thinks that God has more important things on his mind than whether or not she has pierced ears. Perhaps the perception of equality leads women to reject strictures that do not apply to both sexes. If men and women are equals in the private realm, why should they be less equal in the public realm? In a practical sense, as these second- and third-generation Pentecostal women become educated and begin to participate in the work world as professionals, their church doctrines may seem too restrictive. They may, for example, question the strict dress codes that could impede their progress in a world where "dressing for success" can be important.

These four stories both support and contradict the women's notion of gender equality. Marta believes that she needs *some* man to protect her, but knows that God is a better protector than most of the flesh-and-blood men she has encountered. Like Marta, Dorotea believed that she needed a man to help her escape her life of bondage. At the same time, her dedication to the Lord has transcended her dedication to her family. On different occasions, she chose God over her mother, her husband, and her son's family. Maribel and her husband share the bread-winning responsibilities of their household, and both are ordained preachers in their church, yet Maribel describes her husband as the priest in their house. Elsa feels that some of her church's doctrine is excessive, yet she chooses to remain in a church which forbids her to participate.

Elizabeth Brusco warns us not to view women Pentecostals through the lens of Western feminism.[13] As we have seen, Pentecostal women, unlike Western feminists, do not see the family as the origin of their oppression, precisely because men are active participants in the household. And as Brusco also points out, because of shared household responsibilities, Pentecostal women have managed to avoid the double day endured by many liberated Western women. While Maribel may not apply the term feminist to herself, she works within her family and within her church to promote female equality. It is likely that as Pentecostalism becomes more mainstream and as Pentecostal Latinas make places for themselves in the professional world, there will be openings for conversations between self-defined feminists and Pentecostal Latinas.[14]

Whatever the reality may be, it seems to me significant that Pentecostal women perceive an egalitarian relationship between men and women, and that perception liberates them to act accordingly. To a greater or lesser degree, each of my subjects has shared an equal relationship with her man. Until her husband was incapacitated, Dorotea

raised the children while he earned the money, but their equality before God seems to have permitted her to abandon her "wifely duties"
for missionary work. In her new life, Marta and her husband, both former drug addicts, do the Lord's work together as equals. Perhaps because she is relatively new to Pentecostalism, which has brought
such positive changes to her life, she is less likely to reject the strict
doctrine. Elsa and Maribel, who grew up as Pentecostals, have felt
free to reinterpret church practice and doctrine to accommodate their
lives within the religion. Maribel is a wife and mother but insists on
an identity outside the family unit. Elsa, who does not want to have
children of her own, though she might adopt, explodes the myth of
woman as mother.

Perceptions of gender equality have begun to shape the way some
women relate to their churches and have empowered them to reevaluate some church practices. Their perceptions matter because they
have served as a force for change. Thus far, Pentecostalism's adaptability has worked in its favor. We know that newly middle-class
people do not abandon the church. In Latin America and among Latinos in the United States, Pentecostal churches continue to attract
those who feel marginalized from society because of their poverty or
their culture. The sense of community and belonging and the emphasis on the centrality of family offered by these churches would appear to transcend, at least for now, doctrinal structures.

We have seen that strict doctrine has not driven educated women
in search of a new religion. However, it is necessary to acknowledge
that the freedom that women feel to question their religion could potentially lead to its self-destruction as new generations of educated,
working women continue to reinterpret church doctrine and practice
to suit themselves. If the churches are to grow and be meaningful to
future generations of more educated women, they will have to become more flexible in terms of doctrine. Maribel's church may indeed
represent the future of Pentecostalism. In fact, I learned recently
that Dorotea, who is Maribel's mother-in-law, has begun to attend
Maribel and Juan's church.

NOTES

I gratefully acknowledge the comments and encouragement of Adriaan
Noordam, Stacey Schlau, Jill Stephen, Hannah Stewart-Gambino, and Virginia Wiles.

1. Edward L. Cleary, "Pentecostals, Prominence, and Politics," introduc-

tion to *Power, Politics and Pentecostals in Latin America*, ed. Cleary and Hannah Stewart-Gambino, 1–24.

2. Anthony L. LaRuffa, "Pentecostalism in Puerto Rican Society," in *Perspectives on Pentecostalism: Case Studies from the Caribbean and Latin America*, ed. Stephen D. Glazier.

3. John Burdick, "Struggling against the Devil: Pentecostalism and Social Movements in Urban Brazil"; Rowan Ireland, "The *crentes* of Campo Alegre and the Religious Politics of Protestantism in Brazil"; and Paul Freston, "Brother Votes for Brother: The New Politics of Protestantism in Brazil," all in *Rethinking Protestantism in Latin America*, ed. Virginia Gerrard-Burnett and David Stoll; and Kathleen Harder, "The Expanding Politicization of the World Pentecostal Movement," in *Conference Papers 1992*, Society of Pentecostal Studies, 6–7.

4. Cornelia Butler Flora, "Pentecostal Women in Colombia," *Journal of Interamerican Studies and World Affairs* 17:4 (1975), 411–424.

5. Elizabeth Brusco, "The Reformation of Machismo: Asceticism of Masculinity among Colombian Evangelicals," in Gerrard-Burnett and Stoll, *Rethinking Protestantism*, 143–158; and Carol Ann Drogas, "Private Power or Public Power: Pentecostalism, Base Communities and Gender," in *Power, Politics and Pentecostals*, ed. Cleary and Stewart-Gambino, 55–76.

6. LaRuffa, "Pentecostalism," 60.

7. Anna Adams, "Brincando el Charco: A Case Study of Pentecostalism's Journey from Puerto Rico to New York to Allentown, Pa.," in *Power, Politics and Pentecostalism*, ed. Cleary and Stewart-Gambino, 163–178.

8. Samuel Solíván, "Sources of Hispanic/Latino American Theology," in *Hispanic/Latino Theology. Challenge and Promise*, ed. Ada María Isasi-Díaz and Fernando F. Segovia, 134–148.

9. Edwin Colón, interview with the author, June 7, 1994.

10. As is frequently the case in popular Christianity, "God" and "Lord" are used interchangeably.

11. Flora, "Pentecostal Women," 414.

12. Cecilia Loreto Mariz and Maria das Dores Campos Machado, "Pentecostalism and Women in Brazil," in *Power, Politics and Pentecostals*, ed. Cleary and Stewart-Gambino, 41–54.

13. Brusco, "Reformation of Machismo."

14. At the Annual Delaware Valley Women's Studies Conference in September 1999, "Puerto Rican Women at the Turn of the Century: The Challenge of Double Colonization," Elsa and Maribel joined me in a session on Puerto Rican women's changing spirituality.

| CHAPTER 6 | **LATINA ACTIVISTS** |

TOWARD AN INCLUSIVE
SPIRITUALITY OF BEING IN
THE WORLD

JEANETTE
RODRÍGUEZ

Latinas have a unique contribution to make to their communities, churches, and nation. As the foundation of the family, pillars of our communities, preservers of the culture, and transmitters of the faith, Latinas are particularly suited to lead their communities forward. Theologian Elizabeth Dreyer states, "A sense of community is both a prerequisite and an outcome of meaningful work. Beyond one's intimate circle the road of spirituality leads to consciousness and care of ever wider community groups."[1] As a U.S. Latina feminist theologian influenced initially by political theology as well as by U.S. Latina feminist theology, I am particularly interested in the context out of which Latina women manifest and live out their faith.[2] What role does spirituality play in their commitment to service, activism, and leadership? In this chapter I intend to explore how spirituality may inform a Latina's style of service/leadership in her family, faith community, the marketplace, society. Feminist theologian Ann Carr provides a helpful framework for understanding spirituality. Carr writes that spirituality in its broadest sense "can be described as the whole of our deepest religious beliefs, convictions, and patterns of thought, emotion and behavior in respect to what is ultimate."[3] For some, the "ultimate" is identified as God, spirit, work, or family. While spirituality embraces, contains, and manifests our deepest beliefs, thoughts, and behavior, theology articulates these processes in a more systematic, intellectual, and reflective way.

U.S. Latina feminist theology as articulated by theologian María Pilar Aquino draws its inspiration both from Latin American liberation theology and feminist liberation theology.[4] Theology in general is a coherent discourse which seeks to respond to the great questions of humanity: who or what is God, what is humanity, what is our relationship to God, what does it mean to live a good life? These questions in and of themselves do not belong solely to the realm of theology. However, these questions become theological when they arise out of a community of believers and their possible responses are grounded on faith. In this case the believers are Latina women. Theology done by women, in this case by Latina women, deals with concrete experiences. Daily life is their point of departure.[5] For Latinas, a religious view of faith as mediated through their culture has played a primary role in their lives. Through their faith as lived out in their spirituality, they have found a source by which to recognize significant values that they draw from for developing self-esteem, confidence, and a commitment to resist all forms of sustained injustices.[6]

Latinas living in the United States face a daily struggle to maintain their identity as Latinas and as women in a society that explicitly discriminates against both. They are constantly being challenged to define themselves, their roles, desires, assets, and liabilities. Hence my interest: is there a connection between their community involvement/activism and spirituality? If so, what does it encompass? What motivates, ignites, fuels their commitments to serve their communities?

The interest in the relationship between service and spirituality came to me when I met Latina women from the National Hispanic Leadership Institute. These are highly motivated, well-educated women committed to service and justice while working in a white, male-dominated environment, and yet they retain their cultural identity or Latinidad. Research on identity, politics, and women connects these issues to discourses and movements organized around questions of religious, ethnic, and national identity.[7] In our conversations, I found them to reject most kinds of institutionalized religious affiliation. As I got to know them, I witnessed a deep, private, intimate spiritual motivation for what they were doing. Although many were raised, educated, and/or supported by their churches, they had become disillusioned by the perceived lack of commitment to the poor or to sustained indigenous leadership on the part of the church. As these Latina leaders grew in knowledge and confidence, they began to function as creators of their destiny, engaging in social critique and church reform. Perhaps this is where the disillusionment began. Nevertheless, most of these women credit their churches, primarily Roman Catholic, as being instrumental in identifying them as leaders, calling them to work in their communities, and offering them an opportunity to step into leadership roles.

In reflecting on leadership, I'd like to highlight the four qualities described by Peter Koestenbaum. He identifies courage, integrity, vision, and realism as constitutive qualities in any leadership. He understands that courage involves the ability to act; integrity the capacity for truth; visioning the ability to imagine, without which we cannot maintain, promote, or inspire hope; and realism the ability to analyze, to critique, the actual skills and competencies for change.[8] Cleo Molina, a Latina activist, provides a useful definition of leadership that includes spirituality as a core element. Leadership, according to Molina, "depends on an ability to *frame issues correctly,* call forth authentic *actions,* use *ethical sensibilities,* and *touch the spiritual.*"[9] Molina's definition includes spirituality as a core element of leadership.

How and where do Latinas live, exemplify, and model this? The Latino community and communities of people of color are in general some of the most vulnerable in the country. Every indicator of poverty, crime, employment, education, and health-related issues identifies us as a people living in a daily struggle to maintain a basic standard of living and heading toward a difficult future. Poverty rates for Hispanic families, working Hispanic families, and Hispanic children remain disproportionately high.[10] In 1998, the number of Hispanic women totaled 14.7 million, accounting for 48.6 percent of the total Hispanic population. The National Council of La Raza (NCLR) in a 1998 report provides us with the following facts:

- Hispanic women are more likely than white and black women to be under 18 years of age.
- Hispanic women are more likely than white women, but less likely than black women, to be single mothers.
- Hispanic young women have the highest birth rate of all adolescents.
- High school and college completion rates for Hispanic women are lower than those for white and black women.

- The unemployment rate for Hispanic women is higher than that for white women, but lower than that for black women; Puerto Rican women have the highest unemployment rate among Hispanic subgroups.
- Hispanic women workers have lower median earnings than white women workers and median earnings similar to those of black women workers.
- Hispanic women are more likely to be poor than their white and black counterparts; Puerto Rican women are the poorest Hispanic women subgroup.
- Hispanic women are less likely to have private or government health insurance than white or black women.
- Hispanic women are disproportionately affected by AIDS compared to white and black women.[11]

AUTHENTICITY AND LIVED EXPERIENCE

My work as a teacher and U.S. Latina theologian has allowed me to witness the power of belief and its foundational place in leadership. It is this power of belief that frames issues in a meaningful way, grounds ethical sensibilities, and leads to action from a place of *authenticity*, an area that we have not sufficiently accessed, nurtured, or utilized. The foundation of the Latina endeavor must be grounded in an understanding of who we are. Although *who* we are is deeply personal, for the Latina, it is not individualistic. Like spirituality, who we are is formed by our families, teachers, friends, community, class, culture, gender, and by our social location in a historical moment. We are influenced by beliefs, intellectual position, and ethical decision-making. This entails not just awareness, but an authentic living out of that knowledge derived from both formal and informal education. While formal education often codifies cultural stories and presents them as history and texts, stories of human relationships with historical depths, myths, proverbs, and songs tell us who we are and who we can be. These narratives, relationships, and spirituality are lived out and mediated through culture.

Latinas continue to share with me stories that reflect a spirituality undergirding their choices of a career in service or movement into leadership positions. Lilly, born in Texas, working in public utility service, shares these reflections:

I always realized from the time I was a little child that we are here not just for ourselves; we are here for more than ourselves. The purpose of our being a human is to care about others and to provide service, service not necessarily in a formal way. I kept hearing as I was growing up it doesn't matter how poor you are, you might have something to be able to give to somebody else that might have a greater need for something you might have more than what you do . . . There's one term that would summarize it for me and that is service; this notion was instilled in me by my Catholic religion and my grandparents. My belief is still part of who I am and what I do; it's not different than my being Hispanic. I still believe in God. I think the pieces are hard to articulate and that people get embarrassed in trying to articulate those pieces or don't want to credit that to the church. I do think it's spirit in action, particularly females, that we act with spirit. I don't think any of us would be doing this if we thought we were doing this for ourselves.

Cecilia, a Chicana from Texas, offered a story that in reflection formed her sense of community and care:

The story that she [mother] told me had to do with World War II. She described the neighborhood in which she lived. The homes were close together and everyone knew each other. It was a very close, tight-knit community. After all, really all were Chicanos. The story takes place in the middle of the night, during World War II, very late at night. It was one of the most fearful times of night for that community because sometime during the middle of the night they [community] would hear this bell. It was the bell of a bicycle messenger coming to deliver a letter to a family there in that community. The letter was from the military letting them know that someone had lost a son, a father, or a husband in the war.

The way my mother told the story made it seem like it always happened very late at night, in the dead of night, when everyone was asleep. So the sound of the bell was unmistakable. People would wake up when they heard that bell. Most everyone had a son in that war; every household was waiting for the sound of the bell to stop in front of their home. And what my mom would describe was that as the bell traveled down the street the lights would go on for people waiting to see where it was going to stop. And, as it passed your house there was always a sense of relief in that household but eventually the bell would stop and there would be this dead quiet and then the next sound that you would hear would be this wail. You know, coming from someone's home. She would tell the story to me and it never failed to evoke emotion in me and in her.

I think the emotion I feel says something about how I experience history. I experience history through my mother. You know in that particular story somehow I feel like I knew the 1930s and 1940s. My mother and I would spend a lot of time talking about the old days, what it was like when she was young. And I think in doing this she passed on a sense of how hard it was for her and how she wanted advantages not just for me but for our people . . . all people. I think that was always the most explicit thing in her story. It was to give me a sense of some of the things she had gone through in the hopes that I would learn something from it and be very interested in what it was like, you know back then in history.[12]

Cecilia, who today works as a director for public housing in a large city, is still very much connected to the roots of her Chicana experience. Latina leadership does not operate above and/or against one's community but rather draws from its roots, is ingrained in its roots, and continually connects Latinas to the cultural memory of their narrative experience. Cecilia's story is another example of how she remains connected to her community.

Many Latinas' efforts to improve the quality of life in their communities are the consequences of their histories, the histories of their ancestors, and of the people with whom they share their lives. Whether this work is paid or unpaid, what women do in their socially assigned responsibilities extends beyond nurturing and reproducing families; it creates community and the conditions necessary for life. The core message of a liberating religious vision entails the attainment of the fullness of life. The spirituality of U.S. Latina women, in particular, manifests itself from the existing communities and social movements of Latina/Chicana feminism as they have developed in the complexity of the First World but elaborated from the opposite side of triumphal hierarchical world powers.

Because of this consciousness, Latina women seek to identify and respond to the real needs of those who suffer; to not only address but to expose for all to see the consequences of this world order. These insights, fueled and nurtured by their faith, center around concern for eliminating violence against all people and in particular against women and children. The engaging and motivating insights that come from U.S. Latina feminist religious understanding are anchored in the belief that the function of one's faith is not only to explain and interpret its meaning, but also to assist in the transformation of reality itself.

FAITH AND ACTION

Religious traditions remind us that a relationship with God is difficult to maintain if we do not love our neighbor. Our relationship with God must affect all aspects of our lives, all human reality. As we

Latinas become increasingly aware of the injustices sustained and suffered, we reject any concept of salvation that does not affect the present and future reality. This becomes clear as Latinas express their faith experience and choice. Interviews that I have conducted reveal the depth of their concerns.

Many of these interviews were conducted with groups of women. When Cecilia shared her story, a friend of hers in the group wrote the following poem:

Abuela's Story Remembered

She told me the story
of a barrio
on a few blocks of street
between St. Henry's and the underpass
almost in the shadows
Sonora Street Southside San Antonio

"It was during World War II, mijita
when almost every family
prayed for silence
But near midnight
the bicycled messenger's bell
lit each light on the block.
We took what was at hand as offerings
whispered prayers
and spoke soft memories only mothers can bear.
On the nights of the bicycled messenger's bell
we clung one to another, stilled our breathing
knowing in a moment the world ends a second
time.

Each one here lost another.

Did I tell you mijita que pequeño era mi barrio?"

R. CASTRO

The spirituality that emerges from this story and its pregnant images of night, bell, lights, whispered prayers, indicates how one copes with life and death and how life and death are dealt with here in community. The story demonstrates how one learns to be attuned to one's environment and to care. When the messenger's bell rings, all the lights go on, not only the lights of the person receiving the message.

The community is in tune—aware of the impending tragedy—a witness to sorrow as experienced in the wail. For Cecilia, it is this story, in her telling it and in her friend's capturing it in poetic form, which keeps her connected to her community. She is a leader because she is part of the ethos, the morals, and convictions of her community. She knows their stories, their hopes, aspirations, fears, and sorrows. Faith also has to do with how we interpret these places in our lives where we run up against limits. In this story these women are crashing into their limits all the time. They crash into their pain, suffering, loss, death, silence, shadows, all the different words that are used here. This is their faith testament.[13]

In addition to personal story, each of us inherits a cultural story. Each of us, consciously or not, belongs to a culture, a culture that is ideologically, socially, and politically constructed. Many women, and Latinas in particular, live out of multicultural realities. I am a member of the U.S. dominant culture by virtue of place of birth, formal education, and socialization. I identify myself as a Latina or Ecuadorian by virtue of blood, heart, family, and ancestry. Somewhere in the middle is a synchronicity or *mestizaje* of all these things. An example would be my Roman Catholicism; a blend of Western Roman thought and indigenous spirituality.

Latinas' religious views and experiences of faith as mediated through our culture have played a primary role in our lives and the lives of our families. It is in our faith that we have found the source with which to recognize our values. It is in our faith that we have developed our self-esteem. In our faith we have found the strength to resist the aggressive processes of religious, spiritual, and cultural colonization. In faith, we carry the authority of our own conviction and experience.

Two other examples of this inspiration and collective struggle are illustrated in an article by Elizabeth Martínez, "The Pursuit of Latina Liberation." In April 1995, Latina/o and other students from a number of schools in the Bay Area held walkouts to protest the lack of response to the educational needs of the Latina/o community. They demanded educational reform that included more bilingual counselors, more retention programs, and a relevant multicultural curriculum. Martínez contends that during the San Francisco walkouts, it was women who called loudest and most clearly for unity and peace.

The second example Martínez uses is leadership Chicanas exercised through Fuerza Unida (meaning united force or strength), an organization formed in San Antonio, Texas, after Levi Strauss laid off

1,100 garment workers in 1990. Chicana workers and other community women, who would not define themselves as leaders or feminists and yet demonstrated leadership behavior by leading what Martinez calls "objectively feminist lives," responded to the needs of working women with labor organizing and other forms of collective struggle. Martínez concludes, "From often being shy or nervous because of their lack of formal, higher education, Fuerza Unida women have become administrators and amateur labor lawyers, steadily developing as leaders."[14]

ACTIVISM AND SPIRITUALITY OF WOMEN

It seems to me that the lesson for us is to ask: How important is it for us to be conscious and intentional about the way we talk about life? These women may not be conscious and intentional about God, but they are very intentional about life.[15] Through the centuries, women have been responsible for the daily functions of life—making the fire, baking the bread, giving counsel, and organizing the economic household—centuries of life-sustaining work that gives one a healthy respect for the concrete and "ordinary." This intentionality is the connection between faith and leadership. Latinas' leadership is one of inclusiveness, of enabling others to realize their potential, and of being "a part of" instead of "separate from." Both Latina leadership and spirituality deal with concrete experiences, which means dealing with the things of daily significance. Daily life then becomes the point of departure, and women's spirituality and leadership are work done with the body, the heart, the hands, and the head. It is the language of poetry and symbol and narrative, of community and ritual, that best expresses the understanding and wisdom of the faith. Such language expresses a person's deepest and most genuine aspirations and desires.[16]

It is apparent to me that leadership has to do with breaking barriers between people. It fosters and creates community, engendering respect and participation from all its valued members. The commitment to respect human dignity and liberation leads one into the service of justice. Brazilian theologian Ana María Tepedino consistently reminds us that "the cry of women comes from within the massive cry of the poor and oppressed in the midst of the exploitation and misery in which the majority of the population lives," and this is why those of us who wish to ground our work in faith or in spirituality must reflect from a woman's point of view and make this voice heard "as a service to all of those alienated from society."[17] For example, Third World women offer a distinct perspective on ecological crises, due to their intimate involvement in struggles for survival.

To say that women and nature are intimately associated is not to say anything revolutionary. After all, it was precisely just such an assumption that allowed the domination of both women and nature. The new insight provided by rural women in the Third World is that women and nature are associated, not in passivity but in creativity and in the maintenance of life.[18]

THE JEWISH AND THE CHRISTIAN TRADITIONS OF RESISTANCE AND LIBERATION

We find, thanks to the contribution of feminist theologians, accounts of spiritual resistance in the Hebrew scriptures among the women of Exodus. When recalling the book of Exodus one usually thinks of the Israelites leaving the land of Egypt, with Moses leading and guiding them. Theologian and storyteller Megan McKenna, however, opens with the focus on women. The Exodus account tells the events around the birth of Moses, but it is the women who are the active players here.[19]

It is the midwife who begins our liberative salvation history by refusing to cooperate with the pharaoh's orders to kill every firstborn son of the Hebrew people. Two midwives, Shiprah and Puah, unfamiliar names to many, follow the dictates of their God over the oppressive dictates of a merciless and unjust king. It is the midwives' courage, faith, and belief in a God of life, that helps them overcome their fear for their own safety to disobey the pharaoh's command to kill the Hebrew boys. It is the mother of Moses, out of love for her son, and her daughter who honors her mother and loves her brother, who are willing to give up the son, the brother for life, so that the son, the brother might live. The pharaoh's own daughter goes against the wishes of her father to save a life.

Scripture tells us that the pharaoh's daughter, whom I assume knew the ruling of her father, finds this baby and is moved to compassion. Together, all of these women saved this child destined by God to manifest God's glory by leading God's people to new life. But only life can beget life. As I read about the role all these women played in our salvation history, what immediately came to mind was the ordinary prophets and saints of Latino women who live in the community, who act in the community for the same purpose: to give life. To give life abundantly. They do this against the discrimination and marginality of their social situation. Elba, a Puerto Rican from New York has this to say:

Ever since I was a little girl I had a desire to help people. I was very religious. I always thought God spoke to me . . . that God had a mission for me . . . that I was going to live a long life. Today, I am not so sure that I will live a long life, but I think I am fulfilling the mission, which is the work of advocating for services to Latino children.

Currently, I am executive director of a community-based organization that is mid-size. Our budget is one million. I founded this organization fifteen years ago with a group of Latino professionals who cared about Latino families caught up in the foster care system that had no one to speak on their behalf. I wanted to create an agency that would speak out about the need to place children in Latino homes so that they would have continuity of care and be able to grow up with a healthy sense of self. I did not have any funding to create the organization but believed in the power of commitment and good faith in other people. With a group of six people we had a party in my house and fund-raised nine hundred dollars—enough to get us started.

CONTEXTUALIZING THE SPIRITUALITY OF LATINAS

Leadership among Latina women is formed by concrete everyday experiences that impact their lives and the people in their communities. Their perspective has to do with physical and spiritual needs as they are embodied as experience. Their impetus is toward the attainment of the fullness of life grounded in human dignity, shared solidarity, respect, inclusion, and interrelatedness—values learned in one's formation and translated into a leadership style. Foundational to this is "caring" and a vision of how things could be.

Jackie, the director of a Latino/a family agency and a Mexican American from California, illustrates this:

My grandmother was a very special person in my life. I grew up in Texas and we were poor. I was very aware of our status because every day at school I was ostracized by the predominately white children who did not like my clothes, my hair, my skin, my name, or my lunches. My grandmother would deliver my lunch to me every day. I always had a warm taco with beans and meat or rice and a small thermos of milk. Everyone else had white bread sandwiches with cold cuts. I always felt pained at lunchtime because part of me didn't want to see my grandmother and the other part of me felt so guilty for feeling that way. She knew that children made fun of me and of her, but she acted as if she was oblivious to it. She always brought certain differences to my attention, never explicitly saying what she really meant but laying a foundation of thought in my head. If a different colored plant grew out of place she would comment on how its difference made things more interesting. She would brush her long hair at night and comment on how some people did not like it when gray hair began to grow into their natural color but she said that she liked it because it meant something different and it gave more strength to her dark hair. She said everything in nature should be appreciated because it was part of God's design. As I got older things did not get any easier. I wondered why my only happy place was in my home when other children got to be happy both in their homes and at school. Finally, things began to change. The Chicano movement began to blossom and I grabbed hold tight to it. I felt like it was my knight in shining armor coming to save me from this cruel society I had grown up in. I became very militant to the point of becoming cruel to those persons who were different from me. I lost my grandmother's words about the importance of differences. I became an angry and sad person. I took a break from the movement because I wanted to think about where I was and where I was going. By this time my grandmother had been dead five years and I suddenly began to miss her terribly. I began to recall all of my best memories together with her and her knack for always pointing out the beauty of differences in life. I began to think more about her words and they took on more meaning. That was about twenty years ago and today I have finally come full circle. I appreciate myself and others, all thanks to my grandmother.[20]

For Latinas, religious and cultural oppression plays the major role in the formation of their worldview.[21] To understand Latinas, we must appreciate their psychosocial reality. To understand the effect of a foundational spirituality, we must understand how experience is perceived and valued, and how it motivates behavior.[22] In the case of Jackie and despite the overwhelming pressures of domination and assimilation, today she seeks to transform what could be structures of oppression into dynamic patterns of faith and hope as an advocate. Elba also depends on her sustaining faith to continue the struggle against injustices toward Latino children and families. She reflects:

In recent years, I have received national exposure and am becoming a spokesperson for Latino children and families' child welfare concerns. I get tremendous satisfaction from effecting changes and influencing people to do the right thing for children. Attending meetings where I speak up and have my voice heard because I've been articulate and made my arguments effectively gives me great satisfaction. Unfortunately, most meetings are not a success.

When I have too many unsuccessful meetings or too many *no's* on the fund-raising side and I feel I can't do this any more, I get angry at the injustices and, that drives me to get up and try again. I have come to realize that anger motivates me.

But I also hold deep sustaining beliefs. My deepest beliefs and values are to live my life being as honest as I can be with everyone, to live up to my work, that is, following through with an agreement and commitments, to value and respect human life and other living things, and of course, to speak up against injustices perpetrated on myself and others.

Many Latinas' psychosocial religious development has been brought about, as well as hindered, by a legacy of culturally construed Catholicism. For many people in the Hispanic/Latino community, as in general for people who have been marginalized on many levels, the religious worldview is the primary worldview: that is, they understand everything within a religious context. Latinas have been marginalized as *mestizas* in a patriarchal society and church. As a result, many Latinas are reclaiming their indigenous roots and spirituality; they struggle to integrate themselves to their specific pre-Columbian religious tradition. Integration, however, may take the form of reclaiming the Spanish language, strengthening and reinterpreting key symbols such as Malinche and Our Lady of Guadalupe, providing and introducing ancient rituals, and transferring communal/inclusive ritual practices into their organizational leadership style.[23]

A NEW PARADIGM OF EXISTENCE

As Gloria Anzaldúa contends, "The future will belong to the *mestiza* . . . [it] depends on the breaking down of paradigms, it depends on the straddling of two or more cultures. By creating a new mythos— that is, a change in the way we perceive reality, the way we see ourselves and the ways we behave—*la mestiza* creates a new consciousness."[24] An example of a woman who integrates her indigenous worldview with the practice of organizational leadership is Guatemalan Nobel Peace Prize winner Rigoberta Menchú. She is a product of an indigenous/religious formation coupled with the skills needed to function in a totally different epistemological context.

Similarly, Latinas in leadership positions are products not only of an indigenous or particular Latino group, but are also shaped by the academy and ways of thinking that at times conflict with a more intuitive, affective way of knowing. "*La mestiza* constantly has to shift out of habitual formations; from convergent thinking, analytical reasoning that tends to use rationality to move toward a single goal (a Western mode), to divergent thinking, characterized by movement away from set patterns and goals and toward a more whole perspective, one that includes rather than excludes."[25] In addition to this concept of *mestizaje*, there is another source which helps to understand this challenge for integration and value of inclusivity.[26] The second source comes from pre-Columbian Nahuatl philosophical thought. This particular epistemological position, writes Miguel León-Portilla, is "an aesthetic conception of the universe; to know the truth is to understand the hidden meanings of things through flower and song *(flor y canto)*."[27] This refers to a more intuitive and heart-directed way of understanding and interpreting reality. The phrase "flower and song" is an example of *difrasismo*, the Spanish term for a form used in Nahuatl language to connote a complementary union of two words or symbols to express one meaning. The phrase *flor y canto* is not only a metaphor; it is a means by which to express a worldview, one that many of us inherit. The Nahuatls believe that only through flower and song, only through *flor y canto*, can truth be grasped. Truth intuited through poetry derives from a particular kind of knowledge that is the consequence of being in touch with one's own inner experience as lived out communally. The seeker of this truth is mediated through the cultural constructs of the community as understood through the individual. In the Nahuatl worldview, the concept of the individual is manifested through *rostro y corazón*, face and heart. Understanding the language and the affectivity of the heart is paramount to this worldview. The individual *rostro y corazón*—pursuing the mysteries of life through *flor y canto*— reflects the emphasis on the intuitive nature of thinking in Nahuatl philosophy. It is not a Western European understanding based solely on linear thinking patterns but is dynamic, fluid, open, creative, and searching. Both paradigms are legitimate, though incomplete if taken alone. I believe that the task of U.S. Latina leaders, grounded in a conscious and authentic spirituality, similarly is not solely interpretation and analysis. The task is to imagine hopeful and healing ways of thinking and feeling which influence how we proceed with institutional change that breaks with sustained injustices.

Reflecting on the lives of Latinas connects us to the power and wisdom of *flor y canto*. We can learn something from how women live out and relate to their concrete experiences of daily life in the stories offered earlier in this paper. We can learn something from their concern and focus on the needs of our communities and their desire for bread, water, shelter, land, and relationships. These are the elements of daily significance for women. The potential for guidance, direction, and leadership is done not only with the body, but the heart, the hands, and the head. We live in and through a complex interaction of what sustains us individually and communally.

CONCLUSION

The behavior that sustains us, what Elizabeth Johnson describes as "creating new life, working to sustain, renewing, grieving over destruction, inspiring critique, and teaching people to be wise,"[28] is none other than the work of what some religious traditions attribute to the spirit. If we examine these processes, we find that generations of women have had the power to emulate these activities of the spirit. Our spirituality thus becomes the inspiration of our leadership, which is expressed in everything that we do that sustains life. It involves learning how to live in a way that encapsulates the whole of our deepest convictions, our ways of thinking, feeling, and especially in our ways of acting.

Latina leadership challenges dominant culture's reality by interpreting experiences through *flor y canto*. Their *mestiza* consciousness functions as an asset for Latinas in leadership in terms of challenging stereotypical paradigms. Carol Becker describes such interpretations' potential as assets:

The best way to see a paradigm clearly is to get outside of it, by putting ourselves into another one . . . If paradigms help us sort and interpret information, they also help us make judgments, and it is here that they affect women in leadership today. For example, if we accept the prevailing white male system as a paradigm, we are likely to find women wanting in their leadership, no matter what they do.[29]

Following Becker, the *mestizaje* inheritance of Western philosophy and education, a syncretic religion, and indigenous spirituality can provide an ethos that values relationship, inclusivity, and reverence for story and leads to social justice. The Latina's spiritual leadership shifts the male, Western enlightenment leadership paradigm. As one observes how Latina women describe their faith, their understood legacy of service, and their powerful leadership, the connection between service, leadership, and an embodied spirituality becomes clear.[30]

NOTES

1. Elizabeth A. Dreyer, *Earth Crammed with Heaven: A Spirituality of Everyday Life*, 91.
2. Political theology is that theology which connects theory and practice and insists that any statement about God and salvation be translated into a concern about the human condition as contextualized in its political and social dimension. See Johannes Baptist Metz, *A Passion for God: The Mystical-Political Dimension of Christianity;* and Betsy A. Brenneman, "Political Theology: A Process, Feminist Perspective" (master's thesis, Graduate Theological Union, 1977).
3. Ann Carr, "On Feminist Spirituality," in *Women's Spirituality: Resources for Christian Development*, ed. Joan Wolski Conn, 49.
4. See María Pilar Aquino, *Our Cry for Life. Feminist Theology From Latin America*.
5. Ibid., 110–111.
6. Ibid., 27–29.
7. For more on this subject see *Identity, Politics, and Women: Cultural Reassertions and Feminisms in International Perspective*, ed. Valentine M. Moghadam.
8. Peter Koestenbaum, *Leadership: The Inner Side of Greatness: A Philosophy for Leaders*.
9. Cleo Molina, "Personal Theory of Leadership" (graduate paper, Seattle University, spring 1996), 4–5.
10. Sonia M. Pérez and Eric Rodríguez, "U.S. Hispanic Demographic Profile: Developments, Implications, and Challenges," National Council of La Raza, Policy Analysis Center, Office of Research, Advocacy, and Legislation, April 1998.
11. Hispanic Women Fact Sheet, National Council of La Raza, Census Information Center, November 1998.
12. Jeanette Rodríguez, *Stories We Live: Cuentos Que Vivimos*, 18–19.
13. Ibid., 19–20.
14. Elizabeth Martínez, "The Pursuit of Latina Liberation," *Signs: Journal of Women in Culture and Society* 20, no. 4 (1995): 1024–1025.
15. Rodríguez, *Stories We Live: Cuentos Que Vivimos*, 16–21.
16. Aquino, *Our Cry for Life*, 110–111.
17. Ana María Tepedino, "Feminist Theology as the Fruit of Passion and Compassion," in *With Passion and Compassion. Third World Women Doing Theology*, ed. Virginia Fabella and Mercy Amba Oduyoye, 165.
18. Vandana Shiva, "Let Us Survive: Women, Ecology and Development," in *Women Healing Earth*, ed. Rosemary Radford Ruether, 70. See also Shiva, ed., *Close to Home: Women Reconnect Ecology, Health, and Development*.
19. Megan McKenna, *Not Counting Women and Children: Neglected Stories from the Bible*.
20. Rodríguez, *Stories We Live*, 29–31.
21. Ibid., 33–34.
22. Ibid., 29–32.

23. Malinche and Our Lady of Guadalupe are key feminine symbols in Mexican and Mexican-American culture. Both of these symbols have elicited negative stereotypes: Malinche as one who betrayed her people and Guadalupe as a passive oppressive symbol. For a revisionist perspective of both of these symbols see my book *Our Lady of Guadalupe: Faith and Empowerment among Mexican-American Women*, especially 72–76 and 85 for material on Malinche.

24. Gloria Anzaldúa, "La conciencia de la mestiza: Towards a New Consciousness," in *Making Face, Making Soul. Haciendo Caras: Creative and Critical Perspectives by Feminists of Color*, ed. Gloria Anzaldúa, 379.

25. Ibid., 378–379.

26. On the notion of *mestizo* and *mestizaje* see Virgilio Elizondo, *The Future is Mestizo, Life Where Cultures Meet; Mestizo Christianity, Theology from the Latino Perspective*, ed. Arturo J. Bañuelas; and María Pilar Aquino, "Theological Method in U.S. Latino/a Theology: Toward an Intercultural Theology for the Third Millennium," in *From the Heart of Our People: Latino/a Explorations in Catholic Systematic Theology*, ed. Orlando O. Espín and Miguel H. Díaz, 35–37.

27. Miguel León-Portilla, *Aztec Thought and Culture: A Study of the Ancient Nahuatl Mind*, 182.

28. Elizabeth A. Johnson, *She Who Is: The Mystery of God in Feminist Theological Discourse*, 82–83.

29. Carol E. Becker, *Leading Women*, 51.

30. Sections of this chapter appear in a shorter, modified version, "Toward an Understanding of Spirituality in U.S. Latina Leadership," in *Frontiers: A Journal of Women's Studies* 20, no. 1 (1999), and are reprinted with permission.

PART II   U.S. LATINA
           FEMINIST
           THEOLOGICAL
           INSIGHT

CHAPTER 7

LATINA FEMINIST THEOLOGY
CENTRAL FEATURES

MARÍA PILAR
AQUINO

We have not one movement but many . . . Ours are individual and small group *movidas*, unpublicized *movimientos*—movements not of media stars or popular authors but of small groups or single *mujeres*, many of whom have not written books or spoken at national conferences . . . Now here, now there, *aqu y all* , we and our *movimientos* are firmly committed to transforming all our cultures.   GLORIA ANZALDÚA

We are the feminists among the people of our culture.
                                        CHERRÍE MORAGA

The social movements acting today in the global space are carriers of projects and specific agendas related to millennial discriminations—of gender, of ethnicity, of sexual orientation—and to problems that are increasingly global: environment, peace, human rights, etc. In this ambivalent, contradictory space still in process of being constructed . . . globalization is a new "field of dispute" *(terreno de disputa)* for the world feminisms to impel new rights and new transnational, multicultural connections recreating the diversity of feminist outlooks, and nourishing a new vision of what human living could be.   GINA VARGAS

I am opening my contribution to this book with the words of three feminists of Latin American ancestry to clearly indicate its focus and direction.[1] The growth and development of the powerful tradition of Latina/Chicana[2] feminist theories correspond to the contemporary growth and development of a plural sociopolitical movement and of a plural sociopolitical subject, both constituted as a new sociopolitical force for the achievement of justice, equality, human rights, true democracy, and a greater quality of life for all, which together can be summarized in the term *liberation*. This social force irrupted across the Americas in the second half of the twentieth century and continues to generate a plural and consistent process of critical action and insight for the transformation of the current dominant paradigm of social living.

The formal articulation of Latina/Chicana feminist thought is intrinsically connected with these historical movements. It did not emerge as a body of metaphysical convictions removed from real sociopolitical subjects. As noted in a 1971 conference report, from its early stages this thought asserted that liberation is not authentic if the elimination of kyriarchal[3] domination is overlooked or dismissed: "We are in a struggle for the liberation of our people. In this struggle, we must recognize that there are many forms of oppression. There is class, race, and women's oppression, which is tied into the same thing—capitalism. We cannot just separate these types of oppression and leave them separated."[4] The Latina feminist struggle of women and men against all forms of the kyriarchal hegemony has been, and continues to be, plural in its expressions and in its spaces of social insertion. Because feminist thought is constitutive of our *movidas*, or movements, it involves and evolves everywhere, in rural and urban areas, in the kitchen and the streets, in our minds and our communities, in schools, hospitals, and churches, *entre sábanas y libros*. C. Orozco simply says, "Feminism is necessary for liberation."[5] Latina feminist theology is also developing in the context of these plural sociopolitical subjects and movements for transformation. It did not come to light based on a metaphysical subject that exists only in one's mind, but in connection with historical movements and subjects. As the cognitive space of our religious experiences for justice and liberation, this theology contributes to the aims of that sociopolitical force that is bringing about new visions of an alternative paradigm for social living.

Consequently, the purpose of my chapter is threefold.[6] First, arguing against the myth that feminism is a foreign concept and experience for Latinas, I present some understandings and orientations shared in common by Latina/Chicana feminism and Latina feminist theology as historical background of their evolving conversation. Second, by including *indicative* data to describe the current context of reality, I want to bring to light the chilling panorama confronted by Latina/Chicana feminism and Latina feminist theology, so that we engage in changing that context from our various locations and activities. Third, I seek to describe the central features of Latina feminist theology, including its major methodological characteristics, principles, and tasks. From my perspective, I suggest that this theology can and should be characterized as an *intercultural* activity.

CENTRAL UNDERSTANDINGS AND ORIENTATIONS

The Latina feminist tradition has exposed the monocultural character of dominant Euro-American feminism.[7] The very active myth in the minds of many scholars that feminism is nonexistent among Latinas is just that: a myth.

This myth can only survive in the minds of those who claim to "know" reality but ignore that such "knowledge" is only the expression of monocultural experiences, traditions, symbols, and languages. In a similar manner, what M. S. Copeland says about black theologians can be equally applied to Latinos/as: "Black theology must expunge the myth that feminist concerns are white women's concerns."[8] Those Latinos/as who operate with kyriarchal ideologies simply ignore the plural dynamics of feminism among Latina grassroot movements. The reality, however, is that Latina/Chicana and Latin American feminisms have been denied visibility and influence in the dominant theoretical construction of both U.S. feminism and Latino/a culture. V. Ruíz points out that

Survey texts and relevant specialized monographs in U.S. Women's history overlook Chicana feminism. Although scholars recognize the 1960s and 1970s as the era of the modern feminist movement, they have left Chicanas out of their stories. Countering these chilling silences, a growing body of scholarly studies and literary works offer eloquent testimonies of Chicana feminist thought inside and outside the academy.[9]

A brief look at the pioneers of Latina/Chicana feminism shows how strongly they fought against the belief held by many that feminism does not have a Latina/Chicana cradle. They rejected the idea that Latina feminists are merely a tainted copy, a bad replica of white upper- and middle-class feminism. For example, A. Castillo notes that "there indeed existed a solid initiative toward Chicana feminist thought . . . as early on as the late 1960s."[10] C. Sandoval asserts that "by 1971, grassroots organizations of 'U.S. third world feminists' began to form across the United States."[11] In 1973, M. Cotera wrote that "research and detailed analysis of our cultural patterns and traditions of strong women prove that we have a long, beautiful history of Mexicano/Chicano feminism which is not Anglo-inspired, imposed, or oriented. In fact, the entire community should be proud of the feminists in our history."[12] In 1974, A. NietoGómez stated that *"feministas* uphold that feminism is a very dynamic aspect of the Chicana's heritage and not at all foreign to her nature."[13] In 1976, NietoGómez wrote against those who believed that feminism is a foreign notion for Latinas: "I resent the usual remark that if you're a feminist you have somehow become an Anglo or been influenced by Anglos . . . Why? Because of what it is saying—that you, as a Chicana, a Chicana woman, don't have the mentality to think for yourself!"[14] Along the same lines, four feminist scholars wrote a beautiful article in the early 1990s "not only to trace the growth of Latin American feminisms . . . but also to dispel the myth that Latin American women do not *define themselves as feminists.*" These authors stated that "not only is the Latin American [feminist] model unique in its organization of women, but it has also garnered a political base that could, and most certainly should, be the envy of feminists elsewhere."[15]

This brief look at the irruption of contemporary Latina/Chicana feminism is the historical basis of the prescriptive title coined by B. Pesquera and D. Segura for their essay: "There Is No Going Back: Chicanas and Feminism."[16] In my case, as a Latina Catholic woman born in Mexico of grassroot migrant farmworker parents, with many years of experience and involvement with various feminist movements throughout the Americas, I find these perspectives inspiring and empowering for all in society, and in the churches.

In this article, I want to highlight several understandings and orientations of Latina/Chicana feminism. It is a *mestiza* theory, method, spirituality, and praxis that has egalitarian social relations in everyday life as its principle of coherence, and it seeks to intervene in concrete reality for the historical actualization of social justice.[17] Latina/Chicana feminism is a critical framework to analyze systemic injustice, both locally and globally, to determine effective strategies for its elimination and the actualization of authentic justice. The critically reflective daily life experiences of grassroot, working-class Latina women are the starting point for our *mestiza* feminist theories and transformative practices.

Latina/Chicana feminism is a plural and often conflictive reality that, in its struggle against inequality among women and between women and men, has built a *common sense* about social relationships of power.[18] It is both a goal and a process, and it is also a personal quest and struggle. Its goal is the transformation of the hegemonic kyriarchal relationships of domination. It is a process because it engages in the continuing challenge of male privilege and in decolonizing ourselves by engendering an oppositional feminist consciousness.[19]

Another constitutive element of our struggle is the reappropriation and exercise of our right to be subjects of knowledge and of theoretical construction. We cannot afford to leave this task in the hands of those who oppress us with their excluding theories and ideologies.[20] In today's context, Latina scholars are called to expand our analytical views, to move beyond the limited U.S. literary criticism to critical systemic analyses of geopolitical, geocultural, and geoeconomic reach. Speaking of Chicana feminism, B. Harlow says that it has become "exemplary in important ways for the history of the United States women's movement more generally."[21] In sum, we have an evolving tradition that continues to inspire our feminist theories, methods, spiritualities, and socio-ecclesial practices.

Many of us Christian women, Roman Catholic and Protestant alike, have nurtured our faith experience and spirituality within the space created by contemporary feminist liberation theologies. Many of us Catholic women of Latin American roots grew up influenced by these theologies in the context of the church of Medellín.[22]

From Medellín we learned that the people of God are the true church, whose mission—consistent with the gospel of liberation—is to eliminate the sins of oppression, exploitation, violence, and dehumanization.[23] With Medellín, we understood that the historical dimension of Christian faith is the praxis of liberation, that the church's identity has a sociopolitical dimension, and that the social and the epistemic location of the faith is the world of the poor and oppressed. Medellín did not suffocate the sociopolitical forces that seek new egalitarian cultures, new social relationships, and greater social justice. For many of us, the space opened by Medellín led us to engage in the feminist struggle for the transformation of kyriarchal churches and religions and allowed us to claim our space as subjects of theological construction and imagination.[24]

If today Latina feminist theologians are still few in number, we were "invisible" thirty years ago! We "were not there" and we could not "be there" as partners in dialogue with the pioneers of Latina/ Chicana feminism. But we cannot say the same at the present time. In C. Moraga's words, *We are here,* "we are the feminists among the people" of God within our cultures.

Along the same lines, M. Lagarde's words eloquently express our present reality when she says,

Feminism also occurs quietly. It takes place not only in public struggles but also in new forms of human sharing and of everyday life. It happens around coal stoves and kitchen tables, in the food markets, in hospitals, and in churches. It is found in classrooms, in concert halls, and in productive projects . . . To associate the entire cause with only a few prominent feminists makes invisible millions of other feminists.[25]

Latina feminist theology adopts the understandings and orientations of Latina/Chicana feminism. This theology explicitly acknowledges the feminist struggles of the Latina community. It is internally connected with the history, the legacy, and the current developments of the feminist sociopolitical and ecclesial subjects and movements on both sides of the border. We take seriously the basic premise of all liberation theologies, according to which theological thought emerges from the actual political actors and social movements for social transformation.

Many of us Latina/Chicana *mestizas* who struggle everywhere for justice and liberation have called ourselves *feminists.* The main reason we have chosen deliberately not to call ourselves *mujeristas,* as Ada María Isasi-Díaz does in her theological perspective,[26] is that there are no *mujerista* sociopolitical and ecclesial subjects or movements in the United States or in Latin America. Puerto Rican feminist theologian R. Rodríguez notes that "'mujerismo' has negative connotations for the Latin American feminist movement."[27] A theory with no real, self-aware sociopolitical subject leads to what M. Lamas in her criticism of *mujerista* thought calls "a sectarian group that glorifies difference," producing "discursive dislocations and false oppositions" that weaken the political force of feminism.[28]

As a prominent feminist anthropologist in Latin America, M. Lamas has defined *mujerismo* as an essential conceptualization of women that "idealizes the 'natural' conditions of women and exalts the relationships among them" sacralizing the woman's being.[29] Throughout the continent and the Caribbean, the *mujerista* position is indisputably understood as an ideology rooted in both the assumption of a homogeneous identity of women and a unitarian and unifying women's strategy for change. In general, due to their lack of knowledge and of exposure to critical feminist theories in Latin America, many U.S. theologians have naively and erroneously asserted that *mujerista theology* is *"the"* unitarian expression of the U.S. Latinas' theological activity. However, it is necessary to dispel this myth and to correct this error. Given the long-standing political meaning that such ideology has for Latin American feminists, and in view of its countermoving effects, I suggest that our theology must be clearly characterized by a *non-mujerista* orientation.

Those of us who self-identify as Latina feminist theologians, therefore, consciously seek to develop our theological languages in dynamic conversation with the plural feminist experience and thought of Latinas/Chicanas. We seek to accompany the spiritual experience of the grassroot Latina feminist women and men who struggle for authentic liberation in view of a new civilization based on justice, equality, and integrity for all. This position also differs from that of L. Martell Otero, who, writing from the Protestant *evangélica* perspective, argues that the *mujeres evangélicas* do not relate with feminist nor *mujerista* theologies because both are "predicated on *teología de liberación*. Most *evangélicas* look upon this theology with some suspicion, especially those who come from a politically conservative viewpoint."[30] The Latina feminist theologian, developing critically the reflective language of faith, wants to use the power of theology with its liberating traditions as a religious force which contributes to personal and social transformation and to the elimination of suffering born of violence and social injustice.[31]

But let us now briefly look at the social context of our theological activity.

CURRENT CONTEXT OF REALITY

Latina feminist theology expresses, in religious language, our commitment and vision "of a new model of society and of civilization free of systemic injustice and violence due to patriarchal domination. It seeks to affirm new paradigms of social relationships that are capable to fully sustain human dignity and the integrity of creation."[32] The relevance and urgency of this language can be appreciated better in relation to the context of reality where our theological activity takes place. This context determines the methodological characteristics, the principles of theologizing, and the tasks ahead for Latina feminist theology.

What factors might reflect the true face of our present reality? I have given priority to *indicators* related to people's quality of life, their access to goods, to knowledge, and to social inclusion, as these benefit or harm the various social subjects at the global and local levels. I have chosen this route because I want to *provide specific data* supporting the recent orientation of feminist theory and theology toward what S. Saldívar-Hull calls "material geopolitical issues that redirect feminist discourse,"[33] what C. Sandoval calls "another kind of critical apparatus" that attends to "global-geopolitical struggles,"[34] and what E. Schüssler Fiorenza calls "a critical systemic analysis of domination."[35] I simply want to show, based on an honest look at quantitative material, the naked facts that cry out for the reconstruction of the feminist critical apparatus.

At the end of the twentieth century, much of the available information demonstrates that the four most prominent characteristics of the global reality are in unceasing growth: poverty, inequality, social exclusion, and social insecurity. We have begun the twenty-first century, therefore, with major questions about the possible contributions of religions in general, and of feminist theologies in particular, to the historical actualization of social justice, equality, human rights, and the well-being of all around the globe. These characteristics are the product and consequence of the current capitalist, neoliberal global economic paradigm.

As I have noted elsewhere, this paradigm "presents itself as the ultimate response to the human search for happiness and humanization. It not only imposes itself as the dominant force of geoeconomic, of geopolitical, and of geocultural reach, but also carries a particular conception of civilization, of understanding humanity, and of what social relations should be."[36] A. M. Ezcurra observes that although this dominant paradigm is mobile and changing, its invariable thesis is that the capitalist market constitutes the optimum instrument for human development and for the sustainable management of ecological resources.[37] The current capitalist market, as Jesuit scholar X. Gorostiaga indicates, "attempts to present as unavoidable a homogeneous and neoliberal globalization of the world market based on privatization, on competition, and on liberalization of the economies, under the aegis of the international financial institutions,"[38] especially the World Bank and the International Monetary Fund.

The market's globalization project contains a rhetoric of "democratic values" and a "firm internationalist will" for a "global democratization."[39] Its communications technology is globalizing a culture that promotes individualistic values of competition and self-gratification. However, in terms of real human development, of democratic participation, and of ecologically responsible management, the naked facts prove that such a project is failing dramatically. The driving law of perfecting technology so that it can save money by reducing employment is resulting in massive human exclusion. F. Morales-Pérez rightly notes that "long ago, misery, hunger, institutionalized violence, injustice, and oppression were globalized for three-fourths of humanity."[40]

The unceasing deterioration of the quality of life for the majority of humans, the growing violence, the fragmentation and polarization of societies, and the continuing exclusion of women can be seen in the following data. I must stress from the outset that I use and present data *only as indicative* of the conflicting locations, positions, and experiences of the various social subjects, not as statistics "carved in stone."

THE WORLD'S PANORAMA[41]

The dream of the capitalist neoliberal global economy to establish global integration through global markets, global technology, global ideas, and global well-being has truly become a nightmare for the majority of the world's population. According to the United Nations 1999 Human Development Report, the globalization of markets, instead of resulting in global integration, has deepened and expanded economic imbalance and social inequality. In this global paradigm, it is the world's rich who benefit most at the expense of the poor, most of whom are women and children. Such a paradigm is controlled by the world's seven richest countries, led by the United States of America, by the transnational banks and corporations, and by the new mega-billionaires. According to X. Gorostiaga, these are the hegemonic subjects of the capitalist neoliberal global economy.[42] These subjects can be further identified as a *kyriarchal power elite* who, as rightly pointed out by E. Schüssler Fiorenza, maintain "an overarching system of male domination."[43] These subjects are also directly responsible for the "complex multiplicative interstructuring of gender, race, class, and colonial dominations and their imbrication with each other."[44] In a mobile *kyriarchal paradigm,* the poor countries and oppressed peoples have little influence and little voice in today's global policy-making forums.

For example, in terms of population, the United Nations celebrated the "Day of Six Billion" on October 12, 1999. Of this population figure, 19 percent are located in the affluent countries of the Northern and 81 percent in the poor countries of the Southern Hemisphere. As of April 2000, the United States represented only 4.53 percent of the world's population yet consumed 25 percent of the world's resources. In global terms of distribution of goods and resources, by the late 1990s the one-fifth of the world's people living in the highest-income countries had 86 percent of the world's products and resources, while the bottom one-fifth had just 1 percent. Of the 82 percent of world export markets, the bottom one-fifth had just 1 percent. Of the 68 percent of foreign direct investment, the bottom one-fifth had just 1 percent. Of the 74 percent of world telephone lines, today's basic means of communication, the bottom one-fifth had just 1.5 percent. The world's richest countries, with only 19 percent of the global population, have 71 percent of global trade in goods and services and 58 percent of foreign direct investment. Infant mortality in 1998 (calculated as 1 infant death per 1,000 live births) were: 6 in Western Europe, 6 in North America, 33 in Latin America and the Caribbean, 51 in the Near East and North Africa, 59 in Asia, and 92 in sub-Saharan Africa. A baby born in sub-Saharan Africa is far more likely to die in infancy than a child born anywhere else. A child born in Latin America or Asia can expect to live between seven and thirteen fewer years, respectively, than a child born in one of the world's more affluent regions.

More than a quarter of the 4.5 billion people in developing countries still do not have some of life's most basic choices: survival beyond age 40, access to knowledge, and minimum private and public services. In the poor countries, one in seven children of primary school age is out of school, and nearly 1.3 billion people do not have access to clean water. About 840 million are malnourished. An estimated 1.3 billion people live on incomes of less than $1 a day. In contrast, the world's 200 richest people more than doubled their net worth in the four years prior to 1998, to more than $1 trillion. The assets of the top 3 billionaires are more than the combined assets of all the least developed countries and their 600 million people.

These imbalances are more alarming given the environmental degradation that threatens people worldwide and undercuts the livelihoods of at least a half-billion people. Deforestation benefits the one-fifth of the world's people who live in the richest countries because they consume 84 percent of the world's paper.

As for distribution of workload in the family and resources for advancement, high levels of inequality prevail in terms of gender.[45] At the world level, women have fewer opportunities to access advanced education and positions of influence. The global market economy gives few incentives and few rewards for it. Everywhere in the world, societies have allocated women much of the responsibility and the burden for household care. Women spend two-thirds of their work in unpaid activities, while men only one-fourth. Families, nations, and corporations have long counted on free or underpaid caregiver services from a female labor force. Women increasingly participate in labor markets, yet they continue to carry the burden of unpaid caregiver services. In addition, the traffic of women and girls for sexual exploitation—500,000 a year in Western Europe alone—is one of the most heinous violations of human rights, estimated to be a $7 billion business.

As for communications technology, the Internet plays a significant role in the globalization of markets and of global conversations.[46] However, 88 percent of users live in industrialized countries that collectively represent just 17 percent of the world's population. English prevails in almost 80 percent of all Web sites, yet less than one in ten people worldwide speaks it. The literally well-connected have an overpowering advantage over the unconnected poor, whose voices and concerns are being left out of the global conversation. In terms of gender, men prevail as Internet users worldwide: 93 percent in China, 84 percent in Russia, 83 percent in Japan, 75 percent in Brazil, and 62 percent in the United States of America. The gap in the production of knowledge is greater than the gap in distribution of income and resources: 96 percent of the world's research is concentrated in the 19 percent of highest-income countries, and half of it is centralized in the United States.

THE U.S. PANORAMA

Although the United States is the leading subject of the capitalist neoliberal global economy, poverty affects the lives of millions of its people. As of April 1, 2000, the United States had nearly 275.6 million inhabitants, of whom about 134.8 million were male and 140.8 million were female. The total Latino/a population was well over 35 million at the beginning of the twenty-first century, given the March 1997 total documented at 29.7 million. The Latino/a population was further identified by national/ethnic descent in millions as approximately: 18.8 Mexican; 3.2 Puerto Rican; 1.3 Cuban; 4.3 Central and South American; and 2.2 "other Hispanic." The population of Mexican descent remains the largest group and continues to expand. Between 1980 and 1997, the Mexican share of U.S. Latino/as rose from 59 percent to 64 percent. In terms of poverty by race in 1997, white non-Latinos/as showed the lowest percentages at 8.8 percent, followed by 17.3 percent for Cubans, 21 percent for Central and South Americans, 28.4 percent for black non-Latinos/as, 30 percent for "other Hispanics," 31.2 percent for Mexicans, and 36.1 percent for Puerto Ricans.[47] Numbers show that U.S. pets are treated better than humans: in 1998, there were 64.1 million cats and 63.8 million dogs in the United States, while only 1 percent of legally blind people used guide dogs; U.S. pet owners spent $9.3 million on cat and dog food, $100 million on cat treats, and $1 billion on dog treats.[48] These amounts could have provided better human nutrition, health, and education for the poor around the world.

Current documentation shows that the poverty rates for children, minorities, and families headed by women are well above the average of all U.S. people. Of the 12.2 million U.S. households maintained by women in 1995, 1.5 million were headed by Latinas. Data from the year 2000 are expected to show a significant increase in households maintained by Latinas. Women continue to earn less than men, in part because of differences in educational levels and years of work experience, but also because of traditional gender bias in salary levels. Poor women heads of families with dependent children have limited opportunities to attend school, which further obstructs employment opportunities.

Latina women are one of the fastest-growing population groups in the nation. Of these, by the end of 1996, the largest subgroup was women of Mexican origin (5.7 million), followed by women of Puerto Rican origin (1.1 million), and women of Cuban origin (485,000). The remaining 2.3 million were of other Hispanic descent. The highest rate of unemployment, however, continued to plague women of Mexican and Puerto Rican descent in 1996. White Cuban-American women, who generally have higher educational attainment than the non-white Latinas, have a lower unemployment rate. Most non-white Latinas (*mestizas*, blacks, and Native Americans) are exploited in job categories that require few skills and little training, offer low wages, and give no opportunities to attend school.[49]

In terms of age and education,[50] data demonstrate that the Latino/a population in the United States is young. It is estimated that 50 percent are under the age of 26, and only 4 percent of Latinos/as are over the age of 65. This represents a higher school-age population and a trend of *what the future workforce will be* in the United States. Among the nation's population ages 25 and over in 1995, 83 percent were at least high school graduates and 24 percent had at least a bachelor's degree. In the Latino/a community, however, 53.7 percent were high school graduates and only 9.3 percent held a bachelor's degree or higher.

Among younger adults, Latinos/as have the lowest educational level, while non-Latino/a whites and Asians have the highest. Nearly 40 percent of Latinos/as ages 25 to 44 in 1998 never finished high school, compared with 18 percent of Native Americans, 14 percent of blacks, 10 percent of Asians, and 7 percent of non-Latino/a whites. The unemployment rate for teenage Latinas was 25.1 percent in 1996. Contributing to this is their higher high school dropout rate and generally greater difficulty communicating in English.

Poor non-white Latinas are less likely than other minority groups to attend or graduate from college. U.S. Native Americans also have a relatively low likelihood of graduating from high school or college. Poverty, uneven access to good schools and cultural and linguistic barriers explain some of this lower educational attainment among Latinos/as and Native Americans. In light of this general panorama, I believe that further critical analysis is needed to examine the widening gap among Latinas along lines of socioeconomic status, race, and ethnicity.

LATINA WOMEN IN THE U.S. THEOLOGICAL PANORAMA

We begin the twenty-first century with the conscious determination of continuing our struggles against the exclusion of Latina women from the theological activity. Our capacity and ability to articulate the epistemic rationality and conceptual theological language have been denied to Latina women, especially to *mestizas*, blacks, and Native Americans. The fact that we are very few women theologians throughout the Americas is not due to our lack of will or vocation, but to the impact on our lives of the interlocking systemic forces of colonization, of racist and sexist exclusion, and of socioeconomic injustice. A. Castillo notes that "because we have been historically barred from the writing profession [it is assumed] that we have nothing of interest, much less of value to contribute."[51] Latina women in the United States, notably the non-white poor, are perceived to be "excellent" for occupations such as cashiers, janitors, dry cleaners, maids, textile operators, cooks, harvesting *campesinas*,[52] and so on, but rarely are we pictured as university professors, scientists, researchers, or any other professions that involve the pursuit of knowledge. In this context, T. Córdoba rightfully calls us to acknowledge that "colonization is the historical legacy that continues to haunt us, even today . . . the University is an unfriendly place for us."[53] This call demands that we undertake a critical and rigorous feminist analysis of the power forces that prevent Latinas from access to higher education. The truth is, as D. González notes, that "our situation in the academy is not improving radically or rapidly."[54] Such analysis cannot overlook the analytical tradition of Chicana feminism, noted by A. García, of the connection between capitalism, racism, and kyriarchy.[55] I could not agree more with S. Saldívar-Hull when she says that "the realities of women of color under capitalism in the United States urge the Latina women to write."[56]

For Latina theologians, intellectual activity certainly requires the radical transformation of the theological academic space through a concerted effort of U.S. theologians and churches everywhere. We need to bring about effective means and resources to support the contribution of Latina women to the theological construction in general and to feminist theology in particular. In support of this, I want to present the current *indicative* data of the situation of Latinas in the U.S. theological arena. I am focusing on the most prominent theological organizations in the United States.[57]

Before I proceed, I need to clarify several points. My objective in this section is not an exhaustive study but rather an initial approach to the percentages that indicate the involvement of Latinas in the U.S. theological arena. To my knowledge, this is the first such attempt in the history of U.S. Christianity. I want to clarify that in my view, the generic term "Latina" proved insufficient or limited in exploring how the majority of *non-white* Latinas are affected in our access to theology. By way of further clarification of this section, I must point out that the data provided by some theological organizations represent only estimates due to the absence in their documentation of declarative categories of race and of ethnicity. And finally, in my focus on percentages, I am not including the membership policies of the theological organizations that I address next.

1. *The American Academy of Religion (AAR).* As of March 2000, AAR records indicated a total membership of 10,238. Of the 8,866 who declared gender, 65.55 percent were male and 34.45 percent were female. Latinos/as represented only 1.58 percent of the total membership, 1.09 percent male and 0.49 percent female. This 0.49 percent included Protestant and Roman Catholic Latinas.

2. *The Catholic Theological Society of America (CTSA).* As of March 2000, the CTSA records indicated an estimated total membership of 1,400. Of this total, 76.07 percent were male and 23.93 percent were female. Latinos/as represented only 1.29 percent of the total membership, 0.86 percent male and 0.43 percent female.

3. *The College Theology Society (CTS).* As of January 2000, the CTS records indicated a total membership of 879. Of this total, 62.68 percent were male and 37.32 percent were female. Latinos/as were estimated to represent only 1.48 percent of the total membership, 0.79 percent male and 0.69 percent female.

4. *The Black Catholic Theological Symposium (BCTS).* The situation of U.S. black Catholic theologians is very similar to that of Latinas/os. Their general number is very low, and their contributions are easily dismissed by the hegemonic theological academy. As is the case of Latinas (both white and non-white), the number of black female theologians is disproportionately low compared to that of males. Also, in spite of the growing number of black Latinas (many of whom are of Puerto Rican and of Cuban descent), no BCTS member is of Latino/a origin or descent. As of March 2000, the BCTS total membership was documented at 71. Of this total, 69.01 percent were male and 30.99 percent were female. In the three existing membership categories, 50 were full members, 68 percent of them male and 32 percent female; 12 were associate members, 75 percent of them male and 25 percent female; 9 were affiliate members, 67 percent of them male and 33 percent female.

5. *The Academy of Catholic Hispanic Theologians of the United States (ACHTUS).* As of April 2000, ACHTUS records indicated 90 as its total membership. Of this total, 58 percent were Latinos, 24 percent were Lati-

nas, and 18 percent were non-Latinos/as. In the four existing membership categories, 35 were active members, 77 percent of them male and
23 percent female; 37 were associate members, 70 percent of them male
and 30 percent female; 4 were honorary members, 100 percent of them
male; and 14 were affiliate members, 50 percent of them male and
50 percent female. In the active membership category (those who hold
doctoral degrees in theology, scriptures, ministry, or religious studies),
only 8 of us are active Catholic women theologians. Of these 8 Latinas,
who include whites and *mestizas,* 3 are of Cuban descent, 2 of Mexican
descent, 1 of Ecuadorian descent, 1 of Salvadorean descent, and 1 of
other Hispanic descent. There are no blacks or Native Americans in the
ACHTUS membership. In terms of academic position, only 3 Latinas hold
the associate rank, and 1 holds the assistant rank.

6. *The Journal of Hispanic/Latino Theology (JHLT).* Jean-Pierre Ruíz, the
journal's editor, states that "by the conclusion of this volume year [2000],
we will have published more than 92 articles by 69 different authors—
50 men and 19 women." [58] Of the 19 women authors, 11 are Latinas,
3 are blacks, and 5 are European-Americans.

For J. P. Ruíz, the historical exclusion of Latina women from the theological activity is a challenge of primary importance that must be addressed. For him, "the numbers speak clearly about the real and pressing
need to hear the voices of women . . . If our theologies are going to make
a difference in redressing the multiple structural and institutional oppression of women, then we must do more, lest we continue to be even
unwittingly complicit through silence and neglect. At the same time, our
advocacy must avoid the sort of patronizing behavior by which Latino
male theologians claim to speak *for* Latinas in ways that keep them from
speaking *for themselves.*" [59]

CENTRAL FEATURES OF LATINA FEMINIST THEOLOGY

For many of us grassroot Latina, black, and Native American women,
access to higher education and to intellectual life is a struggle, not a
luxury or a given. This is true for Roman Catholics and for Protestants alike. Latina feminist theology as reflective religious language,
as conceptual elaboration, as cognitive space, as intellective process,
as critical reflection on our faith experiences, and as systematic articulation of our socioreligious practices seeking justice, becomes for
us a key language with which we say who we are and how we seek to
affect the present and future direction of society, culture, academy,
and the churches. In M. S. Copeland's words, "In conformity with our
baptismal vocation, we are naming ourselves *as* church—not some-

thing to which we belong, but who *we are.*" [60] In the present context of a globalized *kyriarchal paradigm* where unceasing growth of poverty, inequality, social exclusion, and social insecurity prevail, G. Anzaldúa's remarks become more central: "We need theories that examine the implications of situations and look at what's behind them . . . We need to de-academize theory and to connect the community to the academy." [61] Our theological activity and religious experience, as Orlando Espín ably suggests, can and should become a "prophetic critique" of such globalization and a space of "fierce defense of local rights." [62] Our activity stands as a constitutive "knot" of the global feminist network that strengthens the sociopolitical and ecclesial forces seeking, as E. Schüssler Fiorenza insists, "not just to understand but to change relations of marginalization and domination." [63] With this in mind, I want to present a brief sketch of the foundations of Latina feminist theology. I have chosen to speak of foundations because the following aspects are the primary conditions for the existence of this theology; they determine its direction, its methodological characteristics, its principles of articulation, and its future tasks.

PRECONDITIONS OF THEOLOGICAL CONSTRUCTION [64]

Latina feminist theology understands that if the whole of theology is to make an impact on today's reality, at least five preconditions are required of theologians everywhere: entering *Nepantla*; fostering *la facultad*; *honesty* with the real; *empapamiento* of hope; and an *evolving* truth. *Nepantla* refers to our willingness to infuse our theologies with an authentic dialogical dimension. It means that we choose to enter, as Orlando Espín suggests, "there where abundant dialogue occurs," "there where relationships happen," or "there where we are 'both-and.'" [65]

In this new era of globalization, entering Nepantla means for theologians that we are willing to engage in new explorations about God and ourselves from the creative "border" locations. According to G. Anzaldúa, "*Nepantla* is the Nahuatl word for an in-between state, that uncertain terrain one crosses when moving from one place to another, when changing from one class, race, or gender position to another, when traveling from the present identity into a new identity." [66]

Elaborating on Anzaldúa's notion of *la facultad*, Chela Sandoval explains this term as "a developed subjectivity capable of transformation and relocation, movement guided by the learned capacity to read, renovate, and make signs on behalf of the dispossessed."[67] As theologians confronting our lived realities with the Gospel's message, we need consistency in our efforts at cultivating our powers of *la facultad* for theology to maintain its vitality and dynamism.

Honesty with the real is a deliberate option for seeing our world as it is, marred by suffering born out of social injustice. For us, the most honest way to deal with this suffering is by joining others in a common effort against social injustice.[68]

Empapamiento refers to our ability of "saturating ourselves," of "imbuing ourselves," of "permeating ourselves" with hope so that we explore more freely the open possibilities of our reality and bring about the open possibilities of our transforming imagination.

An *evolving*-becoming truth as a precondition refers to our understanding of "truth" not as a finished product created by Western monocultural kyriarchal ideologies and religions, but as an evolving process of egalitarian exchange of *culturally plural truths*. Only through dialogical engagement do we all become contributors to the "truth process."[69] These preconditions indicate that our activity needs to continue developing in the direction of *intercultural* theological construction.

MAJOR METHODOLOGICAL CHARACTERISTICS

This theology articulates our vision of justice and liberation from within the plural and dynamic reality of our *mestiza* intercultural communities. It gathers in a systematic way the motives, reasons, beliefs, values, and perceptions that both validate and challenge our existence. In the words of Olga Villa-Parra, "We are always hungry for understanding, we engage in the eternal human search for reason, for grouping things together so that we make sense of them. We want to understand what drives us in life."[70]

Consequently, the methodological characteristics of this theology include the historicity of the personal and communal reality that we *are*, which gives us the freedom to open hopeful possibilities and to deal courageously with limitations. It also focuses on the daily-life plural experiences of excluded Latina women as the starting point of critical reflection. The anthological imagination as a *modus operandis* deliberately exercises "what we have come to call *teología de conjunto.*"[71] Latina feminist theology apprehends the intercultural nature of our being, our knowledges, theories, and experiences;[72] and our analyses in theological construction adopt an interdisciplinary approach.

KEY PRINCIPLES[73]

Like any other Christian theology, Latina feminist theology has the reality of divine revelation as its fundamental principle of knowledge and discernment. Such revelation always takes place and is interpreted in historical terms. The core content and ultimate finality of God's revelation is resumed in the term *salvation*. As the most precious gift of God to humans and to the world around us, salvation is understood by Latina feminist theology as liberation from every oppression.[74] Thus the historical process of liberation from poverty, social injustice, and exclusion becomes the most effective and credible manifestation of God's salvation.[75] This salvation/liberation, as E. Schüssler Fiorenza stresses, "is not possible outside the world or without the world. G*d's vision of a renewed creation entails not only a 'new' heaven but also a 'renewed,' qualitatively different earth freed from kyriarchal exploitation and dehumanization."[76] Accordingly, our perception and discernment of God's revelation and salvation/ liberation are guided by egalitarian grounding principles.

The faith of the people in popular religion is evident in the religious imagination that permeates the everyday life of the Latino/a community. There is no doubt that the majority of practicing Protestants and Roman Catholics in this community are women. There is no doubt that our communities, whether by culture, by personal conviction, or by the mere human orientation to the transcendent, are constituted by a deep sense of the sacred. This sense involves the whole of our everyday lives. There is no doubt that religious faith is a major dimension in the life of grassroot Latinas. Due to the blending of kyriarchal European religious colonization with the kyriarchal indigenous religious traditions, religious faith has contributed to deepen our oppression and exclusion. However, there is no doubt either that throughout our history, popular religion has provided the liberating principles of Christian faith to support and validate the grassroot people's struggles of resistance and emancipation. Grassroot women are both the majority and the primary carriers or subjects of popular religion,[77] and their various movements speak of their articulation of a religious faith aimed at the transformation of kyriarchal domination. In this sense, the term "popular" becomes an analytical category because it not only refers to the grassroot majorities, but also to socio-ecclesial groups that organize and mobilize themselves to change oppression and exclusion.[78] Critically aware of its force in furthering liberating purposes, Latina feminist theology takes the faith experience of women and men in popular religion as its principle of coherence.

The feminist option for the poor and oppressed also underlies this theology. As the indicative percentages of the previous section show, the everyday life of grassroot Latinas is marked by sociopolitical, economic, cultural, academic, ecclesial, and theological exclusion. In the present context, we should not and cannot give up an explicit option of standing with poor and oppressed women. In feminist terms, this is an option for the authentic life and humanization of all, an option for the life-giving cause of popular social groups, an option for ourselves as excluded humanity struggling for justice. For many of us, this option is not only the most honest course in a context of widespread exclusion, but also the most coherent way of being authentically Christian.

In its transformative practice for liberation, Latina feminist theology seeks to join efforts to eliminate the systemic kyriarchal forces that daily erode the dignity of women and of those around us. Consequently, it is from within our plural practices for transformation aimed at justice and liberation that we discern, recognize, and name God's revelation. There may be other languages that reflect critically on our practices, but what makes Latina thought *theological* is that it formally focuses on our day-to-day practices sustained by the liberating visions and traditions of Christian religion and faith.[79] There may be other religious languages that reflect on our religious customs and traditions, but what makes Latina thought *liberative* is that it deliberately focuses on our daily activities aimed at transformation toward greater justice. Our theological activity starts from these plural endeavors seeking justice and liberation and returns to them in a fecund and a creative tension. With this principle, we are asserting that theology's identity and meaning are only found in the very content and finality of God's revelation, which is liberation. We aim our theological endeavors at the systemic transformation of kyriarchal domination for a new way of living so that God's liberation is actualized.

Socio-ecclesial equality is likewise a guiding principle of Latina feminist theology. The sociopolitical principle of *equality* is a moral and a theological imperative for us in our current context. The consequences of inequality are lived only by us, the "despised identities"[80] of society, of the theological academy, and of the churches. Therefore, the struggle for equality must give coherence to our theories, theologies, methodologies, and practices.

CONCLUSION: FOUR MAJOR TASKS

I want to close my contribution to this book by highlighting some of the urgent tasks faced by Latina feminist theology in the present and future. I would argue that the first task is precisely that of continuing to develop in a consistent and a systematic way the various aspects involved in its theological foundations. This task must include a feminist critical approach to our sources of theological construction, such as *mestizaje*, popular religion, Scripture and Magisterium, interdisciplinary studies, and intercultural theories and philosophical hermeneutics. All these contemporary and traditional sources must be expanded and enriched *from* the lived experiences of grassroot Latinas in our privileged space of *la vida cotidiana*. As for *mestizaje*, I want to mention the importance of continuing to explore the provocative reflections suggested by Z. Glass not only for black theology but for our entire theological activity.[81] As for Scripture as a traditional source of religious insight, with no doubt, I believe that *la biblia* occupies a central place in our religious identity, and it is important for Latina grassroot women. Because of these, I want to emphasize the urgency we have of encouraging and supporting the development of Latina feminist biblical hermeneutics. As for related studies and theories, I want to note the increasing pertinence of Latina/o and Chicana/o literature as a key source in our feminist theological activity.

The second task is that of continuing to claim our right to theological intellectual construction. This is a requirement not only to confront neocolonization, but more importantly to empower the socio-ecclesial popular forces committed to bringing about new realities in which equality, true democracy, and justice prevail. In this vein, I find no justification, no rational explanation, no acceptable excuse for maintaining such a low number of Latina theologians in Roman Catholicism and in Protestantism. In the case of Roman Catholics, which I know best, according to the bishops' own documentation, "80 percent of U.S. Hispanics are Catholic . . . [and] . . . by the second decade of the next century, the Church in the United States will very likely be over 50 percent Hispanic."[82] Facing this reality, I believe that the Roman Catholic bishops can and must take the responsibility of providing effective means and resources for the theological education of Latinas. But their contribution must accept that this needed formal education of Latinas is for the development of a theology that both affirms justice and liberation and overcomes kyriarchal theologies. This responsibility extends to the bishops and their equivalents in the Protestant churches' hierarchies. No Christian church leader is excused from this responsibility.

The third task is that of more deeply connecting theology and spirituality in feminist terms. The feminist articulation of theology and spirituality is particularly urgent for several reasons, including the continuing self-alienation of grassroot Latina women that is maintained through their daily exposure to kyriarchal Christianity and religion; the growth of diverse Christian groups that promote among oppressed Latina women a metaphysical religious experience characterized by a naive, individualistic, and irrational religiosity that conceals the integral meaning of freedom and self-determination; and the need we have in the grassroot ministerial setting for educational processes that sustain the intellective and reasoned dimensions of religious faith. Feminist spirituality provides creative spaces and conceptual frameworks for a critical interpretation and celebration of our faith experiences in tune with our liberating traditions.

The fourth task that I want to suggest is that of continuing our critical theological analyses of the impact of capitalist neoliberal globalization on the everyday life of grassroot Latinas. If salvation is to have any meaning in our lives, theology must help us to discern how that impact advances or prohibits justice, liberation, and human dignity. In facing these tasks, the collaborative work between Protestant and Roman Catholic Latina feminists is a must. In the final analysis, as faith seeking understanding, our theological activity is nothing more than our critical appropriation of the possibilities opened by God's revelation in our lives and our faith response to it seeking to actualize historically the possibilities of salvation.

NOTES

1. See Gloria Anzaldúa, "Haciendo Caras, una entrada. An Introduction," in *Making Face, Making Soul Haciendo Caras. Creative and Critical Perspectives of Feminists of Color*, ed. Gloria Anzaldúa, xxvii; Cherríe Moraga, "Entering the Lives of Others: Theory in the Flesh," in *This Bridge Called My Back: Writings by Radical Women of Color*, ed. Cherríe Moraga and Gloria Anzaldúa, 23; and Gina Vargas, "Nuevas dinámicas de la globalización," in

Feminismos Plurales: VIII Encuentro Feminista Latinoamericano y del Caribe, by Women-Mujeres ALAI, Area de Mujeres, at http://www.alainet.org/mujeres/feminismos/011.html. My translation from Spanish.

2. I use the term Latinos/as for persons "born or raised in the United States of Latin American ancestry." See glossary in *From the Heart of Our People. Latino/a Explorations in Catholic Systematic Theology*, ed. Orlando O. Espín and Miguel H. Díaz, 262. The term Chicanas/os is referred to as "persons of Mexican descent born or residing in the United States" in the preface to *Between Borders: Essays on Mexican/Chicana History*, ed. Adelaida R. del Castillo, vi. I use the term Latina/Chicana to indicate that not all Latinas are of Mexican ancestry. See also "The Basics: Who are Chicanas?" in *Making Face, Making Soul, a Chicana Feminist Homepage*, at http://www.chicanas.com/whowhat.html#Who.

3. On the meaning of this contemporary term which replaces the term "patriarchal/patriarchy" see Elisabeth Schüssler Fiorenza, *But She Said. Feminist Practices of Biblical Interpretation*, 7–8, and *Jesus Miriam's Child, Sophia's Prophet. Critical Issues in Feminist Christology*, 14.

4. Sandra Ugarte, "Chicana Regional Conference," in *Chicana Feminist Thought. The Basic Historical Writings*, ed. Alma M. García, 155.

5. Cynthia Orozco, "Sexism in Chicano Studies and the Community," in *Chicana Voices: Intersections of Class, Race, and Gender*, ed. Teresa Córdova et al., 14.

6. My thanks to the Louisville Institute's Christian Faith and Life Sabbatical Grants Program for making possible my research for this chapter.

7. For a study of monocultural/intercultural philosophies see Raúl Fornet-Betancourt, *Hacia una filosofía intercultural latinoamericana* and *Interculturalidad y Globalización. Ejercicios de Crítica Filosófica Intercultural en el Contexto de la Globalización Neoliberal*. For a discussion of monocultural theories and theologies see María Pilar Aquino, "Theological Method in U.S. Latino/a Theology: Toward an Intercultural Theology for the Third Millennium," in *From the Heart of Our People*, ed. Orlando Espín and Miguel H. Díaz, 6–48.

8. M. Shawn Copeland, "Black, Hispanic/Latino, and Native American Theologies," in *The Modern Theologians. An Introduction to Christian Theology in the Twentieth Century*, ed. David F. Ford, 366.

9. Vicky L. Ruíz, *From Out of the Shadows. Mexican Women in Twentieth-Century America*, 100.

10. Ana Castillo, *Massacre of the Dreamers. Essays on Xicanisma*, 35.

11. Chela Sandoval, "Mestizaje as Method: Feminists-of-Color Challenge the Canon," in *Living Chicana Theory*, ed. Carla Trujillo, 356.

12. Martha P. Cotera, *The Chicana Feminist*, 9.

13. Anna NietoGómez, "La Feminista," in *Chicana Feminist Thought*, ed. Alma M. García, 89.

14. Anna NietoGómez, "Chicana Feminism," *Chicana Feminist Thought*, ed. A. M. García, 53.

15. Nancy Saporta Sternbach, Marysa Navarro-Aranguren, Patricia Chuchryk, and Sonia E. Alvarez, "Feminisms in Latin America: From Bogotá to

San Bernardo," in *The Making of Social Movements in Latin America. Identity, Strategy, and Democracy,* ed. Arturo Escobar and Sonia E. Alvarez, 209. My italics.

16. Beatríz M. Pesquera and Denise A. Segura, "There Is No Going Back: Chicanas and Feminism," in *Chicana Critical Issues. Mujeres Activas en Letras y Cambio Social,* ed. Norma Alarcón et al., 95–115.

17. See Sandoval, "Mestizaje as Method," 352–370; and Gloria Anzaldúa, *Borderlands. La Frontera. The New Mestiza,* 352–370.

18. See Sonia E. Alvarez, "Estados Unidos: Feminismos Diversos y Desplazamientos Desiguales," *Fempress,* Red de Comunicación Alternativa de la Mujer, at http://www.fempress.cl/base/fem/alvarez.html.

19. This understanding is from Cynthia Orozco, "Crónica Feminista," *La Gente* (February-March 1983): 8. My thanks to Professor Orozco for sending me hard-to-find pioneering materials of Latina/Chicana feminist thought.

20. See Anzaldúa, "Haciendo Caras, una entrada," xxv-xxvi.

21. Barbara Harlow, "Sites of Struggle: Immigration, Deportation, Prison, and Exile," in *Criticism in the Borderlands. Studies in Chicano Literature, Culture, and Ideology,* ed. Héctor Calderón and José David Saldívar, 156.

22. This expression refers to the conclusions of the Latin American Catholic Bishops conference which took place in Medellín, Colombia, from August 26 to September 6, 1968. See Second General Conference of Latin American Bishops, *The Church in the Present-Day Transformation of Latin America in the Light of the Council,* 2d ed. (Washington, D.C.: United States Catholic Conference, 1973).

23. See for example Gustavo Gutiérrez, *The Power of the Poor in History;* and Ignacio Ellacuría, *Conversión de la Iglesia al Pueblo de Dios. Para Anunciarlo y Realizarlo en la Historia.*

24. See for example María Pilar Aquino, "Presencia de la mujer en la tradición profética," *Servir* 88–89 (1980): 535–558; Aquino, "Women's Participation in the Church. A Catholic Perspective," in *With Passion and Compassion. Third World Women Doing Theology,* ed. Virginia Fabella and Mercy Amba Oduyoye, 159–164; and Aquino, "La Visión Liberadora de Medellín en la Teología Feminista," *Teología con Rostro de Mujer,* edited by José Luis Burget and Rafael Aragón, Alternativas 16/17. Managua, Nicaragua: Editorial Lascasiana, 2000, 141–172.

25. Marcela Lagarde, "Claves Eticas para el Tercer Milenio," *Fempress,* at http://www.fempress.cl/base/fem/lagarde.html. My translation from Spanish.

26. See Ada María Isasi-Díaz, *Mujerista Theology: A Theology for the Twenty-First Century* and *En la Lucha. In the Struggle: Elaborating a Mujerista Theology.* See also my criticism of *mujerismo/mujerista* in "Teología Feminista Latinoamericana," a chapter of the excellent book *El Siglo de las Mujeres,* ed. Ana María Portugal and Carmen Torres, 233–251.

27. Raquel Rodríguez, "La Marcha de las Mujeres. Apuntes en torno al movimiento de mujeres en América Latina y el Caribe," Revista *Pasos,* no. 34 (1991): 11, note 6. My translation from Spanish.

28. Marta Lamas, "Ampliar la Acción Ciudadana," *Fempress,* at http://www.fempress.cl/base/fem/lamas.html. My translation from Spanish.

29. Marta Lamas, "De la identidad a la ciudadania. Transformaciones en el imaginario político feminista," Facultad de Ciencias Sociales, Universidad de Chile, March 2000, at http://rehue.csociales.uchile.cl/publicaciones/moebio/07/. My translation from Spanish.

30. Loida Martell Otero, "Women Doing Theology: Una Perspectiva Evangélica," *Apuntes* 14/3 (1994): 72–73.

31. María Pilar Aquino, "Construyendo la Misión Evangelizadora de la Iglesia. Inculturación y Violencia Hacia las Mujeres," in *Entre la Indignación y la Esperanza. Teología Feminista Latinoamericana,* ed. Ana María Tepedino and María Pilar Aquino, 63–91.

32. See María Pilar Aquino, "Feminist Theologies," in *Dictionary of Third World Theologies,* ed. Virginia Fabella and R. S. Sugirtharajah, 88–89.

33. Sonia Saldívar-Hull, "Feminism on the Border: From Gender Politics to Geopolitics," in *Criticism in the Borderlands,* ed. Calderón and J. Saldívar, 208.

34. Sandoval, "Mestizaje as Method," 352, 355.

35. Schüssler Fiorenza, *Jesus Miriam's Child,* 12.

36. María Pilar Aquino, "Economic Violence in Latin American Perspective," in *Women Resisting Violence. Spirituality for Life,* ed. Mary John Mananzan and Mercy Amba Oduyoye et al., 102.

37. Ana María Ezcurra, "El neoliberalismo es un paradigma cambiante," *Revista Electrónica Latinoamericana de Teología,* at http://www.uca.edu.ni/koinonia/relat/204.htm.

38. Xabier Gorostiaga, S.J., "Mezcla ingobernable de Somalia y Taiwán o puente socialmente estable entre el norte y el sur del continente, entre el Atlántico y el Pacífico," Segundo Encuentro Mesoamericano de Filosofía, Universidad Centroamericana, at http://www.uca.ni/ellacuria/02goros.htm.

39. Ezcurra, "El neoliberalismo."

40. Francisco A. Morales-Pérez, "Lo globalizado como clave hermenéutica para una historización de la globalización desde América Latina," Segundo Encuentro Mesoamericano de Filosofía, at http://www.uca.edu.ni/ellacuria/morales.htm.

41. This section is based on *The United Nations Human Development Report 1999,* at http://www.undp.org/hdro/report.html; U.S. Census Bureau, "Notes on the World POPClock and World Vital Events," at http://www.census.gov/ipc/www/popwnote.html; U.S. Census Bureau, "World Population Profile: 1998–Highlights," at http://www.census.gov/ipc/www/wp98001.html; U.S. Department of Commerce Economics and Statistics Administration, "World Population at a Glance: 1998 and Beyond International Brief," at http://www.census.gov/ipc/www/wp98.html; U.S. Census Bureau, "International Data Base (IDB)," at http://www.census.gov/ipc/www/idbnew.html.

42. Xabier Gorostiaga, S.J., "Análisis Socioeconómico de América Latina y el Caribe," conference paper presented at the Latin American Encounter "Amerindia," Guatemala City, Guatemala, February 7–12, 2000.

43. Elisabeth Schüssler Fiorenza, "Ties That Bind: Domestic Violence against Women," in *Women Resisting Violence,* ed. Mananzan and Oduyoye, 43.

44. Elisabeth Schüssler Fiorenza, *Rhetoric and Ethic. The Politics of Biblical Studies*, 5.

45. *U.N. Human Development Report 1999*.

46. See Xabier Gorostiaga, S.J., "La Civilización de la Copa de Champagne. Hechos," handout distributed during his conference presentation at the Latin American Encounter "Amerindia"; *U.N. Human Development Report 1999*; Emilio de Benito, "Internet agrava la distancia entre Ricos y Pobres," *El País Digital*, no. 1165, July 12, 1999, and "E-Muro," *El País Digital*, no. 1167, July 14, 1999, at http://www.elpais.es/. According to the U.S. Department of Commerce, the disparity of Internet usage by gender in the United States is coming closer to disappearing. See U.S. Department of Commerce, National Telecommunications and Information Administration, and Economics and Information Administration, "Falling through the Net: Toward Digital Inclusion," October 16, 2000, at http://www.ntia.doc.gov/ntiahome/fttno/Falling.htm#33.

47. On this paragraph see U.S. Population Reference Bureau, "A New Look at Poverty in America," September 1996, at http://www.prb.org/topics/poverty_welfare.htm; U.S. Census Bureau, "Demographic Indicators: 2000," at http://www.census.gov/main/www/popcld.html; U.S. Census Bureau, "Detailed Tables," at http://www.census.gov/population/www/socdemo/Hispanic/ho97-1-05.html; U.S. Census Bureau, "Poverty by Race/Ethnicity," Internet release date August 7, 1998, at http://www.census.gov/population/socdemo/Hispanic/cps97/tabo5-4.txt.

48. John MacIntyre, "Amount That Americans Spend on Pets Each Year," *Southwest Airlines' Magazine, Spirit* (June 1998): 157; Gorostiaga, "La Copa de Champagne."

49. On this paragraph see U.S. Population Reference Bureau, "New Look at Poverty"; U.S. Department of Labor Women's Bureau, "Facts on Working Women, Women of Hispanic Origin in the Labor Force," at http://www.dol.gov/dol/wb/public/wb_pubs/hisp97.htm.

50. National Conference of Catholic Bishops Secretariat for Hispanic Affairs, "Demographics," at http://www.nccbuscc.org/hispanicaffairs/demo.htm; U.S. Population Reference Bureau, "America's Racial and Ethnic Minorities," at http://www.prb.org/pubs/bulletin/bu54-3/part5.htm#edu; U.S. Department of Labor Women's Bureau.

51. Castillo, *Massacre of the Dreamers*, 4.

52. See the list of "leading occupations for Latina women," in U.S. Department of Labor Women's Bureau, "Facts on Working Women."

53. Teresa Córdova, "Power and Knowledge: Colonialism in the Academy," in *Living Chicana Theory*, ed. Trujillo, 15, 20.

54. Deena J. González, "Speaking Secrets: Living Chicana Theory," in *Living Chicana Theory*, ed. Trujillo, 47.

55. Alma M. García, "The Development of Chicana Feminist Discourse, 1970-1980," *Gender and Society* 3, no. 2 (June 1989): 217-238.

56. Saldívar-Hull, "Feminism on the Border," 207.

57. I want to thank the following persons for providing me with the data included in this section: Joe DeRose from the AAR Membership Services; Mary Ann Hinsdale, Executive Secretary of the CTSA; Brother Alexis Doval,

Executive Secretary of the CTS; M. Shawn Copeland, from the BCTS; Francisco Lozada, Executive Secretary of ACHTUS; and Jean-Pierre Ruíz, Head Editor of the JHLT. A word of special thanks to Carmen Nanko, the Treasurer of ACHTUS, for the most updated information on the ACHTUS membership and to my colleague Lance Nelson at the University of San Diego for creating the percentages spreadsheet of the theological organizations that I researched.

58. Jean-Pierre Ruíz, "The Current State of Latina/o Theological Research: A Catholic Perspective. From *We Are a People* to *From the Heart of Our People*" (paper presented at "Grounding the Next American Century: A National Conference on Funding Latino/a Theological Research," Center for the Study of Popular Catholicism, University of San Diego, February 25–26, 2000), p. 15.

59. Ibid., 16.

60. M. Shawn Copeland, "Method in Emerging Black Catholic Theology," in *Taking Down Our Harps. Black Catholics in the United States*, 122.

61. Anzaldúa, "Haciendo Caras, una entrada," xxv-xxvi.

62. Orlando O. Espín, "La Experiencia religiosa en el contexto de la globalización," *Journal of Hispanic/Latino Theology* 7, no. 2 (November 1999): 26–28.

63. Schüssler Fiorenza, *Rhetoric and Ethic*, 7.

64. For additional theological background on this paragraph see my "Theological Method," 20–23.

65. Orlando O. Espín, "Immigration, Territory, and Globalization: Theological Reflections," *Journal of Hispanic/Latino Theology* 7, no. 3 (2000): 56.

66. Gloria Anzaldúa, "Chicana Artists: Exploring nepantla, el lugar de la frontera," *NACLA Report on the Americas* no. 1, vol. 27 (1993): 39.

67. See Sandoval, "Mestizaje as Method," 359. See also Anzaldúa, *Borderlands*, 38–39.

68. Jon Sobrino, *The Principle of Mercy. Taking the Crucified People from the Cross*, 35–36.

69. On this notion of "truth" see Fornet-Betancourt, *Hacia una filosofía intercultural*, 23–25.

70. Olga Villa-Parra (speech delivered at "Grounding the Next American Century" conference, University of San Diego).

71. This insight comes from Jean-Pierre Ruíz, 8. The "anthological imagination" is also clearly visible among Latina/Chicana feminist scholars who cooperate to assemble reflections and books. On the term *teología de conjunto*, see the glossary in *From the Heart of Our People*, ed. Espín and Díaz, 263.

72. See Fornet-Betancourt, *Hacia una filosofía intercultural*.

73. For additional theological background on this paragraph see my "Theological Method," 23–32.

74. María Pilar Aquino, "Salvation/Liberation," in *Our Theology: Manual de Teología Latina en los EE.UU.*, ed. Allan Figueroa Deck, Ismael García et al.

75. For further reading on "salvation" as "liberation" see Ignacio Ellacuría, "The Historicity of Christian Salvation," in *Mysterium Liberationis. Fundamental Concepts of Liberation Theology*, ed. Ignacio Ellacuría, S.J., and

Jon Sobrino, S.J., 251–289; and Ignacio Ellacuría, "Salvación en la Historia," in *Conceptos Fundamentales del Cristianismo*, ed. Casiano Floristán and Juan José Tamayo, 1252–1274.

76. Schüssler Fiorenza, *Jesus Miriam's Child*, 27.

77. Orlando O. Espín, *The Faith of the People. Theological Reflections on Popular Catholicism*, 4–5, and "An Exploration into the Theology of Grace and Sin," in *From the Heart of Our People*, ed. Espín and Díaz, 127–132.

78. On the term "popular" as analytical category see Helio Gallardo, "Notas sobre la sociedad civil," Revista *Pasos* 57 (1995): 24.

79. María Pilar Aquino, "Perspectives on a Latina's Feminist Liberation Theology," in *Frontiers of Hispanic Theology in the United States*, ed. Allan Figueroa Deck, 23–40.

80. Copeland, "Method in Emerging Black Catholic Theology," 121.

81. Zipporah G. Glass, "The Language of Mestizaje in a Renewed Rhetoric of Black Theology," *Journal of Hispanic/Latino Theology* 7, no. 2 (November 1999): 32–42.

82. National Conference of Catholic Bishops Secretariat for Hispanic Affairs, "Demographics."

CHAPTER 8

THE UNNAMED WOMAN
JUSTICE, FEMINISTS, AND THE
UNDOCUMENTED WOMAN

DAISY L.
MACHADO

The person of Hagar in the Genesis narrative has been used as a symbol by womanists. Delores Williams finds similarities between the story of Hagar and the reality of African-American women, especially Hagar's role as slave who is sexually used by her master and is mistreated by the master's wife.[1] The story of Hagar is one filled with pain and human failing. It is a multi-vocal story that speaks to the reader on many levels, and the tale it tells is one that encompasses gender, race, abuse of power, shame, cultural values, and social roles.

Yet when speaking from my social and geographic location, as a Latina who lives in the borderlands of Texas, I discover in the narrative of the *unnamed woman* found in Judges 19 a biblical paradigm that talks about the reality of the world in which I live and in which the *undocumented woman* can be found.[2] In my own reading, Hagar is not only a slave, she is also a foreigner, alien, outsider whose outside legal status only increases her vulnerability.

The concubine of the Judges narrative shows us the horrors of violence inflicted upon a woman who, though not a slave, is, like Hagar, a foreigner, outsider. The marginal legal status of the concubine leaves her defenseless, voiceless, and ultimately meaningless. I do not intend the biblical narrative to parallel the thousands of stories of women who cross the southern border into the United States, women who come to *el norte* from Mexico, Central America, and the Caribbean seeking to find safety, shelter, food, and the hope of a new life.

However, the stories of the women I have met in South Texas, in the various shelters there and the INS center in Port Isabel,[3] contain many of the horrific elements of this tragic biblical narrative. Shrouded in the cloak of invisibility created by their poverty and non-legal alien status, these women, like the unnamed woman in the Bible, are powerless and vulnerable. And like the unnamed woman, thousands of the undocumented women who cross the border into the United States have faced rape, violence, and even torture. Yet they remain faceless to us, hard to envision; their pain and suffering go unnoticed. These women fade and recede further into the margins of this society. Their humanity and their plight are lost to us in the politicized anti-immigrant public discourse so prevalent across the nation. They remain *unnamed* and mostly *unprotected*. They belong to us, though, to the community of all women who, motivated by faith and a strong commitment to justice, believe that these voiceless and displaced women are our sisters. These women represent us. They are us because like us they are created in the image of God. And above all the injustice that afflicts them is not only an affront to their humanity and dignity but also a challenge to our own gender-based discourse about justice and the self-worth of women across the globe.

In this essay I want to invite the reader to examine the issues related to the undocumented alien in the United States. I want to talk about the border and its levels of meaning—geographic, emotional, racial, cultural, linguistic. I want to talk about immigration as a movement of displaced people and place it in a more global context. I also want to examine the heightened anti-immigrant attitudes that seem to be everywhere in North America in an effort to understand the historical and racial factors that help keep them alive. But first I want to share the story of one undocumented woman. I want to share her story to give this woman and all undocumented women a public voice. Her silence must be broken if we can ever hope to claim a truly liberative woman's discourse about justice and inclusivity. I want to give the unnamed woman a name. I want to give her a face. I want her to become real to us and not remain simply a number in the endless statistics kept by the INS on illegal border crossers.

THE BIBLICAL NARRATIVE: JUDGES 19

The narrative in Judges 19 is considered by Phyllis Tribble as one of four "texts of terror" found in the Hebrew Bible.[4]

It depicts the horrors of male power, brutality, and triumphalism; of female helplessness, abuse, and annihilation. To hear this story is to inhabit a world of unrelenting terror that refuses to let us pass by on the other side. Belonging to the close of the book of Judges, the story reflects a time when leaders were lacking, God seldom appeared, and chaos reigned among the Israelite tribes.[5x]

The narrative revolves around two central characters. One is the Levite who was "sojourning in the remote hill country of Ephraim" (19:1); the second is his concubine. This woman, simply called a concubine in the text, is the Levite's secondary wife as demonstrated in verses 4, 7, and 9, where the Levite is called the woman's husband and her father is called the Levite's father-in-law. This distinction is important because as a secondary wife she is a "woman subject to her husband's control and answerable to his directives."[6] Her namelessness is also significant because it is a "marker of a woman's subordination in the biblical text."[7] Indeed the concubine does not utter one word in the entire narrative.

The story unfolds when the concubine makes a decision to leave her husband, the Levite. By making this decision the woman moves from object to subject, and it is an unexpected action by a woman who had no control over her life and destiny. The text itself is unclear about why she leaves. Two manuscript traditions have survived and offer two explanations for the concubine's leaving.

The Hebrew (MT) and Syriac claim that "his concubine played the harlot" against the Levite, while the Greek and Old Latin maintain that "his concubine became angry with him" . . . Ancient manuscripts give contradictory answers; the story itself allows either reading. All versions agree, however, upon the second action of the concubine: she left the Levite for "her father's house at Bethlehem in Judah and was there some four months" (19:2; cf. 19:3b).[8]

The Levite follows the woman to her father's house in Bethlehem with the purpose of bringing her back to his house. Indeed, as the Judges 19 story unfolds, we find that its entire plot concerns the concubine's inability to exert any control over her own fate.[9] Her father receives the Levite with joy and raises no objections. After five days of feasting in his father-in-law's house the Levite fulfills his mission by taking the woman with him. It does not seem to matter what the woman wants. Whatever autonomy she had sought to manifest in running away in the first place is easily quashed.[10] The Levite's party goes as far as the village of Gibeah, where they decide to spend the night. They have some problems finding a place to sleep, and eventually an old man from "the hill country of Ephraim" takes them in (v. 16).

It is worth noting that this entire episode takes place in the village of Gibeah, where the Levite and his concubine are foreigners or aliens. As a further ironic twist, the Ephraimite, the only person who offers them hospitality, is himself a sojourner in the town. We find a sojourner offering hospitality to other sojourners, thereby fulfilling the social obligation the natives of the town would not. However, because the Ephraimite is in this town temporarily his offer of hospitality is itself limited.

The Levite and the concubine may have a place to sleep, but there is no guarantee of their safety. This stands in direct contrast to the nights spent in the house of the concubine's father in Bethlehem. There the father-in-law is on native soil. His hospitality is not limited, and the couple were safe. And it is at this point in the narrative that the horror begins.

That night a group of men come to the house of the Ephraimite demanding that the Levite come out so "they may know him" (v. 22). The old man refuses to endanger the Levite and instead offers the men his virgin daughter and the concubine. Once again we find women in a position of powerlessness over their own fate. For the concubine, her secondary status makes her even more vulnerable and leaves her defenseless. Such is her condition that even this Ephraimite, who has no direct authority over her, can still subject her to his will. When the men refuse the women, the Levite himself pushes his concubine out the door and puts her life in peril.

She is a pawn in the hands of men, and, like a pawn on a chess board, she is valuable only up to a point. If it becomes necessary, the man in control of her movements is willing to sacrifice her in the interest of protecting his more important pieces, in this case, himself.[11]

The concubine must face her attackers alone, and the night's terrors are about to begin. She is raped and tortured throughout the night, and no one comes to her aid. Finally, when the sun comes up the woman is released. She manages to return to the house of the

Ephraimite, where she falls at the doorway. Violated and betrayed, she has nowhere else to go. She is in an unknown town, an alien with no one to care for her. Daybreak discovers this terrible crime against the concubine.

The Levite, who opens the door because he was preparing to leave the village, finds her collapsed by the doorway "with her hands on the threshold" (v. 27) as if trying to claim for herself a final space of safety and acceptance. His words are cruel. He tells her to get up, but there is no answer. The Levite shows no remorse for his actions the night before nor compassion for the tortured and discarded woman lying before him.

Her silence, be it exhaustion or death, deters the master not at all. What he set out to do in the light of the morning, he does. Putting her on the donkey, "the man rose up and he went away to his place" . . . His mission is completed, though not as the narrator proposed it.[12]

Once home the Levite wastes no time and taking a knife he cuts her limb by limb and distributes the twelve pieces throughout the territory of Israel. The cycle of violence against the concubine is complete.

Neither the other characters nor the narrator recognizes her humanity. She is property, object, tool, and literary device. Without name, speech, or power, she has no friends to aid her in life or mourn her in death . . . Captured, betrayed, raped, tortured, murdered, dismembered, and scattered—this woman is the most sinned against.[13]

The story concludes (v. 30) with three imperatives for the people of Israel: consider what you have seen, take counsel on what action to take, and speak. The imperatives are a challenge to respond to the suffering of the dead woman. To remain silent is to condone the violence and terror. Silence covers complicity. For today's reader the imperative challenges women of faith to respond yet again.

When we direct our hearts to her, what counsel can we take? What word can we speak? . . . First of all, we can recognize the contemporaneity of the story. Misogyny belongs to every age, including our own . . . Woman as object is still captured, betrayed, raped, tortured, murdered, dismembered, and scattered. To take to heart this ancient story, then, is to confess its present reality. The story is alive and all is not well.[14]

A PERSONAL NARRATIVE: THE STORY OF ELENA[15]

In March 1999 I made a trip with a group of seminary students to South Texas. This class was to be an "immersion experience" for twelve seminary students that would introduce them, face to face, with the realities of life along the U.S.-Mexico border. One of the sites we visited was *Proyecto el Buen Samaritano* (Good Samaritan Project), which is housed in a Latino Christian Church (Disciples of Christ) congregation in Los Fresnos called Iglesia Cristiana Ebenezer. The pastor of this small congregation, the Reverend F. Feliberto Pereira, is himself a sojourner in South Texas. Having spent some years in a concentration camp in Cuba, upon his release he came to the United States, where he reentered the ministry serving in the Christian Church. He came to South Texas twenty-five years ago and has for all those years focused his ministry and the resources of both the congregation and the denomination on the needs of the immigrants who arrive daily.

The Rev. Pereira believes that as an immigrant who has suffered violence, he is called to help the many others who come to this country having left all they know and love behind and who now face an unknown future. He is the founder and director of the Good Samaritan Project, which not only provides temporary shelter for women and men who have crossed the border but also with food and clothing. The Rev. Pereira, who is well-known to other people and organizations involved in immigrant/border issues, also helps to get many of the women and men who come to the church pro bono legal aid, medical care, counseling, and pastoral care. The church buildings that house the project have been built through the volunteer labor of hundreds of congregational mission groups that have traveled to South Texas through the years. They are simple wooden structures, well-maintained, and are known by almost everyone in the nearby communities to be a safe place for the undocumented immigrant.

In stark contrast to the simple facilities that house this project, the many large Euro-American church facilities near Los Fresnos have larger buildings and many more physical amenities but are closed to the immigrant. They offer no hospitality, no safe place, no welcome at their doors.

I met Elena, a 29-year-old native of El Salvador, and her two young children at the Good Samaritan Project. She had been in the country less than a year when we met. Her son was in kindergarten and was spending mornings away from his mother. He was learning English, and Elena's face showed great pride in the little boy who kissed her goodbye to leave for school. Her second child was a daughter who was still breastfeeding and was about two years old. She was a quiet child, clinging to her mother, suspicious of strangers. Elena explained that she believed her daughter acted this way because she was pregnant with her when she experienced the great violence in her life.

It was difficult for Elena to just sit and talk. She nervously cleared the breakfast table as I waited to speak with her. She kept her back toward me, and I realized that she was embarrassed for me to sit across from her and look directly at her face. Elena had no idea it was just as hard for me to look directly at her. As a matter of fact it took great effort on my part to conceal my shock when we were first introduced by the Rev. Pereira. I was embarrassed at my reaction and hoped that I had managed to keep my facial expressions under control when we shook hands. You see, Elena had no nose on her face. Between her soft brown eyes was a gaping wound.

When Elena finally sat down, she picked up her daughter and began to breastfeed her. I understood the comfort of this act for Elena. These two children were all the family she had left in the world. To hold her child close to her, the very act of feeding her child from her own body must have provided her with a sense of hope. Her future was uncertain, and she was waiting to hear from the INS about her second petition for asylum. She had already been turned down once. The INS had doubts that if Elena returned to El Salvador she would face persecution, torture, or death. Elena expressed her great sense of frustration. "Look at my face. Anyone who looks at my face knows that if I return to El Salvador I will be killed by the same men that did this to me." The INS, however, believed otherwise. I then asked Elena to tell me what happened. She began to breathe deeply, and I noticed that her hands trembled. The little girl who had begun to fall asleep as she drank her mother's milk opened her eyes as if awakened by the tension and apprehension visible in her mother's entire body. Elena's story was not only difficult for her to share with me but also difficult for me to hear.

Elena was raised in a country village in El Salvador. She was young during the great military and political upheavals that shattered her country during the 1980s; however, a decade later she still could not escape the violence. Her husband and some of her brothers, neighbors, and friends had been suspected and accused by the military of being anti-government guerrillas. Military personnel began to visit their village, and soon the men hid in the countryside. In an effort to find out where the men were hiding, Elena was taken by the soldiers and forced to talk. She told me of the rapes despite the fact her pregnancy was visible. She told how one of the soldiers inserted the end of his weapon into her vagina. Her husband and all the men were found by the soldiers, and in a voice consumed with pain, Elena told me how she was forced to watch her husband being shot to death before her eyes. She described the terror of feeling the weight of his lifeless body collapse onto hers.

When it was all over, Elena had lost her husband, her family, her community. She explained that the soldiers told her they were letting her live, and then she told me of the pain as they began to cut off her nose. Elena was being made into a living human "billboard" to remind dissenters of the fate that awaited anyone who opposed the government. I waited for Elena to compose herself, barely able to grasp the violence, horror, and terror of her story. She was not describing events that took place at the height of the great Central American bloodshed of the mid- to late 1980s. What Elena had experienced and was telling me had taken place in 1997!

Elena's story stood in stark contradiction to the claims of the U.S. government that in Central America peace had been finally won, government repression had ended, and countries were on the mend. The countries of Central America do not make it into the U.S. English-language news media any more. Except for the disaster from Hurricane Mitch in 1999, which hit Honduras hardest, Central America seemed to have fallen off the U.S. radar. The U.S. public had truly accepted the axiom that no news is good news. Elena is living proof this was not so. She is living proof that government repression and torture continue unabated in El Salvador.

Like the unnamed woman, Elena had no control over her fate. Like the unnamed woman, her value to those soldiers was relative and could be again—if they needed to, they would kill her. She had no value to these men except as a means to frighten others and to make visible their capacity for violence. Her rape and her torture were done as a show of power and domination. And like the unnamed woman whose body was dismembered and then sent to the tribes, Elena's nose was cut off and the disfigurement used to send a message to her community. Elena had no protection. Elena had no one to turn to.

Frightened and alone, Elena took her two children and left El Salvador, arriving at the "threshold" of the U.S.-Mexican border seeking a space of safety and acceptance. What I know of Elena today is that she has still not been deported and continues to fight to stay in the United States. Her pro bono lawyers are doing what they can to show the INS that there is reason to believe that Elena's life is in peril if she returns to El Salvador. She is still powerless. She is still vulnerable. She has no control over the outcome of her petition for asylum. She is an undocumented woman, an illegal border-crosser who broke the law when she entered the United States with no visa. She is the unwanted illegal immigrant who must wait in South Texas while those in power decide over her ultimate fate.

THE BORDER AS REGION

I want to talk about the border. I am both fascinated and frightened by the geographical markings on a map that are transformed into the concrete immigration plazas where documents are checked and one gets the sense that "Big Brother is watching." In Texas the Border Patrol takes the U.S.-Mexican border very seriously, and the militarization of this southern border is one that makes me shudder. The military gear worn by Border Patrol personnel, the rifles they carry, the trained dogs, and the bright lights that make nighttime at the border seem like noon, all these are reminders that the possibility of violence is always there.

However, what is truly interesting to me is that the U.S.-Mexico border remains a 2,000-mile stretch of a "thin, porous membrane"[16] that people cross and sometimes remain, as if suspended, awaiting the next step in their life's journey.

[W]e are learning that the U.S. / Mexico Border is a region unto itself, one that supersedes the more abstract state boundaries on either side and which is considered by the powers that be—whether in Washington, D.C.; México, D.F.; Austin, Texas; or Sacramento, CA—as irrelevant except as a place of passage for goods and people. We find that we are living in a "de-constitutionalized" zone where the Bill of Rights can be ignored because of "sovereignty" issues (illegal immigration, drug smuggling, etc.) or just because the border region is poor and, in vast areas, sparsely populated. The region becomes disenfranchised, and the wishes and well-being of its citizens ignored. As a matter of habit and convenience, border residents get left holding the dirty end of the stick.[17]

So the border becomes a place where human lives are in a very real way trapped, whether for a few days or months or even years, in a reality that is filled with human suffering, poverty, neglect, and despair.

In Texas all you need to do is walk the streets of places like Austin, Dallas or Houston, then spend the same amount of time wandering through Browns-ville, Laredo or El Paso. Compare the institutions and public works that require state and federal funding—schools, highways, and universities—and you'll witness first hand the difference between power and impotence.[18]

Statistics show that in the South Texas valley, 39.7 percent of all Latinos live below the official U.S. government poverty level; that 35 percent of the total workforce is unemployed; that 57 percent of the adult residents have not completed high school; that 36.5 percent of all housing is substandard; and that 11 percent of all South Texas valley residents live in *colonias*, most of which lack water, electric-ity, sewerage, paved roads, and adequate police and fire protection.[19]

Perhaps this is why Chicana writer Gloria Anzaldúa calls the border "an open wound." It seems to have no healing as thousands of women, children, and men continue to cross to *el norte* in search of what cannot be found on native soil. However, once having crossed the border, they find a reality experienced nowhere else in the nation. To talk about the border necessitates the inclusion of the theme of immigration and of the undocumented immigrant. To talk about the immigrant and immigration in the context of the borderlands of the United States means to also talk about national attitudes toward the sojourner (foreigner or alien). It is a complex conversation. It makes many Euro-Americans uncomfortable, and the irony is a clear and bitter one: in this nation, created by immigrants and waves of immigration, there is a fear and even hatred of the immigrant.

For Chicano writer Rubén Martínez there is a long history in this country of a love/hate relationship with the Latino immigrant in the borderland states. He writes that what this love/hate relation-ship is about is "loving the cheap labor, hating the natural conse-quence of Anglos having to share space—and a slice of the economic pie—with big Spanish-speaking, mostly Catholic families."[20] Much of this has been shaped and continues to be fueled by the national self-perceptions held by North Americans.[21] These self-perceptions can be traced to the arrival of the first Western Europeans to this hemisphere.

The European settlers came to conquer and in the process "in-vented" a new reality.[22] A key element of this new reality was the de-velopment of the particular concept of U.S. nationalism that was tied to the idea of belonging to a group of people, a nation, chosen to fulfill the unique task of settling and "civilizing" a "wild frontier" where the non-chosen or "outsiders" were to be conquered or eliminated. The racism inherent in this nationalism is obvious, and its hold on the United States has been difficult to eliminate.

The history of Texas, for example, is the story of the reconquest of the Mexican people who were identified as outsiders and relegated to this status through racism and segregation, which also guaranteed their poverty. As most were Spanish-speaking Roman Catholics, their language and religion further distanced them from the dominant groups. This notion of the Mexican-American as un-American has today been extended to immigrants from Central and South America. Many in the dominant culture see these immigrants as unwanted people.

Clearly the largest influx of immigrants coming across the U.S.-Mexican border throughout the 1980s was from Central America.

One recent study estimates that three-quarters of a million to 1.3 million Central American migrants are living in the United States. The U.S. General Accounting office estimates the number of undocumented Salvadoreans in the United States at six to eight hundred thousand.[23]

The question most people ask is, "Why do these people migrate?" It must be made clear that every decision to leave one's country is a difficult one and not made lightly.

The combined effects of political crisis, war, and the economic crisis aggravated by political conditions have transformed a normal migration flow into massive displacement and exodus. In terms of internal displacement, it has been estimated, that by 1987 up to a million Central Americans (including a quarter-million Nicaraguans, one hundred thousand to a quarter-million Guatemalans, and a half million Salvadoreans) had been displaced within their own countries.[24]

Coming across the U.S.-Mexican border were not just immigrants looking for a better economic future for themselves and their families, but a displaced people ravaged by war and military violence, people whose lives, psyches, and hopes had been shattered by an external violence fueled by U.S. foreign policy related to the fear of the spread of communism throughout Central America.

The issue of forced migration is a fundamental issue of basic human rights on several levels. The Universal Declaration of Human Rights states that individuals have a fundamental right to live free of governmental persecution and to leave their country of origin . . . [However] the right to grant asylum is a right reserved to governments . . . The delicate process of balancing state rights against individual rights is an unresolved issue which is brought to the fore by the analysis of uprooted people.[25]

Research shows that many people are displaced and uprooted from their nations of origin to become part of different flows of refugees for three key reasons: some refugees form a politically induced flow; other refugees migrate because of underdevelopment; and still more seek relief from an oppressive combination of forces. "The relationship between economic underdevelopment and repressive political institutions is a close (albeit poorly understood) one, but it cannot be ignored in trying to understand the causes of forced migration."[26] These three factors—politics, underdevelopment, and repression—all played and continue to play key roles in the migration of millions of Central Americans to the United States.

A CALL TO JUSTICE

The reality of a national self-perception shaped by an exclusive mentality that segregates, stereotypes, all the while denigrating, means that to talk about the undocumented woman in the borderlands of the United States one must also talk about justice. How is justice, as preached by the Hebrew prophets and promised by God, made manifest in this border region to the immigrant who is female and undocumented and therefore an illegal immigrant?

In talking about justice, Karen Lebacqz says that "[t]here will be no single way of defining justice and no single theory of justice that satisfies all."[27] Accepting Lebacqz's claim about the variety of approaches to justice, I will use the model put forth by liberation theologians which begins with praxis and which includes a "dialectical reflection: reflecting on practice in the light of faith and on faith in the light of practice."[28] In this reflection the bias is for the poor and the oppressed. Here again the terms are redefined so that the poor are not only those who are materially deprived but also those who are marginalized by the dominant society. The marginalized are poor and in many ways are forced to keep their poverty because they lack "full access to and participation in socio-economic and political processes."[29]

The undocumented immigrant woman belongs to the group of those whom Gustavo Gutiérrez calls "nonpersons." These nonpersons are "suffering misery and exploitation, deprived of the most elemental human rights, scarcely aware that they are human beings at all."[30] As she sits in the detention center in Port Isabel, Texas, this woman has little to say about her future. As she works in the fields or cleans someone's home or cleans tables in a restaurant or sews in a sweatshop, this woman lives in the constant fear of losing all she has if her undocumented status were detected or if the INS were alerted to her presence. She is the ultimate outsider with no alternatives, no legal rights, no voice, no access to protection from those who have the power to exploit her labor or even her body. Fear, humiliation, exploitation, poverty, and even physical abuse are part of her reality, and to talk about justice for these women means to call into question the very structures of our society that are capable of such injustice.

The undocumented immigrant woman, her suffering, and her struggle cannot be omitted from what women are saying in their theological, ethical, and political discourse. The undocumented immigrant woman's voice must be included in the social analysis we do as women, for she is performing the innumerable underpaid menial jobs that help contribute to the lifestyle of comfort and privilege so many enjoy in this country. As we move into the new millennium, the critical perspectives feminists and womanists have developed on society and its patriarchal structures must be broadened to include the plight and reality of the most marginal in our midst, the undocumented woman. To exclude these women from the analysis being done by feminists and womanists has consequences for the entire field of women's studies which "ultimately . . . prevent[s] a full understanding of gender and society."[31]

There is a blind spot in our discourse on justice that does not allow us to see the vast number of truly voiceless and unnamed undocumented women who live within this nation's borders. It seems that rarely, if ever, have undocumented women been treated as explicit subjects of the concerns of women in theology. I think this is related to what I have already said about the national self-perceptions that still influence our discourse, no matter how progressive it may be. Women, feminists and womanists, still speak from a culturally and historically shaped social location that in very real ways limits their perspective.

Linda S. Bosniak, addressing the absence of a focus on the issue of justice in the debates over Proposition 187, also makes some observations to help explain why those whom she calls "progressives" had such a limited perspective. I think her analysis helps to further clarify what I believe is happening within the discourse of women in theology.

Here is the problem: Despite progressives' commitment to challenging systemic forms of subordination and marginalization, the political and legal landscape they are concerned with is most often a national landscape, and the boundaries they seek to dismantle are, most often, political and legal boundaries that exist within the already bounded community of the nation-state. Most progressive scholarship produced in this country devotes nearly exclusive attention to relationships among people who are already presumed to be national community members . . . Sometimes, this frame is made explicit, as when scholars directly invoke the United States or "America" or the constitutional Republic as their community of normative concern.[32]

As long as women uncritically hold to and accept the belief in the legitimacy of national borders, the scholarship and social analysis they make about justice and about the community of women in the nation will be incomplete. This is because "it is precisely enforcement of these borders which produces the immigrants' powerlessness here in the first place."[33] As Bosniak explains,

Even if undocumented immigrants are not specifically denied access to education and health care, and other social services . . . the constant threat of deportation will continue to structure their lives in this country, and will ensure their continued marginalization and domination.[34]

While we in the theological academy enjoy the luxury of time in which to research and write, and while we have available to us a space in which to share our ideas, the urgency of the reality of the unnamed women of the border challenges us to rethink what our task is about. Elena's disfigured face is a witness to the violence, vulnerability, powerlessness so many women experience. She is no longer a statistic. You know her story. You have seen her face. You have heard her voice. The biblical imperative calls to us: consider what you have seen, take counsel on what action to take, and speak.

NOTES

1. Delores S. Williams, *Sisters in the Wilderness, The Challenge of Womanist God-Talk*, 1–12.

2. While I will not address the issue of the undocumented immigrant who is male, this does not mean that he does not suffer many of the same realities as the undocumented immigrant who is female. However, the issue of gender is one that is very important because being female increases the level of vulnerability of the immigrant and makes her situation more precarious.

3. The U.S. Immigration and Naturalization Service (INS), under the Department of Justice, has oversight for the U.S. Border Patrol, which polices the borders of this country. The largest detention center for undocumented migrants (known as *el corralón* or the "big corral") is located in Port Isabel, Texas. Here women and men await their deportation hearings.

4. Phyllis Tribble, *Texts of Terror*, 65–91. See also Susan Ackerman, *Warrior, Dancer, Seductress: Women in Judges and Biblical Israel*, 216–252.

5. Tribble, *Texts of Terror*, 65.

6. Ackerman, *Warrior, Dancer*, 236.

7. Ibid., 236.

8. Tribble, *Texts of Terror*, 66, 67.

9. Ackerman, *Warrior, Dancer*, 237.

10. Ibid., 237.

11. Ibid., 238.

12. Tribble, *Texts of Terror*, 79.

13. Ibid., 81.

14. Ibid., 86–87.

15. The name of the woman whose story this is has been changed.

16. Bobby Byrd and Susannah Byrd, eds., *The Late Great Mexican Border*, viii.

17. Ibid., viii–ix.

18. Ibid., ix.

19. *Catholic Ministry*, a newsletter published by the Diocese of Brownsville, Texas, February 1991.

20. Rubén Martínez, "The Undocumented Virgin," in *Goddess of the Americas. La Diosa de las Américas*, ed. Ana Castillo, 104.

21. I use the term "North American" when talking about the people of the United States. I hold that to use the term "American" to refer to U.S. residents is chauvinistic and denies the reality that there are millions of other *americanos* who also inhabit this western hemisphere known as the "Americas."

22. See Myra Jehlen, *American Incarnation: The Individual, The Nation, and the Continent*. Jehlen uses Edmundo O'Gorman's idea that the discovery of America (meaning the United States) was really an "invention," that is a "construction by history." See pages 22–42.

23. Nora Hamilton and Norma Stoltz Chinchilla, "Central American Migration: A Framework for Analysis," in *Challenging Fronteras: Structuring Latina and Latino Lives in the U.S.: An Anthology of Readings*, ed. Mary Romero, Pierrette Hondagneu-Sotelo, and Vilma Ortiz, 91.

24. Ibid., 90.

25. Elizabeth G. Ferris, *Beyond Borders: Refugees, Migrants, and Human Rights in the Post-Cold War Era*, xxi–xxii.

26. Ibid., xxii.

27. Karen Lebacqz, *Six Theories of Justice*, 9.

28. Ibid., 101.

29. Ibid.

30. Ibid.

31. Maxine Baca Zinn, Lynn Weber et al., "The Costs of Exclusionary Practices in Women's Studies," in *Making Face, Making Soul, Haciendo Caras*, ed. Gloria Anzaldúa, 33.

32. Linda S. Bosniak, "Undocumented Immigrants and the National Imagination," in *The Latino/a Condition, A Critical Reader*, ed. Richard Delgado and Jean Stefancic, 103.

33. Ibid., 103.

34. Ibid., 104.

CHAPTER 9

**JUSTICE CROSSES
THE BORDER**
THE PREFERENTIAL
OPTION FOR THE POOR
IN THE UNITED STATES

CARMEN
MARIE NANKO

Since Medellin in particular, the Church, clearly aware
of its mission and loyally open to dialogue, has been
scrutinizing the signs of the times and is generously
disposed to evangelize in order to contribute to the construction of a new society that is more fraternal and
just; such a society is a crying need of our peoples.
Thus the mutual forces of tradition and progress, which
once seemed to be antagonistic in Latin America, are
now joining each other and seeking a new, distinctive
synthesis that will bring together the possibilities of the
future and the energies derived from our common roots.
And so, within this vast process of renewal that is inau-
gurating a new epoch in Latin America, and amid the
challenges of recent times, we pastors are taking up the
age-old episcopal tradition of Latin America and preparing ourselves to carry the Gospel's message of salvation
hopefully and bravely to all human beings, but to the
poorest and most forgotten by way of preference.[1]

CELAM, Puebla, 1979

Arising from the heart of the Latin American
experience, the expression "preferential option
for the poor" appeared on the horizon in 1979 at
Puebla de Los Angeles, Mexico, in the final document of the Third General Conference of the
Latin American Episcopate.[2] More than a year
later, it was repeatedly affirmed by name by Pope

John Paul II during his 1980 visit to Brazil. In his July 10, 1980 address to the Brazilian bishops, he explained:

You know that the preferential option for the poor was strongly proclaimed at Puebla. It is not a call to exclusiveness, it is not a justification for the bishop to omit to announce the word of conversion and salvation to one or another group of persons on the pretext that they are not poor. After all, what is the context that we do give this term? . . . it is a call to special oneness with the small and weak, those that suffer and weep, those that are humiliated and left on the margin of life and society.[3]

In its journey across the Americas, the notion of preferential option as articulated at Puebla faced and continues to face the problems associated with border crossings—detainment and misunderstanding—as well as the challenges of creating a new life in a new place and transforming the place of encounter. In the encounter with the United States, the question raised echoes the question of John Paul II in Brazil, "After all, what is the context that we do give to this term?"[4]

Within the context of U.S. Hispanic/Latino/a theology, the principle of the preferential option for the poor is appropriated as a foundational characteristic of theologies of liberation. In the words of María Pilar Aquino, we "must reaffirm that the option for the poor and oppressed does not belong to a past theological paradigm; rather, it remains a fundamental Christian imperative—a required norm for the protection of our rationality."[5] It is precisely this significance that invites a closer examination of the mediation and appropriation of this principle within the United States. Therefore, this essay traces the use of the expression through representative pastoral statements by U.S. bishops, individually and collectively. This will make it possible to gauge a context for ascertaining the current level of understanding, communication, reception, and appropriation of the preferential option for the poor within the Roman Catholic Church in the United States. If this principle is to transform the place of encounter and in turn be transformed by its appropriation in this new place, then it is crucial to the ongoing conversation to track its journey.

A survey of the signs of the times suggests the urgency with which the preferential options for the poor *and the young* must be revisited and re-imagined within the context of the United States, in particular from the perspectives of Latino/a theologians whose reflections tend to privilege *lo cotidiano*, everyday experience. Statistics provide a window into the complexities that constitute the daily reality of U.S. Hispanic experiences. Theologians need to contend with these glimpses, as they often prove to be signs of contradiction.

The Census Bureau reports that Latino/a life is characterized by approximately one in four households living in poverty, yet the poverty rate in the U.S. declined in 1999 for the third consecutive year with all measured racial and ethnic groups setting or equaling historic lows. For Hispanics this translates into a drop of six hundred thousand, leaving 22.8 percent of the Latino/a population in poverty, the lowest percentage recorded since 1979.[6] As of 1998, Hispanic children constituted the largest minority group of youth in the United States, and one-third of these children are growing up poor in homes headed by females. Women do not fare well, as 46 percent struggle to survive on incomes below $10,000, in comparison to 24 percent of Latino men.[7] At the same time, the discretionary income of U.S. Hispanics is greater than the Gross Domestic Product of Mexico, and Latino/a purchasing power grows at a rate of more than $1 billion every three weeks.[8]

In the United States, the digital divide has descended into a "racial ravine" where the information rich outpace the information poor with cyberspeed, yet gender disparity in Internet usage has virtually disappeared. Discrepancies in access, abetted by the cost factor, take a toll on minorities and female-headed households that utilize the Internet to conduct job searches and pursue on-line courses in order to improve current status. While "no one should be left behind as our nation advances into the 21st Century, where having access to computers and the Internet may be key to becoming a successful member of society," the reality is that the digital divide remains, impacting those who need the technology the most as a resource.[9]

Theologians can ill afford to ignore the reality that for increasing numbers of U.S. Hispanics, liberation involves upward mobility and an SUV. As Hispanics rapidly move into the vast middle, the experience of Jeff Valdez, creator of the cable television family "The Garcia Brothers," is both enlightening and alarming. The show was test-marketed using two different types of Latino families, recent immigrants struggling to make it versus an assimilated suburban middle-class family. Hispanic focus groups "vociferously voted against the downscale family. They asked, 'Why do we have to always be poor and drive lousy cars and speak in accents?'"[10] The painful

legacy of poverty and the abiding stereotypes call for structural answers and contextual reflection—crucial elements of the transformative praxis of Latino/a theology.

ACROSS THE BORDER: THE U.S. CONTEXT

Prior to the September 1984 "Instruction on Certain Aspects of the
'Theology of Liberation'" by the Congregation for the Doctrine of
the Faith (CDF),[11] references to a preferential option for the poor
appear in the pastoral letters and addresses of the bishops of the
United States sporadically and primarily from those bishops who
were either themselves from under-represented racial and ethnic minority communities or whose ministries were involved with these
communities.

One of the earliest references occurs in an address to the Catholic
Press Association in May 1980 by African-American Bishop James
Lyke, O.F.M., then an auxiliary bishop of Cleveland and a member of
the Committee for the Campaign on Human Development (CHD).
Regarding the experience of the Catholic Church in Latin America
and its predilection for the poor as a learning opportunity for the
Catholic Church in the United States, Lyke presents the efforts of
CHD as an example of a "preferential, though not exclusive, love of
the poor." He cites the criteria for CHD-funded programs as evidence
for this determination. The majority of people served must fall below
the poverty line, the projects must be controlled by the poor, and
"projects should encourage various racial and ethnic groups, as well
as the poor and not so poor, to work together for justice."[12]

From Lyke's perspective, "CHD is a case where the church listens
to the poor and is evangelized by them. The campaign does not dictate the methods to be used . . . CHD receives applications from poverty groups which have themselves designed their own methods
of addressing the causes of their poverty and oppression."[13] Furthermore, CHD funding supports self-help projects that seek to foster
structural change by attacking the causes of poverty or by affect-
ing the legal, policy- and decision-making processes that maintain
poverty.

Essential to the preferential option for the poor, according to Lyke,
is the need to empower the poor, to bring about structural and systemic change, and to appreciate the poor as an evangelizing force.
From his perspective, the poor evangelize the Church by opening eyes
to injustices, sinful structures, and oppressive systems; by communi-

cating a sense of urgency; by inviting a greater fidelity to the Gospel; by calling for a reexamination of lifestyles, especially in terms of consumption; by raising minds and hearts to the social dimensions of the Christian message. The poor "tell us that we are not saved as individuals but as a people and that all doctrine is social doctrine."[14] While remaining optimistic, Lyke recognized that "[m]any of us perhaps feel that it would be a mistake to let the poor evangelize the church, because this would drag the church down. On the contrary, the church would be renewed if we let ourselves be evangelized."[15]

The application of the notion of preferential option for the poor to specific concerns and populations is evident in two statements impacting Hispanics/Latinos/as that appear between 1981 and 1983. Reflecting on 1981 as the 50th anniversary of Pius XI's social encyclical *Quadragesimo Anno*[16] and the 450th anniversary of the appearance of Our Lady Of Guadalupe, the bishops of the Santa Fe province explored three themes that they attribute to Pope Pius XI, themes with particular relevance for their region as the "site of the confluence of three major ethnic cultures—Anglo, Mexican and Native American."[17] One of these themes, the Church's preferential option for the poor, is identified as a "reoccurring papal concern about material poverty," with roots in scripture and the Church's history. For these bishops, to be poor "is to die of hunger, to be illiterate, to be exploited and not know that you are being exploited. To be poor in this context is to be without choices. To be rich and powerful in terms of papal literature is to have a variety of alternatives and options from which a person may choose a course of action."[18]

The bishops insisted that the Church's predilection for persons who are poor or oppressed does not imply the canonization of a particular social class, nor does it offer an assurance of "blanket salvation for the poor and condemnation for the rich."[19] However, they maintained that the option as a response to the sinful human condition of poverty carries social and religious consequences. "Persons with choices and therefore with power can do something to ameliorate the human condition for those in need and thereby contribute to the human development of the impoverished . . . Persons with choices meet the Lord in a special way in the poor and their positive response to them can be personally redemptive, a 'measure' . . . of conscience, a way to the kingdom."[20] This interpretation is illustrated in the encounter between the Virgin Mary and the bishop mediated by Juan Diego, "a lowly Aztec Indian who had no stature in the new society of the Spaniards and who could not even speak Spanish, the language of the bishop."[21] Viewed through the lens of the Tepeyac experience, "the powerful are given the option to respond to God's intention through the presence of the poor."[22]

In the pastoral letter on Hispanic ministry, *The Hispanic Presence: Challenge and Commitment*, approved by the U.S. bishops at their 1983 national meeting, the term appears in a context that appears to identify Hispanics with the poor. "We call all U.S. Catholics to work not just for Hispanics but with them, in order to secure their empowerment in our democracy and the political participation which is their right and duty. In this way we deepen our preferential option for the poor which, according to Jesus' example and the church's tradition, must always be a hallmark of our apostolate (Puebla, 1134)."[23]

The year 1984 emerged as a turning point in terms of the exposure the option for the poor receives in the statements of the U.S. bishops. In early September the CDF released its "Instruction on Certain Aspects of the 'Theology of Liberation.'" The congregation was quick to explain that this warning should not be interpreted as "a disavowal of all those who want to respond generously and with an authentic evangelical spirit to the 'preferential option for the poor' . . . It is, on the contrary, dictated by the certitude that the serious ideological deviations which it points out tend inevitably to betray the cause of the poor."[24] Concerned by interpretations of the option for the poor that "transform the fight for the rights of the poor into a class fight within the ideological perspective of the class struggle,"[25] the CDF also affirms the positive meaning associated with preference given to the poor "without exclusion, whatever the form of their poverty, because they are preferred by God."[26]

In 1984 the option for the poor was very much on the minds of the U.S. bishops, with the November release of the first draft of their pastoral letter on the U.S. economy. The influence of the preferential option for the poor is evident in the three priorities guiding its direction: the basic needs of the poor should be fulfilled; increased participation by the marginalized takes precedence over the preservation of privileged concentrations of power, wealth, and income; and investment should be targeted toward meeting human needs and increasing participation.[27]

First it imposes a prophetic mandate to speak for those who have no one to speak for them, to be a defender of the defenseless . . . It also demands a compassionate vision which enables the church to see things from the side of the poor, to assess lifestyle as well as social institutions and policies in terms of their impact on the poor. Finally and most radically, it calls for an emptying of self, both individually and corporately, that allows the church to experience the power of God in the midst of poverty and powerlessness.[28]

Throughout the draft, preferential option for the poor serves as a frame of reference for shaping the approach toward domestic and international economic issues.

The year 1984 concluded with a strong affirmation of the Church's commitment to the option for the poor by Pope John Paul II in his address to the College of Cardinals and in his Christmas *Urbi et Orbi* message. Acknowledging the emphasis placed on the option by the Latin American bishops and reiterating his own commitment to the poor as a dominant motive of his pastoral action, John Paul II affirmed: "I have made and I do make that 'option' my own; I identify with it."[29] He defended the "Instruction on Certain Aspects of the 'Theology of Liberation'" from distorted interpretations by contending that the document "constitutes an authoritative confirmation of it and effects a clarification and deepening of it at the same time."[30]

After two additional drafts (one in 1985 and another in April 1986), the U.S. bishops' pastoral letter on the U.S. economy, *Economic Justice for All*,[31] was approved in November 1986. In this pastoral, preferential option for the poor is affirmed as a "fundamental criterion for making moral judgments about economic policy."[32] It was understood by the bishops as a moral priority that obliges all members of society to "assess lifestyles, policies, and social institutions in terms of their impact on the poor. This 'option for the poor' does not mean pitting one group against another, but rather, strengthening the whole community by assisting those who are most vulnerable . . . we are called to respond to the needs of *all* our brothers and sisters, but those with the greatest needs require the greatest response."[33]

This meant recognizing as urgent objectives: the fulfillment of the basic needs of the poor, a priority that precedes "the fulfillment of desires for luxury consumer goods, for profits not conducive to the common good, and for unnecessary military hardware;"[34] increased active participation in economic life by those currently excluded or vulnerable; investment of wealth, talent, and energy in efforts benefiting the poor or economically insecure; the evaluation of social and economic policies and the organization of the work world in light of their impact on the stability and integrity of family life.[35]

The attention paid to the poor did not go without notice even in the earliest stages of the drafting process. As Joseph Bernardin, Cardinal Archbishop of Chicago, noted, "The letter makes space in the policy debate for the fate of the poor in a way which has not been evident for some years now. We need to make space for the faces of the poor in our personal consciences and in the public agenda because the facts tell us that poverty is not so marginal in this nation as we might think."[36]

There were noticeable changes from the first draft to the final version in the treatment of preferential option for the poor. *Economic Justice for All* credits the agency of the poor by adding that decisions can be judged not only in terms of what they do *for* and *to* the poor but by "what they enable the poor to do *for themselves.*"[37] Later on they add that the poor are not exempted from the obligations of solidarity and justice. "The guaranteeing of basic justice for all is not an optional expression of largesse but an inescapable duty of the whole of society."[38]

In November 1996, the U.S. bishops approved a one-page anniversary statement, *A Catholic Framework for Economic Life*, outlining ten principles drawn from Catholic teaching on the economy. Third on the list was that "a fundamental moral measure of any economy is how the poor and vulnerable are faring."[39]

In his remarks introducing the framework to the bishops, Bishop William Skylstad, chair of the Committee on Domestic Policy, suggested that it "calls us to focus on moral principles, not the latest polls; on the needs of the weak, not the contributions of the strong; and the pursuit of the common good, not the narrow agendas of powerful economic interests . . . We need to be very clear. Our defense of the poor, our pursuit of economic justice is fundamentally a work of faith."[40] Who are the "least of these" whose lives and dignity are to be defended?

This is about children of God with names and faces, with hopes and fears. This is about the women who are cleaning our hotel rooms this morning for the minimum wage. This is about immigrants who will bus our dishes this afternoon. This is about the people who knock on our rectory doors, rely on our food pantries and live in cardboard boxes under bridges. This is about children dying in Africa this morning. This is not about the president or the speaker of the House. It's about people who make our sneakers and haul our trash. It's about people in corporate America trying to resist short-term pressures for long-term contributions to the common good. It's about the 55-year-old executive who is downsized and the family farmer who can't make it anymore.[41]

He concludes by reminding his brother bishops that ten years after their pastoral on the economy there was still work to do, and he urges them to support and actively utilize this latest tool in applying and sharing the economic teaching of the Church in the United States.

MAPPING THE TRENDS

Twenty years after the introduction of the preferential option for the poor into the theological and pastoral vocabulary and thirteen years after the formalization of the principle in the consciousness of the U.S. bishops, there is striking evidence that while this option was born in the heart of the Americas, the journey north has met with obstacles. The difficulty in appropriating the principle in the United States is evident in the bishops' 1998 document on the implementation of social teaching on all levels of Catholic education. Acknowledging that the Church's social teaching must no longer be treated as tangential or optional, the bishops admit that many Catholics do not comprehend these teachings as essential to the faith. Recognizing the power of education as integral to the transmission of this social mission and message, the bishops are also aware that "in too many schools and classrooms these principles are often vaguely presented; these values are unclear; these lessons are unlearned."[42]

This challenge to understanding is in part due to the manner in which discourse about preferential option for the poor has been framed, communicated, and understood. It can even be argued that the option for the poor crossed into the United States via Alitalia with the papal statements and curial pronouncements as primary vectors. Prior to 1984, attempts were made to credit the Catholic Church in Latin America for its instrumental role in articulating the principle. Yet the distancing of the concept of the preferential option for the poor from its Latin American roots also begins early in the U.S. formulations.

The first draft of the U.S. bishops' pastoral on the economy mentions the emergence of the expression at Puebla as significant to Church thought. In an address at The Catholic University of America in Washington, D.C., shortly after the release of that draft, Cardinal Bernardin acknowledges that this concept was "rooted in the Scriptures, developed with originality by the Catholic Church in Latin America and now becoming a guide for ministry in the universal Church under the leadership of John Paul II."[43] By the third draft, the Puebla reference was relegated to a footnote citation that begins with the Congregation for the Doctrine of the Faith's 1986 *In-*

struction on Christian Freedom and Liberation,[44] released barely two months before the appearance of the draft.

In the pastoral letter of the Santa Fe province bishops, the option for the poor is attributed to Pius XI, tenuously connected to a phrase in *Quadragesimo Anno.* The phrase in question appeared in the context of a discussion of the responsibility of civil authority for the protection of the common good. Quoted by the Santa Fe bishops to indicate papal provenance for the option for the poor is the latter portion of a line from section 25: "in protecting the rights of private individuals, chief consideration ought to be given to the weak and the poor."[45]

The Santa Fe province bishops were also strongly influenced by John Paul II's desire to be voice of the voiceless and conscience of the consciences:

For the chief spokesman of the universal church to assume the role of advocate for the poor is consistent with the Catholic doctrine that the pope is the vicar of Christ. To be his vicar is to present the cause of the poor to those who can make a difference. In a word to speak for those who have no choices, to speak to those who do have choices and who therefore can choose to respond or to refuse to respond.[46]

The selective memory reflected in U.S. episcopal formulations unfortunately models the very marginalization and voicelessness they seek to correct. In effect, the gradual muting of Latin American voices and the mediation of the preferential option of the poor through the offices of the Pope and Congregation for the Doctrine of the Faith perpetuated relationships grounded in privilege and power rather than justice. Is it the authority of the Vatican that lends credibility to the claims of the poor or is it the agency and conditions of the poor, vulnerable, powerless, and silenced?

The marginalization of the poor and vulnerable is further evident in the language used to communicate this moral imperative. The agency of the poor is diminished both by what is said and by how it is expressed. The impression often given is that the poor exist to enlighten or evangelize or raise the consciousness of the non-poor. Whether it is Bishop Lyke's claim that the Church would be renewed if we *allowed* "ourselves" to be evangelized by the poor or the Santa Fe bishops' perspective that the powerful are given the option to respond to God through the presence of the poor, the result, despite the best of intentions, objectifies the poor. Those without power or privilege are relegated to the realm of depersonalized others with whom an encounter is instrumental in bearing utilitarian, if not salvific, benefits for those among the privileged and powerful who choose to respond.

Consistent references to the poor and vulnerable in the third person further increase marginalization while diminishing agency. The repeated use of third-person pronouns in speaking of the poor and first-person pronouns when speaking of the Church or the United States sets up a dichotomous "us" and "them" that undermines talk of solidarity. This stigmatizes the poor further by implying their disconnectedness from the Church and the nation. For example, in the 1983 pastoral on Hispanic ministry the U.S. bishops call "all U.S. Catholics to work not just for Hispanics but with *them*, in or to secure *their* empowerment in *our* democracy," thus deepening "*our* preferential option for the poor."[47] Granted the increased appreciation for the concept of empowerment that enables U.S. bishops to move from initiatives that do for and do to the poor toward enabling the poor to do for themselves, however, this carelessness with language is counterproductive in terms of creating a sense of community, let alone true empowerment. The degree of separation between privileged and powerless articulated by this use of language is not a matter of nitpicking or trivialization, for such discourse ensures that agency remains in the hands of those with the choices and options.

This difficulty with discourse underscores a fundamental inability to conceptualize the preferential option for the poor as a manifestation of solidarity. Much of the controversy surrounding the appropriation of the principle is generated by an inability to conceive of it as an option *for* community, not against community. This is evident in the insistent refrain of non-exclusivity that accompanies the mention of the preferential option for the poor. In the Puebla document, the Latin American bishops grant this concern fleeting attention, choosing instead to keep the focus on the poor: "This option does not imply exclusion of anyone, but it does imply a preference for the poor and a drawing closer to them."[48] In the 1986 "Instruction on Christian Freedom and Liberation" the Congregation for the Doctrine of the Faith cautioned, "The special option for the poor, far from being a sign of particularism or sectarianism, manifests the universality of the Church's being and mission. This option excludes no one."[49] In his 1991 social encyclical letter *Centesimus Annus*, John Paul II notes that the preferential option for the poor is "never exclusive or discriminatory toward other groups."[50] In their pastoral on the economy, the U.S. bishops write that the "option for the poor" is not "an adversarial slogan that pits one group or class against another. Rather it states that the deprivation and powerlessness of the poor wounds the whole community."[51] This refrain is echoed in the words of Bishop Kinney to the people of the diocese of St. Cloud: "The option for the poor . . . is a helpful way of understanding how we should respond to anyone in need."[52]

The temptation to frame the principle in adversarial terms, especially in the context of the United States, comes as no surprise. "Preference" carries baggage. In a climate charged with discussion of the pros and cons of affirmative action, "preferential" implies, for some, partiality and special treatment. This implication is clear in economist Milton Friedman's critique of *Economic Justice for All:*

> We want greater opportunities for everybody. It is a mistake to regard the so-called poor as a special class. Not only are the poor at any time human beings like the rest of us, but the poor at one time are not the same as the poor at other times, and the very concept of who are 'the poor' is a matter of perception, not of fact.[53]

Friedman downplays the hard reality of poverty by making poverty and the poor a matter of perception rather than fact. Who *are* the poor? In crossing the border from Puebla to the United States, the definition of "poor" expands exponentially. In the Puebla document, poverty is perceived through the lens of material deprivation and denial of access to means of economic sustenance.[54] In the subsequent appropriation of the principle, the option for the poor is not limited to material poverty but expanded to incorporate cultural and spiritual poverty as well. In a 1983 address to priests in El Salvador, John Paul II notes that the ordained minister is "called to make a preferential option for the poor, but he cannot disregard the fact that there is a radical poverty wherever God is not alive in the hearts of people who are slaves to power, to pleasure, to money, to violence. He must extend his mission to these poor too."[55]

In his 1984 *Urbi et Orbi* message, John Paul II renewed the Church's commitment to the preferential option for the poor, identifying the countless multitudes of the modern poor. He affirmed solidarity with the victims of famine, drought, and hunger; with refugees; with the unemployed; with those experiencing solitude and abandonment through sickness, old age, or misfortune; with widows and orphans; with those martyred for preaching the Gospel and living the social teaching; with the kidnapped; with families suffering from the moral upheaval unleashed by consumerism; with those struggling to escape drugs, violence, and criminal organizations.[56] The pope went on to express solidarity with "victims of those other forms of poverty which strike at the spiritual and social values of the individual."[57] In this grouping he included those deprived of the right to freedom of movement, personal security, and life; those excluded by virtue of discrimination based on race or nationality; those denied expression of thought or of profession and practice of faith; those excluded or imprisoned for dissenting legitimately from a regime's ideology; those subjected to psychological violence, violating the sanctity of the conscience.[58]

In the United States the option for the poor is frequently amended to include the vulnerable, a category harkening back to the scriptural concern for the poor as well as widows, orphans, and strangers in the land, groups of people whose conditions suggest dependence and powerlessness. This expanded understanding of the marginalized does not lessen the rhetoric of inclusion. This is certainly reflected in the statement of Rembert Weakland, O.S.B., Archbishop of Milwaukee and head of the economic pastoral's drafting committee, when he presented the first draft at the 1984 national meeting: "As one would expect from Catholic bishops, we have a special emphasis on the poor . . . But neither our pastoral vision nor our policy perspective is limited to our concern for the poor. They also extend to the near poor and the not-so-near poor."[59]

It is this ongoing refrain repeatedly raised on behalf of the not-so-near poor and the near poor that betrays a profound obstacle in the comprehension and acceptance of this principle within the U.S. context. Since the option for the poor arose within a Latin American context marked by great disparity between the very rich and the very poor, the lacuna in U.S. discourse is located in the underdevelopment of an understanding and articulation of the role of those who find themselves in the vast middle. While there is no disputing the existence of a disparity in wealth, access, and resources between the very rich and the very poor, in the United States these represent extremes, with the majority of people falling economically somewhere between these two poles. The failure to account for that middle ground has prevented the development of a U.S. interpretation of the preferential option for the poor that invites embrace.

As Allan Figueroa Deck has noted, "Poverty in the United States is not the reality of the mainstream, but that of the minority (albeit growing in recent times). The norm for most North Americans as well as for the growing numbers of United States Hispanics is the middle-class way of life."[60] Citing work done by sociologist Andrew Greeley, Deck continues that even U.S. Hispanics tend not to relate psychologically as well to identifications of themselves as poor even though all too many frequently meet the statistical definition of poverty. This inability to recognize the middle ultimately undermines solidarity and is counterproductive to the transformational power and intent of the option for the poor and vulnerable.

The challenge missed is how to enable individuals to evaluate personal choices, attitudes, lifestyles, savings, investments, and consumption habits in such a way as to appreciate the impact on others, especially the neighbors at the margins. How does personal conversion effect structural transformation? How is one led to recognize interdependence not in terms of "vague compassion or shallow distress" but as a "persevering determination to commit oneself to the common good . . . to the good of all and each individual because we are all really responsible for all"?[61] Unfortunately, in dealing with personal response the emphasis has been on charity, not justice, thus fostering the sense of vague compassion that does not lend itself to just relationships rooted in interdependence, but to one-sided dependence. Attention has primarily been concentrated on conscientization of those with power and privilege and to a lesser degree on the empowerment of the poor and vulnerable.

In his remarks to the Special Assembly for America, Bishop Ricardo Ramírez of Las Cruces, New Mexico, exhorted the bishops to "maintain as a major concern the weakest among us and recognize this as part of the law of charity and not just a gesture of benevolence."[62] This repeated identification of the principle as a manifestation of a distorted notion of charity rather than justice rooted in solidarity reduces the transformative potential of the option for the poor.

Catholic social teachings appear amorphous on this matter, contributing to the confusion that strips the poor and marginalized of their agency and voice. In *Sollicitudo Rei Socialis*, John Paul II identified the "option or love of preference for the poor" as a "special form of primacy in the exercise of Christian charity."[63] Yet in *Centesimus Annus*, the pope sends what seem to be conflicting messages. Early in the letter he writes:

[I]t will be necessary above all to abandon a mentality in which the poor—as individuals and as peoples—are considered a burden, as irksome intruders try-ing to consume what others have produced. The poor ask for the right to share in enjoying material goods and to make use of their capacity to work, thus cre-ating a world that is more just and prosperous for all.[64]

The impression is that the poor are active participants in transform-ing the world, partners in solidarity asking for their just place at the table.

Later in the same encyclical the pope claims, "Justice will never be fully attained unless people see in the poor person, who is asking for help in order to survive, not an annoyance or a burden, but an oppor-tunity for showing kindness and a chance for greater enrichment."[65] The power of the first statement is mitigated by the blandness of the second, in which the poor are placed in a position of inequality as sup-plicants of charity, objects who provide others with an instrumental opportunity. Although the pope did go on to say that this aid should be drawn from substance and not surplus goods and that it required a change of lifestyles and consumption models to enable the marginal-ized to enter into the sphere of human and economic development, damage is done to the notion of preferential option as an expression of justice. In the U.S. context this encourages an interpretation of the option for the poor as a hybrid of charity and justice, whereby charity is evident in the contributions of time, money, and resources, whereas justice is effected by the enactment of socioeconomic change through public policies, institutions, and legislation. As Bishop Ramírez ob-serves, "While U.S. Catholics are generous in their charitable contri-butions, they lack a 'social conscience' and fail to go beyond charity to work for justice."[66]

Further attenuating the transformative power of the preferential option for the poor is a failure to appreciate its intergenerational po-tential. The preferential option for young people seems to have been detained at the border, without an opportunity to pack for the jour-ney. In the final Puebla document, this option follows the option for the poor and is discussed in some detail in part 4, chapter 2.[67] Unfor-tunately, the inclusion of this option has been interpreted as "playing down to some degree the uniqueness of the phrase 'option for the poor' and in this way making it less threatening and more widely ac-cepted."[68] What this disregards is the disproportionate presence of the young among the poorest and most vulnerable and the implica-tions of that fact for the future. Left unexplored are the possibilities for transformation that exist if an option is made for youth and if in turn the young themselves make an option for life on the margins.

The lack of attention to the option for the young did not go unnoticed. In the 1984 "Instruction on Certain Aspects of the 'Theology of Liberation'" the Congregation for the Doctrine of the Faith noted, "We should recall that the preferential option described at Puebla is twofold: for the poor and for the young. It is significant that the option for the young has in general been passed over in silence."[69] The precarious condition of youth did receive priority attention at the III Encuentro in 1985. In the "Prophetic Pastoral Guidelines," preceded by a preferential option for the poor and marginalized, and numbered third among the sixty-eight articles affirmed at the gathering, is a "preferential option for Hispanic youth so that they will participate at all levels of pastoral ministry."[70] This commitment to the young is fueled both by a concern for the experience of marginalization that is often heightened by poverty and issues of cultural identity and by faith in the prophetic voice of youth. The pastoral dimensions of the commitment are articulated in greater depth in articles 30 through 38. Though the term "preferential option for the young" is not explicitly cited, it appears to inspire the underutilized 1991 U.S. bishops' pastoral "Putting Children and Families First: A Challenge for Our Church, Nation and World."[71]

The discussion of preferential option for the poor in the Puebla document includes the young at the top of its list of the many faces of the poor. Insistence on a preferential option for the young by no means distracts from the uniqueness of the preferential option for the poor. On the contrary, each heightens the urgency of the other. At Puebla a preferential option for the poor and a preferential option for young people were discussed in the context of evangelization. Both the poor and the young "constitute the treasure and the hope of the Church in Latin America, and so evangelization of them is a priority task."[72] Recognition is given that such evangelization serves to benefit the young who are seeking "to construct a better world" and the continent benefits as this evangelization guarantees "the preservation of a vigorous faith."[73] The young, like the poor, emerge as both the evangelized and, in turn, the evangelizers.

Shoved to the margins of the discourses on the options for the poor and the young is the role of gender as a marginalizing factor. While it is assumed that women are included among the poor and young, occasional references note their unique situation. In the Puebla document this occurs in a footnote recognizing that the women who constitute the poor are "doubly oppressed and marginalized."[74] In the discussion of youth, "negative features of women's liberation and a certain *machismo*" are identified as the culprits "blocking the sound advancement of women as an indispensable factor in the construction of society."[75]

Within the context of the United States, women are also addressed as an afterthought with references focused on their role in relationship to the raising and care of children. One exception appears to be the U.S. bishops' 1988 "National Pastoral Plan for Hispanic Ministry," grounded in the working document and conclusions of III Encuentro. Within the context of the discussion of a "preferential missionary option for the poor and marginalized, the family, women, and youth,"[76] the reality of a triple discrimination endured by women is acknowledged:

- Social (*machismo*, sexual and emotional abuse, lack of self-esteem, exploitation by the media),
- Economic (forced to work without proper emotional and technical preparation, exploited in regard to wages and kinds of work, bearing full responsibility for the family, lacking self-identity);
- Religious (her importance in the preservation of the faith is not taken into account, she is not involved in decision-making yet bears the burden for pastoral ministry).[77]

While the well-intentioned objective is "to promote faith and effective participation in Church and societal structures on the part of these priority groups . . . so that they may be agents of their own destiny (self-determination) and capable of progressing and becoming organized,"[78] the plan offers a weak form of concrete address, avoiding further discussion of the ramifications of the previously identified multiple levels of discrimination. Action is limited to a call for regional meetings with a focus on ministries by women.[79]

In the conversation about the options, women are denied agency and voice, as their experiences of poverty and youth are mediated by others. Ignored is the empowerment of women and girls, whether on the margins or in the vast middle, to embrace, live, and shape these options as their own. The voices of Latina theologians have not been silent. María Pilar Aquino writes, "The women's perspective gives a special place to one aspect of the option for the poor: it wants to reach the questions, historical and spiritual experiences, knowledge, memory, desires, and expectations of women, not only as part of this suffering world, but primarily *as women.*"[80]

DIRECTIONS: REDRAWING THE MAP

Roberto Goizueta has noted that "when read in the context of contemporary U.S. society, the preferential option for the poor—as developed most systematically by Latin American theologians—is susceptible to misinterpretation."[81] It is clear that U.S. bishops' statements about the preferential option for the poor explicitly draw neither on the work of Latin American bishops and theologians nor on the work of U.S. Hispanic/Latino/a theologians. As my survey of pastoral statements reveals, the primary dialogue partner remains Rome. It is surprising to realize the absence of Hispanic/Latino/a theological voices in the episcopal formulations that articulate a national investment in this option.

At the very least, enlightened self-interest should dictate that it is high time for this theological voice to enter the conversation, if not shape its course and development on the national level. As James Hickey, Cardinal Archbishop of Washington, suggested in 1984, the fashioning of "our own preferential option for the poor" remains a pressing challenge, taking into account the context of the United States with its unique spectrum of abundance as well as marginalization.[82]

There is a need to bridge, in a balanced manner, the distance between the Latin American roots of the option for the poor and its formal articulations in the United States. This requires a recognition that "Latin American references to the poor and a spirituality forged from the perspective of the popular masses and their legitimate struggles for revolutionary change can seem strangely out of place and somewhat off target for the United States Hispanics."[83] At the same time, it requires a reclaiming of the option for the poor as enunciated at Puebla to counteract the trend of

reversion to a more abstract, spiritualized understanding of the option for the poor. Solidarity with the poor, now defined as the culturally marginalized, can be effected simply through "consciousness raising" rather than through a practical identification with the political and economic struggles of the poor.[84]

Investment in the transformative potential and lived experience of a preferential option for those on the margins requires outreach to and engagement by those who populate the vast middle ground as well as to and by the young. This is especially urgent for U.S. Latinos/as. Statistics reveal endemic marginalization for Hispanics: a disproportionate number live in poverty; the population is characterized demographically by its youthfulness; the school dropout rate is alarming; anti-immigrant resentment and violence are growing; discrimination toward the public use of the Spanish language finds protection in the law. On the other hand, the Hispanic experience is also marked by an attraction to and increased presence in that vast middle described appropriately by one African-American writer as "someone who is one step out of poverty and two paychecks from being broke. I have income but not true wealth."[85] Frequently in the particular case of the Latino/a immigrant, at least one of those checks is being sent to support family in the nation of origin.

It is this ground, with its ambiguous promise of the "American dream," that Latino writer Junot Díaz portrays in his short stories, a social geography replete with moderate- to low-income apartment complexes "surrounded by the malls, cineplexes and municipal pools of the middle class."[86] Commenting on how often writers of color who like himself were reared in suburban and middle-class environments portray low-income people in their works, Díaz observes that "it shows that even writers are responding to pre-set notions of who 'we' are and how 'we' are supposed to be viewed."[87]

From a U.S. Latino/a perspective, the preferential option for those on the margins entails accompanying the poor, as well as bringing the middle to the edges that some would rather forget. In order to ensure that amnesia does not become a permanent condition, "you must simultaneously touch the center of society and move the center— sometimes *drag* the center to the margins where the poor and powerless can be found."[88]

The encounter between Latinos/as established in the United States and more recent immigrants reinforces the urgency with which this twofold responsibility must be assumed. One Latina, raised in the United States since the age of three, calls the widening cultural gap between newcomers and Latinos/as who immigrated decades ago "willful distancing," observing that there exists "very little help from established Latinos to the newcomers . . . There's little social conscience. But that is not necessarily unique to Latinos."[89]

Unfortunately, the "Americanization" of Hispanics with respect to the poor and marginalized is apparent in attitudes that perpetuate the "otherness" of recent immigrants and that frame poverty in terms of personal and moral failure. This is evident in the words of a 51-year-old highly accomplished Salvadoran who became a U.S. citizen in 1979 and in thirty years has gone from being a dishwasher to one of the few Hispanic administrators in the District of Columbia public school system. "There's a big difference for us who came first," she tells the *Washington Post*. "It was harder to make it, yet we had the strong moral values. For us, the United States was *una casa ajena* [someone else's home], so we had to show the best of us even to those who thought we were invading. We had to show we had something to offer. But this generation is totally different."[90]

The gap and its correlative dichotomy between "us" and "them" is manifest in the admission by a successful son of Colombian immigrants who is a neighbor to newcomers from rural Central America: "They come for economic reasons or human rights reasons . . . it's kind of alien to me because my family is fairly well off . . . As far as exposure to these people, I haven't had that much. There's distance. My ties to the first generation aren't very strong at all."[91]

Hispanic theologians need also be cognizant of both the privileged (if not comfortable) position we occupy in the middle by virtue of our education and employment and the marginalization we encounter in the academy, the society, and the churches on the basis of the voices and experiences we attempt to bring to the table. It is from this unique social location that Latino/a theologians can view through bifocal lenses perspectives both from the margins and the middle ground to cultivate and model relationships born of the mutuality that solidarity presupposes. "Solidarity helps us to see the 'other'—whether a person, people or nation—not just as some kind of instrument . . . but as our 'neighbor,' a 'helper' (cf. Gn. 2:18-20), to be made a sharer on a par with ourselves in the banquet of life to which all are equally invited by God."[92]

It is not to be a voice for the voiceless but to ensure that those silenced have access, especially in this advanced technological age, to the basics, resources, and structures to find and exercise their own voices.

In order to be transformative, the preferential option for the poor and vulnerable necessitates practical engagement in daily, personal, and public life. However, the discourse regarding the option remains primarily on the abstract level with minimal description. This is illustrated in the 1998 U.S. bishops' pastoral "Sharing Catholic Social

Teaching: Challenges and Directions." It would seem that a statement specifically targeting the need to integrate social teaching in all areas of Catholic education would take care to communicate in concrete and accessible language a heritage they admit is unknown by many Catholics. The document was informed by a task force report that highlighted the reality that for too many Catholics in the United States, social teaching is not viewed as essential to the faith and that in educational settings the teaching is not sufficiently integral and explicit.[93] The task force drew on assessments from people in ministries across the nation that underscored the confusion surrounding the understanding of the preferential option for the poor. It is worth noting that in the final task force report, the phrase "preferential option for the poor" was replaced by "compassion for the poor" and the specific concern regarding the understanding of the option is not referenced. The section on the preferential option for the poor that finally appeared in the U.S. bishops' education document is all too brief. Once again the option for the poor is articulated without pictures, a surprise considering the intended audience is comprised of educators charged with conveying the message to and engaging the creativity and commitment of the young. Lacking imagination, the passage merely reiterates what has come before.

When the bishops use concrete examples, these tend to be limited, drawn mainly from the provision of social services, emergency interventions, and the enactment of political or legislative change. For example, Bishop Kinney's pastoral letter explains that the option for the poor means "we strengthen, not diminish, already existing programs such as food shelves, parish-sponsored meals for needy persons, shelters for the homeless . . . It could mean legislation on wages to ensure that Bill and other workers do not work full time and still remain in poverty. It could also mean striving for changes in our health care system that will guarantee every person's right to basic medical treatment."[94]

Implicitly operative in this example as well is a characteristically hybrid interpretation of the preferential option for the poor found in U.S. formulations that appears to place charity in the sphere of the personal and justice in the sphere of the public. This is underscored in the report of the Content Subgroup of the aforementioned task force on social teaching and Catholic education. In its description of the option for the poor as a basic principle of Catholic social teaching, the subgroup understands the response to all, especially those with the greatest needs, as accomplished "through acts of charity, through meeting the immediate needs of those who are poor and vulnerable, as well as through our own participation in society, shaping political and economic institutions that meet basic needs, promote justice, and ensure the participation of all."[95]

A lack of images and concrete examples hampers the communication, understanding, and integration of the preferential option for the marginalized in the U.S. Catholic lived experience and imagination. The Church has failed to heed its own advice that those "who preach should always bear in mind that the ability to hear is linked to the hearer's language, culture, and real-life situation."[96]

The challenge to re-imagine and re-articulate the preferential option for the poor and vulnerable in a manner that invites engagement and commitment requires the discovery and recovery of windows that offer glimpses into how the option for those on the margins can be lived. In Dalton, Georgia, self-described "carpet capital of the world," a major influx of Mexican and Central American immigrants was greeted with innovations designed "not only to ease the immigrants' transition to American life, but to create a new, more bilingual community."[97] Facing classrooms where the enrollment increase in Spanish-speaking students threatened to paralyze the school system, the community responded by seeking to make all students fluent in both English and Spanish. This entailed the establishment of a partnership with the University of Monterrey in northern Mexico whereby graduates of that university were granted temporary work visas in order to staff schools with bilingual instructors, and U.S. teachers were sent to Monterrey for intensive language and culture classes.

The community as a whole has benefited from this option made for the most vulnerable, in this case the stranger in the new land. Immigrant workers have well-paid jobs to support their families; the town has improved economically; all the children of the town have the opportunity to be fully bilingual; second- and third-generation Hispanics living in Dalton have been enabled to reclaim their linguistic and cultural heritage; and a partnership grounded in a mutual exchange has developed between two towns on either side of the border. A main consideration in the design of this bilingual program, known as the Georgia Project, was the intention to avoid "the regrettable yet frequent mistake made in numerous schools throughout the world: to place languages in competition, as if one were a more legitimate human communication vehicle."[98]

In 1993, in Alexandria, Virginia, a group of nurses opened a neighborhood health clinic in response to growing numbers of Hispanic school children without immunizations and of uninsured Latinas without prenatal care giving birth at home, all too often to babies with preventable birth defects. "'I don't see what we do as charity, and I don't see the city's role as providing charity,' Executive Director Susan Abramson said. 'I do see our role as investing in a population that needs investment. To protect and promote its own welfare as a city, the city needs to help all its citizens be productive, healthy residents.'"[99]

In Washington, D.C., a public service advertisement sponsored by United Cerebral Palsy was posted in Metro stations throughout the region. The ad depicted such beneficial features of the transit system including elevators, flashing lights signaling the approach of a train, announcements indicating impending stations, a tone warning passengers about the opening and closing of car doors. The question posed in the ad, "Did you know people with disabilities make your commute easier?" was answered with the simple statement "Access for One Means Access for All."

Fashioning a contextualized preferential option for the marginalized in the United States needs articulation and illustration. This is a task Hispanic theologians are in a position to appreciate, considering the primacy accorded experience and location as valid loci for theological reflection in a contextual framework. This is a task that the work of Latina feminist theologians has prepared us to embrace by their emphasis on the daily lived reality of the Hispanic experience and by including a deliberate option for women in the preferential option for the poor.[100] This is a task that requires recognition of the reciprocal connection between *teologías de conjunto* and *pastoral de conjunto*, a relationship Latino/a theologians foster in order to keep "the practice of theology from becoming a self-enclosed, self-preoccupied endeavor by binding both its questions and its reflections to the lived reality and the living faith of the churches and communities within which and for the sake of which it takes place."[101] This is a task that requires reclaiming domestic imagery.

As theologians who share in the Latino/a experience in the United States understand, for many here the preferential option for the poor is a preferential option for family scattered across the Americas. This is a task that requires the imagination and openness to recognize the preferential option for the poor and vulnerable in the daily encounters of ordinary lives lived in solidarity.[102]

NOTES

1. Third General Conference of the Latin American Episcopate, convened at Puebla, Mexico, January 1979, *Final Documents: Evangelization in Latin America's Present and Future,* no. 12, in *Puebla and Beyond,* ed. John Eagleson and Philip Scharper, 125–126.

2. Ibid., nos. 733 and 1134–1165, pp. 222, 264–267.

3. Pope John Paul II, "Communion, Participation, Evangelization," no. 6.9, *Origins* 10:9 (July 31, 1980): 135.

4. Ibid.

5. María Pilar Aquino, "Theological Method in U.S. Latino/a Theology. Toward an Intercultural Theology for the Third Millennium," in *From the Heart of Our People. Latino/a Explorations in Catholic Systematic Theology,* ed. Orlando O. Espín and Miguel H. Díaz, 31.

6. U.S. Census Bureau, "United States Department of Commerce News," September 26, 2000, available on the World Wide Web at http://www.census .gov/Press-Release/www/2000/cb00-158.html.

7. U.S. Census Bureau, "The Hispanic Population: 1999," June 23, 2000, available at http://www.census.gov/population/socdemo/hispanic/cps99/ 99gifshow/sld024.htm.

8. Hispanic Association on Corporate Responsibility, "Recent Hispanic Market Study," May 21, 1999, at http://solutions-e.com/HispRecent.htm.

9. U.S. Department of Commerce, National Telecommunications and Information Administration (NTIA), and Economics and Statistics Administration (ESA), "Falling Through the Net: Toward Digital Inclusion," October 16, 2000, at http://www.ntia.doc.gov.

10. Dale Russakoff, "Keeping up with the Garcias," *Washington Post,* September 23, 2000, A8.

11. Congregation for the Doctrine of the Faith (CDF), "Instruction on Certain Aspects of the 'Theology of Liberation,'" *Origins* 14:13 (September 13, 1984): 193, 195–204.

12. Bishop James Lyke, OFM, "When the Poor Evangelize the Church," *Origins* 10:3 (June 5, 1980): 37.

13. Ibid.

14. Ibid., 36.

15. Ibid.

16. Pope Pius XI, "Quadragesimo Anno: On Reconstructing the Social Order," in *Justice in the Marketplace,* ed. David Byers, 44–90.

17. Bishops of Santa Fe Province, "The Southwest's Converging Ethnic Groups," *Origins* 11:39 (March 11, 1982): 623.

18. Ibid., 621–622.

19. Ibid., 622.

20. Ibid., 622–623.

21. Ibid., 623.

22. Ibid.

23. National Conference of Catholic Bishops (NCCB), "The Hispanic Presence: Challenge and Commitment," no. 15, *Origins* 13:32 (January 19, 1984): 539.

24. CDF, "Instruction on Certain Aspects," 195.

25. Ibid., 201.

26. Ibid.

27. NCCB, "Catholic Social Teaching and the U.S. Economy," nos. 102–106, *Origins* 14:22/23 (November 15, 1984): 352–353.

28. NCCB, "Catholic Social Teaching," no. 52, p. 347.

29. Pope John Paul II, "One Church, Many Cultures," no. 9, *Origins* 14:30 (January 10, 1985): 501.

30. Ibid., no. 10, p. 501.

31. NCCB, *Economic Justice for All: Pastoral Letter on Catholic Social Teaching and the U.S. Economy* (Washington, D.C.: United States Catholic Conference, 1986).

32. Paul D. McNelis, S.J., "The Preferential Option for the Poor and the Evolution of Latin American Macroeconomic Orthodoxies," in *The Catholic Challenge to the American Economy: Reflections on the U.S. Bishops' Pastoral Letter on Catholic Social Teaching and the U.S. Economy*, ed. Thomas J. Gannon, 138.

33. NCCB, *Economic Justice for All*, no. 16, x-xi.

34. Ibid., no. 90, pp. 46–47.

35. Ibid., nos. 91–93, pp. 47–48.

36. Cardinal Joseph Bernardin, "The Fact of Poverty: A Challenge for the Church," *Origins* 14:33 (January 31, 1985): 544.

37. NCCB, *Economic Justice for All*, no. 24, p. 12.

38. Ibid., no. 120, p. 60.

39. NCCB, "A Catholic Framework for Economic Life," (November 1996): 1. At http://www.osjspm.org/10points.htm.

40. "Bishop Skylstad Introduces Catholic Framework for Economic Life," 2. At http://www.osjspm.org/10skylst.htm.

41. Ibid.

42. NCCB, "Sharing Catholic Social Teaching: Challenges and Directions," *Origins* 28:7 (July 2, 1998): 105.

43. Bernardin, "Fact of Poverty," 545.

44. CDF, "Instruction on Christian Freedom and Liberation," *Origins* 15:44 (April 17, 1986): 713, 715–728.

45. Bishops of Santa Fe Province, "Converging Ethnic Groups," 622, referencing Pope Pius XI, "Quadragesimo Anno," no. 25.

46. Ibid.

47. NCCB, *Hispanic Presence*, no. 15, emphasis mine.

48. CELAM, *Final Documents*, no. 733, 222.

49. CDF, "Instruction on Christian Freedom and Liberation," no. 68, 723.

50. Pope John Paul II, "Centesimus Annus," no. 57, *Origins* 21:1 (May 16, 1991): 21.

51. NCCB, *Economic Justice for All*, no. 88, p. 46.

52. Bishop John Kinney, "Pastoral Letter on Social Justice Concerns," *Origins* 28:13 (September 10, 1998): 227.

53. Milton Friedman, "Good Ends, Bad Means," in *Catholic Challenge*, ed. Thomas Gannon, 99–100.

54. CELAM, *Final Documents*, nos. 31–39, pp. 128–129.

55. Pope John Paul II, "The Priest, the Man of Dialogue," no. 6, *Origins* 12:40 (March 17, 1983): 642.

56. Pope John Paul II, "The Beatitude of the Poor," no. 8, *Origins* 14:30 (January 10, 1985): 498.

57. Ibid.

58. Ibid.

59. Archbishop Rembert Weakland, "The Economic Pastoral and the Signs of the Times," *Origins* 14:24 (November 29, 1984): 394.

60. Allan Figueroa Deck, "The Spirituality of United States Hispanics: An Introductory Essay," *U.S. Catholic Historian* 9:1–2 (Winter 1990): 137–146, cited in *Mestizo Christianity: Theology from the Latino Perspective*, ed. Arturo Bañuelas, 228.

61. Pope John Paul II, "Sollicitudo Rei Socialis," no. 38, *Origins* 17:38 (March 3, 1988): 654.

62. Bishop Ricardo Ramírez, "Poverty in the United States," *Origins* 27:26 (December 11, 1997): 444.

63. Pope John Paul II, "Sollicitudo Rei Socialis," no. 42, p. 656.

64. Pope John Paul II, *Centesimus Annus*, no. 28, p. 12.

65. Ibid., no. 58, p. 21.

66. Bishop Ramírez, "Poverty in the United States," 444.

67. CELAM, *Final Documents*, nos. 1166–1205.

68. Donal Dorr, *Option for the Poor: A Hundred Years of Catholic Social Teaching*, 394–395, note 4.

69. CDF, *Instruction on Certain Aspects*, 198.

70. NCCB Secretariat for Hispanic Affairs, "Prophetic Voices: The Document on the Process of the III Encuentro Nacional Hispano de Pastoral," no. 3 (1986), in *Hispanic Ministry: Three Major Documents* (Washington, D.C.: United States Catholic Conference, 1995), 33.

71. NCCB, "Putting Children and Families First: A Challenge for Our Church, Nation and World," (Washington, D.C.: United States Catholic Conference, 1991).

72. CELAM, *Final Documents*, no. 1132, p. 263.

73. Ibid., no. 1131, p. 263.

74. Ibid., no. 1135, p. 264.

75. Ibid., no. 1174, p. 268.

76. NCCB, "National Pastoral Plan for Hispanic Ministry," no. 51 (1988), in *Hispanic Ministry*, 79.

77. Ibid., no. 54, p. 79.

78. Ibid., no. 56, p. 80.

79. Ibid., no. 63, p. 81.

80. María Pilar Aquino, *Our Cry for Life: Feminist Theology from Latin America*, 113.

81. Roberto S. Goizueta, *Caminemos con Jesús: Toward a Hispanic/ Latino Theology of Accompaniment*, 173.

82. *Origins* 14:13 (September 13, 1984): 197.

83. Deck, "Spirituality of United States Hispanics," 228.

84. Roberto Goizueta, "The Preferential Option for the Poor: The CELAM Documents and the NCCB Pastoral Letter on U.S. Hispanics as Sources for U.S. Hispanic Theology," *Journal of Hispanic/Latino Theology* 3, no. 2 (November 1995): 75.

85. DeNeen Brown, "Her Sisters' Keeper," *Washington Post Magazine*, January 23, 2000, 16.

86. Samuel Freedman, "Suburbia Outgrows Its Image in the Arts," *New York Times*, Sunday, February 28, 1999, Arts and Leisure section 2, p. 27.

87. Junot Díaz, quoted in Freedman, "Suburbia."

88. Bishop Donald Pelotte, "Six Challenges for Justice Ministries," *Origins* 21:10 (August 1, 1991): 158.

89. Sylvia Moreno, "La Nueva Vida/Latinos in the Washington Region: Established Latinos, Newcomers Perceive Gap," *Washington Post*, January 23, 2000, A18.

90. Ibid.

91. Ibid.

92. Pope John Paul II, "Sollicitudo Rei Socialis," no. 39, pp. 654–655.

93. See the Summary Report of the Task Force on Catholic Social Teaching and Catholic Education, at http://www.nccbuscc.org/sdwp/projects/socialteaching/summary.htm.

94. Bishop Kinney, "Pastoral Letter," 227.

95. Task Force on Catholic Social Teaching and Catholic Education, "Report of the Content Subgroup," at http://www.nccbuscc.org/sdwp/projects/socialteaching/subgroup.htm.

96. NCCB, *Hispanic Presence*, 534.

97. William Branigan, "Georgia Town Finds Ways To Cross a Language Barrier," *Washington Post*, February 27, 1999, A22.

98. Ibid.

99. Sylvia Moreno, Philip Pan, and Scott Wilson, "La Nueva Vida/Latinos in the Washington Region: Hope and Hardship," *Washington Post*, January 23, 2000, A17.

100. María Pilar Aquino, "La Mujer/Women," in *Prophetic Vision. Pastoral Reflections on the National Pastoral Plan for Hispanic Ministry*, ed. Soledad Galerón, Rosa María Icaza and Rosendo Urrabazo, 142–162 and 316–335.

101. Jean-Pierre Ruíz, "U.S. Hispanic/Latino Theology: The 'Boom' and Beyond," at http://www.adelphi.edu/~catissue/RUIZ96.htm.

102. My thanks to Jean-Pierre Ruíz for his helpful comments on an earlier draft of this essay.

CHAPTER 10

**IGNORED VIRGIN OR
UNAWARE WOMEN**

A MEXICAN-AMERICAN
PROTESTANT REFLECTION ON
THE VIRGIN OF GUADALUPE

NORA O.
LOZANO-DÍAZ

Since all human beings have a story, a context, a
perspective, theology cannot be articulated in
a vacuum. The last decades have witnessed an
increased tendency to acknowledge the theologian's perspective in the theological task. As a
consequence, the classical notion of an objective, general, universal, unchanging theology
has been challenged as a theology that can be
oppressive, irrelevant, and false. According to
Stephen B. Bevans, the contextualization of theology is a theological imperative if theology
is going to be a pertinent theology.[1] Theology
needs to be grounded in a specific context where
a particular group of people, a community, can
recognize it, relate to it, welcome it, and be challenged by it.

Among the contextual theologies that have
flourished in the last decades are several feminist and women's theologies that affirm the need
to take the experiences of women as a theological foundation.[2] As I ponder on the foundations of a Latina women's Protestant theology,
I affirm the need to incorporate as a theological source the Latina Protestant women's experiences which are grounded in a specific context,
the Latino culture. Traditionally, Latino Protestantism has had a tense relationship with the
Latino culture. It has dismissed many elements
of the culture due to their connections with

Catholicism. I believe there is a need to reevaluate the roots and motivations behind this reaction toward culture. Furthermore, there is a
need to reevaluate the whole Protestant relationship to culture in order to challenge what is oppressive in it and to recuperate what is
powerful and life-giving. As I explore the topic of the Lady of Guadalupe, I want to present some preliminary thoughts toward this goal.

I want to identify myself as a Protestant woman who looks at life
and theology from a bridge.[3] By looking from this bridge, as Leticia
Guardiola-Sáenz has described it, I want to recognize and honor
the experiences that identify me as a Mexican as well as a Mexican-
American woman.[4] In some areas of the border, the Mexican and U.S.
lands are geographically united by a bridge. This bridge helps me to
imagine a cultural bridge where I can stand in order to incorporate my
experiences in both of these cultures.

THE IGNORED VIRGIN

I grew up in a Mexican Protestant home. My parents have been active
members in the Baptist church for as long as I can remember. As I was
growing up in this Baptist home, the Lady of Guadalupe was not present in my immediate environment. Little by little, however, given her
extensive presence in Mexico, I became aware of the existence of the
Lady of Guadalupe. Early in my elementary school years I remember
seeing the golden medals with the image of the Lady of Guadalupe
that many of my classmates wore as a sign of devotion and protection.
I remember hearing on national television slogans such as "Todos los
mexicanos somos Guadalupanos" (Every Mexican is a Guadalupano).
During my teen years, I learned about the apparition of the Lady of
Guadalupe to Juan Diego thanks to a television show with one of my
favorite actresses.

According to the Catholic story, the Lady of Guadalupe appeared
in 1531 to an indigenous man called Juan Diego. She referred to herself as "Tlecuauhtlacupeuh," which the Spaniards heard as "Guadalupe." She addressed Juan Diego as her son and told him that she was
his mother. She asked Juan Diego to build a temple for her and promised to comfort all who suffer.[5] My Protestant family, however, told
me that this story was only a superstition, that the apparition never
happened.

Just as in my home, the Lady of Guadalupe was pretty much ignored in my Protestant church. In fact, the Lady of Guadalupe is not
even acknowledged at all in the Protestant tradition. If Protestant

people refer to the Virgin, they talk about the Virgin Mary, the biblical Mary who was the mother of Jesus. However, this happens seldom, if ever.

The reason for overlooking the Virgin Mary may be found in the way in which the Hispanic American Protestantism was developed. The Hispanic American Protestantism harbored since the beginning a radical anti-Catholic feeling:

Against the baroque style and ostentation of the Catholic temples, the Evangelical halls were places without any decoration. The most that Protestants would allow was some biblical texts on the walls. Many of them would consider it a sign of idolatry to hang a cross, even an empty one, or to have pictures with the image of Jesus. Against the Roman ritualism, the Evangelicals reacted by having a spontaneous worship service, many times an improvised one . . . If the Catholic Church was bound with the State and the political powers, the Evangelicals preached indifference and abstention before all social and political matters. At other times they would proclaim an open opposition against any social or political participation.[6]

Given that the Virgin Mary is so central to Catholicism, she became also a casualty of this anti-Catholic perspective. The Protestants, in an effort to differentiate themselves from the Catholic Church, rejected and dismissed even the biblical Mary. They did this simply by ignoring her.

There are two ways in which the Virgin Mary has been overlooked in the Protestant churches. First, when one studies the *círculos femeniles* (women's church groups), one notices that no group uses the name of Mary as its name. One finds these groups adopting the names of other women biblical characters—Esther, Deborah, Martha, Mary (Lazarus's sister), Ruth, Sarah, Lydia, Rachel—or the groups are named after a local or foreign woman missionary.[7] Likewise, most Hispanic Protestant families would never name their daughters María or Guadalupe. They would feel very proud of the names of other biblical women, but not that of Mary.

A second way the Virgin Mary is ignored in Protestant churches is the lack of reference to her in traditional Protestant sermons and Bible studies. Sometimes she is mentioned during Christmas or Easter, but the rest of the year she is mostly ignored.

However, this effort of Protestant families and churches to ignore the Lady of Guadalupe is almost futile. As soon as a Protestant family in Mexico gets on a bus to go home after church, for example, they will see a small poster of the Lady of Guadalupe on the dashboard. Protestant children today have the same experiences I had growing up. They constantly hear that "todos los mexicanos somos Guadalu-panos." Much of what I have said about Mexico is also true among Mexican-Americans. A Hispanic Protestant woman from the barrio will find images of the Lady of Guadalupe in many of her neighbors' houses and in the windows of Hispanic stores. She will find images of Guadalupe in the graffiti on walls, on posters in the grocery store, or on the T-shirt of the store clerk. Protestant Mexican-American women will certainly see their favorite soap opera characters praying to the Lady of Guadalupe every time they face a problem.

In spite of the Protestant efforts to ignore the Lady of Guadalupe, she is still present in the lives of people of Mexican descent. Her presence has permeated all of Mexican culture in such a way that she is not only present, but she also plays a role in the lives of Mexican and Mexican-American Protestant women.

UNAWARE WOMEN

Since the Lady of Guadalupe is a reality that affects the lives of Mexican and Mexican-American Protestant women, it is important for them to become aware of her presence and how it affects them. To do so, they would need a pertinent way to deal with her. A starting point would be for Mexican and Mexican-American Protestants to look at the Lady of Guadalupe as an element of their culture. Given the fact that the Lady of Guadalupe has to do with belief, to argue over whether she really appeared to Juan Diego is not helpful. The important element from a Protestant perspective is that the Lady of Guadalupe, due to her extensive presence in society, has become a part of the Mexican and Mexican-American culture.[8]

However, many Mexican and Mexican-American Protestant people would deny the idea that the Lady of Guadalupe has anything to do with Protestant women. They would affirm that since the Lady of Guadalupe is a Catholic figure, she cannot influence the lives of Mexican and Mexican-American Protestant women. Yet, the reality is different! She long ago became much more than a Catholic devotional figure: she became a cultural symbol that affects all people of Mexican descent.

The reason for this unawareness or denial of the way in which the Lady of Guadalupe affects Mexican and Mexican-American Protestants may be connected to the Protestant view of culture. Protestant people have been taught to live primarily as citizens from heaven and not from earth.[9] Thus many Protestants have been encouraged to live their Protestantism outside their culture. This idea of living outside the culture is related to the anti-Catholic perspective mentioned above. Since the culture is seen as permeated with Catholic views, it is necessary, as much as possible, to withdraw oneself from it. In many cases, as soon as a person converts to the Protestant faith, he or she is required to stop dancing, smoking, drinking, playing cards, watching movies, seeing plays, attending bull fights or horse races. The new believer is taught to see life dualistically: the church and the world are opposite and conflicting realities. Thus new believers are required to retreat from the world, from any political or social commitment,[10] and from the culture in general. Although this idea of a heavenly citizenship is a valid one, it is also true that while Mexican and Mexican-American Protestants are on earth, they are also citizens and members of an earthly culture: the Latino one. Even though some Protestants have tried to live outside earthly culture, this is not feasible. Every human being lives in a culture, and even if a person does not want to acknowledge it, the culture affects her.

Mexican and Mexican-American Protestants live in a culture in which the Catholic tradition is a key element. Therefore, they are cultural Catholics who live in a cultural Catholic ethos. They live surrounded by Catholic symbols that affect their lives.[11] The roots of this cultural Catholicism are found in history. In the sixteenth century the American continent witnessed a violent clash between Spanish culture and the Aztec/Nahuatl cultures. The Spaniards were zealous Catholics who regarded Catholicism not only as a religion, but as a way of life. As the victors, the Spanish imposed their religion and way of life on the indigenous people. It is hard to know exactly how long it took for the Catholic religion to become the authentic religion of the people or what elements from the Christian and indigenous religions had to be combined for the people to accept the Catholic faith.[12] However, regardless of the feelings of the indigenous people and of any syncretism that may have happened, the final result was that the Catholic religion and way of life became the official ones in New Spain.

This Catholic ethos was the ground where the Mexican and Mexican-American Protestantism was developed. Although Protestants began developing their own Christian values and lifestyles, they continued to live surrounded by Catholic culture. They became cultural Catholics, Protestants who lived their faith in a Catholic social environment.

However, these cultural dynamics changed for Mexican and Mexican-American people. Mexican people have continued to live in a predominantly Catholic environment, while Mexican-Americans have experienced a third element in these dynamics: the dominant Anglo-Protestant culture. Mexican-American Protestants have lived their Protestantism inside an immediate Hispanic Catholic culture, yet this Hispanic Catholic culture exists in a predominantly Anglo-Protestant environment. This means that on the one hand Mexican-American Protestants are in tension in terms of religious beliefs with the immediate Catholic culture and in agreement with elements of the Anglo-Protestant culture. On the other hand, in most cases Mexican-American Protestants are in agreement in ethnic terms with the Hispanic Catholic culture and in tension with the Anglo ethnic environment.[13]

Mexican and Mexican-American Protestants need to be aware of the cultural elements that surround them. Furthermore, they need to examine and evaluate these elements. When I was growing up, my siblings and I were not allowed to have a Christmas nativity scene; neither were we allowed to participate in the *posadas* because they were Catholic traditions. However, we always had a Christmas tree and waited for Santa Claus to bring us some toys. The Christmas tree and Santa Claus traditions are not Christian traditions, but we always participated in them without a question because they represent the Protestant way of celebrating Christmas that the missionaries gave us. Mexican and Mexican-American Protestants need to evaluate their cultural experiences by following Jesus's spirit of liberation and empowerment for all human beings, to take what is life-giving in the culture and to dismiss what is oppressive.

IS THE LADY OF GUADALUPE A SOURCE OF OPPRESSION OR LIBERATION FOR MEXICAN AND MEXICAN-AMERICAN PROTESTANT WOMEN?

The important issue for us to focus on and evaluate is whether the Lady of Guadalupe presents an oppressive or liberating model for Mexican and Mexican-American Protestant women.

The writer Octavio Paz has described the Virgin of Guadalupe as a sign of passivity that is an illustration of the feminine condition.[14] In a collection of essays written by the Franciscan Friars of the Immaculate, the Lady of Guadalupe is presented as a sorrowful figure and as an example of perfection, purity, and submission.[15] Sandra Messinger Cypress mentions that traditionally the Virgin of Guadalupe has been seen as a saintly woman who has embodied attributes such as virginity, piety, helpfulness, forgiveness, goodness, and devoted and selfless motherhood.[16] Following these writers, one can conclude that the characteristics assigned to Guadalupe are not very liberating for women. These characteristics may be positive in some instances, but when they are abused they become oppressive. Yet these are the characteristics that have been emphasized for Mexican and Mexican-American women. They are at the heart of the cultural patterns of behavior that are normative for these women.

In the book *The María Paradox*, authors Rosa M. Gil and Carmen Inoa Vázquez describe in a more practical way how these characteristics affect the lives of Latinas. They refer to this view of the Virgin Mary as *marianismo*, which defines the traditional ideal role of women following patriarchal views of the Virgin Mary herself.

> Marianismo is about sacred duty, self-sacrifice, and chastity. About dispensing care and pleasure, not receiving them. About living in the shadows, literally and figuratively, of your men—father, boyfriend, husband, son—your kids, and your family.[17]

The ten commandments of *marianismo*, according to the authors, are as follows:

1. Do not forget a woman's place.
2. Do not forsake tradition.
3. Do not be single, self-supporting, or independent-minded.
4. Do not put your own needs first.
5. Do not wish for more in life than being a housewife.
6. Do not forget that sex is for making babies—not for pleasure.
7. Do not be unhappy with your man or criticize him for infidelity, gambling, verbal and physical abuse, alcohol or drug abuse.
8. Do not ask for help.
9. Do not discuss personal problems outside the home.
10. Do not change those things which make you unhappy that you can realistically change.

Obviously *marianismo* is an outdated cultural structure that is oppressive for Mexican-American women. Gil and Vázquez highlight that the ultimate expression of *marianismo* is the noble sacrifice of self,[18] and thus it erodes the self-esteem of Mexican-American women. Although not all the elements of *marianismo* affect all Mexican and Mexican-American women in the same way and with the same intensity, I do believe that all are affected by *marianismo*. Consequently, they need to challenge these cultural stereotypes in order to discover and develop themselves and their self-worth. They need to do this in order to live fully as human beings made in the image of God.

One way to do this is to look for new readings of the Lady of Guadalupe. Traditionally, the readings of Guadalupe have been from a patriarchal view, so these new readings need to come from a feminist liberative perspective that brings freedom and a holistic life for Mexican and Mexican-American women.

Among the scholars who perceive the Virgin as a liberating figure is theologian Jeanette Rodríguez. For her, the encounter between the Virgin and Juan Diego liberated him so that he was able to relate differently to God and the world around him. This is repeated today when Mexican-American Catholic women encounter the Lady of Guadalupe: it is a liberating event for them. Rodríguez stresses that Mexican-American Catholic women know only parts of the Guadalupe event and that they need to learn more about it so as to find in it more options for liberation and empowerment.[19]

Virgilio Elizondo is another Catholic theologian who sees the Virgin as a liberating figure. He sees the apparition of the Lady of Guadalupe in 1531 as a life-giving event for the conquered indigenous people. By appearing to Juan Diego, an Indian man, the lowest of the low, the Lady of Guadalupe brought new hope and life to the indigenous people. She gave them back their dignity. Spaniards had raped many indigenous women, and the *mestizo* offspring of this violence were seen as a race of illegitimate children. Through her apparition to Juan Diego, the Lady of Guadalupe radically changed this. She legitimized the *mestizo* race by becoming its mother. Through the Virgin, the indigenous people went from degradation to pride, from rape to purity, dignity, equality, and freedom.[20]

Although the liberating endeavors presented by Rodríguez and Elizondo are valid ones, I believe that they are not very helpful for Mexican and Mexican-American Protestant women. The first reason for this is that both writers approach this liberative view of the Virgin through the eyes of the Catholic faith and regard the Catholic faith as a central element.[21] Since most Mexican and Mexican-American Pro-

testant women do not have faith in the Virgin, these liberating attempts do not represent an option for them. Second, as Catholic endeavors, these writings do not address the Protestant Church's rejection of Mary.

However, this is not an excuse to continue ignoring the Lady of
Guadalupe and the effects she has on the lives of Mexican and Mexican-American women in general. As we saw earlier, the traditional
image of Guadalupe has had oppressive effects for women; therefore,
Mexican and Mexican-American Protestant women need to deal with
her as a cultural symbol to find liberation from this patriarchal model
of womanhood.

But what is the difference between a cultural symbol and a religious symbol? A symbol is a reality of the senses that reveals a meaning related but not limited to its form. It evokes and invites us to look
beyond what is immediately apparent to consider deeper or overarching meanings and realities.[22] A cultural symbol reveals something
about the culture and invites us to seek a meaning about the culture
beyond the symbol itself. It is widely present and visible in the whole
culture of a group. It may or may not have a religious background. It
affects the whole population whether in a religious or a non-religious
way. On the other hand, a religious symbol reveals something about
a transcendent, mysterious reality that the senses cannot apprehend,
and it invites us to participate in a deeper understanding and relationship with this reality. It has a religious background. It must be approached through faith and has a religious effect on some people. In
the case of the Lady of Guadalupe, she is a cultural symbol for the
whole Mexican and Mexican-American population and only a religious symbol for the people who see her and relate to her through
their faith. An example of this is found in the flag that Miguel Hidalgo y Costilla used in the proclamation of the Mexican independence in 1810. This flag has in the center the image of the Lady of Guadalupe and as a background the official Mexican colors—green,
white, and red. It has become a national symbol that both Catholics
and Protestants recognize as part of history. For Catholic people it
also has a religious meaning, while for Protestant people it only has a
cultural, historic meaning.[23]

Therefore, if Mexican and Mexican-American Protestant women
cannot approach the Lady of Guadalupe as a religious symbol, they
can look at her through other liberating efforts approached from cultural and feminist perspectives. These efforts are an attempt to redis-

cover the Virgin and to rectify the model that she presents for women.

In a powerful essay titled "Guadalupe the Sex Goddess," Sandra Cisneros, a Mexican-American writer, presents how the traditional image of the Lady of Guadalupe as a pure and virginal mother affected negatively her relationship with her body and her sexuality. In searching for her own liberation, Cisneros found that she needed a more liberating image of the Lady of Guadalupe. By looking at history, she found indigenous perspectives and understandings of the Lady of Guadalupe that the Church has tried to erase. Cisneros found Tonantzin, an Aztec goddess who is a feminine part of the Aztec supreme dual deity. Inside Tonantzin, Cisneros found a pantheon of other mother goddesses of fertility and sex, such as Tlazolteotl, the patron of the sexual passion, and Coatlicue, the creative/destructive goddess who is not passive and silent but always gathering force around her. By rediscovering the Lady of Guadalupe's roots and meanings as an Aztec goddess who honored sexuality, Cisneros was able to reclaim a more holistic sexuality for herself and for all women of Mexican descent.[24]

As a Protestant woman, I believe that approaches that present the Lady of Guadalupe as a cultural symbol will make an impact in Protestant circles. This approach gives Mexican and Mexican-American Protestant women a way of dealing with the Lady of Guadalupe without having to embrace Catholic understandings of her.

Another resource to challenge the traditional image of the Lady of Guadalupe is the Bible, the book that holds greatest authority for Protestant Mexican and Mexican-American women. Through an alternative feminist reading of the Bible that is both liberative and empowering, these women can recover and embrace the biblical Mary and confront the oppressive views of Mary and Guadalupe. If traditionally the Virgin Mary has been perceived as a passive woman, an alternative feminist reading of Luke 1:26–38 can suggest the opposite. The fact that she became a vessel to fulfill God's plan gives the idea of becoming a passive object. However, verse 38 suggests that she was in reality a subject. She decided out of her free will to take the mission that God had for her. She did not consult anybody about becoming a mother, not even her future husband. Thus this passage hints that Mary was an active and assertive woman who made her own choices.

Another characteristic that traditionally has been ascribed to the Virgin is submission. However, Luke 1:46–55 suggests that perhaps the biblical Mary did not have a very submissive mind. This passage presents Mary's song of praise to celebrate the merciful acts of God. The thinking reflected in this song gives the idea of a Mary who was well aware of social injustices and who celebrated the acts of God to reverse the social order in favor of the poor and oppressed.

A third characteristic of the traditional Mary is that the role of devoted motherhood was her only function in life. However, Acts 1:12– 14 offers a glimpse of a Mary who also was busy with other activities. According to the passage, along with other women, Mary was a committed and active disciple of the Jesus movement who was involved in the original group of disciples who started the church.[25]

These alternative views suggest a different Mary than the traditional one. They invite us to think about Mary as a subject with a strong will and social consciousness, who was active, assertive, and involved with functions other than motherhood. This Mary and her liberating qualities can be a model for Mexican and Mexican-American Protestant women in their struggles to achieve liberation and justice because she provides them with a new biblical model of how to be a woman. Once these women grasp and experience the alternative options that this model presents, they will be able to use it also as a pertinent tool to confront and challenge the oppressive characteristics that have been ascribed to the Lady of Guadalupe. As a consequence, the traditional image of the Lady of Guadalupe as a cultural symbol will have less power to influence how these women live their lives.

CONCLUSION

Protestant Mexican and Mexican-American women need to stop ignoring the Lady of Guadalupe. She long ago became much more than a Catholic devotional figure—she became a cultural symbol. As a cultural symbol elaborated by a patriarchal culture, however, certain characteristics have been ascribed to the Lady of Guadalupe that affect women negatively. If Mexican and Mexican-American Protestant women ignore the Lady of Guadalupe, they will be unable to discover how these patriarchal expectations of women are oppressive. Furthermore, they will not be able to fight the oppressive models of what it means to be a woman.

On the other hand, if Mexican and Mexican-American Protestant women become aware of the importance of the Lady of Guadalupe and contribute to a different reading of her, they will benefit from it. They will realize that they can have more control and power over important societal symbols. This will help Protestant women to challenge and do away with oppressive cultural symbols, and this in turn will help them to develop a better sense of self and to generate greater self-esteem. As these new readings emerge, the Lady of Guadalupe and Mexican and Mexican-American Protestant women alike will find liberation.

NOTES

The original version of this paper was presented at the 1998 Annual Meeting of the American Academy of Religion. I want to thank the audience in that presentation for their helpful and engaging comments. Also, I am indebted to Leticia Guardiola-Sáenz and Ada María Isasi-Díaz for reading the first draft of this paper and providing helpful suggestions.

1. Stephen B. Bevans, *Models of Contextual Theology*, 1–10.

2. See María Pilar Aquino, *Our Cry for Life: Feminist Theology from Latin America;* Ada María Isasi-Díaz, *En la Lucha: In the Struggle. Elaborating a Mujerista Theology;* Rosemary Radford Ruether, *Sexism and God-Talk: Toward a Feminist Theology;* and Delores S. Williams, *Sisters in the Wilderness: The Challenge of Womanist God-Talk.*

3. Even though my particular identification is Baptist, I decided to use in this paper the term Protestant in general because I believe that these reflections go beyond the Baptist Mexican and Mexican-American world. At least this is what I have found in my conversations about this topic with other Mexican and Mexican-American Protestant people. Although I believe that what I present here is a predominant position regarding the Lady of Guadalupe among Mexican and Mexican-American Protestant people, I recognize that there are exceptions to this picture. The Episcopal and Lutheran traditions are more open to the Virgin Mary/Guadalupe. However, they represent a minority among the Hispanic Protestant traditions.

4. Leticia Guardiola-Sáenz, "A Mexican-American Politics of Location: Reading from the Bridge," paper presented at the American Academy of Religion (AAR) annual meeting in Philadelphia, 1995.

5. Franciscan Friars of the Immaculate, *A Handbook on Guadalupe,* 179–180 and 193–204.

6. Pablo Alberto Deiros, *Historia del cristianismo en América Latina,* 722. (My own translation.)

7. For instance, Sara Alicia Hale, an American missionary who worked in Mexico, and Hortencia Morales, a Mexican missionary who worked in northern Mexico, are namesakes of such groups.

8. Donald Demarest, "Guadalupe Cult . . . in the Lives of the Mexicans," in Franciscan Friars, *Handbook on Guadalupe,* 112–115.

9. Philippians 3:20 (New Revised Standard Version).

10. Deiros, *Historia del cristianismo,* 714, 722–723.

11. Ada María Isasi-Díaz and Yolanda Tarango, *Hispanic Women: Prophetic Voice in the Church*, x.

12. Charles Gibson, *Los aztecas bajo el dominio español: 1519–1810*, 101–106.

13. Justo L. González mentions his experience regarding these dynamics in his book *Mañana: Christian Theology from a Hispanic Perspective*, 22–26.

14. Octavio Paz, *El laberinto de la soledad*, 94.

15. Franciscan Friars, *Handbook*, v and Friar Maximilian, F.F.I., "Our Lady's Submission to the Church," 205.

16. Sandra Messinger Cypress, *La Malinche in Mexican Literature*, 6–7.

17. Rosa María Gil and Carmen Inoa Vázquez, *The María Paradox: How Latinas Can Merge Old World Traditions with New World Self-Esteem*, 7.

18. Ibid., 8.

19. Jeanette Rodríguez, *Our Lady of Guadalupe: Faith and Empowerment among Mexican-American Women*, 159–165.

20. Virgilio Elizondo, *Galilean Journey: The Mexican-American Promise*, 11–13. See also Virgilio Elizondo, *La Morenita: Evangelizadora de las Américas*.

21. Elizondo, *La Morenita*, 79, 86; Rodríguez, *Our Lady*, 6–17, 159.

22. Shawn Madigan, C.S.J., "Symbol," in *The New Dictionary of Catholic Spirituality*, ed. Michael Downey, 953–955; and *Catholic Dictionary*, ed. Peter M. J. Stravinskas, 463.

23. In conversations with other Hispanic scholars regarding these symbols, it became clear to me that Catholic and Protestant Hispanic people seem to have different worldviews that affect the way each group apprehends these symbols. For Hispanic Catholic people the categorization of cultural and religious symbols seems to be sharp, while for Hispanic Protestant people it seems to be less rigid.

24. Sandra Cisneros, "Guadalupe the Sex Goddess," in *Goddess of the Americas, La Diosa de las Américas: Writings on the Virgin of Guadalupe*, ed. Ana Castillo (New York: Riverhead Books, 1996), 46–51.

25. See Ivoni Richter Reimer, *Women in the Acts of the Apostles. A Feminist Liberation Perspective*, 231–233; Elisabeth Schüssler Fiorenza, *In Memory of Her. A Feminist Reconstruction of Christian Origins*, 52–53; and Schüssler Fiorenza, *Discipleship of Equals. A Critical Feminist Ekklesia-logy of Liberation*, 114.

CHAPTER 11

PATHWAYS TO A *MESTIZA* FEMINIST THEOLOGY

GLORIA
INÉS LOYA

I will be exploring the rich contributions that the Hispana-Latina is making in an evolving *mestiza* feminist theology with its roots in the history, culture, and faith of Latin America, as well as describing how this theology is becoming an original and unique liberating presence within the United States.[1]

The Hispana-Latina in the United States has basically remained an unrecognized or unknown voice, *una voz desconocida* in the theological forum. Yet the Hispana-Latina has been profoundly present in the service of the Church, in the U.S. workforce, and as a leader in churches and local communities. But has she been invited to share her thoughts, her dreams, and her experiences in the Church and in the theological forum? Through consultation and communication with a number of Latina leaders and ministers in the Church who work in the Hispano-Latino/a community in California, a means of dialogue and exchange was created to be able to gather and record the rich stories, the deep faith life, and new insights that come from the collective memories of Hispana-Latinas. The voices of Hispana-Latinas, who are *mestizas*, and their stories formulate the nucleus of this essay. The ideas, opinions, thoughts, feelings, and values shared by the women are sacred as they reflect a sense of the divine and "holy ground," or that "soil" from which our identity and personhood is cultivated from our faith and culture. Therefore, the material cannot be reduced to merely data and numbers. The data express human experience.

The process of dialogue in the study is based on one-on-one interviews, as well as by meeting with small gatherings in parishes or in homes. And ultimately some three hundred women responded to a "closed questionnaire." I began with an "open questionnaire" that allows for varied opinions and narratives, but it became almost impossible to capture the core data. I am convinced that no study is totally objective. A closed questionnaire allowed for various opinions and views while making it more feasible to respect the experiences of the women and to tabulate the data in a responsible and reasonable manner.

These groups were composed of ten to thirty women who had already been formed as women's discussion groups, as parish training groups, or in more informal local neighborhood groups. Each group had a visible woman leader who had responsibility for coordinating the gatherings and their content. They were for the most part participating in or at least in touch with the church. Before meeting with each group, I met with the coordinator and asked her to initiate the dialogue with the women. The coordinator would then invite the women to express their thoughts and perceptions regarding their lives, their culture, and their faith. Later on some of the women were invited to share their personal histories through interviews. Finally, a questionnaire was distributed to those who wished to answer it, as another means of listening to the women.

The process of respectful dialogue became a strong guide in the course of visiting the groups, of listening to the women, and of inviting them to respond to a questionnaire. Three hundred women answered and returned the questionnaires through their women's groups. The questionnaires were prepared in Spanish and in English. This was the initial step in entering into the culture of Hispana-Latinas in Southern California (Los Angeles, Santa Ana) and in Northern California (San Francisco Bay area), as well as in some parts of the Central Valley (Stockton, Sacramento).

The study provided a rich forum for ongoing theological reflection with the women in the groups. The participants were assured that their responses would be anonymous. As I prepared the questionnaire, I consulted with other women. We felt that Latinas are already "interviewed" and "questioned" by officials of state and other agencies. I wanted the women to know that their responses would not be used in any way except for the purpose of the study. I really think this provided a sense of trust. The initial invitation for the women to participate within already formed groups established a greater bond between them. The women took the study seriously, yet with enthusiasm. They pointed out that they felt encouraged that their opinions and views were being recognized as important for furthering the life of the community and of the Church. This was the beginning of developing a means of entering into the complexity of the culture and faith through the perceptions and experiences of the women.[2]

First, I will summarize and synthesize some of the thoughts the women expressed in the study, as well as two cases from the interviews. This information and the data become a foundational step in creating a pathway toward a *mestiza* feminist theology, based on the women's lived experience and wisdom. Nine graphs representing the respondents' views will be interpreted. For this discussion, the material presented will at least give one a "snapshot" of the women's views. The questionnaires yielded still more pertinent information based on cross-tabulations comparing the responses to education, to employment, and so forth.[3] Nevertheless, I believe that the interviews and the nine graphs in this discussion contribute toward a *mestiza* feminist theology.

Next I will discuss two central cultural and historical feminine figures which emerged from the initial roots of *mestizaje:* María de Guadalupe and Malinalli/Malintzin.[4] The two feminine figures that emerged in sixteenth-century Mexico are crucial in furthering a second pathway for this feminist theology. I am aware that as a Mexican American, the presence of Guadalupe and of Malintzin are interpretive keys for a Latina-Hispana-*mestiza* theology. Having presented much of this information to other Latina-Hispanas, I have consistently found support in that Malintzin and Guadalupe are core figures for all *mestizas,* not only for those of us of a Mexican-American or Chicana heritage. From the experience of the merging, clashing, and birthing of the indigenous spiritual cosmos with the Iberian Christian world comes the painful and hopeful presence of what theologian Virgilio Elizondo has named the "new *mestizo*" people in the United States.

In the figures of the two women, Malinalli—also called Malintzin—and Guadalupe, the Hispano-Latino/a people find the source for their identity as a new people of two philosophical, racial, and spiritual worlds merged into one as a new race of indigenous and European mixtures: the new *mestizo* people. Malintzin and Guadalupe are the central interlocutors opening the pathways toward a *mestiza* feminist theology. Clearly, a *mestiza* feminist theology not only informs feminist theology but also contributes to Hispanic theology in the United States.

By describing and in interpreting this "sacred material," I hope to unearth some of those factors, views, values, and new questions that contribute to a *mestiza* feminist theology. By including the cultural and historical figures of the feminine presence, I think that it will be possible to see that the presence of the feminine in our collective memory is intimately connected in our understanding of ourselves, of our communities, of our spiritual heritage, and of our thirst and commitment for justice. In this study it can be said that Hispana-Latinas urgently want to participate in the church community and in the theological forum, because from this Roman Catholic living tradition, Latinas can formulate a new ethic which embraces and includes *mestizas* as moral agents who are leaders in the family and in society.

From within their small communities and women's groups, Hispana-Latinas collectively engage in the doing of theology and in the creation of a *mestiza* feminist theology. As has been stated by theologian María Pilar Aquino:

An unprecedented fact in our midst is the birth of a theological trend that consciously and critically seeks to respond to the faith experience, needs, and liberating ends of the Hispanic/Latino people. This theology, brought about as a collective effort, proposes to articulate systematically our self-understanding as subjects and actors of faith and history in the circumstances of the present.[5]

FIRST PATHWAY: LISTENING TO THE EXPERIENCE OF HISPANA-LATINAS

I have selected two narrations as an illustration of *mestizas* who are becoming the subjects of their lives and whose leadership in the family and in the community enrich U.S. society and the Church. They are presently living and working in the Hispano-Latino/a community.

Interview: Eva

I am from El Salvador, one more refugee from the war. I was a student when my studies were prolonged because of the intervention of the government.

One evening the police began shooting toward the house. We were frightened and we thought that, at any moment, they would come in and kill us. Later my husband received a death threat. My husband was obliged to abandon us, and we have never seen him again. Because of everything that happened, I lived in fear.

I felt that the best thing to do for my children was to leave our country, so ridden, at that time, with violence and war. A relative helped me to get to San Francisco, where survival has also been difficult. I had no legal papers. I was welcomed by a Protestant church. They supported me in many ways, and they gave me confidence in myself. We continue to work where we can find work, and we try to give a decent life to our children.

In the testimony of Eva, there is a special quality of what it means to have courage and to continue to have hope. Eva is a gentle woman with tremendous inner strength who never allowed the evil forces of violence and of war to rob her of her dignity and of her personhood. She lives out her commitment patiently in working in her church community. Her story represents one of the millions who had to flee from the homeland of Central America and who today contemplate whether to return. Her faith in God and in her family continues as a source of hope. Her voice, her story, and presence enrich a *mestiza* feminist theology.

Interview: Margarita

I was born in Mexico. I began to get involved in the Hispano community and in the church after I made my Cursillo de Cristiandad. Since my marriage my husband and I have also helped in Marriage Encounters. I have also begun to learn and to participate in the community organization in our parish. This group focuses on social justice issues that are facing our local church and neighborhood. In this project I have worked to combat the selling and distribution of illegal drugs in our area. I have also begun to give presentations to Hispano groups regarding the growing danger of AIDS in our community. And I am also going to community college to finish my bachelor's degree. I have heard that only 7 percent or less of Hispana-Latinas finish their college education.

As a mother I have also become aware of the importance of my responsibility in the home. Our children need our support. I share my frustrations, my joy, and my struggles in the family. I have learned that as a woman, I thought that there is equality for women in education, at work, and in the church. But I realize that there is so much more to be done to bring this about for the future. I hope that I will be able to guide my daughters when they experience these things. I also hope that I can be a support to them as they choose their call and vocation in following the Lord. I also recognize that I have an exceptional husband who supports me and who animates me when I feel down. Most of all, he respects my decisions and he respects me as a person and as a mother.

Family and the vocation to marriage are part of the identity of Margarita, as she cares for her household as a partner with her husband. She also serves in the wider community. While she is very involved in family and in various types of ministries in the Hispano community, she seems also to recognize her need for personal goals, as for example, her striving to complete her university studies. Her voice is needed in the developing of a *mestiza* feminist theology. I have been enriched by her leadership ability, as have the Church and society.

These two interviews are an important, yet small, reflection of what so many other Hispana-Latinas have lived. There are many, many more stories that need to be told so that we can reclaim and reconcile our past, as our history is the place of God's abiding presence and grace. Our personal and collective history holds life. Both of these Latinas are women of a clear vision for themselves and for their families. Their vision is supported by their spirituality, because each is a woman of deep faith.

To further examine the insights and views of Hispana-Latinas, I illustrate in the following graphs some of the information shared by women through questionnaires. I wanted to develop questions that were simple and direct so the women could respond freely. The responses were gathered and compiled for furthering dialogue and theological reflection among women. There was so much initial information that it is still being analyzed.

For this essay, some of the core information that has been tabulated is presented in light of comparisons that were made with reference to the various age groups among the women. The ages ranged from sixteen years to eighty-five years of age. Another factor is that 85 percent of the women identified with the Roman Catholic faith. This is not unusual since the groups that participated were almost all from Roman Catholic parishes, or women's groups. This made the distribution and communication easier; however, in the future, it would be advantageous to seriously reach beyond the Roman Catholic community of Hispana-Latinas. What follows is a simple demonstration and description of their responses in percentages.

This is not a scientific study, nor is the questionnaire meant to be used to arrive at sweeping conclusions. However, the responses do give some interesting insights, and the women seem to raise some critical questions, all of which inform a *mestiza* feminist theology. The participants are women of deep faith, and they also have serious concerns regarding the Hispano-Latino/a community.

GENERAL INTERPRETATION OF THE WOMEN'S RESPONSES FROM THE QUESTIONNAIRE—AS COMPARED WITH AGE

Graph 1, below, shows the results based on the question regarding the women's employment and their ages. I believe that the question of employment is important because in the United States there is a serious lack of understanding as to the major contribution that Latinos/as have made to the labor force. I have reviewed much of the literature and have discovered that indeed, Latinos and Latinas have long held a vital place in the U.S. labor force. Since the early nineteenth century, *mestizos/as* have worked long hours for low pay in agriculture and industry throughout the nation. In New York, women have worked and continue to work in "sweatshops." Since the 1930s Mexicanas have worked in canneries and packing houses. During the Great Depression, Latinas began to organize labor unions in California. Latino/a families continue to work in agriculture. The

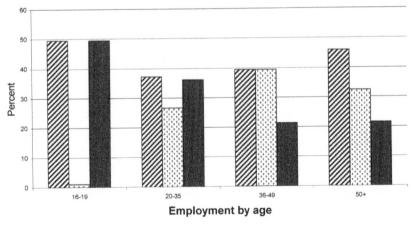

Employment by age

☑ Unemployed ▦ Full-time ■ Part-time

1. Employment

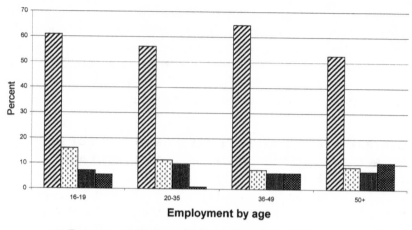

Employment by age

🞥 Parents ⬚ Mother ■ Grandparents ▨ Grandmother

2. To Whom Faith Is Owed by Age

multibillion-dollar agribusiness of California and other states has been built on the "backs" of *mestizas* and of their families. When César Chávez began the Farm Workers Union in the 1960s, the leadership of the Latina was essential, as for example was the nonviolent, prophetic voice of Dolores Huerta.[6]

At this beginning of the new millennium, a growing number of Latinos and Latinas have had the opportunity to continue their academic studies, unlike our parents. We now recognize *mestizas* as professionals in every state: lawyers, doctors, teachers, high-tech experts, social workers, nurses, and so forth. Yet in this study only about ten of the women noted that they had completed university studies.

The question of employment is important to be able to appreciate how the *mestizo/a* community has contributed to building this nation, even while receiving so little in just wages in return. The majority of women who answered this question were working in service and secretarial fields, as store clerks, accountants, and domestic and office workers.

The older women have a higher percentage of full-time employment, with 39.34 percent of the 36- to 49-year-olds working full-time, and 32.43 percent of the women 50 and older working full-time. It must be noted that 50 percent of the teenagers who responded are working part-time. These Hispana-Latinas are clearly in the work force. It should also be noted that the working teens contribute to the family income from their salaries. This raises the concern that educators have pointed out that working teens often have trouble doing well in high school. Latinas are not simply at home, they are and historically have been engaged in the workforce as well as in the family.

In the question regarding to whom they attribute their faith, the respondents stated that they owe their faith to their parents. This is quite strong in each age group. Among the teens, 60.80 percent said they owe their faith to their parents, as did 56.10 percent of the young adults. Among the women 36–49 years of age, 64.56 percent attributed their faith to their parents, and 52.63 percent of those 50 and older also said this. It does challenge the church as to how the family, especially the parents, are supported in developing children's faith. For example, in his apostolic exhortation *Evangelii Nuntiandi*, Pope Paul VI stresses that the family is the "domestic church" in which the various aspects of the entire church should be found.[7] From this graph it can be said that the Latino/a family is the domestic church from which the faith must be cultivated by the parents who are the "pastors" of the small community. Are church resources committed to this reality?

Because it is often stated in churches and in the larger society that Latinos/as are a people of faith, I wanted to ask a question that would allow the respondents to express whether or not this is true. This question compared importance of the faith or of religion in their lives

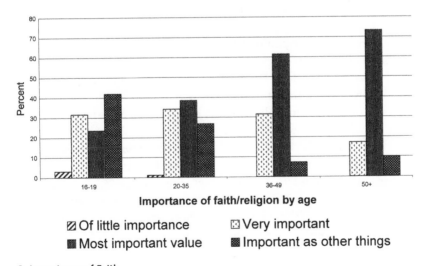

Importance of faith/religion by age

☑ Of little importance   ▨ Very important
▓ Most important value   ▦ Important as other things

3. Importance of Faith

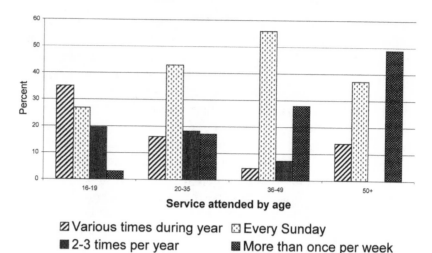

Service attended by age

☑ Various times during year ⊠ Every Sunday
■ 2-3 times per year ▨ More than once per week

4. Service Attendance

with other values. The women 36 and older said their faith is the most important value in their lives: 61.43 percent of the women ages 36–49 and 73.17 percent of those 50 and older said their faith or religion is their most important value. Not one woman mentioned anything more valuable than the faith or religion, that is, no one wrote education, material possessions, or other responses. Faith as a major value is important to all the age groups, and its significance is strongest in the opinions of the older women. Could the tendency, in this study, for its increasing importance as related to age come from one's evolving maturity?

In the question regarding the regularity or frequency of attending religious or liturgical services, only nine women said they never attend services. Therefore, these nine were not included in the graph. It would have been difficult to include such a small number as showing real significance. Certainly, it would be advantageous to be able to return to the nine who said they never attend, to ask them why. From the perspective of respect for the women, this would not be possible. The remaining number of women do participate in services. The women 36–49 tend to worship each Sunday (55.88 percent), and nearly half (48.84 percent) of those 50 and older attend services even during the week. Although the teens show lower participation, 26.80 percent attend services every Sunday, and 35.05 percent attend various times during the year. More than 40 percent of the 20- to 35-year-olds attend every Sunday.

Regarding the respondents' views on whether Hispana-Latinas should assume a greater responsibility for the church, 164 women answered that they want to assume responsibility in the church by participating in decision-making. The graph illustrates that 52.34 percent of the teens see decision-making as important, and all other age groups express this interest and concern, though in somewhat lower numbers than the teens. This could indicate that indeed, many Hispana-Latinas want to be responsible subjects within the Christian community, and they yearn to contribute rather than to passively receive. The women also express their desire for more training or education in the faith. Many stated that by participating in ministry, women can assume a greater responsibility in the church.

In the question as to how they think the church responds to the necessities of the community, 71.43 percent of the women 50 years and older said the church responds little to the necessities of the community. All ages stated they perceived the response of the church to be little. It is interesting that the older women who answered the questionnaire, and who seem to participate even in weekly eucharist, also are aware that the church can and should respond more to the needs of the community. They expect more from the church in regard to the needs of the community.

Regarding how the women see the place of the Hispana-Latina in the church, most of the women expressed that there is a growing openness but that more must be done so that women can feel that

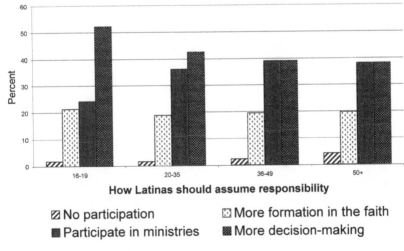

How Latinas should assume responsibility

◩ No participation   ▨ More formation in the faith
■ Participate in ministries   ▨ More decision-making

5. Responsibility to Church

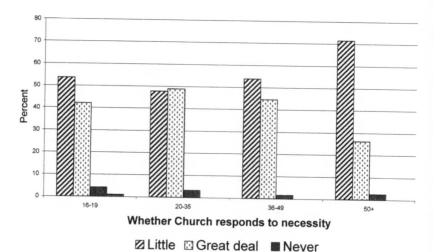

Whether Church responds to necessity

☑ Little   ▨ Great deal   ■ Never

6. Church and Community

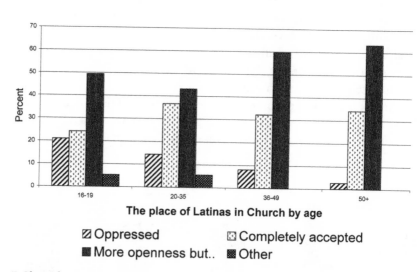

The place of Latinas in Church by age

☑ Oppressed   ▨ Completely accepted
■ More openness but..   ▨ Other

7. Place of Latina in Church

their gifts and leadership are totally welcomed within the church. Among the women 50 and older, 63.16 percent see a growing openness toward the gifts of women in the church; and 49.47 percent of the teens do. Of the women 36–49 years old, 59.68 percent see a growing openness, though they said more needs to be done. They see that they are welcomed and that they are accepted by the church;

however, there is also a reluctance or caution among them that the *mestiza* and her gifts are not totally accepted.

In graphs 8 and 9, it should be kept in mind that the women could opt for multiple answers or responses. In graph 8, four urgent issues or problems emerged from the women: the lack of education, discrimination against the Hispano-Latino/a community, the scarcity of good jobs, and poverty. Among all age groups, 163 women said a lack of education is the most urgent problem that the community must change. Discrimination was cited by 161 women; 105 cited the lack of jobs; and 91 stated that poverty was a problem. I can only conclude that the women are insightful and clear regarding these urgent issues.

When the women were asked to indicate how women can best use their intelligence and creativity in the pastoral ministry of the Hispano-Latino/a community, 139 of the 300 women said "through study and reflection." The need for training and education are basic to this group of women. The concern for study and reflection as a basis for using their creativity and intelligence was strongest among the younger adults and those 36–49 years old. Of the whole group, 111 women stated that they should use their intelligence and creativity in social justice, while 104 said their intelligence can best be expressed in leadership. Of the women, 121 saw the parish as the place for women to use their creativity and intelligence.

In the introductory remarks of this essay, I suggested that the His-

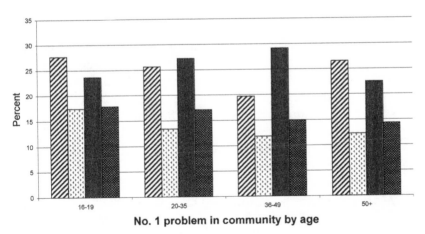

No. 1 problem in community by age

⊘ Discrimination ⊡ Poverty ▦ Lack of education ▦ Lack of jobs

8. Urgent Problems

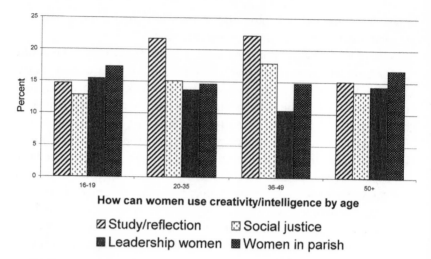

How can women use creativity/intelligence by age

▨ Study/reflection ⬚ Social justice
■ Leadership women ▦ Women in parish

9. Creativity/Intelligence

pana-Latina has remained an unrecognized voice—*una voz descono-cida*—in the church and in society. However, these three hundred women have contributed to changing this by expressing their views. There have been differing points of view, and there have even been conflicting perspectives in some of the responses, all of which inform the process of creating a pathway toward a *mestiza* feminist theology rooted in the contributions and thinking of women.

The cogent views of the women as expressed through the graphs bring new insights that contribute to the theological forum. The data gleaned and interpreted inform the theological process. The women in the study, particularly the older ones, seem to be loyal and faithful to the church. They also are capable of critical and thoughtful reflection in that they desire to have a stronger voice in the decisions that are made within the church. The women are responsible subjects of theology, of the church, and of society. Their views suggest that they are leaders who see themselves as ministers, rather than as objects who passively receive from ecclesial and societal institutions without a voice or without thoughtful and prayerful reflection.

The content of the expressions and opinions of the women is further enriched when the cultural and historical roots of *mestizaje* are also examined and explored. Therefore, in what follows, I will describe a second pathway that can lead toward a *mestiza* feminist theology. I will discuss two key feminine symbols and images that emerge from the struggle for life and for spirituality.

SECOND PATHWAY: HISTORICAL AND CULTURAL
ASPECTS FOR A MESTIZA FEMINIST THEOLOGY

Before the arrival of the Iberians in the Americas, indigenous peoples such as the Mayas, the Toltecs, and the Aztecs had developed great and magnificent civilizations. In the ancient Mayan histories, such as the creation stories in the document called the *Popol Vuh*, there is a strong theme that the Creator God was Mother and Father of the earth. In the spiritual world of the Indians, God created and blessed the universe with life.[8] From these ancient times, the Latino/a community has preserved a living tradition of an image of God that holds the characteristics of a Mother and of a Father. The Creator God is described with human and divine qualities, as one who initiates, who invites, and who blesses the universe with new life. Our community's perception of a life-giving God is actualized historically and culturally in four interrelated dimensions: *mestizaje*, the feminine presence in *mestizaje*, María de Guadalupe, and the voices of *mestizaje* in the Southwest United States.

MESTIZAJE

The long, complex, dramatic fusion of the two worlds and the two cosmo-visions between the Spanish-European and the indigenous-American is what Virgilio Elizondo has called *mestizaje*.[9] Through this gradual evolution and merging and blending of cultures, of values, of languages, and of spiritualities a new people came to be in the Americas. This period cannot be merely romanticized, for the sixteenth century in the New World was an epic of pain, of pillage, and of conquest.

In *La historia general de las cosas de la Nueva España*, the work of Franciscan Friar Bernardino de Sahagún, this era is described as he listened to the natives of New Spain and as he wrote about their lives.[10] While the conquerors searched for treasures and plundered, the missionary, at least the first missionaries of New Spain, were imbued with an idealism of a new evangelization. During the Reformation, Europe was submerged in social and religious turmoil. Spain considered itself to be the faithful Catholic nation that held steadfastly to the "true faith." History confirms that those early missionaries such as Fray Bernardino de Sahagún, Fray Toribio de Benavente, and Fray Pedro de Gante did respect the "soil" or the spiritual and cultural cosmos of the Indians.[11] They respected that the faith of Christianity could take root, only if it was cultivated within the "soil" of the indigenous cosmic spiritual world. Unfortunately, the conquerors who came with the sword plundered and destroyed the world of the indigenous. Julia Esquivel reminds us that no one felt the invasion of the conquerors more than the women of the Americas; they lived in a situation of vulnerability and of defenselessness, and they and their children would suffer prolonged uncertainty and suffering.[12] Hispana-Latinas return to this our collective memory because it holds the truth and the seeds for understanding ourselves and our *mestizo/a* communities.

THE FEMININE PRESENCE OF *MESTIZAJE*

There is need for theological reflection regarding *mestizaje* that begins with the two powerful images and figures of *mestizaje*, Guadalupe and Malinalli Tenepal (also called Malintzin). From these two major figures of our past, not only can we understand a *mestizo/a* faith, but also we can unlock key principles of a *mestiza* feminist view of our personhood.

Malinalli Tenepal, or Malintzin, was also named doña Marina by the Spaniards, while history gave her the name of La Malinche. She was the beautiful, intelligent figure of the Indian woman that continues to live in the consciousness of the *mestizo/a* memory. She was the daughter of Chief Xaltipán, who gave her to another chief, Olutal, who gave her to Spanish Captain Juan de Grijalva. Again, she was given like property to another Spaniard, Portocarrero, who later returned to Spain. During the time that Malintzin lived with Portocarrero, she learned the Spanish language, and she was able to speak Nahuatl and Maya as well. When Hernán Cortéz marched into Mexico, he took her for himself. She became indispensable to Cortéz, because she knew three languages. She was his translator and interpreter.[13]

Malintzin remains strongly embedded in the collective memory of Hispano-Latinos/as and continues to be remembered as the tragic figure of *mestizaje*. In common parlance her name is understood, even in the Hispano-Latino/a communities of the Southwest, as synonymous with "traitor." Latina researchers have begun to reconstruct the place and presence of Malintzin in a careful and methodical manner. Malintzin clearly stands, contrary to some opinions, as a symbol of an intelligent woman whose struggle to survive during the conquest holds her as a interlocutor or as a bridge between the indigenous spiritual cosmos and the Iberian Christian world.

History has blamed Malintzin for the Conquest in the same way that some have blamed Eve for the Fall . . . She was in fact a courageous woman. She was not a traitor. She stands in the history of Latinos as the mother of the *mestizo* people. She became the bridge between the Iberian and the indigenous worlds.[14]

From the union between Cortéz and Malinalli-Malintzin, a son named Martín was born. His birth became the real as well as the symbolic expression of the painful birthing of a *mestizo* people. What is so profound regarding Malinalli Tenepal is that her story and so many legends continue through the oral tradition in Mexico, as well as in the Southwest United States. I have heard it said in the Latino/a community of California: "Don't go near that lake, because la Malinche is there." When she is seen with respect as the mother of the *mestizo* people, I believe that the shadow of her image is changed and transformed into a sign of hope. In such a reinterpretation Malinalli stands out as a courageous image. She becomes the bridge between two cultures and two racial worlds. Hispana-Latinas writing in the United States, such as Jeanette Rodríguez, have clarified the misrepresentation placed on Malintzin's image and on her role in history and in the consciousness of the people of the Americas. I am suggesting that such a new understanding of her place in history and in the psyche of *mestizaje* opens a pathway for a *mestiza* feminist theology. According to Rodríguez,

What emerges from the reinterpretation of Malinche is a female historical figure, lifted out of her proper time and place made into a cultural scapegoat who was blamed for a tragic clash between cultures . . . In summary, the Mexican woman historically has been depicted as treacherous, passive, and willingly violated (i.e. Malinche). An alternative view is a young woman who was able to assess her situation and able to act according to a value system that acknowledges and honors her understanding and world view as well as concern and compassion for the people around her.[15]

MARÍA DE GUADALUPE

Through the image of the woman Guadalupe, a new spiritual world begins to open, and there begins the joining of the Indian spiritual cosmos and the Christian word, proclaimed from the Hill of Tepeyac. Through her, the story of the conquest is transformed into the story of salvation history, or of the struggle for liberation and for spiritual, psychological, and cultural rebirth. Through the person of Guadalupe and carried within her body, the word of God comes to light for the people of the Americas.[16]

With her messenger, Juan Diego, we see that he recognizes her as the Teotl, or as the mother of the Nahuatl God and the mother of the Iberian-European God, "Dios."[17] Through the person of Juan Diego, the indigenous, the *mestizos/as*, and the *españoles* see and begin to receive and to believe in the God of María de Guadalupe. She communicates through the signs and symbols of the indigenous spiritual and cultural world. Through her person, her message of hope and of liberation is communicated. She is not Mary the meek and mild, but rather she is the liberating and prophetic figure for the people. No other religious or spiritual figure penetrates the heart of the *mestizo* people as she does, and this is especially true within the Latino/a communities of the United States. Her strong feminine presence and tender voice on the Hill of Tepeyac call *mestizos* to a living faith. I do not believe that anyone can describe this fully, yet at the heart of her presence during the pain of the conquest, her word has been one of compassion and of liberation.

Through the genre of *flor y canto*,[18] she enters into the faith and culture of the indigenous and of the Iberians. The story of Tepeyac was communicated by the woman by using the symbolic language of the Nahuatl. For the Aztecs, through their language of Nahuatl, a single idea was expressed in two distinct words. The words were synonymous and conveyed the same meaning. It was a metaphorical and symbolic means of communicating the sacred and the transcendent. This language metaphorically expressed their thinking that the only path to God's self-expression or revelation was through poetry and music, or in flower and in song. In this manner, the indigenous understood God's communication to them.

She "understands the soil" or the faith and culture of the people, and from there she proclaims the word from Tepeyac, a word of liberation. Thus, she is one with the *mestizo* people in the Americas, and through *flor y canto*, poetry and song, the struggle and thirst for justice become a liberating praxis in the Americas. Her figure and presence in creating a pathway for a *mestiza* feminist theology is central, for this is no romantic symbol, but rather Guadalupe is a source of strength and of grace in a transformational and liberating praxis within our society. The memory of her words, recorded in the *Nican Mopohua*, speaks about liberation from misery and suffering for the actualization of a new life:

I very much want and ardently desire that my hermitage be erected in this place. In it I will show and give to all people all my love, my compassion, my help, and my protection because I am your merciful mother and the mother of all the nations that live on this earth who love me, who would speak with me, who would search for me, and who would place their confidence in me. There I will hear their laments and remedy and cure all their miseries, misfortunes, and sorrows.[19]

In the writing of Julia Esquivel, there is a powerful interpretation of the image of Guadalupe as Esquivel reflects on the Maya cosmogony in which the sun corresponds to the male and the moon to the female. She says that the scars and wounds of the peoples of the Americas will heal and find reconciliation and that equality of a true nature for women and for men will shine without detriment to either, precisely as soon as there is equal brightness between the sun and the moon. It can be said that the figure of Guadalupe who stands in front of the sun and who stands over the moon, has already announced this egalitarian and liberating vision as here among us.[20] By embracing the message of the woman of the Hill of Tepeyac, the people of faith begin to create a liberating praxis in the Americas.[21]

VOICES OF *MESTIZAJE* IN THE SOUTHWEST UNITED STATES

The creation of a *mestiza* feminist theology has begun from those Hispana-Latina women who gather to tell their stories of struggle and of life, who bring their shared faith and wisdom as a spiritual force which leads to hope and to liberation. In small groups of women, as has been demonstrated with the responses given by the women in the questionnaires, a process of theological reflection or of life reflection becomes a foundation for mutual support and exchange and for clarifying strategies and plans for transforming our lives and society. There is something unique and original in that much of the work of such a theology is evolving from the Hispana-Latinas living in the United States. This theology is one that is inclusive, and it is taking place among *mestizas* who feel disconnected from the church as well as among *mestizas*, Protestant and Catholic, who work from within the Christian community. By shared learning and through communal discernment, groups of women are defining and forging new horizons for their lives. There is a need to continue to link and to connect, especially with the younger members of the community, as these new pathways are opened. This is stated by Lara Medina:

Chicanas venturing into often undefined spiritual arenas continue a tradition of religious agency as lived by many of our *antepasados, abuelas, madres, y tías.* Our *consejeras, curanderas, rezadoras, espiritistas,* and even *comadres,* practiced and still practice their healing ways in spite of, in lieu of, or in conjunction with the sacraments and teachings offered by the Christian churches.[22]

Some of the most enlightening discussions on theology and spirituality from the *mestiza* perspective are being held among Chicanas. Women like Gloria Anzaldúa, Adelaida Del Castillo, and Norma Alarcón have critically analyzed the implications and impact of the figure of Malinalli Tenepal-Malintzin.[23] They see that the image of this great woman must be freed from her historical bondage in order that all *mestizas* might find the pathway to liberation and to their full humanity and dignity. She then becomes a key figure as the first woman of the Americas who has a place and a voice in the new era. This is not mere folklore, for this image contributes to the formation of a *mestizo/a* psychic consciousness that will either view Malinalli, and women in general, as traitors-*malinchistas,* or women will be perceived as strong, prophetic, intelligent, and embodied human persons.

A *mestiza* feminist theology must be grounded in Guadalupe, who, as has been described, has a prophetic place not only in indigenous and *mestizo/a* history but also in our rich spiritual history. Too often Malinalli Tenepal-Malintzin and María de Guadalupe have been viewed as oppositional figures: the "whore" and the "virgin." This is quite troublesome, yet the fact is that history has managed to limit the most powerful feminine figures to either the virgin or the whore. For example, there have been some interpretations of the scriptures that present us with either "Eva" or with "Ave" (Eve and Mary). Eve and Mary represent not this juxtapositioning, but rather women of depth, of intelligence, and of a profound faith in God, as they discover their call in salvation history.

It seems to me that the human-spiritual image of Guadalupe goes beyond the limiting roles placed on women in history. She dissolves all of our human categories, because she is a paradigmatic figure that brings new meaning to our spiritual and racial understandings. Through her human body we can begin to imagine the powerful presence of a woman who communicates with all cultures and races and who invites gender inclusiveness. She stands as a Christian figure but also as an ecumenical figure for all peoples. As *mestizas,* we have a special responsibility in continuing to see Guadalupe as central to our human-spiritual identity, while inviting peoples of other cultures to respect and reverence her as a strong source of grace and of moral agency.

In this essay, I have presented both women as necessary to a true understanding and interpretation of *mestizaje* which welcomes men and women as equal partners. The figures of both Malinalli and Guadalupe are essential in creating the foundations for a *mestiza* feminist theology. Malinalli-Tenepal is a woman of great dignity who survived her oppression and who became the racial and cultural mother and voice for the Americas. Guadalupe furthers our human dignity and is the pathway to transforming a culture of death into a culture of life, to "building a new temple." She calls and invites all who believe in her and in her word to create a new society in the Americas.

CONCLUDING REMARKS

This reflection began with the thoughts and insights of three hundred women. The views of *mestizas* form a critical part of a feminist theology. In the process the women discover their voice and their dignity and leadership. Much more time should be spent in this slow yet central manner of networking, of sharing, and of theological reflection from the experience of *mestizaje*. Planning pastoral projects and time for communal prayer and liturgical celebration among the women can then flow from such gatherings. Women's reflections should continue to focus on key cultural and spiritual images of our history and faith for a fuller understanding of ourselves as moral leaders following the pathway which leads to liberation. Following the models set by some of the *mestiza-chicana* authors, our work needs to include musicians, artists, and writers. They contribute richly to this theology, and they remind us that our work also includes a *mestiza* spirituality, which I believe can be named a spirituality of *flor y canto* (of flower and song, music and poetry). From this indigenous genre of *flor y canto* the spiritual and transcendent accompanies a *mestiza* feminist theology. Our serious searching and researching must be integrated with humor and with *fiesta*. No one expresses this better than Sandra Cisneros.

Anguiano Religious Articles

Rosaries Statues Medals
Incense Candles Talismans
Perfumes Oils Herbs

A statue is what I was thinking, or maybe those pretty 3-D pictures, the ones made from strips of cardboard that you look at sideways and you see the Santo Niño de Atocha, and you look at it straight and it's La Virgen, and you look at it from the other side and it's Saint Lucy with her eyes on a plate or maybe San Martín Caballero cutting his Roman cape in half with a sword and giving it to a beggar, only I want to know how come he didn't give that beggar all of his cape if he's so saintly, right.[24]

Little Miracles, Kept Promises

Virgencita . . .

Don't think it was easy going without you. Don't think I didn't get my share of it from everyone. Heretic. Atheist. Malinchista. Hocicona. But I wouldn't shut my yap. My mouth always getting me in trouble. Is that what they teach you at the university? Miss High-and-Mighty. Miss Thinks-She's-Too-Good-for-Us . . . Malinche. Don't think it didn't hurt being called a traitor.

I don't know how it all fell in place. How I finally understood who you are. No longer Mary the mild, but our Mother Tonantzin. Your church at Tepeyac is built on the site of her temple. Sacred ground no matter whose goddess claims it.[25]

Through theological reflection and discourse, a *mestiza* feminist theology becomes a place and process in which women are welcomed and invited to participate in doing theology in community. This theological and spiritual journey nurtures, challenges, and sustains us in the struggle for justice and dignity.[26] Women who are creating these new pathways of faith and of spirituality are grounded and committed to:

- *Shared Wisdom: Sabiduría.* By sharing life stories, women find new wisdom and God's grace, even in the experiences of chaos and crisis. Such wisdom or *sabiduría* gives substance and flavor *(sabor)* to life.
- *Community: Koinonía.* In the base communities, faith is fostered through support of one another. In the community, prayer and celebration-fiesta thrive. In this ambiance women learn about themselves within the context of Hispano-Latino/a culture.
- *Moral Leadership.* Through doing theology and by God's transforming grace, women become moral leaders. Through critical theological reflection, the art of discernment, to be able to make moral choices and judgments in the name of liberation becomes a reality. Women who become moral leaders have a commitment to the Gospel imperative to love of neighbor and to social justice (Luke 4:18–21).

NOTES

1. For the purpose of my essay I will use the terms Hispana and Latina interchangeably. Both terms have been used to designate the social and ethnic *New People* who emerged through *mestizaje* and conquest from the sixteenth century, when the indigenous peoples of the Americas and the European Iberian peoples mixed. See the glossary in *From the Heart of Our People. Latino/a Explorations in Catholic Systematic Theology*, ed. Orlando O. Espín and Miguel H. Díaz, 261–262; and *Mestizo Christianity: Theology from the Latino Perspective*, ed. Arturo J. Bañuelas.

2. Entering into the cultural context includes those inner working systems and signs and symbols which can only be "thickly" described in their configurations and complexities, as explained by Geertz. See Clifford Geertz, "Thick Description, Toward an Interpretive Theory of Culture," in *The Interpretation of Cultures, Selected Essays*, (Basic Books, 1973), 14. See Robert Schreiter, *Constructing Local Theologies:* "Only through trying to catch the sense of a culture holistically and with all its complexity will we be in the position to develop a truly responsive local theology" (28).

3. For a more complete review of this study, see Gloria Inés Loya, "The Mexican American Woman in California: Pathways Towards a Pastoral Project" (Doctor of Ministry project, Pacific School of Religion, Graduate Theological Union, 1996).

4. See Virgilio Elizondo, who continues to deepen our awareness and understanding of the reality of *mestizaje*, in *The Future Is Mestizo, Life Where Cultures Meet:* "From a realization of the uniqueness of the Mexican *mestizo*, as proclaimed in that inscription at the Plaza de las Tres Culturas in Mexico City, I moved to a discovery of the new *mestizaje* of the Southwest that was pulling Anglos and Mexican-Americans alike into the formation of a new humanity. As some would say, this was the emergence of the new cultural nation of Mexicamerica. As I consciously rewalked the historical pilgrimage, no longer through the categories of conquest but through the categories of birth, I saw the identity of the new being in a new light" (73).

5. María Pilar Aquino, "Directions and Foundations of Hispanic/Latino Theology: *Toward a Mestiza Theology of Liberation*," in Bañuelas, *Mestizo Christianity*, 192.

6. See Albert Camarillo, *Chicanos in California, a History of Mexican Americans in California*.

7. Pope Paul VI, *Evangelii Nuntiandi: On Evangelization in the Modern World* (Washington, D.C.: United States Catholic Conference, 1975), 51.

8. Albertina Saravia, ed., *El Popol Vuh*, 1.

9. Virgilio Elizondo, "*Mestizaje* as a Locus of Theological Reflection," in *Frontiers of Hispanic Theology in the United States*, ed. Allan Figueroa Deck, 104–123.

10. Robert Ricard, *The Spiritual Conquest of Mexico, An Essay on the Apostolate and the Evangelizing Methods of the Mendicant Orders in New Spain: 1523–1572*, 42. Fray Bernardino de Sahagún worked on this historical and linguistic work for some thirty years. It was written in Castilian and in Nahuatl and expressed the beliefs and customs of the indigenous of New

Spain. It is said that he was meticulous as well as fastidious in preparing new missionaries, especially in the linguistic understanding of theological concepts.

11. Enrique Dussel, ed., *Historia general de la iglesia en América Latina,* 28–48.

12. Julia Esquivel, "Conquered and Violated Women," in *The Voice of the Victims, 1492–1992,* ed. Leonardo Boff and Virgilio Elizondo, 68–77.

13. Nancy O'Sullivan-Beare, *Las Mujeres de los Conquistadores: la Mujer Española en los Comienzos de la Colonización Americana,* 85.

14. Gloria Inés Loya, "Considering the Sources/Fuentes for a Hispanic Feminist Theology," *Theology Today* 54, no. 4 (January 1998): 494.

15. Jeanette Rodríguez, *Our Lady of Guadalupe: Faith and Empowerment among Mexican-American Women,* 75.

16. Virgilio Elizondo, *La Morenita: Evangelizadora de las Américas,* 55–56. Also see Elizondo, *Guadalupe, Mother of the New Creation.*

17. Elizondo, *Guadalupe,* 12.

18. Miguel León-Portilla, ed., introduction to *Cantos y Crónicas del México Antiguo,* 7–46.

19. Elizondo, *Guadalupe,* 8, and *La Morenita,* 76.

20. Esquivel, "Conquered and Violated," 76–77.

21. Marcello de Carvalho Azevedo, *Inculturation and the Challenges of Modernity,* 7. Azevedo discusses the relationship between the Christian message and culture. He goes beyond what the anthropologists propose, as he speaks on behalf of the faith which transmits meanings, and representations between those who belong to a particular culture. These symbols, meanings, and representations are foundational for a genuinely liberating praxis.

22. Lara Medina, "Los espíritus siguen hablando: Chicana Spiritualities," in *Living Chicana Theory,* ed. Carla Trujillo, 189.

23. Gloria Anzaldúa, *Borderlands/La Frontera. The New Mestiza;* Norma Alarcón, "Chicanas' Feminist Literature: A Re-Vision through Malintzin, OR Malintzin: Putting Flesh Back on the Object," in *This Bridge Called My Back: Writings by Radical Women of Color,* ed. Cherríe Moraga and Gloria Anzaldúa, 182–190; Norma Alarcón, "Traddutora, Traditora: A Paradigmatic Figure of Chicana Feminism," in *Scattered Hegemonies: Postmodernity and Transnational Feminist Practices,* ed. Inderpal Grewal and Caren Kaplan, 110–133; and Adelaida del Castillo, "Malintzín Tenepal: A Preliminary Look into a New Perspective," in *Chicana Feminist Thought: The Basic Historical Writings,* ed. Alma M. García, 122–126.

24. For a wonderful insight into the *mestizo-chicano* reality in the Southwest, Sandra Cisneros captures the power, the faith, the humor, and she does it with such wit. Her stories always take us into the depths of the *mestizo* experience. See Sandra Cisneros, *Woman Hollering Creek and Other Short Stories,* 114.

25. Ibid., 127–128.

26. For an excellent and exciting view of a theology for the present and future see Ada María Isasi-Díaz, *Mujerista Theology: A Theology for the Twenty-First Century.*

CHAPTER 12

NOTES TOWARD A CHICANAFEMINIST EPISTEMOLOGY (AND WHY IT IS IMPORTANT FOR LATINA FEMINIST THEOLOGIES)

NANCY
PINEDA-
MADRID

Epistemology,[1] which deals with the origin, nature, and limits of knowing, and with the validity of what constitutes knowledge, plays a preeminent role in Latinas' drive toward full humanity.[2] The very process of creating and validating "knowledge" vitally contributes to the "humanization" of subordinated populations like Latinas. This is so precisely because Latinas, and others, lack the institutional power to re-order the boundaries of what the dominant society defines as knowledge. Even though oppression may be described as racism, sexism, classism, heterosexism, and so forth, or be understood as the cumulative and interconnected effect of several "isms" (which is often the case for Latinas and others), ultimately oppression means being prevented from naming our world and ourselves. At its root, oppression—as both a social and an internalized phenomenon—has to do with who controls the creation and validation of knowledge, with *epistemology*; and with the ability to act on that knowledge, with *humanization*. As theorist Audre Lorde warns, "[I]t is axiomatic that if we do not define ourselves for ourselves, we will be defined by others—for their use and to our detriment."[3]

In recent decades the work of a growing number of theorists, particularly feminist theorists,[4] strongly undermines the idea that knowledge and the process of knowing can be conceptualized ahistorically and acontextually. As a result, the very possibility of a general theory of knowledge is now seriously suspect. What we have commonly referred to as "knowledge," they rightly argue, is bound up in a "structure of inequality which is gendered,"[5] and I would add, bound in multiple ways to a global systemic inequality. This insight, among other effects, calls attention to the inherent relationship between epistemology and politics. On the one hand, epistemology must never be reduced to politics; but on the other, any credible epistemology cannot ignore the sociopolitical dimensions of knowledge.

Nonetheless, epistemological commitments, whether implicit or explicit, serve as the rational foundation for all intellectual work and have implications for the pursuit of truth. In striving toward the truth of God, theologians invariably assume an epistemology.

The primary aim of this essay is not to engage in an exhaustive study of the emerging discourse of Chicana feminisms, although this essay does draw on the work of some prominent Chicana theorists; nor is it to detail the multiple and significant connections between such discourse and Latina feminist theologies. Rather, the primary aim of this essay is to offer a prolegomenon toward a possible ChicanaFeminist epistemology *by naming two important "anchoring" themes (la familia and Chicana womanhood)* whose epistemic interpretations matter in Chicanas' drive toward their full humanity.[6] The significance of a Chicana feminist epistemology lies in its ability to provide a theoretical foundation for Latina feminist theologies, which in turn strengthens the force of their assertions.

Why connect an epistemology grounded in *Chicana* feminism to the development of *Latina* feminist theologies? Self-identified Chicanas have written almost all the work used in this essay. Their work as theorists or artists or both deliberately engages Chicana experience. Their work embodies an important and historical field of study thus far not substantially employed by U.S. Latina theologians. Moreover, U.S. Latina theologians hold as one of their central goals the articulation of theology *from* the perspective of women of Latin American ancestry, a large number of whom are Chicanas. Chicana theory has much to contribute to the future of U.S. Latina theologies.

This three-part essay begins by situating the project of a possible ChicanaFeminist epistemology in context. Some preliminary questions are examined: Who is a ChicanaFeminist? Who has a legitimate role in shaping ChicanaFeminist thought? What distinguishes an epistemology as ChicanaFeminist? The second part names the two anchoring themes to be explored and provides an analysis of their significance. In the final part, I briefly explore the contribution which a ChicanaFeminist epistemology can make to Latina feminist theologies.

THE WHO AND WHAT OF A CHICANAFEMINIST EPISTEMOLOGY

Throughout this essay the words "Chicana" and "Feminist" are run together (ChicanaFeminist) to signify the integral reality embodied in this field of discourse.[7] But they are kept separate when they refer to a person or group of people because for some, they are not co-extensive. "ChicanaFeminist" cannot be reduced to simply "a different version of feminist theory," nor to "a different version of race theory." It could be just as easily written "FeministChicana." ChicanaFeminist is a *gestalt* of a particular race and gender consciousness which theorists attempt to capture in ideas and concepts. It typically includes a critical consciousness of class and sexual orientation as well. It cannot simply be understood as a critique or deconstruction of feminist or race theory. It has integrity of its own.

Who is a Chicana feminist? And who has a legitimate role in defining ChicanaFeminist thought? The two extreme positions, one "materialist" and the other "idealist," assist in framing a response to these questions. A materialist position asserts that the life experience that comes with being born a woman of Mexican ancestry makes one a Chicana feminist. Here the deciding factor is biology. Adherents of this position argue that in the United States, most women of Mexican ancestry repeatedly face situations that reinforce the worldview that as a brown person, as a female person, and often as a poor person, she is less than human. Upon reflection, such experiences may provoke a critical awareness of how social structures collude in forming a worldview that deems Chicanas inferior.

At the other end of the spectrum, arguments can be made for the exclusive norm of a critical and political consciousness as determinative of a Chicana feminist. This is the idealist position. On this view, any person who seeks to subvert the hegemonic paradigm, which strives to keep Chicanas subordinate, deserves the title "Chicana feminist." And therefore, such persons, as a result of their ideological commitments, have a legitimate role in shaping Chicana-Feminist thought.

The most compelling response to the questions incorporates elements of both positions. The very origins of the term "Chicana/o" suggest as much. In the 1960s, some U.S.-born people of Mexican descent "recuperated, appropriated and recodified the term Chicano to form a new political class,"[8] one that embodied a critical consciousness aimed at breaking through the hyphenated existence of "Mexican-American" to a more integral identity. Feminist Chicanas assumed significant roles from the outset of the development of this new political class. Contemporary discussions of the term reflect much of its origins. Theorist Norma Alarcón observes:

Thus, the name Chicana, in the present, is the name of resistance that enables cultural and political points of departure and thinking through the multiple migrations and dislocations of women of "Mexican" descent. The name Chicana is not a name that women (or men) are born to or with, as is often the case with "Mexican," but rather it is consciously and critically assumed and serves as a point of redeparture for dismantling historical conjunctures of crisis, confusion, political and ideological conflict, and contradictions of the simultaneous effects of having "no names," having "many names," not "know[ing] her names," and being someone else's "dreamwork." . . . in the Mexican-descent continuum of meanings, Chicana is still the name that brings into focus the interrelatedness of class/race/gender into play and forges the link to actual subaltern native women in the U.S./Mexican dyad.[9]

Chicana as a point of "redeparture" foregrounds the importance of a "class/race/gender" critical and political consciousness as well as the life experience of Mexican/indigenous women. While others may contribute to the shaping of ChicanaFeminist thought, the primary responsibility for defining and validating it must rest with those who are Chicanas. A particular authenticity and congruity belongs exclusively to those who not only ascribe to its critical and political consciousness but also materially experience the reality of being a Chicana.[10]

Therefore, Chicana feminist theorists and artists play a unique role when they interpret Chicana experience through writing, activism, art, scholarship, teaching, and intellectual work. This role originates from three sources. First, their day-to-day life experience as Chicanas, according to theologian María Pilar Aquino, gives them a singular view of the world emergent from the diverse means by which Chicanas (and all human beings) reproduce themselves, appropriate the world, and engage in relationships which in turn influence the wider social context.[11] Second, in cooperation with other Chicanas, Chicana feminist theorists and artists can generate a particular vision that emerges from the dialectic of critical reflection and emancipatory action, which must include both the knowledge of Chicanas that emerges from daily living and the knowledge of Chicanas who engage in intellectual work as a profession. Third, through their work Chicana feminist theorists and artists can create the necessary and relatively autonomous space in which an uninhibited discussion of ChicanaFeminism can occur, which in turn can enable the growth of an inner core of authority and confidence in what it means to be a Chicana feminist. The collective work of Norma Alarcón, Cherríe Moraga, Gloria Anzaldúa, and Ana Castillo, to name only a few,[12] exemplifies such an autonomous space. This autonomous "space" does not reflect a separation from life. On the contrary, this space allows the reality of Chicanas to be explored fully and critically and to be named with authority. In brief, Chicana feminist theorists and artists play a preeminent role in the creation and validation of knowledge which furthers Chicanas' emancipatory goal.[13]

What, then, distinguishes an epistemology as *ChicanaFeminist*? A brief survey of feminist epistemologies will clarify the need for an explicitly ChicanaFeminist epistemology.

For almost two decades a growing number of feminist theorists from across the academic spectrum have brought to light not only the significance of gender to the production of knowledge but also the inherently political character of validating knowledge-claims.[14] Political scientist Christine Sylvester loosely categorizes feminist epistemologies into three groups. First, *feminist empiricist epistemologies*, which start from "the premise that modern science provides a valuable way of knowing the activities of women in the world and, therefore, [modern science is] a potentially helpful tool for recovering . . . [women's] contributions to civilization." These epistemologies judge the scientific approach to knowledge as "contaminated" only by virtue of its "social biases against women." This contamination can be remedied by "incorporating more feminist women and problematiques into research enterprises."[15] But ultimately these epistemologies leave the mechanics and politics of knowledge production largely unchallenged. To put it more colloquially, the rules of the game are not under scrutiny. Only who has a seat at the game table is called into question. The commitments of these epistemologies imply that when "reason" and "rationality" are used well, they ultimately lead everyone to reliable and unbiased knowledge. An effective ChicanaFeminist epistemology would have little in common with empiricist epistemologies because a ChicanaFeminist epistemology would need to call into question the game itself—a much more radical concern than is operative in this group.

Feminist standpoint epistemologies, the second group, begin "from the perspective of women's lives . . . because [this perspective] leads to socially constructed claims that are less false—less partial and distorted"—than claims that privileged men can socially construct."[16] In a general sense, a standpoint refers to a group of people who "share socially and politically significant characteristics."[17] Yet feminist standpoint epistemologies face a host of challenges. Women's ways of knowing "may be distorted by patriarchy" and distorted by the racist, classist, and heterosexist biases embedded in the social network of relationships which shape women's lives. As Alarcón argues, if the ideal woman is assumed to be the self-sufficient individual, as is the case in much feminist theory, then the "native female's" and "woman of color's" ways of knowing can be greatly marginalized if not summarily excluded.[18] Standpoint epistemologies "can homogenize the diversity of women's experiences in the world" by making "biological difference" the primary difference and therefore the "ultimate foundation of truth."[19] However, some feminist theorists who take these limitations seriously have theorized the idea of "standpoint" so as to reflect the complexity and significant differences in women's lives.[20] Admitting the challenges which surface in the attempt to describe "standpoint," they nonetheless consistently recognize, and thereby call attention to, "women as agents of knowledge and theory."[21] In addition, standpoint epistemologies poignantly challenge epistemologies that claim objectivity while articulating the perspectives of only a few elites. They move toward embodying what theorist Cherríe Moraga refers to as "theory in the flesh," namely a theorizing which emerges out of the daily experiences of women rather than one which begins with some faceless, abstract, "generic" woman. But do these epistemologies go far enough?

Postmodern feminist epistemologies, the third and final group, incorporate strands of the skepticism of postmodern thought regarding the "social formation of subjects" with strands of "standpoint feminism." Drawing from postmodern thought, these epistemologies take a critical approach toward the universalizing interpretations of gender, race, social relations, knowledge, and so forth which reside in the notion of the "social formation of subjects." Hence, the serious failures of these universalizing interpretations must be exposed. From standpoint feminism, these epistemologies retain the "politics of self-assertion." Within this group, epistemologists tenuously negotiate the intellectual ground between the significance of gender and self-assertion, the hallmark of standpoint epistemologies, on the one hand, and the utter inadequacy of any universalizing, coherent explanations which ignore and appropriate difference and particularity—a central insight of postmodern thought—on the other hand.[22]

Broadly speaking, ChicanaFeminist discourse and its explicit and implicit emerging epistemologies belong in this final group.[23] ChicanaFeminist discourse resonates strongly with the politics of self-assertion characteristic of standpoint feminism, and also with the postmodern critique of theory which ignores difference. In the work of Chicana feminist theorists and artists, differences of class, race, and so forth matter *as much as* gender. For many among the contemporary generation of Chicanas, their participation in the Chicano Movement as well as in the white feminist movement advanced the development of their sociopolitical consciousness.[24] In short, Chicana consciousness is a multilayered reality.

A specific ChicanaFeminist theory of knowledge is necessary because the primacy of Chicanas' multiple consciousness, distinguished by various asymmetrical relations (e.g., race, class, culture, sexual orientation) does not typically characterize Anglo-feminist epistemologies. While some developed Anglo-feminist epistemologies recognize and explore these differences, in the end they use difference largely for descriptive and illustrative purposes, and therefore not as part of their central analytical work. This is inadequate. Alarcón supports this conclusion, calling it the "common denominator" problem. She argues:

. . . [*This Bridge Called My Back's*][25] challenge to the Anglo-American subject of feminism has yet to effect a newer discourse . . . Anglo feminist readers of *Bridge* tend to appropriate it, cite it as an instance of difference between women, and proceed to negate that difference by subsuming women of color into the unitary category of woman/women. The latter is often viewed as the "common denominator" in an oppositional (counter-identifying) discourse with some white men, that leaves us unable to explore relationships among women . . . the female subject of *Bridge* is highly complex. She is and has been *constructed in a crisis of meaning situation* [italics mine] which includes racial and cultural divisions and conflicts. The psychic and material violence that gives shape to that subjectivity cannot be underestimated nor passed over lightly.

The fact that not all this violence comes from men in general but also from women renders the notion of "common denominator" problematic.[26]

Chicanas must engage the complexity of their lived reality in the process of resisting that which needlessly limits or restrains Chicanas' full humanity.

Moreover, a ChicanaFeminist epistemology is necessary because much of Anglo feminist thought proceeds as if becoming a woman can be understood, defined, and clarified fundamentally in "opposition to men." Yet in this country, and many others, race and class as well as gender function as preeminent, organizing principles. A woman becomes a woman not only in opposition to men but also in opposition to other women. The sociopolitical consciousness of being a woman becomes dangerously simplistic, narrow, and distorted when the asymmetrical relations of race, class, and sexual orientation are deemed secondary or irrelevant. Consciousness can be the site of a multi-voiced subjectivity, which means that a woman can come to know her subjectivity through several themes, not merely one. In this schema, it is the experience of several "competing notions for one's allegiance or self-identification" that forms one's subjectivity. Multi-voiced subjectivity requires opting for several themes, a decision which is at once theoretical and political.[27]

It is only through naming and struggling with the dissonance provoked by prevailing but inadequate common-denominator feminisms that Chicanas will begin to glimpse the potential strands for a new ChicanaFeminist epistemology. This essay attempts to catch sight of some of those "potential strands" to examine the evolving, dynamic, and fluid self-understanding of Chicanas and its epistemic, humanizing implications. This constitutes the subject of the next section.

ANCHORING THEMES FOR A CHICANAFEMINIST EPISTEMOLOGY

In peering through the multifaceted kaleidoscope of Chicana particularity, how do we discover the material backdrop for Chicanas' particular *standpoint(s)* on their own experience? The term *standpoint(s)*, and not *standpoint* or *standpoints*, best signifies the shared experience yet enormous differences that exist between Chicanas. Chicana identities are and have been "constructed in a crisis of meaning situation."[28] At these crisis moments the very question of how we know and what knowledge is valid for a particular Chicana or for Chicanas collectively becomes of vital significance. Chicanas' drive toward self-understanding in their familial relationships, in their own womanhood, in their response to claims on their sexual identity and power, and so forth, surfaces a crisis-of-meaning situation. As theologian David Tracy points out, these crisis moments embody occasions in which our humanity is at stake.

Interpretation is a lifelong project for any individual in any culture. But only in times of cultural crisis does the question of interpretation itself become central . . . We need to reflect on what none of us can finally evade: the need to interpret in order to understand at all . . . Every time we act, deliberate, judge, understand, or even experience, we are interpreting. To understand at all is to interpret. To act well is to interpret a situation demanding some action and to interpret a correct strategy for that action. To experience in other than a purely passive sense (a sense less than human) is to interpret; and to be "experienced" is to have become a good interpreter. Interpretation is thus a question as unavoidable, finally, as experience, understanding, deliberation, judgment, decision, and action. To be human is to act reflectively, to decide deliberately, to understand intelligently, to experience fully. Whether we know it or not, to be human is to be a skilled interpreter.[29]

In sum, crisis-of-meaning situations create the space for interpretations that reveal self-understanding even as they embody "knowing." These interpretations disclose themselves as signs, whether verbal or visual, which bear insights about the self, others, and the world; they expose a self-others-world apprehension. These interpretations—while fluid, dynamic, and evolving—constitute the very material backdrop of Chicanas' particular standpoint(s).

Moreover, the liberation of Chicanas weighs in the balance of their interpretations. Their interpretations either perpetuate a silencing of and a disconnection from the self, or they forge the development of interior authority and self-trust. When Chicanas tenaciously and critically cling to their own reality by naming themselves and their world, they not only affirm but actualize their humanity. Through this interpretative process, cognitive authority emerges and deepens.

However, as stated above, a ChicanaFeminist epistemology will ally itself more closely with postmodern feminist epistemology than with standpoint feminist epistemology. At stake in this choice of alliance is how *difference* is taken into account. Obviously, enormous differences are evident among Chicanas. Not all are poor. Not all experience race in a comparable manner. The same may also be said of Anglo women, but the key distinction here is that for a Chicana-

Feminist epistemology, *race* and *class* complement gender as primary categories for analytical work. Chicanas' standpoint(s) reflect(s) not an essentialized understanding of experience but a loosely resonant collection of interpretations which link Chicanas together under the umbrella term Chicana. If the term "Chicana" is to have any meaning at all, and it does, there must be some distinguishing factors, patterns, or processes that bring about broad recognition. The necessary challenge is to avoid essentializing the diverse experiences of Chicanas while explicating the meaning of the term "Chicana." The term standpoint(s) signifies this particular challenge.[30]

Various anchoring themes constitute Chicanas' particular standpoint(s). These anchoring themes reflect points of notable tension, places where Chicanas are and have been "constructed in a crisis of meaning."[31] The notions of *la familia* and *Chicana womanhood*, both anchoring themes, play a potent and pervasive role in shaping the collective Chicana (and Chicano) consciousness. The significance of these two themes lies in their symbolic character, in other words, in their ability to bear such an abundance of meaning that any explication of their meaning is ultimately insufficient. Thus, these themes are vital. Yet many other anchoring themes bear similar import (e.g., work and the struggle to survive; race and ethnicity; language and the shaping of identity; sexuality and power). The following discussion of these two themes argues that Chicanas' drive toward an emancipatory self-understanding utterly depends upon how they interpret these themes.

THE UNSETTLED NOTION OF *LA FAMILIA*

The symbol and idea of *la familia* functions in a compelling fashion for both Chicanas and Chicanos. The efficacious power of *la familia* resides in the deeply rooted communal, relational self-understanding of Chicanas and Chicanos. Notions of the "self" invariably mean "self in community." Accordingly, the social construct of *la familia* constitutes one of the anchoring themes that Chicanas necessarily interpret in their drive toward self-understanding. *La familia* endures as a potent symbol.[32]

One example of the potency of *la familia* can be observed in the ideological and organizational role which it has played in the Chicano movement. *La familia* emerged as the central organizing symbol around which the movement rallied and forged a deep loyalty among its proponents. The language of *carnalismo* associated with the movement expressed this deep loyalty.[33] A *carnal* is someone who is of one's flesh. *Carnalismo* therefore can loosely be translated to mean a sisterhood or brotherhood. But unlike these rough equivalents in English, *carnal* carries a strong material sensibility. Being a *carnal* or *carnala* means being part of an extended family which affirms your presence within the family and anticipates your loyalty. Patricia Zavella explains that the centrality of *la familia* to the ideology of the Chicano movement served to promote ideas of "unity, strength and struggle within adversity."[34] When conflicts and antagonisms surfaced, loyalty to *la familia* was invoked as a means to suppress discord.

The Chicano movement remains a helpful point of reference because many of the challenges evidenced in the movement continue to influence the contemporary Chicana/o community. What follows are examples illustrating how *la familia* continues to be a symbol of contested meanings and a symbol whose interpretation shapes and reflects Chicana knowing, thereby influencing Chicanas' humanizing quest.

During the Chicano movement, Chicanas opted for differing interpretations of their own humanity—some interpretations silenced and cut off dimensions of Chicana womanhood, signaling a distorted commitment to Chicana humanity, whereas other interpretations signaled an enhanced, open-ended commitment to their humanity. In the former instance, Chicanas held that *la familia* implied a tacit acceptance of male dominance. For these Chicanas ("loyalists"), sexual equality was not among the central priorities of the movement. For them, liberation meant liberation of *la raza* (the Chicano people) as defined by the male leadership. Too much was at stake to consider liberation in more far-reaching terms. As feminist Chicana Nieto-Gomez observes:

Many loyalists felt that these complaints from women ("feminists") were potentially destructive and could only divide the Chicano movement. If sexual inequalities existed they were an "in-house" problem which could be dealt with later. However, right then, there were more important priorities to attend to, e.g., Vietnam, *La Huelga*, police brutality, etc.[35]

For these loyalist Chicanas, the collapse of an old worldview of male public leadership remained beyond their imagination and their courage. They were content to wait. When faced with an opportunity to reinterpret Chicana womanhood toward an emancipatory goal, the loyalists opted out. They interpreted Chicana womanhood such that Chicanas' liberation as women was secondary.

Thus Chicana humanity, rather than being made invisible by asymmetrical dyadic race, class, and gender relations of Chicanos and whites, was subverted by a traditionally defined vision of *la familia*. In the process, oppressions became hierarchically ranked, with race occupying the apex, and gender and class part of the second or third tier. At first glance, such a position might have appeared attractive because it entailed an assertion of cultural identity and racial pride, one which linked all Chicanas/os together. But for Chicanas who accepted such a ranking, they did so at the price of minimizing a principle dimension of themselves. Their humanity remained defined by the other. They settled for a position of less-than-full responsibility, and one of compromised autonomy. When taken to an extreme such a position eventually leads to depression, cynicism, and total despair.[36]

But some Chicanas opted for a different path, insisting upon Chicanas' liberation as women. These feminist Chicanas criticized the norm of exclusive male leadership and, as sociologist Alma García explains, found themselves at the center of controversy and accused of being anti-*familia*. The loyalists asserted that these feminist Chicanas had allowed themselves to be influenced by the Anglo women's movement and by the individualism of the Anglo society. In spite of this, feminist Chicanas continued to affirm that self-determination, liberation, and equality for *Chicanas* as well as for Chicanos could not merely be swept under the rug.[37]

This gender fault line within the Chicano movement forced Chicana leaders to wrestle with particular questions: Who are we in public settings? What are the priorities for us as Chicanas? Which public roles should we claim? In the process of engaging these questions and testing different answers, these feminist Chicanas began the risky and painful, but deeply affirming, process of searching for new ways to name themselves and their world. They honored their own contributions to the movement in the face of those who had little regard for them. The traditional, patriarchal interpretation of *la familia* did not hold these Chicanas captive. In the act of redefining themselves, they began to forge an altered understanding of *la familia*.

These feminist Chicanas contested the patriarchal interpretation of *la familia* not only in public, but also in the private sphere of their home life. In this private sphere, these Chicanas reinterpreted their identities such that their own subjectivity and personhood took on a much greater significance for them.[38] Some sought sweeping changes, while others chose not to reject the traditional female role within the family but to open it up by discarding its constricting features and enhancing its importance. Their knowing of themselves and their world had shifted. No longer did they identify themselves exclusively in terms of the roles they played in relation to the male figures in their lives. They now assumed greater responsibility for their particular personhood.

However, these examples only mention interpretations of *la familia* from within a heterosexually circumscribed universe. This begs the same question: Who interprets *la familia?* Some Chicanas, out of fidelity to their own reality and in their drive toward full humanity, have questioned the short-sided boundaries of this heterosexual universe, a move which has again elicited anti-*familia* accusations. In *The Last Generation*, Moraga strongly criticizes the norms that have traditionally defined and confined *la familia*, keeping it a "culturally correct" *familia*. These traditional norms have excluded and continue to exclude the validity of "female sexuality generally and male homosexuality and lesbian specifically," all of which she argues are relevant today.[39] For Moraga, *la familia* can mean Chicanas coming together for the purpose of exploring and celebrating Chicana womanhood, for the purpose of being *la familia* for one another.

In theorist Yvonne Yarbro-Bejarano's examination of Moraga's play *Giving up the Ghost*, she uncovers a vision of *la familia* that places the humanization of women at the center.[40] If such a community does not exist, claims Moraga's protagonist, Corky, she will create it. In the process of interpreting their experience in a manner which honors the fullness of that experience, Chicana thinkers like Moraga provoke new understandings of *la familia*.

How Chicanas interpret *la familia* matters. Their interpretations of *la familia* signify their knowledge and belief about the self-others-world relationship. In their drive toward self-understanding, do Chicanas swallow in silent acceptance the traditional explanations of who they are in the context of *la familia*, or do they struggle toward fullness in their lives, attempting to make sense of reality as they experience it?

CONTESTED "MODELS" OF CHICANA WOMANHOOD

Tracing their origins back to the conquest of Mexico, particular symbols of womanhood continue to play significant roles in shaping the imagination of the Mexican and Chicana/o community. These ideal-

ized and demonized versions of womanhood (e.g., Our Lady of Guadalupe, La Malinche, La Llorona) powerfully symbolize the "good" and
"evil" of female humanity. Even so, simple or definitive interpretations of these symbols always elude the interpreter. Such interpretations are never secured, nor will they ever be. Nonetheless, the significance of these symbols for Chicanas becomes apparent with the
extent to which Chicanas do or do not identify with particular interpretations of these symbols. In this negotiation of identity, Chicanas
actualize their self-understanding.

The oppression experienced by Chicanas (e.g., the cumulative effect of racism, classism, sexism, and heterosexism) finds its ideological legitimacy in particular meanings attributed to symbols and powerful myths. As with any system of domination, those who control
and benefit from the current asymmetrical power relations will seek
to control the interpretation of these symbols so as to perpetuate
their hegemony. More specifically, these symbols, especially those
explored below, have been and still are used to cloak and sanitize oppressive social relations so that ". . . racism, sexism, and poverty appear to be natural, normal, and an inevitable part of everyday life."[41]
What results is the attempt to keep Chicanas at arm's distance, im-
aged as other (exotic, oddly fascinating, mysterious, more "natural").

For those who control current sociopolitical systems, the "otherness" of Chicanas is rooted in an epistemology of oppositional dichotomies such as mind/body, reason/emotion, fact/opinion, and so
forth. These hierarchically ordered dichotomies create patterns of
domination and subordination in which most Chicanas, along with
many women of color, "occupy a position" representing the cumulative subordinate half. Moraga illustrates and affirms this point when
she writes,

At times, they took the worst of Mexican machismo and Aztec warrior bra-
vado, combined it with some of the most oppressive male-conceived idealiza-
tions of "traditional" Mexican womanhood and called that cultural integrity.
They subscribed to a machista view of women, based on the centuries-old vir-
gin-whore paradigm of la Virgen de Guadalupe and Malintzin Tenepal. Guadalupe represented the Mexican ideal of "la madre sufrida," the long-suffering
desexualized Indian mother, and Malinche was "la chingada," sexually stigmatized by her transgression of "sleeping with the enemy," Hernan Cortez.
Deemed traitor by Mexican tradition, the figure of Malinche was invoked to
keep Movimiento women silent, sexually passive, and "Indian" in the colonial
sense of the word.[42]

It remains clear that those who effectively define these symbols hold a major instrument of power. The extent to which Chicanas interpret these symbols so as to resist their assigned position of subordination makes a profound difference. Inside this resistance lives a transformed knowledge of the self for Chicanas, and in transforming themselves Chicanas transform the world. When Chicanas take on a self-understanding which furthers their resistance to positions of subordination, then Chicanas claim power over their own lives and actualize the integral value of their humanity.

Two symbols are worthy of particular attention: *la madre pura y sufrida*, symbolized by Our Lady of Guadalupe; and the whore, *la vendida*, symbolized by La Malinche.

LA MADRE PURA Y SUFRIDA SYMBOLIZED BY THE VIRGIN OF GUADALUPE

Arguably the most influential icon of Chicana womanhood, the Virgin of Guadalupe provokes charged passion around diverging interpretations. Interpretations of Guadalupe reflect a wide range of meanings.[43] Many scholars and artists, but not all, call attention to the apparent connections between the Virgin of Guadalupe and the Virgin Mary. In these discussions her attributes include varying combinations of motherhood, faith, purity, goodness, strength, power, self-abnegation, liberation, and passivity. Others call attention to her association with the mother goddess Tonantzín, one of the Náhuatl deities. This most formidable female goddess had power over the creation and extinction of life and had the capability to act for good or evil. When drawing connections between Guadalupe and Tonantzín, Chicana writers emphasis Guadalupe's more progressive and powerful aspects.

Some Chicanas interpret the Virgin of Guadalupe as the ideal to which they should aspire as wives and mothers. However, this "ideal" often contains an implicit judgment, namely that the value of Chicana womanhood is reflected *exclusively*, or at least ultimately, through the roles of wife and mother. To define the value of Chicana womanhood so narrowly restricts and undermines Chicanas who choose to define their womanhood in other ways. Moreover, some Chicanas uncritically accept the patriarchally defined ideal of "good wife and mother." This ideal, they believe, is symbolized in Guadalupe conflated with the Virgin Mary, which for them upholds a woman who aspires to docility, purity, self-abnegation, obedience, and de-sexualized existence.[44] NietoGomez (as quoted by Alma M. García) critiques the resulting effects of such an interpretation when she writes:

Some Chicanas are praised as they emulate the sanctified example set by [the Virgin] Mary. The woman par excellence is mother and wife. She is to love and support her husband and to nurture and teach her children. Thus, may she gain fulfillment as a woman. For a Chicana bent upon fulfillment of her personhood, this restricted perspective of her role as a woman is not only inadequate but crippling.[45]

Yet, other writers put forward a contrasting interpretation of Guadalupe, one which honors her strength and power precisely as a mother.

Thus for Chicano culture, the Virgin of Guadalupe represents characteristics considered positive for women: unselfish giving, intercession between earth and spirit, and the ideal qualities of motherhood. She is the higher being who can be appealed to on a very personal level . . . Many women feel the Virgin has much more power than the "official" ascendancy given to her by the church. For one thing, she is seen as having a mother's hold over her son—that it is not just through him that she derives her power, but that from the respect he has for her, she only has to look at him for him to obey her commands. In her images in Chicano culture, she stands alone—without her son—and in her dress she wears the ancient symbols of Tonantzín.[46]

Chicanas, such as those whose interpretations of Guadalupe are reflected in the above quote, maintain that Guadalupe can symbolize autonomous and virtuous power, a woman who is not primarily defined by her relationships to men. This interpretation of Guadalupe supports a more expansive ideal of womanhood, one which affirms a self-referential mode of authority. This interpretation de-centers externally imposed, patriarchy-serving interpretations and offers instead a vision of vital Chicana personhood.

In addition to embodying an ideal for wives and mothers, the Virgin of Guadalupe has been used to signify the unattainable goal of *virgin motherhood*. Because Chicanas can never measure up to *virgin motherhood*, some Chicanas interpret this unattainable goal to mean blind endurance, selfless "love," and utter fidelity in the face of the most self-destructive circumstances. For some in such circumstances Guadalupe represents *aguante* (endurance at all cost) and through *aguante*, survival. Yet, other Chicanas in their desire for the fullness of life challenge this crippling interpretation of Guadalupe.

Through the voice of her protagonist, Chayo, writer Sandra Cisneros illustrates the tension between these two divergent interpretations of Guadalupe. Cisneros, recognizing the destructive consequences of *aguante,* forcefully opposes this interpretation of Guadalupe.

Virgencita de Guadalupe. For a long time I wouldn't let you in my house. I couldn't see you without seeing my ma each time my father came home drunk and yelling, blaming everything that ever went wrong in his life on her.

I couldn't look at your folded hands without seeing my abuela mumbling, "My son, my son, my son . . ." Couldn't look at you without blaming you for all the pain my mother and her mother and all our mothers' mothers have put up with in the name of God. Couldn't let you in my house.

I wanted you bare-breasted, snakes in your hands. I wanted you leaping and somersaulting the backs of bulls. I wanted you swallowing raw hearts and rattling volcanic ash. I wasn't going to be my mother or my grandma. All that self-sacrifice, all that silent suffering. Hell no. Not here. Not me.[47]

Cisneros not only critiques the traditional interpretations of Guadalupe but also offers a commanding, robust, and dynamic revision. Cisneros's hoped-for revision of Guadalupe validates Chicanas' drive for fullness. She recognizes that she must idealize Chicana womanhood in a form radically divergent from the one commonly passed down to succeeding generations of Chicanas. Through her revision of Guadalupe, Cisneros invites Chicanas to know themselves as commanding, robust, and dynamic.

How Chicanas interpret the Virgin of Guadalupe matters. Whatever interpretation Chicanas hold will invariably function as a measuring stick of Chicana womanhood. Chicanas must criticize interpretations which idealize them as mute and passive and which narrowly define their possible aspirations. But such a critique, while absolutely essential for growth, comes at a price. Criticism of sociopolitically entrenched interpretations brings pain and suffering. It means being misunderstood by those who cling to accepted but detrimental explanations of themselves and their world. Yet only Chicanas who risk much to forge liberative understandings of themselves can hope to transform themselves and their world.

THE WHORE, *LA VENDIDA,* SYMBOLIZED
IN THE IMAGE OF LA MALINCHE/MALINTZIN

Just as the Virgin of Guadalupe has idealized goodness, the indigenous woman Malintzin has been demonized as the evil woman. She was twice betrayed, once by her family when they sold her into slavery, and again at the age of fourteen when she was given away to the Spanish conquistador, Hernán Cortez. Cortez took particular interest in Malintzin due to her ability to speak both Nahuatl and Maya, which he used to his advantage during the conquest. As Cortéz's mistress, she bore him a child. Afterward, Cortez kept their child and married off Malintzin to one of his soldiers. By the age of twenty-four she had died. Over the years Malintzin has been referred to as La Malinche, which has come to mean a traitor. Blamed for the Spanish conquest of Mexico, her title "Malinche" has often been invoked in attempts to control Chicanas' behavior.[48]

Some Chicanas fail to question longstanding interpretations of the myth of Malinche which link the idea of "the traitor" with that of "the whore." This link has served as an omen. Chicanas who too freely traverse the boundaries of cultural sexual norms become traitors or Malinches to their families and their people. As such, this link functions to repress Chicana sexual drives and behavior and acts to suppress the development of Chicana sexual agency. Alarcón rightly insists that ". . . the male myth of Malintzin is made to see betrayal first of all in her very sexuality, which makes it nearly impossible at any given moment to go beyond the vagina as the supreme site of evil until proven innocent by way of virginity or virtue, the most pawnable commodities around."[49] In this "male myth of Malintzin" woman's behavior is *not* the result of her own decisions, but the result of either her weakness or forces beyond her control. Obviously, such an interpretation paints an immature, passive, and limp portrait of Chicana womanhood.

Revisionist interpretations of La Malinche, like the one put forward by poet Carmen Tafolla, offer a contrasting and hope-filled portrait. In this interpretation, La Malinche acts on her own behalf and that of her people; she is a woman with significant command of her historical and sexual agency. Not only does she act on her own authority, but she sees what neither Cortéz nor Moctezuma can see, the dawning world of *La Raza*. She courageously pursues her vision. Neither "traitor" nor "whore" describes Malinche. Tafolla's poem is simply titled *La Malinche*.

Yo soy la Malinche.

. . .

Of noble ancestry, for whatever that means,
I was sold into slavery by MY ROYAL FAMILY—so

that my brother could get my inheritance.

. . . And then the omens began—a god, a new civilization, the downfall of

our empire.

    And *you* came.

    My dear Hernán Cortés, to share your "civilization"—to play a god, . . .

and I began to *dream* . . .

        I *saw*

            and I *acted.*

I saw our world

    And I saw yours

        And I saw—

           another.

. . .

    They could not imagine me dealing on a level

        with you—so they said I was raped, used,

            chingada

                ¡Chingada!

. . .

But Chingada I was not.

    Not tricked, not screwed, not traitor.

For I was not traitor to myself—

    I saw a dream

        and I *reached* it.

           Another world . . . .

              la raza.

                La raaaaa-zaaaaa . . .[50]

This interpretation of La Malinche sharply undermines any puppet-like portraits of her womanhood. With this poem, Tafolla issues a clarion call to Chicanas that affirms and pushes forward Chicanas' agency. The personhood of Chicanas depends upon naming and denouncing internalized messages which keep Chicanas' historical and sexual humanity underdeveloped. It depends upon Chicanas laying claim to emancipatory visions of their humanity and using these visions to transform how Chicanas know themselves.

    In Chicanas' drive toward fullness, liberative interpretations of symbols like the Virgin of Guadalupe and La Malinche are important for several reasons. First of all, given the contemporary oral nature of Mexico/Chicano culture, "symbolic icons, figures, or even persons" take on highly significant roles in the transmission and organization of "knowledge, values and beliefs."[51] More to the point, the tenacity and vitality of knowledge, values, and beliefs to a large extent depend upon the effective heuristic use of symbolic icons and figures. Second, these symbolic icons and figures can and do prompt strong emotional responses. Such responses intensify Chicanas' need and drive to understand their experience. Third, these symbolic icons and figures retain broad universal appeal, commanding unrivaled attention, and yet they effect a sense of intimate connection. In other words they enable Chicanas to recognize the transcendent, spiritual nature of their humanity. For these reasons, a liberative interpretation has the powerful effect of enabling Chicanas to know themselves differently and, as a result, to act differently in the world.

Having reflected on two important anchoring themes, I now turn to the final topic of this essay: How is the creation of a ChicanaFeminist epistemology important for a Latina feminist theology?

OF THEOLOGICAL IMPORT

Whenever Latina theologians interpret Christian beliefs or religious symbols (such as the nature of grace and sin, Our Lady of Guadalupe) or investigate the meaning of popular religious practices (*posadas, los reyes magos*) or explain the scriptures or church documents, on each of these occasions their epistemological commitments undergird their theological claims. When theologians interpret Latina religious experience, they also reveal their assumptions about *how Latinas know God's revelation.* A theologian's work invariably discloses the theologian's epistemological commitments.[52]

An effective ChicanaFeminist epistemology would allow greater depth and critical insight concerning the nature of the relationship between knowing and liberation. Additionally, it would assist in probing how the knowledge which emerges from an emancipatory interpretation of themes like *la familia* relates to the pursuit of truth in the work of each Latina feminist theologian. What follows are some reflections on the potential contributions an effective ChicanaFeminist epistemology would make to the work of Latina feminist theologians.

First, a ChicanaFeminist epistemology, by examining the nature of the relationship between knowing and liberation, would *contribute to a fuller understanding of what humanization means* and thereby enable Latina feminist theologians to probe more deeply a central concern of their work. The process of developing a mature, valid, and fruitful ChicanaFeminist epistemology would necessitate the creation of a relatively autonomous space, a space in which Chicanas could openly and without restraints explore, deliberate on, and test their own self-understandings. In such a space Chicanas could develop an inner core of cognitive authority based on the self-understanding, both individual and collective, that can develop in and through relationships with other Chicanas seeking the same. The fruit of this labor would provide Latina feminist theologians with greater insight into the meaning of *gloria Dei vivens homo*[53] for Chicanas.

Second, a ChicanaFeminist epistemology would *provide a critical framework* for the work of Latina feminist theologians. As a result of an effective ChicanaFeminist epistemology, Latina feminist theologians could uncover and analyze the gender, racial, and class hegemonies operative in the work of U.S. Latino theologians in particular and in theology in general. For example, much of U.S. Latino theology draws on and develops insights from the story and symbol of the Virgin of Guadalupe. But what vision of womanhood is given legitimacy through the discussion of Guadalupe in the work of U.S. Latino theologians? And how does each theologian account for the varied ways in which this symbol functions in the lives of women, as well as men, in the lives of *mulatos* and *mestizos,* in the lives of the rich and the poor? And how does the social location of the theologian influence what they "know" of this symbol? Much is at stake here. Unarticulated epistemological assumptions often shape how theological debates proceed and where they ultimately settle.[54]

Finally, a ChicanaFeminist epistemology would *provide a theoretical foundation* for a relevant, compelling and in-depth presentation of the Christian faith. Theologians invariably confront two fundamental questions: How do we know what God has communicated? What is the relationship of religious knowledge to the production of knowledge? If we understand "religious knowledge (to be) the product of our interpretative response to our experience, (and) not some absolutely certain grasp of divinely revealed truth,"[55] then what Latinas come to "know" from their experience is fundamental to the very possibility of religious knowledge. By providing a coherent explanation of how Chicanas come to know, a ChicanaFeminist epistemology would allow Latina feminist theologians to demonstrate the significance and value of the Christian faith and tradition in relation to what Latinas "know" of their experience.

Epistemology is presumed and assumed when Latina feminist theologians respond to a number of fundamental questions which reside beyond the bounds of epistemology. For example, to what extent should "Latina experience," and the knowledge emergent from that experience, be privileged in the construction of Latina feminist theologies? Should Latina liberation function as the *sole* norm for Latina feminist theologies? In other words, is the struggle of Latinas to resist the destructive nature of oppression in all its forms the central locus of divine revelation? And if we hold that it is, does such a claim imply that other interpretations of divine revelation are irrelevant? Moreover, even if we believe that the "perspective of the oppressed will yield the deepest religious understanding," should Latina liberation function as the exemplar of this perspective? In brief, exactly how normative is the norm of Latina liberation? In addition, if Latina feminist theologies claim to be Christian, does this demand a particular norm for divine revelation, a norm grounded in scripture and tradition, a norm which calls attention to the integrity of the Christian message? And if a Christian norm is deemed central, how should it be balanced with the norm of Latina liberation? And, how should it be constructed or devised? But if a Christian norm is not deemed central, in what sense can Latina feminist theology still claim to be Christian?[56] In the absence of a carefully developed epistemology, these questions cannot be seriously engaged. While the Latina feminist theologians contributing to this volume have begun to address these fundamental concerns, much work remains to be done.

As long as Chicanas and Latinas long for and actively pursue the fullness of their humanity, and as long as Latina feminist theologians hope to advance the liberation of Latinas, the relationship between knowing and liberation must be of paramount concern. Placing Chicanas at the center of inquiry creates new paradigms of thought, new epistemologies that humanize. Any ChicanaFeminist epistemology must begin and proceed as an iconoclastic endeavor, breaking down life-consuming visions of Chicana womanhood and drawing forth life-giving visions. Such efforts will assist Chicanas and Latinas as they seek to transform their lives and the world.

NOTES

1. Epistemology, the study of knowing, attempts to respond to a wide range of questions: How does knowing occur? What are the grounds of knowing? What are the limitations of knowing? How do we judge the validity and

trustworthiness of knowledge? Finally, what is the relationship between knowledge and truth? See Sandra G. Harding, *Whose Science? Whose Knowledge? Thinking From Women's Lives*, 308. I am especially indebted to María Pilar Aquino, Kirk Wegter-McNelly, Mary Lowe, Larry Gordon, and Jane Redmont for generously offering their ideas, recommendations, and insightful critique of various drafts of this work.

2. Throughout this essay I use the term "Latina" for the purpose of signifying women of Latin American ancestry who live in the United States. I use the term "Chicana" to indicate a more specific population, namely women who are of Mexican ancestry and who identify themselves as Chicanas. The term Chicana indicates a particular consciousness. See Norma Alarcón, "Chicana Feminism: In the Tracks of the Native Woman," in *Living Chicana Theory*, ed. Carla Trujillo, 371–382.

3. Audre Lorde, *Sister Outsider: Essays and Speeches*, 45.

4. The following works represent a rather small sample of some of the most important contributions which have been made in the expanding field of feminist epistemology. See *The Second Wave: A Reader in Feminist Theory*, ed. Linda Nicholson; *Knowing the Difference: Feminist Perspectives in Epistemology*, ed. Kathleen Lennon and Margaret Whitford; *Feminist Epistemologies*, ed. Linda Alcoff and Elizabeth Potter; Harding, *Whose Science?*; Judith P. Butler, *Gender Trouble: Feminism and the Subversion of Identity*; *Feminism/Postmodernism*, ed. Linda Nicholson; *Gender/Body/Knowledge: Feminist Reconstructions of Being and Knowing*, ed. Alison M. Jagger and Susan R. Bordo; *Feminist Thought and the Structure of Knowledge*, ed. Mary McCanney Gergen; Mary Field Belenky and Blythe Clinchy et al., *Women's Ways of Knowing: The Development of Self, Voice, and Mind*; bell hooks, *Feminist Theory from Margin to Center*; Carol Gilligan, *In a Different Voice: Psychological Theory and Women's Development*.

5. Elizabeth Frazer, "Epistemology, Feminist," in *The Oxford Companion to Philosophy*, ed. Ted Honderich, 241.

6. I am indebted to Patricia Hill Collins; her work functioned as a primary interlocuter for this essay. See Patricia Hill Collins, *Black Feminist Thought: Knowledge, Consciousness, and the Politics of Empowerment*.

7. Some works in this emerging field include *Living Chicana Theory*, ed. Carla Trujillo; *Chicana Feminist Thought: The Basic Historical Writings*, ed. Alma García; Tey Diana Rebolledo, *Women Singing in the Snow: A Cultural Analysis of Chicana Literature*; Norma Alarcón, "Traddutora, Traditora: A Paradigmatic Figure of Chicana Feminism," in *Scattered Hegemonies: Postmodernity and Transnational Feminist Practices*, ed. Inderpal Grewal and Caren Kaplan; Ana Castillo, *Massacre of the Dreamers: Essays on Xicanisma*; Cherríe Moraga, *The Last Generation: Prose and Poetry*; *Making Face, Making Soul–Haciendo Caras: Creative and Critical Perspectives by Feminist of Color*, ed. Gloria Anzaldúa; *This Bridge Called My Back: Writings by Radical Women of Color*, ed. Cherríe Moraga and Gloria Anzaldúa; Norma Alarcón, "Chicana's Feminist Literature: A Re-Vision Through Malintzin/or Malintzin: Putting Flesh Back on the Object," in Moraga and Anzaldúa, *This Bridge*, 182–190.

8. Alarcón, "Chicana Feminism," 371.

9. Ibid., 374, 379.

10. Collins, *Black Feminist Thought*, 34.

11. María Pilar Aquino, *Our Cry for Life: Feminist Theology from Latin America*, 38–41. See also the idea of *lo cotidiano* in Ada María Isasi-Díaz, *Mujerista Theology: A Theology for the Twenty-First Century*, 66–73, 131, 134.

12. See note 8.

13. Collins, *Black Feminist Thought*, 20, 32–36; Alarcón, "Chicana Feminism," 380.

14. See note 5.

15. Christine Sylvester, *Feminist Theory and International Relations in a Postmodern Era*, 31–36.

16. Sylvester, *Feminist Theory*, 43.

17. Nancy Hirschmann, *Rethinking Obligation: A Feminist Method for Political Theory*, 167.

18. Norma Alarcón, "The Theoretical Subject(s) of *This Bridge Called My Back* and Anglo-American Feminism," in Anzaldúa, *Making Face, Making Soul*, 357.

19. Sylvester, *Feminist Theory*, 47.

20. Alarcón, "Theoretical Subject(s)"; Hirschmann, *Rethinking Obligation*; Donna Haraway, "Situated Knowledges: The Science Question in Feminism and the Privilege of Partial Perspective," *Feminist Studies* 14, no. 3 (1988): 575–599; Kathy Ferguson, "Interpretation and Genealogy in Feminism," *Signs* 16, no. 2 (1991): 322–339.

21. Sylvester, *Feminist Theory*, 48.

22. Ibid., 52–63.

23. See note 8.

24. Even though the movements of the 1960s significantly shaped the consciousness of contemporary Chicanas, Chicana thinkers Marta Cotera, Anna NietoGomez and Tey Diana Rebolledo, among others, quickly point out and recount the long history of Chicana gender-, race-, and class consciousness and resistance. This long, largely unknown history dates back to the late nineteenth century. See Marta Cotera, "Feminism: The Chicano and Anglo Versions—A Historical Analysis," in García, *Chicana Feminist Thought*, 223–231; Anna NietoGomez, "Chicana Feminism," in García, *Chicana Feminist Thought*, 52–57; and Rebolledo, *Women Singing*, especially chapters 1 and 2.

25. This is a collection of essays, prose, and poetry by women of color in which they explore their dissonant experiences of feminism. See Moraga and Anzaldúa, *This Bridge*.

26. Alarcón, "Theoretical Subject(s)," 358–359.

27. Alarcón, "Theoretical Subject(s)," 360–366. Also see María Lugones, "Playfulness, 'World'-Traveling, and Loving Perception," in Anzaldúa, *Making Face, Making Soul*, 390–402.

28. Alarcón, "Theoretical Subject(s)," 359.

29. David Tracy, *Plurality and Ambiguity: Hermeneutics, Religion, Hope*, 8–9.

30. In the field of U.S. Latina/o theology, for a discussion of the dilemma of difference see Isasi-Díaz, *Mujerista Theology*, 66–73; Alejandro García-Rivera, "The Whole and the Love of Difference: Latino Metaphysics as Cosmology," in *From the Heart of Our People: Latino/a Explorations in Catholic Systematic Theology*, ed. Orlando O. Espín and Miguel H. Díaz, 54–83; Alejandro García-Rivera, *The Community of the Beautiful: A Theological Aesthetics*.

31. Alarcón, "Theoretical Subject(s)," 359.

32. In the field of U.S. Latina/o theology, for a discussion of the relational self-understanding of Latinos and Hispanics see Roberto S. Goizueta, *Caminemos con Jesus: Toward a Hispanic/Latino Theology of Accompaniment*, 50. And for a discussion of the notion of *la familia* see Isasi-Díaz, *Mujerista Theology*, 128–147.

33. NietoGomez, "Chicana Feminism," 55; Patricia Zavella, "The Problematic Relationship of Feminism and Chicana Studies," *Women's Studies* 17 (1989): 26; Terry Mason, "Symbolic Strategies for Change: A Discussion of the Chicana Women's Movement," in *Twice a Minority: Mexican-American Women*, ed. Margarita Melville, 105.

34. Zavella, "Problematic Relationship," 26–27.

35. Anna NietoGomez, "La Feminista," in García, *Chicana Feminist Thought*, 89.

36. See Paulo Freire, *Pedagogy of the Oppressed*, 27–31, 163, 169.

37. Alma García, "The Development of Chicana Feminist Discourse, 1970–1980," *Gender and Society* 3, no. 2 (1989): 221, 225.

38. García, "The Development of Chicana Feminist Discourse," 219, 224.

39. Moraga, *Last Generation*, 158.

40. Yvonne Yarbro-Bejerano, "Chicana Literature from a Chicana Feminist Perspective," *Theatre Journal* 38, no. 4 (1986): 144. See also Cherríe Moraga, "Giving Up the Ghost," 1986, in her *Heroes and Saints and Other Plays*, 1–35.

41. Collins, *Black Feminist Thought*, 68.

42. Moraga, *Last Generation*, 156–157.

43. See for example Jeanette Rodríguez, *Our Lady of Guadalupe: Faith and Empowerment among Mexican-American Women*.

44. Rebolledo, *Women Singing*, 52–53.

45. García, "The Development of Chicana Feminist Discourse," 222.

46. Rebolledo, *Women Singing*, 53.

47. Sandra Cisneros, *Woman Hollering Creek and Other Stories*, 127.

48. Tey Diana Rebolledo and Eliana S. Rivero, ed., *Infinite Divisions: An Anthology of Chicana Literature*, 191.

49. Alarcón, "Chicana's Feminist Literature," 183.

50. Carmen Tafolla, "La Malinche," in *Infinite Divisions*, ed. Rebolledo and Rivero, 198–199.

51. Alarcón, "Traddutora, Traditora," 113.

52. Epistemology has been addressed in the work of U.S. Latina theologians. See Aquino, *Our Cry for Life*, 101–102, 109–129; María Pilar Aquino, "Theological Method in U.S. Latino/a Theology: Toward an Intercultural

Theology for the Third Millennium," in Orlando Espín and Miguel Díaz, *From the Heart*, 6–48; Isasi-Díaz, *Mujerista Theology*, 59–85. Epistemology has likewise been addressed in the work of U.S. Latino theologians. See García-Rivera, *Community of the Beautiful*; Orlando O. Espín, "Popular Religion as an Epistemology (of Suffering)," in his *The Faith of the People: Theological Reflections on Popular Catholicism*, 156–179; Alejandro García-Rivera, "Creator of the Visible and Invisible: Liberation Theology, Postmodernism and the Spiritual," *Journal of Hispanic/Latino Theology* 3, no. 4 (1996): 35–56; Roberto S. Goizueta, "U.S. Hispanic Popular Catholicism as Theopoetics," in *Hispanic/Latino Theology: Challenge and Promise*, ed. Ada María Isasi-Díaz and Fernando F. Segovia, 261–288; Goizueta, *Caminemos con Jesus*.

53. This literally means "the glory of God is the human person fully alive." This theological principle was first developed by Irenaeus.

54. See Francis Schüssler Fiorenza, "Systematic Theology: Task and Methods," in *Systematic Theology: Roman Catholic Perspectives*, ed. Francis Schüssler Fiorenza and John P. Galvin, 47–48.

55. Thomas E. Hosinski, "Epistemology," in *A New Handbook of Christian Theology*, ed. Donald W. Musser and Joseph L. Price, 153.

56. Hosinski, "Epistemology," 153; Susan M. St. Ville, "Epistemological Privilege," in *Dictionary of Feminist Theologies*, ed. Letty M. Russell and Shannon J. Clarkson, 84.

SELECTED BIBLIOGRAPHY

Ackerman, Susan. *Warrior, Dancer, Seductress: Women in Judges and Biblical Israel.* New York: Doubleday, 1998.

Acosta-Belén, Edna, ed. *The Puerto Rican Woman: Perspectives on Culture, History and Society.* 2d ed. New York: Praeger, 1986.

Acuña, Rodolfo. *Anything but Mexican.* New York: Verso, 1996.

———. *Occupied America.* New York: Harper and Row, 1988.

Alarcón, Norma. "Chicana Feminism: In the Tracks of the Native Woman." *Cultural Studies* 4, no. 3 (1990): 248–256.

———. "Chicanas' Feminist Literature: A Re-Vision through Malintzin, OR Malintzin: Putting Flesh Back on the Object." In *This Bridge Called My Back,* edited by Cherríe Moraga and Gloria Anzaldúa. New York: Kitchen Table, Women of Color Press, 1983.

Alarcón, Norma, Ana Castillo, and Cherríe Moraga, eds. *The Sexuality of Latinas.* Berkeley: Third Woman Press, 1993.

Alarcón, Norma, Rafaela Castro et al., eds. *Chicana Critical Issues. Mujeres Activas en Letras y Cambio Social.* Berkeley: Third Woman Press, 1993.

Alcoff, Linda, and Elizabeth Potter, eds. *Feminist Epistemologies.* New York: Routledge, 1993.

Allen, Paula Gunn. *The Sacred Hoop.* Boston: Beacon Press, 1986.

Alvarez, Sonia A. *Engendering Democracy in Brazil. Women's Movements in Transition Politics.* Princeton, N.J.: Princeton University Press, 1990.

Alves, Rubem A. *The Poet, The Warrior, The Prophet.* London and Philadelphia: SCM and Trinity Press, 1990.

Andolsen, Barbara Hilkert, Christine E. Gudorf, and Mary D. Pellauer, eds. *Women's Consciousness, Women's Conscience: A Reader in Feminist Ethics.* Minneapolis: Winston Press, 1985.

Anzaldúa, Gloria. *Borderlands. La Frontera: The New Mestiza.* San Francisco: Aunt Lute Books, 1987.

———, ed. *Making Face, Making Soul, Haciendo Caras: Creative and Critical Perspectives by Feminists of Color.* San Francisco: Aunt Lute Books, 1990.

Appelbaum, Richard. "Multiculturalism and Flexibility: Some New Directions in Global Capitalism." In Avery Gordon and Christopher Newfield, eds., *Mapping Multiculturalism.* Minneapolis: University of Minnesota Press, 1996.

Aquino, María Pilar. "The Challenge of Latina Women." *Missiology* XX/2 (1992): 261–268.

———. *La Teología, La Iglesia y La Mujer en América Latina.* Bogota, Colombia: Indo-American Press, 1994.

———. "La Visión Liberadora de Medellín en la Teología Feminista." In José Luis Burget and Rafael Aragón, eds., *Teología con Rostro de Mujer. Alternativas* 16/17. Managua, Nicaragua: Editorial Lascasiana, 2000, 141–172.

———. "Latin American Feminist Theology." *Journal of Feminist Studies in Religion* 14/1 (1998): 89–107.

———. "Mujer y Praxis Ministerial Hoy. La Respuesta del Tercer Mundo." *Revista de Teología Bíblica* 46 (1990): 116–139.

———. *Our Cry for Life. Feminist Theology from Latin America.* Maryknoll, N.Y.: Orbis Books, 1993.

———. "¿Qué Es Hacer Teología Desde la Perspectiva de la Mujer?" IX Congreso de Teología Iglesia y Derechos Humanos. *Evangelio y Liberación* (1989): 175–189.

———. "Santo Domingo: La Visión Sobre las Mujeres Latinoamericanas." *Reflexión y Liberación* 19 (1993): 39–50.

———. "Sin Contar a las Mujeres (Mt 14:21). Perspectiva Latinoamericana de la Teología Feminista." *Pastoral Misionera* 178/179 (1991): 103–122.

———. "Teología Feminista Latinoamericana. Evaluación y Desafíos." *Tópicos '90, Cuadernos de Estudio* 7 (1995): 107–122.

———. "Teología y Mujer en América Latina." *Reflexión y Liberación* 15 (1992): 27–40.

———. "Trazos Hacia una Antropología Teológica Feminista. Una Mirada desde la Teología Feminista Latinoamericana." *Reflexión y Liberación* 23 (1994): 43–58.

———. "The Women's Movement: Sources of Hope." *Concilium* 5 (1999): 90–94.

———, ed. *Aportes para una Teología desde la Mujer.* Madrid: Biblia y Fe, 1988.

Aquino, María Pilar, and Roberto S. Goizueta, eds. *Theology: Expanding the Borders.* Vol. 43. Mystic, Conn.: Twenty-Third Publications, 1998.

Aquino, María Pilar, and Ana María Tepedino, eds. *Entre la Indignación y la Esperanza. Teología Feminista Latinoamericana.* Bogota, Colombia: Indo-American Press and Ecumenical Association of Third World Theologians, 1998.

Arroyo, Anita. *Razón y pasión de Sor Juana.* Mexico City: Editorial Porrúa, 1980.

Audinet, Jacques. *Le Temps du Métissage.* Paris: Les Éditions de l'Atelier, 1999.

Baca Zinn, Maxine. "Chicanas: Power and Control in the Domestic Sphere." *De Colores* 2, no. 3 (1976): 19–31.

Bañuelas, Arturo J., ed. *Mestizo Christianity: Theology from the Latino Perspective.* Maryknoll, N.Y.: Orbis Books, 1995.

Batstone, David, and Eduardo Mendieta et al., eds. *Liberation Theologies, Postmodernity, and the Americas.* New York: Routledge, 1997.

Bauman, Richard, ed. *Folklore and Culture on the Texas-Mexican Border.* Austin: CMAS Books, 1993.

Becker, Carol E. *Leading Women.* Nashville: Abingdon Press, 1996.

Belenky, Mary Field, and Blythe Clinchy, et al. *Women's Ways of Knowing: The Development of Self, Voice, and Mind.* New York: Basic Books, 1986.

Beuchot, Mauricio. "Los Autos de Sor Juana: Tres Lugares Teológicos." In *Sor Juana y Su Mundo: Una Mirada Actual,* edited by Sara Poot Herrera. Mexico City: Universidad del Claustro de Sor Juana, 1995.

Bevans, Stephen B. *Models of Contextual Theology.* Maryknoll, N.Y.: Orbis Books, 1994.

Bidegain, Ana María, ed. *Mulheres: Autonomía e controle religioso na América Latina.* Petrópolis, Brazil: Vozes-Cehila, 1996.

Blea, Irene I. *U.S. Chicanas and Latinas Within a Global Context. Women of Color at the Fourth World Women's Conference.* Westport, Conn.: Praeger, 1997.

Boff, Leonardo, and Virgilio Elizondo. *Voice of the Victims, 1492–1992.* London: SCM Press, 1990.

Bonfil Batalla, Guillermo. *Mexico Profundo.* Austin: University of Texas Press, 1996.

Boza, María del Carmen, Beverly Silva, and Armen Valle, eds. *Nosotras: Latina Literature Today.* Binghamton, New York: Bilingual Review/Press, 1986.

Brown, Robert MacAfee. *Persuade Us to Rejoice: The Liberating Power of Fiction.* Louisville, Ky.: Westminster/John Knox Press, 1992.

Broyles-González, Yolanda. *El teatro campesino.* Austin: University of Texas Press, 1994.

Brueggemann, Walter. *The Prophetic Imagination.* Philadelphia: Fortress Press, 1978.

Busto, Rudy. "The Predicament of *Nepantla:* Chicana/o Religions of the 21st Century." *Perspectives,* no. 1 (fall 1998): 7–21.

Butler, Judith P. *Gender Trouble: Feminism and the Subversion of Identity.* New York: Routledge, 1990.

Byers, David. *Justice in the Marketplace.* Washington, D.C.: United States Catholic Conference, 1985.

Byrd, Bobby, and Susannah Byrd, eds. *The Late Great Mexican Border.* El Paso, Tex.: Cinco Puntos Press, 1998.

Calderón, Héctor, and José David Saldívar, eds. *Criticism in the Borderlands. Studies in Chicano Literature, Culture, and Ideology.* Durham, N.C.: Duke University Press, 1991.

Camarillo, Albert. *Chicanos in California: A History of Mexican Americans in California.* San Francisco: Boyd and Fraser, 1984.

Carcaño, Minerva. "The Hispanic Church Towards the Twenty-first Century." *Apuntes* 17/3 (1997) 67–79.

Casarella, Peter, and Raúl Gómez, eds. *El Cuerpo de Cristo. The Hispanic Presence in the U.S. Catholic Church.* New York: Crossroad, 1998.

Castillo, Ana, *Massacre of the Dreamers: Essays on Xicanisma.* Albuquerque: University of New Mexico Press, 1994.

————. *So Far from God.* New York: W. W. Norton and Company, 1993.

————, ed. *Goddess of the Americas, La Diosa de las Américas: Writings on the Virgin of Guadalupe.* New York: Riverhead Books, 1996.

Castro Gómez, Santiago, and Eduardo Mendieta, eds. *Teorías sin disciplina. Latinoamericanismo, poscolonialidad y globalización en debate.* San Francisco: University of San Francisco, 1998.

Chavez, Linda. *Out of the Barrio: Toward a New Politics of Hispanic Assimilation.* New York: HarperCollins, 1991.

Cisneros, Sandra. *Woman Hollering Creek and Other Short Stories.* New York: Random House, Vintage Contemporaries, 1991.

Cleary, Edward L., and Hannah Stewart-Gambino, eds. *Power, Politics and Pentecostals in Latin America.* Boulder: Westview Press, 1997.

Cobos, Ruben. *A Dictionary of New Mexican and Southern Colorado Spanish.* Santa Fe: Museum of New Mexico Press, 1983.

Collins, Patricia Hill. *Black Feminist Thought: Knowledge, Consciousness, and the Politics of Empowerment.* New York: Routledge, Chapman and Hall, 1991.

Conn, Joan Wolski, ed. *Women's Spirituality: Resources for Christian Development.* New York: Paulist Press, 1986.

Córdova, Teresa, Norma Cantú et al., eds. *Chicana Voices: Intersections of Class, Race, and Gender.* Austin, Texas: University of Texas Center for Mexican American Studies, 1986.

Cotera, Martha P. *The Chicana Feminist.* Austin: Information Systems Development, 1977.

Crossan, John D. *The Dark Interval: Towards a Theology of Story.* Sonoma: Polebridge Press, 1988.

Cypress, Sandra Messinger. *La Malinche in Mexican Literature.* Austin: University of Texas Press, 1991.

de Carvalho Azevedo, Marcello. *Inculturation and the Challenges of Modernity.* Rome: Pontifical Gregorian University, 1982.

de la Cruz, Sor Juana Inés. *The Answer/La Respuesta: Including a Selection of Poems.* Edited and translated by Electa Arenal and Amanda Powell. New York: Feminist Press at the City University in New York, 1994.

————. *Obras completas de Sor Juana Inés de la Cruz.* 4 vols.: Vol. 1, *Lírica personal;* Vol. 2, *Villancicos y letras sacras;* Vol. 3, *Autos y loas;* Vol. 4, *Comedias, sainetes y prosa.* Edited by Alfonso Méndez Plancarte and Alberto G. Salceda. Mexico City: Fondo de Cultura Económica, 1951–1957. Reprint. Mexico City: Instituto Mexiquense de Cultura, Fondo de Cultura Económica, 1995.

Deck, Allan Figueroa. *Frontiers of Hispanic Theology in the United States.* Maryknoll, N.Y.: Orbis Books, 1992.

Deck, Allan Figueroa, Ismael García et al., eds. *Our Theology: Manual de Teología Latina en los EE.UU.* Minneapolis: Fortress Press, forthcoming.

Deiros, Pablo Alberto. *Historia del Cristianismo en América Latina.* Buenos Aires: Fraternidad Teológica Latinoamericana, 1992.

del Castillo, Adelaida R., ed. *Between Borders: Essays on Mexican/Chicana History.* Encino, Calif.: Floricanto Press, 1990.

Delgado, Richard, and Jean Stefancic. *The Latino Condition. A Critical Reader.* New York: New York University Press, 1998.

Detweiler, Robert. *Breaking the Fall: Religious Readings of Contemporary Fiction.* San Francisco: Harper and Row, 1989.

———. *Story, Sign, and Self: Phenomenology and Structuralism as Literary Critical Methods.* Philadelphia: Fortress Press, 1978.

Detweiler, Robert, and Gregory Salyer, eds. *Literature and Theology at Century's End.* Atlanta: Scholars Press, 1995.

Díaz-Stevens, Ana María. *Oxcart Catholicism on Fifth Avenue: The Impact of the Puerto Rican Migration on the Archdiocese of New York.* Notre Dame, Ind.: University of Notre Dame Press, 1993.

Dolan, Jay P., and Allan Figueroa Deck, eds. *Hispanic Catholic Culture in the U.S. Issues and Concerns.* Notre Dame, Ind.: University of Notre Dame Press, 1994.

Dolan, Jay P., and Gilberto Hinojosa, eds. *Mexican Americans and the Catholic Church (1900–1965).* Notre Dame, Ind.: University of Notre Dame Press, 1994.

Dolan, Jay P., and Jaime R. Vidal, eds. *Puerto Rican and Cuban Catholics in the U.S. (1900–1965).* Notre Dame, Ind.: University of Notre Dame Press, 1994.

Dorr, Donal. *Option for the Poor: A Hundred Years of Catholic Social Teaching.* Maryknoll, N.Y.: Orbis Books, 1992.

Downey, Michael, ed. *New Dictionary of Catholic Spirituality.* Collegeville, Minn.: Liturgical Press, 1993.

Dreyer, Elizabeth A. *Earth Crammed with Heaven: a Spirituality of Everyday Life.* New York: Hollis Press, 1994.

Dupré, Louis. *Passage to Modernity: An Essay in the Hermeneutics of Nature and Culture.* New Haven: Yale University Press, 1993.

Dussel, Enrique, ed. *Historia general de la iglesia en América Latina.* Vol. 5, Mexico City: Ediciones Paulinas, 1984.

Eagleson, John, and Philip Scharper. *Puebla and Beyond.* Maryknoll, N.Y.: Orbis Books, 1979.

Elizondo, Virgilio. *The Future Is Mestizo, Life Where Cultures Meet.* Bloomington, Ind.: Meyer-Stone Books, 1988.

———. *Galilean Journey: The Mexican-American Promise.* Maryknoll, N.Y.: Orbis Books, 1983.

———. *Guadalupe, Mother of the New Creation.* Maryknoll, N.Y.: Orbis Books, 1997.

———. *La Morenita: Evangelizadora de las Américas.* Liguori, Mo.: Liguori Publications, 1981; and San Antonio, Tex.: Mexican-American Cultural Center Press, 1980.

Ellacuría, Ignacio. *Conversión de la iglesia al pueblo de Dios. Para anunciarlo y realizarlo en la historia.* Santander, Spain: Sal Terrae, 1984.

———, and Jon Sobrino, eds. *Mysterium Liberationis. Fundamental Concepts of Liberation Theology.* Maryknoll, N.Y.: Orbis Books, 1993.

Escobar, Arturo, and Sonia E. Alvarez, eds. *The Making of Social Movements in Latin America. Identity, Strategy, and Democracy.* Boulder, Colo.: Westview Press, 1992.

Espín, Oliva M. *Latina Healers: Lives of Power and Tradition.* Encino, Calif.: Floricanto Press, 1996.

———. *Latina Realities. Essays on Healing, Migration and Sexuality.* Boulder, Colo.: Westview Press, 1997.

Espín, Orlando O. *The Faith of the People: Theological Reflections on Popular Catholicism.* Maryknoll, N.Y.: Orbis Books, 1997.

———. "Immigration, Territory, and Globalization: Theological Reflections." *Journal of Hispanic/Latino Theology* 7, no. 3 (2000): 46–59.

———. "La Experiencia Religiosa en el Contexto de la Globalización." *Journal of Hispanic/Latino Theology* 7, no. 2 (November 1999): 13–31.

Espín, Orlando O., and Miguel H. Díaz, eds. *From the Heart of Our People. Latino/a Explorations in Catholic Systematic Theology.* Maryknoll, N.Y.: Orbis Books, 1999.

Estés, Clarisa Pinkola. *Women Who Run with the Wolves: Myths and Stories of the Wild Woman Archetype.* New York: Ballantine Books, 1992.

Fabella, Virginia. *Beyond Bonding. A Third World Women's Theological Journey.* Manila: Ecumenical Association of Third World Theologians and Institute of Women's Studies, 1993.

Fabella, Virginia, and Mercy Amba Oduyoye, eds. *With Passion and Compassion. Third World Women Doing Theology.* Maryknoll, N.Y.: Orbis Books, 1988.

Fabella, Virginia, and R. S. Sugirtharajah, eds. *Dictionary of Third World Theologies.* Maryknoll, N.Y.: Orbis Books, 2000.

Fernández, Eduardo C. *La Cosecha. Harvesting Contemporary United States Hispanic Theology (1972–1998).* Collegeville, Minn.: Liturgical Press, 2000.

Fernández, Roberta, ed. *In Other Words: Literature by Latinas in the United States.* Houston: Arte Público Press, 1994.

Ferré, Rosario. *Dos Venecias.* Mexico City: Joaquín Mortiz, 1992.

———. *The House on the Lagoon.* New York: Ferrar, Straus, and Giroux, 1995.

———. *Maldito amor.* Río Piedras, Puerto Rico: Ediciones Huracán, 1988.

———. *Sitio a Eros: Quince ensayos literarios.* 2d ed. Mexico City: Joaquín Mortiz, 1986.

———. *Sonatinas.* Río Piedras, Puerto Rico: Ediciones Huracán, 1989.

———. *Sweet Diamond Dust.* New York: Ballantine Books, 1989.

———. *The Youngest Doll.* Lincoln: University of Nebraska Press, 1991.

Ferree, Myra Marx, and Patricia Yancey Martin, eds. *Feminist Organizations: Harvest of the New Women's Movement.* Philadelphia: Temple University Press, 1995.

Ferris, Elizabeth G. *Beyond Borders: Refugees, Migrants and Human Rights in the Post–Cold War Era.* Geneva: World Council of Churches Publication, 1993.

Florescano, Enrique. *Memory, Myth and Time in Mexico.* Austin: University of Texas Press, 1994.

Floristán, Casiano, and Juan José Tamayo, eds. *Conceptos fundamentales del cristianismo.* Madrid: Trotta, 1993.

Ford, David F., ed. *The Modern Theologians. An Introduction to Christian Theology in the Twentieth Century.* 2d ed. Malden, Mass.: Blackwell Publishers, 1996.

Fornet-Betancourt, Raúl. *Hacia una filosofía intercultural latinoamericana.* San José, Costa Rica: Departamento Ecuménico de Investigaciones, 1994.

————. *Interculturalidad y globalización. Ejercicios de crítica filosófica intercultural en el contexto de la globalización neoliberal.* Frankfurt and San José, Costa Rica: IKO Verlag and Departamento Ecuménico de Investigaciones, 2000.

————, ed. *Theologie im III. millennium: Quo vadis? Denktraditionen im dialog: Studien zur befreiun und interkulturalität.* Frankfurt: IKO Verlag, 2000.

Foster, Patricia, ed. *Minding the Body: Women Writers on Body and Soul.* New York: Doubleday, 1994.

Franciscan Friars of the Immaculate. *A Handbook on Guadalupe.* Minnesota: Park Press, 1997.

Freire, Paulo. *Pedagogy of the Oppressed.* New York: Continuum, 1970; and New York: Seabury Press, 1968.

Fuentes, Annette, and Barbara Ehrenreich. *Women in the Global Factory.* Boston: South End Press, 1984.

Galerón, Soledad, Rosa María Icaza, and Rosendo Urrabazo. *Prophetic Vision. Pastoral Reflections on the National Pastoral Plan for Hispanic Ministry.* Kansas City: Sheed and Ward, 1992.

Gannon, Thomas J., ed. *The Catholic Challenge to the American Economy: Reflections on the U.S. Bishops' Pastoral Letter on Catholic Social Teaching and the U.S. Economy.* New York: Macmillan, 1987.

García, Alma M., ed. *Chicana Feminist Thought: The Basic Historical Writings.* New York: Routledge, 1997.

García, Nasario. *Recuerdos de los Viejitos.* Albuquerque: University of New Mexico Press, 1987.

García Canclini, Nestor. *Transforming Modernity: Popular Culture in Mexico.* Austin: University of Texas Press, 1993.

García Coll, Cynthia T., and Maria de Lourdes Mattei, eds. *The Psychosocial Development of Puerto Rican Women.* New York: Praeger, 1989.

García-Rivera, Alejandro. *The Community of the Beautiful: A Theological Aesthetics.* Collegeville, Minn.: Liturgical Press, 1999.

Gaspar de Alba, Alicia. *Sor Juana's Second Dream.* Albuquerque: University of New Mexico Press, 1999.

Geertz, Clifford. *Interpretation of Cultures, Selected Essays.* New York: Basic Books, 1973.

Gergen, Mary McCanney, ed. *Feminist Thought and the Structure of Knowledge.* New York: New York University Press, 1988.

Gerrard-Burnett, Virginia, and David Stoll, eds. *Rethinking Protestantism in Latin America.* Philadelphia: Temple University Press, 1993.

Gibson, Charles. *Los Aztecas Bajo el Dominio Español: 1519–1810.* Mexico City: Siglo XXI, 1978.

Gil, Rosa María, and Carmen Inoa Vázquez. *The María Paradox: How Latinas*

Can Merge Old World Traditions with New World Self-Esteem. New York: G. P. Putnam's Sons, 1996.

Gilligan, Carol. *In a Different Voice: Psychological Theory and Women's Development.* Cambridge, Mass.: Harvard University Press, 1982.

Glass, Zipporah G. "The Language of Mestizaje in a Renewed Rhetoric of Black Theology." *Journal of Hispanic/Latino Theology* 7, no. 2 (November 1999): 32–42.

Glazier, Stephen D., ed. *Perspectives on Pentecostalism: Case Studies from the Caribbean and Latin America.* Lanham, Md.: University Press of America, 1980.

Goizueta, Roberto S. *Caminemos con Jesus: Toward a Hispanic/Latino Theology of Accompaniment.* Maryknoll, N.Y.: Orbis Books, 1995.

———, ed. *We Are a People: Initiative in Hispanic American Theology.* Minneapolis: Fortress Press, 1992.

González, Justo L. *Christian Thought Revisited. Three Types of Theology.* Maryknoll, N.Y.: Orbis Books, 1999.

———. *Mañana: Christian Theology from a Hispanic Perspective.* Nashville: Abingdon Press, 1990.

Gordon, Avery, and Christopher Newfield, eds. *Mapping Multiculturalism.* Minneapolis: University of Minnesota Press, 1996.

Grewal, Inderpal, and Caren Kaplan, eds. *Scattered Hegemonies: Postmodernity and Transnational Feminist Practices.* Minneapolis: University of Minnesota Press, 1994.

Griswold del Castillo, Richard. *La Familia.* Notre Dame, Ind.: University of Notre Dame Press, 1984.

Guerrero, Andrés G. *A Chicano Theology.* Maryknoll, N.Y.: Orbis Books, 1987.

Gutiérrez, Gustavo. *The Power of the Poor in History.* Translated by Robert R. Barr. Maryknoll, N.Y.: Orbis Books, 1983.

Gutiérrez, Ramón A. *When Jesus Came the Corn Mothers Went Away.* Stanford, Calif.: Stanford University Press, 1991.

Guzmán Bouvard, Marguerite. *Revolutionizing Motherhood.* Wilmington: SR Books, 1994.

Harding, Sandra G. *Whose Science? Whose Knowledge? Thinking From Women's Lives.* Ithaca, N.Y.: Cornell University Press, 1991.

———, ed. *Feminism and Methodology: Social Science Issues.* Bloomington: Indiana University Press, 1987.

Hayes, Diana L., and Cyprian Davis, eds. *Taking Down Our Harps. Black Catholics in the United States.* Maryknoll, N.Y.: Orbis Books, 1998.

Heyck, Denis Lynn Daly, ed. *Barrios and Borderlands: Cultures of Latinos and Latinas in the United States.* New York: Routledge, 1994.

Hinsdale, Mary Ann, and Phillis Kaminski, eds. *Women and Theology.* Maryknoll, N.Y.: Orbis Books, 1995.

Hirschmann, Nancy. *Rethinking Obligation: A Feminist Method for Political Theory.* Ithaca, N.Y.: Cornell University Press, 1992.

Honderich, Ted, ed. *Oxford Companion to Philosophy.* Oxford: Oxford University Press, 1995.

hooks, bell. *Feminist Theory from Margin to Center*. Boston: South End Press, 1984.

Horno-Delgado, Anunción, ed. *Breaking Boundaries: Latina Writing and Critical Readings*. Amherst: University of Massachusetts Press, 1989.

Icaza, Rosa María, Soledad Galerón, and Rosendo Urrabazo, eds. *Prophetic Vision. Pastoral Reflections on the National Pastoral Plan for Hispanic Ministry*. Kansas City, Mo.: Sheed and Ward, 1992.

Isasi-Díaz, Ada María. *En la Lucha. In the Struggle: Elaborating a Mujerista Theology*. Minneapolis: Fortress Press, 1993.

———. *Mujerista Theology: A Theology for the Twenty-First Century*. Maryknoll, N.Y.: Orbis Books, 1996.

Isasi-Díaz, Ada María, and Yolanda Tarango. *Hispanic Women: Prophetic Voice in the Church*. San Francisco: Harper and Row, 1988.

Isasi-Díaz, Ada María, and Fernando F. Segovia, eds. *Hispanic/Latino Theology: Challenge and Promise*. Minneapolis: Fortress Press, 1996.

Jagger, Alison M., and Susan R. Bordo, eds. *Gender/Body/Knowledge: Feminist Reconstructions of Being and Knowing*. New Brunswick, N.J.: Rutgers University Press, 1989.

Jasper, David, ed. *Postmodernism, Literature and the Future of Theology*. New York: St. Martin's Press, 1993.

———. *The Study of Literature and Religion*. Minneapolis: Fortress Press, 1989.

Jehlen, Myra. *American Incarnation: The Individual, The Nation, and the Continent*. Cambridge: Harvard University Press, 1986.

Johnson, Elizabeth A. *She Who Is: The Mystery of God in Feminist Theological Discourse*. New York: Crossroad Publishing, 1992.

Kanellos, Nicolás, ed. *Biographical Dictionary of Hispanic Literature in the United States*. New York: Greenwood Press, 1989.

Kaplan, Ami, and Donald E. Pease, eds. *Cultures of United States Imperialism*. Durham, N.C.: Duke University Press, 1993.

King, Ursula, ed. *Feminist Theology from the Third World: A Reader*. Maryknoll, N.Y.: Orbis Books, 1994.

Kirk, Pamela. *Sor Juana Inés de la Cruz: Religion, Art, and Feminism*. New York: Continuum, 1998.

Koestenbaum, Peter. *Leadership: The Inner Side of Greatness. A Philosophy for Leaders*. San Francisco: Jossey-Bass, 1991.

Kourany A., Janet, James J. Sterba, and Rosemarie Tong, eds. *Feminist Philosophies. Problems, Theories and Applications*. 2d ed. Upper Saddle River, N.J.: Prentice Hall, 1999.

Krstovic, Jelena, ed. *Hispanic Literature Criticism*. Detroit: Gale Research, 1994.

Lamphere, Louise, Patricia Zavella et al. *Sunbelt Working Mothers*. Ithaca, N.Y.: Cornell University Press, 1993.

Lebacqz, Karen. *Six Theories of Justice*. Minneapolis: Augsburg, 1986.

Lennon, Kathleen, and Margaret Whitford, eds. *Knowing the Difference: Feminist Perspectives in Epistemology*. New York: Routledge, 1994.

León-Portilla, Miguel. *Aztec Thought and Culture: A Study of the Ancient Nahuatl Mind*. Norman: University of Oklahoma Press, 1963.

————, ed. *Cantos y crónicas del México antiguo*. Madrid: Historia 16, 1986.

Leonard, Irving. *Baroque Times in Old Mexico: Seventeenth Century Persons, Places, and Practices*. Ann Arbor: University of Michigan Press, 1959.

Lorde, Audre. *Sister Outsider: Essays and Speeches*. Freedom, Calif.: Crossing Press, 1984.

Loya, Gloria Inés. "Considering the Sources/Fuentes for a Hispanic Feminist Theology." *Theology Today* 54, no. 4 (January 1998): 491–498.

Machado, Daisy L. "Abre Mis Ojos a la Dignidad de la Mujer Hispana." *Apuntes* 19, no. 2 (1999): 35–41.

————. "Latino Church History: A Haunting Memory." *Perspectivas, Hispanic Theological Initiative*, no. 1 (fall 1998): 22–34.

Maciel, David R., and Isidro D. Ortíz, eds. *Chicanas/Chicanos at the Crossroads: Social, Economic, and Political Change*. Tucson: University of Arizona Press, 1996.

Madison, Soyini D., ed. *The Woman That I Am: The Literature and Culture of Contemporary Women of Color*. New York: St. Martin's Press, 1994.

Maldonado Jr., David, ed. *Protestantes/Protestants. Hispanic Christianity within Mainline Traditions*. Nashville: Abingdon Press, 1999.

Mallard, William. *The Reflection of Theology in Literature: A Case Study in Theology and Culture*. San Antonio, Tex.: Trinity University Press, 1977.

Mananzan, Mary John, Mercy Amba Oduyoye et al., eds. *Women Resisting Violence. Spirituality for Life*. Maryknoll, N.Y.: Orbis Books, 1996.

Marqués, René. *The Docile Puerto Rican*. Translated by Barbara Bockus Aponte. Philadelphia: Temple University Press, 1976.

Martell Otero, Loida. "Women Doing Theology: Una Perspectiva Evangélica." *Apuntes* 14, no. 3 (1994): 67–85.

Matovina, Timothy, ed. *Beyond Borders. Writings of Virgilio Elizondo and Friends*. Maryknoll, N.Y.: Orbis Books, 2000.

McKenna, Megan. *Not Counting Women and Children: Neglected Stories from the Bible*. Maryknoll, N.Y.: Orbis Books, 1994.

Melville, Margarita, ed. *Twice a Minority: Mexican-American Women*. St. Louis, Mo: C. V. Mosby, 1980.

Méndez Plancarte, Alfonso, ed. *Obras Completas de Sor Juana Inés de la Cruz*. Vol. 1, *Lírica Personal*. 1951. Reprint. Mexico City: Fondo de Cultura Económica, 1988.

Merrim, Stephanie. *Early Modern Women's Writing and Sor Juana Inés de la Cruz*. Nashville: Vanderbilt University Press, 1999.

————, ed. *Feminist Perspectives on Sor Juana Inés de la Cruz*. Detroit: Wayne State University Press, 1991.

Metz, Johannes Baptist. *A Passion for God: the Mystical-Political Dimension of Christianity*. New York: Paulist Press, 1998.

Millington, Mark I., and Paul Julian Smith, eds. *New Hispanisms: Literature, Culture and Theory*. Ottawa, Canada: Dovehouse Editions, 1994.

Moghadam, Valentine M., ed. *Identity, Politics, and Women: Cultural Reassertions and Feminisms in International Perspective*. Boulder, Colo.: Westview Press, 1994.

Mohr, Nicholasa. *El Bronx Remembered: A Novella and Short Stories*. 2d ed. Houston: Arte Público Press, 1986.

———. *In Nueva York*. 2d ed. Houston: Arte Público Press, 1993.

———. *Nilda: A Novel*. 2d ed. Houston: Arte Público Press, 1986.

———. *Rituals of Survival: A Woman's Portfolio*. Houston: Arte Público Press, 1985.

Mora, Pat. *Nepantla. Essays from the Land in the Middle*. Albuquerque: University of New Mexico Press, 1993.

Moraga, Cherríe. *Heroes and Saints and Other Plays*. Albuquerque: West End Press, 1994.

———. *The Last Generation: Prose and Poetry*. Boston: South End Press, 1993.

———. *Loving in the War Years: Lo que nunca pasó por sus labios*. Boston: South End Press, 1983.

Moraga, Cherríe, and Gloria Anzaldúa, eds. *This Bridge Called My Back: Writings by Radical Women of Color*. 2d ed. New York: Kitchen Table, Women of Color Press, 1983.

Musser, Donald W., and Joseph L. Price, eds. *A New Handbook of Christian Theology*. Nashville, Tenn.: Abingdon Press, 1992.

National Conference of Catholic Bishops. "The Hispanic Presence: Challenge and Commitment." *Origins* 13, no. 32 (January 19, 1984).

Nicholson, Linda, ed. *Feminism/Postmodernism*. New York: Routledge, 1990.

———, ed. *The Second Wave: A Reader in Feminist Theory*. New York: Routledge, 1997.

Norris, Scott, ed. *Discovered Country: Tourism and Survival in the American West*. Albuquerque: Stone Ladder Press, 1994.

Orozco, Cynthia. "Crónica Feminista." *La Gente* (February-March 1983): 8.

Ortiz Cofer, Judith. *The Latin Deli: Prose and Poetry*. Athens: University of Georgia Press, 1993.

———. *The Line of the Sun*. Athens: University of Georgia Press, 1989.

———. *Reaching for the Mainland and Selected New Poems*. Tempe, Ariz.: Bilingual Press/Editorial Bilingüe, 1995.

———. *Silent Dancing: A Partial Remembrance of a Puerto Rican Childhood*. Houston: Arte Público Press, 1990.

Ortiz Cofer, Judith, Roberto Duran, and Gustavo Perez et al., eds. *Triple Crown: Chicano, Puerto Rican and Cuban-American Poetry*. Tempe, Ariz.: Bilingual Press/Editorial Bilingüe, 1987.

O'Sullivan-Beare, Nancy. *Las mujeres de los conquistadores: La mujer española en los comienzos de la colonización americana*. Burgos: Alderoa, n.d.

Ovid. *Metamorphoses*. Translated by Charles Boer. Dallas: Spring Publications, 1989.

Palumbo-Liu, David, ed. *The Ethnic Canon*. Minneapolis: University of Minnesota Press, 1995.

Palumbo-Liu, David, and Hans Ulrich Gumbrecht, eds. *Streams of Cultural Capital. Transnational Cultural Studies*. Stanford, Calif.: Stanford University Press, 1997.

Paz, Octavio. *El Laberinto de la Soledad*. Mexico City: Fondo de Cultura Económica, 1997.

———. *Sor Juana: Or, the Traps of Faith*. Translated by Margaret Sayers Peden. Cambridge, Mass.: Harvard University Press, 1988.

Pedraja, Luis G. *Jesus Is My Uncle. Christology from a Hispanic Perspective*. Nashville: Abingdon Press, 1999.

Peters, Patricia A. Introduction to *The Divine Narcissus/El Divino Narciso*, by Sor Juana Inés de la Cruz. Translated by Patricia A. Peters and Renée Domeier. Albuquerque: University of New Mexico Press, 1998.

Picón-Salas, Mariano. *A Cultural History of Spanish America: From Conquest to Independence*. Translated by Irving A. Leonard. Berkeley: University of California Press, 1966.

Pineda, Ana María. "The Challenge of Hispanic Pluralism in a Hispanic Context." *Missiology* 21 (1993): 437–442.

———. "Evangelization of the 'New World': A New World Perspective." *Missiology* 20 (1992): 151–161.

———. "Pastoral de Conjunto." *New Theology Review* 3/4 (1990): 28–34.

Poot Herrera, Sara, ed. *Sor Juana y su mundo: Una mirada actual*. Mexico City: Universidad del Claustro de Sor Juana, 1995.

Portugal, Ana María, and Carmen Torres, eds. *El siglo de las mujeres*. Santiago, Chile: Isis Internacional, 1999.

Radford Ruether, Rosemary. *Sexism and God-Talk: Toward a Feminist Theology*. Boston: Beacon Press, 1983.

———. *Women and Redemption. A Theological History*. Minneapolis: Fortress Press, 1998.

———, ed. *Women Healing Earth*. Maryknoll, N.Y.: Orbis Books, 1996.

Ramos, Juanita, ed. *Compañeras: Latina Lesbians: An Anthology*. New York: Routledge, 1994.

Reagan, Charles E., and David Stewart, eds. *The Philosophy of Paul Ricoeur*. Boston: Beacon, 1978.

Rebolledo, Tey Diana. *Women Singing in the Snow: A Cultural Analysis of Chicana Literature*. Tucson: University of Arizona Press, 1995.

Rebolledo, Tey Diana, and Eliana S. Rivero, eds. *Infinite Divisions: An Anthology of Chicana Literature*. Tucson: University of Arizona Press, 1993.

Richter Reimer, Ivoni. *Women in the Acts of the Apostles. A Feminist Liberation Perspective*. Minneapolis: Fortress Press, 1995.

Ricard, Robert. *Spiritual Conquest of Mexico, an Essay on the Apostolate and the Evangelizing Methods of the Mendicant Orders in New Spain: 1523–1572*. Berkeley: University of California Press, 1982.

Ricoeur, Paul. *The Symbolism of Evil*. Translated by Emerson Buchanan. Boston: Beacon, 1967.

Rivera-Pagán, Luis N. *A Violent Evangelism: The Political and Religious Conquest of the Americas*. Louisville, Ky.: Westminster John Knox Press, 1992.

Rodríguez, Daniel, and Rodolfo Espinoza, eds. *Púlpito Cristiano y Justicia Social*. South Holland, Ill.: Ediciones Borinquen, 1994.

Rodríguez, Jeanette. *Our Lady of Guadalupe: Faith and Empowerment among Mexican-American Women*. Austin: University of Texas Press, 1994.

————. *Stories We Live: Cuentos que vivimos.* New York: Paulist Press, 1996.

Rodríguez, José David, and Loida Martell-Otero, eds. *Teología en Conjunto: A Collaborative Hispanic Protestant Theology.* Louisville: Westminster John Knox Press, 1997.

Rodríguez, Olga, ed. *The Politics of Chicano Liberation.* New York: Pathfinder Press, 1977.

Rodríguez, Raquel. "La Marcha de las Mujeres. Apuntes en torno al movimiento de mujeres en América Latina y el Caribe." *Pasos,* no. 34 (1991): 9–13.

Romero, C. Gilbert. *Hispanic Devotional Piety: Tracing the Biblical Roots.* Maryknoll, N.Y.: Orbis Books, 1991.

Romero, Mary, Pierrette Hondagneu-Sotelo, and Vilma Ortiz, eds. *Challenging Fronteras: Structuring Latina and Latino Lives in the U.S.: An Anthology of Readings.* New York: Routledge, 1997.

Rowe, William, and Vivian Schelling. *Memory and Modernity: Popular Culture in Latin America.* New York: Verso, 1991.

Ruíz, Vicky L. *From out of the Shadows. Mexican Women in Twentieth-Century America.* New York: Oxford University Press, 1998.

Russell, Letty M., and Shannon J. Clarkson, eds. *Dictionary of Feminist Theologies.* Louisville, Ky.: Westminster John Knox Press, 1996.

Sánchez, Rosaura, and Rosa Martínez Cruz, eds. *Essays on La Mujer.* Los Angeles: University of California Chicano Studies Research Center, 1977.

Sandoval, Chela. "Mestizaje as Method: Feminists-of-Color Challenge the Canon." *Living Chicana Theory,* edited by Carla Trujillo. Berkeley: Third Woman Press, 1998.

————. "U.S. Third World Feminism: The Theory and Method of Oppositional Consciousness in the Postmodern World." *Genders,* no. 10 (spring 1991): 1–24.

Santiago, Esmeralda. *América's Dream.* New York: HarperCollins, 1996.

————. *When I Was Puerto Rican.* New York: Random House, Vintage, 1993.

Santiago, Roberto, ed. *Boricuas: Influential Puerto Rican Writings—An Anthology.* New York: Ballantine Books, 1995.

Saravia, Albertina, ed. *El Popol Vuh.* Mexico City: Editorial Porrúa, 1971.

Schreiter, Robert. *Constructing Local Theologies.* Maryknoll, N.Y.: Orbis Books, 1985.

Schüssler Fiorenza, Elisabeth. *But She Said. Feminist Practices of Biblical Interpretation.* Boston: Beacon Press, 1992.

————. *Discipleship of Equals. A Critical Feminist Ekklesia-logy of Liberation.* New York: Crossroad, 1993.

————. *In Memory of Her. A Feminist Reconstruction of Christian Origins.* New York: Crossroad, 1985.

————. *Jesus Miriam's Child, Sophia's Prophet. Critical Issues in Feminist Christology.* New York: Continuum, 1994.

————. *Rhetoric and Ethic. The Politics of Biblical Studies.* Minneapolis: Fortress Press, 1999.

————, ed. *The Power of Naming. A Concilium Reader in Feminist Liberation Theology.* Maryknoll, N.Y.: Orbis Books, 1996.

Schüssler Fiorenza, Elisabeth, and María Pilar Aquino, eds. *In the Power of Wisdom: Feminist Spiritualities of Struggle.* Concilium 2000/5, London: SCM Press, 2000.

Schüssler Fiorenza, Elisabeth, and Mary Collins, eds. *Women Invisible in Church and Theology.* Concilium 182, Edinburgh, Scotland: T and T Clark, 1985.

Schüssler Fiorenza, Elisabeth, and M. Shawn Copeland, eds. *Feminist Theology in Different Contexts.* Concilium 1996/1, London: SCM Press, 1996.

Schüssler Fiorenza, Francis, and John P. Galvin, eds. *Systematic Theology: Roman Catholic Perspectives.* Minneapolis, Minn.: Fortress Press, 1991.

Scott, Nathan. *The Broken Center.* New Haven: Yale University, 1966.

Secker, Susan L. "Women's Experience in Feminist Theology: The 'Problem' or the 'Truth' of Difference." *Journal of Hispanic Latino Theology* 1, no. 1 (November 1993): 56–67.

Second General Conference of Latin American Bishops, *The Church in the Present-Day Transformation of Latin America in the Light of the Council.* 2d ed. Washington, D.C.: United States Catholic Conference, Division for Latin America, 1973.

Sedillo López, Antoinette, ed. *Latina Issues: Fragments of Historia (Ella) (Herstory).* New York: Garland Publishing, 1999.

Segovia, Fernando F., and Mary Ann Tolbert, eds. *Reading from This Place: Social Location and Biblical Interpretation in the United States.* Vol 1. Minneapolis: Fortress Press, 1995.

Seidman, Steven, ed. *The Postmodern Turn: New Perspectives on Social Theory.* New York: Cambridge University Press, 1994.

Shiva, Vandana, ed. *Close to Home: Women Reconnect Ecology, Health and Development.* London: Earthscan Publications Ltd., 1994.

Shorris, Earl. *Latinos. A Biography of the People.* New York: W. W. Norton and Company, 1992.

Silen, Juan Angel. *Las bichas: Una interpretación de la literatura feminista y feminina en Puerto Rico.* Rio Piedras, Puerto Rico: R. Valdivia y Alvarez Dunn, 1992.

Sjoo, Mónica and Barbara Mor. *The Great Cosmic Mother.* San Francisco: Harper and Row, 1987.

Sobrino, Jon. *Spirituality of Liberation.* Maryknoll, N.Y.: Orbis Books, 1988.

Sola, María M., ed. *Aquí cuentan las Mujeres: Muestra y estudio de cinco narradoras puertorriqueñas.* Río Piedras, Puerto Rico: Ediciones Huracán, 1990.

Soliván, Samuel. *The Spirit, Pathos, and Liberation. Toward a Hispanic Pentecostal Theology.* Sheffield, England: Sheffield Academic Press, 1998.

Sotomayor, Marta. "Towards the Year 2000: Visions of the Future." *Apuntes* 19, no. 1 (1999): 8–20.

Stevens-Arroyo, Antonio, and Ana María Díaz-Stevens, eds. *An Enduring Flame: Studies on Latino Popular Religiosity.* New York: Bildner Center for Western Hemisphere Studies, 1994.

Stravinskas, Peter M. J., ed. *Catholic Dictionary.* Huntington, Ind.: Our Sunday Visitor Publishing Press, 1993.

Sylvester, Christine. *Feminist Theory and International Relations in a Post-modern Era.* Cambridge: Cambridge University Press, 1994.

Tarango, Yolanda. "The Hispanic Woman and Her Role in the Church." *New Theology Review* 3/4 (1990): 56–61.

Tavard, George. *Juana Inés de la Cruz and the Theology of Beauty: The First Mexican Theology.* Notre Dame, Ind.: University of Notre Dame Press, 1991.

Teish, Luisah. *Jambalaya.* San Francisco: Harper and Row, 1985.

Tracy, David. *Plurality and Ambiguity: Hermeneutics, Religion, Hope.* San Francisco: Harper and Row, 1987.

Tribble, Phyllis. *Texts of Terror.* Philadelphia: Fortress Press, 1984.

Trujillo, Carla, ed. *Chicana Lesbians: The Girls Our Mothers Warned Us About.* Berkeley: Third Woman Press, 1991.

———, ed. *Living Chicana Theory.* Berkeley: Third Woman Press, 1998.

Valis, Noel, and Carol Maier, eds. *In the Feminine Mode: Essays on Hispanic Women Writers.* Lewisburg, Pa.: Bucknell University Press, 1990.

Vasconcelos, José. *La Raza Cósmica: Misión de la Raza Iberoamericana.* Mexico City: Asociación Nacional de Libreros, 1983.

Vélez, Diana, ed. *Reclaiming Medusa: Short Stories by Contemporary Puerto Rican Women.* San Francisco: Spinsters/Aunt Lute Books, 1988.

Vélez-Ibañez, Carlos. *Border Visions.* Tucson: University of Arizona Press, 1996.

Vigil, Angel. *The Corn Woman.* Englewood, Colo.: Libraries Unlimited, 1994.

Vigil, Evangelina, ed. *Woman of her Word: Hispanic Women Write.* 2d ed. Houston: Arte Público Press, 1987.

Villafañe, Eldin. *The Liberating Spirit: Toward an Hispanic-American Pentecostal Social Ethic.* Grand Rapids, Mich.: W. B. Eerdmans, 1993.

Villanueva, Alma. *Mother, May I?.* Pittsburg: Motheroot Publications, 1978.

Viramontes, Helena María. *The Moths and Other Stories.* Houston: Arte Publico Press, 1985.

Vuola, Elina. *Limits of Liberation. Praxis as Method in Latin American Liberation Theology and Feminist Theology.* Helsinki: Soumalainen Tiedeakatemia, 1997.

Walker, Barbara G. *The Woman's Encyclopedia of Myths and Secrets.* San Francisco: Harper and Row, 1983.

Webster, John C. B., and Ellen Low Webster, eds. *The Church and Women in the Third World.* Philadelphia: Westminster Press, 1988.

Weigle, Marta. *Brothers of Light, Brothers of Blood.* Albuquerque: University of New Mexico Press, 1976.

———. *The Lore of New Mexico.* Albuquerque: University of New Mexico Press, 1986.

Williams, Delores S. *Sisters in the Wilderness: The Challenge of Womanist God-Talk.* Maryknoll, N.Y.: Orbis Books, 1993.

Wright, T. R. *Theology and Literature.* Oxford and New York: Basil Blackwell, 1988.

Zavella, Patricia. "The Problematic Relationship of Feminism and Chicana Studies." *Women's Studies,* no. 17 (1989): 26–27.

CONTRIBUTORS

ANNA ADAMS was born in New York, daughter of a Puerto Rican Jewish mother and Russian Jewish father. She received her Ph.D. in history from Temple University in 1992. Currently she is Associate Professor of History at Muhlenberg College, where she teaches courses in Latin American history, Latino history, women's studies, and Spanish. She has just completed a bilingual book, *Hidden from History: Escondida de la Historia: The Latino Community/La Comunidad Latina of Allentown, Pa.* Her work on Latino Pentecostalism stems from her research in the Allentown community.

MARÍA PILAR AQUINO, a *mestiza* daughter of *bracero*-migrant farm workers, was born in Nayarit, Mexico, and raised in the Sonora/Arizona border. She earned her doctoral degree at the Pontifical University of Salamanca, Spain, in 1991. Currently she is Associate Professor of Theology and Religious Studies and Associate Director of the Center for the Study of Popular Catholicism at the University of San Diego. She is the author of *Our Cry for Life. Feminist Theology from Latin America,* 1993; *La Teología, La Iglesia y La Mujer en América Latina,* 1994; the editor of *Aportes para una Teología desde la Mujer,* 1988; and the co-editor with Roberto S. Goizueta of *Theology: Expanding the Borders,* 1998; with Ana María Tepedino of *Entre la Indignación y la Esperanza. Teología Feminista Latinoamericana,* 1998; with Elisabeth Schüssler Fiorenza of *In the Power of Wisdom: Feminist Spiritualities of Struggle,* 2000; and with Dietmar Mieth of *Return of Just War,* 2001. She has published numerous articles on the feminist experience of Latinos/as and Latin Americans in the Church and in theology. In 2000, the University of Helsinki, Finland, conferred upon María Pilar the degree of Doctor of Theology *Honoris Causae.*

TERESA DELGADO, a Puerto Rican, is a Ph.D. candidate at the Union Theological Seminary in New York City. She graduated *magna cum laude* from Colgate University in 1988 and received her M.A. from Union Theological Seminary in 1993. She has facilitated courses and workshops at Union and Auburn seminaries on the emerging theological voices of Latinas in the United States. In addition, she has been active in the community through grassroots organizations such as Harlem Initiatives Together and the Center for Community Leadership. She is currently working on her dissertation, which is focused on the development of an emancipatory Puerto Rican theological perspective using literature as a critical source. Teresa lives in Mount Vernon, New York, with her husband, Pascal Kabemba, and their three children.

MICHELLE A. GONZÁLEZ was born of Cuban parents in Miami, Florida. She is currently Assistant Professor in the Theological Studies Department at Loyola Marymount University, Los Angeles. She received her Ph.D. in Systematic Theology at the Graduate Theological Union in Berkeley, California, in 2001. She received her M.A. from Union Theological Seminary in 1994 and a B.S. from Georgetown University in 1990. Her research interests include theological method, U.S. Latino/a theology, feminist theologies, and theological aesthetics. She is currently working on her dissertation, "A Latin American *Ressourcement:* The Theological Contribution of Sor Juana Inés de la Cruz in Light of Hans Urs von Balthasar's Methodology."

LETICIA GUARDIOLA-SÁENZ, a Mexican-American, is a Ph.D. candidate in New Testament at Vanderbilt University. The focus of her research has been on the Gospels, and she has published articles in this area. The title of her dissertation is "Jesus the Border-Crosser: A Hybrid Representation from the Gospel of John." She received her M.A. in theology and ethics in 1990 and her M.Div. in 1992 from Northern Theological Seminary in Lombard, Illinois. She holds a Bachelor in Accounting (1983) and a Bachelor in Spanish Literature (1987) from the Tecnológico de Monterrey, Mexico. Her academic interest focuses on border theory, postcolonial studies, feminist hermeneutics, cultural studies, and the contextual reading of the New Testament. At present she is the associate editor of the Spanish edition of *The Upper Room*, a devotional guide published by the United Methodist Church in Nashville, Tennessee, and she teaches New Testament at Andover Newton Theological School.

GLORIA INÉS LOYA, P.B.V.M., a Mexican-American, is Adjunct Professor and coordinator of the Instituto Hispano at the Jesuit School of Theology at Berkeley, California. She received her D.Min. at the Pacific School of Religion, Graduate Theological Union in Berkeley in 1996; her S.T.L. at the University of Salamanca, Spain, in 1989; and her M.Ed. at Antioch College with the Mexican American Cultural Center in San Antonio, Texas, in 1979. Her areas of interest are theology of ministry, pastoral counseling, inculturation, Hispanic/Latina feminist theology, theological reflection, and field education. She has published in the areas of spirituality, religious life from a Hispanic cultural context, and Hispanic feminist theology. She is a member of the religious order Sisters of the Presentation of Mary.

NORA O. LOZANO-DÍAZ, a Mexican, is a Ph.D. candidate at Drew University. She holds a B.A. from the Universidad Regiomontana in Monterrey, Mexico (1984) and a M.Div. from Eastern Baptist Theological Seminary (1991). Her academic interests are centered in the areas of systematic, Hispanic, Latin American, and women's theologies. She is currently working on her dissertation, "Confronting Suffering: A Woman's Theological Challenge to the Traditional View of Suffering in the Mexican and Mexican American Realities." She lives in San Antonio, Texas, with her husband, Paul Kraus, and her daughter, Andrea, and son, Eric.

DAISY L. MACHADO, born in Cuba, emigrated with her parents to New York City at the age of three. She received a Master's in Social Work degree from Hunter College School of Social Work in 1978 and a Master's in Divinity degree from Union Theological Seminary in 1981, when she also was ordained. She received her Ph.D. from the University of Chicago in 1996, making her the first Latina Protestant in the United States to complete a doctorate in any field in theology. She has served inner-city Latino congregations in Connecticut, in Spanish Harlem in Manhattan and Brooklyn, New York, and in Houston and Fort Worth, Texas. From 1996 to 1999 Daisy served as the first Program Director of the Hispanic Theological Initiative. In 1999 she was awarded the Distinguished Alumna Award by her alma mater, Brooklyn College. Currently she is Associate Professor of Church History and Latino Church Studies at Brite Divinity School, Texas Christian University, in Fort Worth, Texas. Her dissertation, "Of Borders and Margins: Hispanic Disciples in Texas, 1888–1945," is to be published by Oxford University Press as part of the American Academy of Religion Dissertation Series. She is currently writing a book on the history of Latino Disciples of Christ in the United States and Canada.

CARMEN MARIE NANKO, an Hispanic laywoman, is Director of Campus Ministry at Trinity College in Washington, D.C., where she also teaches theology. The holder of a D.Min. from the Catholic University of America (1991), she is an active member of the Academy of Catholic Hispanic Theologians in the United States (ACHTUS) and serves ACHTUS as treasurer. She is the author of *Campus Ministry: Identity, Mission and Praxis,* 1997. Carmen has extensive experience as an administrator and educator at the secondary school level. She is an active member of the Catholic Theological Society of America and the National Catholic Educational Association and is a frequent lecturer on topics that range from Catholic Social Teaching to Catholic-Jewish Relations.

GAIL PÉREZ, a Chicana, teaches Ethnic Studies and Creative Writing at the University of San Diego. She received her Ph.D. from Stanford in 1992. She has written on multi-ethnic education and critical pedagogy as well as on Chicano/a writers. While at Stanford she was a Wallace Stegner Fellow in Creative Writing. Currently she is working on a video ethnography with Latino students and is also researching the literature and culture of the U.S.-Mexican border.

NANCY PINEDA-MADRID, a Chicana of first-generation Mexican parents, spent her early childhood in New Mexico and her adolescent years in El Paso, Texas. She is completing her doctoral studies in systematic and philosophical theology at the Graduate Theological Union in Berkeley, California. She received her M.Div. from Seattle University in 1991 and a B.B.A. from Loyola Marymount University in 1983. Her research interests include feminist theologies, U.S. Latina/o theology, and philosophies of religion. Her dissertation will consider a soteriological interpretation of the symbol of Our Lady of Guadalupe. She has taught at the Graduate Theological Union and the University of San Francisco. She has more than ten years of experience in pastoral leadership, primarily in the Roman Catholic Archdiocese of Seattle.

JEANETTE RODRÍGUEZ is a New York Latina, daughter of Ecuadorian parents. She received her Ph.D. from the Graduate Theological Union in Berkeley, California, in 1990. She is currently an Associate Professor and Chair of the Theology and Religious Studies Department and holds the Piggott-McCone Endowed Chair for Scholarship at Seattle University. She served a term as president of the Academy of Catholic Hispanic Theologians in the United States. She is the author of *Our Lady of Guadalupe: Faith and Empowerment Among Mexican American Women*, 1994, and *Stories We Live*, 1996, as well as a number of articles on U.S. Hispanic theology, spirituality, and cultural memory. Jeanette was recipient of the U.S. Catholic Award for the year 2000. She lives in Seattle with her husband, Tomás, and her children, Gabriella and Joshua.

INDEX

CPSIA information can be obtained
at www.ICGtesting.com
Printed in the USA
FSHW020513141119
64054FS